PENNSYLVANIA TROUT & SALMON FISHING GUIDE

Mike Sajna

Frank Amato Publications • P.O. Box 02112 • Portland, OR • (503) 653-8108

Thanks

More people than I can remember answered questions or provided me with information to help put this book together. I would especially like to thank the various members of the Fish Commission and Department of Environmental Resources Bureau of Forestry and Bureau of State Parks, who supplied me with information of one sort or another. Occasional mistakes aside, Pennsylvania's conservation officers do an outstanding job in the face of relentless pressure. Thanks also to Dave Kolesar for running me all over central Pennsylvania; Joe Lester for his suggestions and filling me in on Little Mahoning Creek; B.C. for keeping me company during a trip to northwestern Pennsylvania; Cindy Shegan for help with the photography and Art Zelienski for his photographs. A very special thanks also goes to the public libraries of Pennsylvania, especially the Norwin Public Library, the Greensburg Public Library and the Carnegie Free Public Library in Pittsburgh where I did most of my research. They are treasures that deserve more support than they get. Finally, thanks to all the fishermen of Pennsylvania who I met along these streams and through conversation gained some knowledge of a waterway.

Copyright 1988 Mike Sajna   Mike Sajna photos.
Book Design: Joyce Herbst - Typesetting: Chris Mazzuca
ISBN 0-936608-72-2

About the Author

Mike Sajna has lived in Pennsylvania all of his life and began fishing its waters as a child. He is a graduate of California State University in California, Pennsylvania, the outdoor columnist for *Pittsburgh Magazine* and a member of the Forbes Trail Chapter of Trout Unlimited. His free-lance work has appeared in a wide variety of magazines and newspapers.

Dedication

For Ruth, who suffered all the neglect,
My mother, who did all the worrying,
And, of course, my dad, who started it all.

Contents

Introduction

When I first read Vincent Marinaro's *A Modern Dry-Fly Code* back in the early 1970s, I was immediately overcome by both the quality of its story and its writing. Before I turned the final page, I made up my mind to try the Letort, Big Springs, the Yellow Breeches and all the other limestone streams so lovingly portrayed by the author. My fantasies, after four years of college, had wrought havoc on my fishing career, including successfully matching wits with a five-pound, wild brown in Fox's Meadow, and even meeting Marinaro and Charlie Fox. I could half see us meeting them along the banks of the Letort, and, as occasionally happens with trout anglers, spending the rest of the afternoon swapping tales. We all dream.

Probably because the Letort was already so famous in my mind, I never considered there would be any problem finding it. If memory serves me right, I may have even imagined signs pointing the way. Like at Old Faithful, Niagara Falls, or some other national treasure. Sometimes our emotions trample our rational centers of thought. For when I reached Carlisle that first time, what I found was a tangled series of side streets and a majority of the population whose main connection to the stream was through a small municipal park, a place where the legendary waters run buried between concrete walls. It took me over an hour, including stops at a gas station and sporting goods store, before I finally set eyes on the spot where Marinaro and Fox's fishing hut once stood.

In the fifteen or so years since my first trip to the Letort, I have managed to waste days, countless hours when I could have been fishing. Searching for other Pennsylvania trout streams, I've driven past turnoffs for Cedar Run, Walnut Creek, Donegal Spring Creek, Little Lehigh Creek and God only knows how many others. And I know I have not been alone in my folly. One friend confessed it took him two and a half hours to find the Letort on his first visit. He drove over it time and again.

While there is nothing unusual about missing a road or making a wrong turn when looking for a new stream, what is strange is that a state as famous for its trout fishing as Pennsylvania has never had a proper guidebook written about it, or at least none I am familiar with. Enough magazine articles have been written about individual streams to fill several volumes, but nobody has

ever tried to put it all together in one place. Which is where this book comes in. After so many years of wrong turns, my balloon sharp senses finally told me what Pennsylvania needs is a guidebook to its trout streams. Or at least the best and most famous of its trout streams.

Because I favor the old style of outdoor writing, the style that instructs through story, instead of the boring nuts and bolts material found in most of today's outdoor magazines, I also thought such a book should contain as much local color as possible. I've always found a stream a lot more enjoyable to fish if I know something about its past. Among my favorite parts of Charles Brooks' outstanding guide to the Madison River watershed, *The Living River,* are those which touch on the old days along that famous river, the days of the Mountain Man and early tourists. So, I've included a touch of history and legend on as many streams as possible in this book. Some of it is quite surprising. Working on this book has done nothing, if not deepen my love for the state where I was born. It is a wonderful place to live and fish. No trout fisherman can ever consider his experience complete without a stay in Pennsylvania.

The Streams

To pretend to be on intimate terms with all the streams in this book would be ludicrous. Pennsylvania has almost 15,000 miles of both stocked and unstocked trout streams. A person could spend a lifetime and never get to know all of them well. And since streams are living organisms, always in motion and changing, the waterway a person was familiar with last year may be a much different place two years from now. Anybody who doubts a stream possesses a life of its own should try writing about a few of them. Storms, pollution, droughts. . .those are just three things with the capability of changing a stream from one trip to the next. There is no way to keep up with it all. In the year and a half I was sitting at my desk writing this book, Dave Kolesar, a good friend of mine who lives in central Pennsylvania, called me on three different occasions to tell me of fish kills. There is no way for a guidebook to keep up with such changes.

But if I could never know as much about a stream as an angler who fishes it regularly, I could at least visit it, try to write down the easiest directions to it and dig up a bit of history. Which is essentially what I've done in this book. Regulars on every stream listed will know a lot more about their water than what is contained here. These pages are for people new to a stream or area. They are only a starting point. I ask the forgiveness of regulars on every stream for any shortcomings they might find.

In picking the streams, I used a combination of my own experience, suggestions from friends and acquaintances, tackle shop owners, conservation officers, magazines, books and pamphlets and, most of all, material available from the Fish Commission. For convenience, it is all arranged into the six regions used by the Fish Commission's law enforcement division.

To readers living in more remote sections of the United States, it may seem strange to focus on "stocked" water. But Pennsylvania annually sells upwards of a million fishing licenses. And the majority of those people fish for trout. At least during the early part of the season. There is no way on earth a cold water fishery could survive in Pennsylvania without an extensive stocking program. To make up for this need to fish for hatchery plants, however, what I did was try to pick streams that are more than a "put-and-take" affair, though in a few cases I've made exception for history or parks. I've also avoided wild trout water, except in a couple of instances. They are too fragile to draw attention to. Anglers who want to fish such waters will have to find them somewhere else. But that is not to say the streams here are empty of wild fish. Many of them contain wild trout in their headwaters, as well as good numbers of "holdovers," stocked trout that have managed to survive from one season to the next and thus become "wild."

No matter what streams an angler chooses to explore, however, he, or she, should keep in mind a couple of things. First, almost all Pennsylvania trout streams get crowded. This is especially true early in the season, before the opening of the walleye, pike and then bass seasons pull fishermen away. Of course some streams will be more crowded than others, and it is always possible to stumble across a quiet spot. But, generally speaking, do not expect to be alone on a stream from the start of the season in mid-April until at least when the season on walleye and pike opens in mid-May. From then on, though, the pressure continually decreases until by mid-June, when bass season opens, it is possible to find the same stretches of streams that were filled with shoulder-to-shoulder "fishermen," completely devoid of people.

Unfortunately, mid-June also marks the time when Pennsylvania's freestone streams begin to warm and drop. In many places, the water remains good in July, depending upon the rain, even well into July. But by the end of June look for many streams to be too low and warm to fish, which is what makes the limestone spring creeks of central Pennsylvania, with their constant flow and temperature, often crowded during summer.

Hatches

On a number of streams, particularly the famous ones, I was fortunate enough to come up with some general material on hatches. I've included this as a starting point. But remember, the quality and timing of a hatch can vary from year to year, no two years being exactly alike. Still, what I have included should give the fly fisherman, especially those new to the sport, an idea of what to expect and try during different times of the season.

For those streams where there was no readily available information on hatches of aquatic insects, or a lack of good hatches, I've added a list of fly patterns which have proven successful on a wide variety of trout streams all across Pennsylvania. They are nor-

mally arranged for their effectiveness from the opening of the season on. But beginners should not be afraid to break away from the list and try some of the other flies in their box. Pennsylvania's freestone streams, those created by runoff water from the mountains, are generally not very fertile breeding grounds for aquatic insects. So trout in freestone streams cannot afford to be too picky. If they want to eat, they often have to take whatever is floating by. For that reason, freestone waters frequently offer much better dry fly fishing than the fabled limestone creeks.

As a point of reference, the major Eastern hatches, common names, include:

April: Blue Dun, Early Brown Stonefly, Blue Quill, Quill Gordon, Caddis, Hendrickson and Black Quill.

May: Light Stonefly, Sulphurs, Blue Dun, Caddis, Gray Fox, March Brown, Light Cahill, Isonychia, Green Drake, Brown Drake and Blue-Winged Olive.

June: Sulphurs, Blue Quill, Blue-Winged Olive, Caddis, Light Cahill and Yellow Drake.

July: Isonychia and Tricorythodes.

Signs and Roads

As I've already said, Pennsylvania is my home and I love it. But if there is one thing in which it is woefully deficient it is signs. If the Bureau of Travel wants more people to vacation in the state and leave with a good impression, the best thing it could do, at least in my opinion, is purchase some signs. Anybody who has tried to navigate the state's back roads knows exactly what I am talking about. Sometimes it seems as though nothing matches the map or the description in the guide book. Township Road 333 is not really Township Road 333 on the sign, but Mill Road. Legislative Route 45678 was Pennsylvania Route 456 when the book was written, but PennDOT (the Pennsylvania Department of Transportation) changed it last year to Pennsylvania Route 654. It is a vicious cycle.

Pennsylvania's state-maintained secondary roads are known as legislative routes. They are generally identified by a small, about 10-inch square white sign, attached to a stop sign or a four-foot high post at the end of a road. At least that is the way things used to be. For PennDOT is presently in the process of turning all of its legislative routes into state routes. So what was L.R. 12345 last week, or even yesterday, may be S.R. 5432 today. The state route signs are bigger and there are more of them, but the change-over is not complete. Where it was possible, I've used the new state route numbers. On the roads where they were not yet in place when I went through, I've used the old legislative route number, but tried to place the road by a landmark, such as a bridge, a large rock, the ruins of a farm house and so forth. In some cases it doesn't matter, since both the new state route number and the old legislative route number mark a road.

Township-maintained roads are even worse than those belonging to the state. Their condition is generally rougher and frequently there are no signs at all identifying them. At other times, as I've mentioned already, Township Road 123 may actually appear as Mill Road. Again I've tried to place turns on township roads to some landmark.

Any angler looking to try a new stream should get a map. Plenty of free ones are available from PennDOT. But one of the best state maps for trout fishermen is the "Pennsylvania Recreational Guide" of the Bureau of State Parks. It is available, free of charge, at most park offices. It shows the location of all state parks, many of which include trout streams, along with state game lands and forests. But it is light on secondary roads. For those roads, an angler would do well by purchasing a copy of the

Pennsylvania Atlas & Gazetteer. It is published by the DeLorme Mapping Co., P.O. Box 298, Freeport, Maine 04032, and available in a growing number of bookstores and tackle shops. But don't look for either legislative route or state route numbers in it. Caught in the middle of the great change-over, I guess the mapmakers decided to forget the whole thing.

Many of the streams in this book also contain addresses of state forest and state park offices where free maps can be had of forest and park areas. **When writing for them, please enclose a stamped, self-addressed envelope for reply.** Most of the offices are quite prompt in their response. Anybody who plans on fishing in Allegheny National Forest also should be certain to purchase a map (cost $1) of the forest from one of the ranger stations. It is invaluable.

The Fish Commission publication *Trout Fishing in Pennsylvania* also is a good supplement. It contains some rather crude maps, but still shows all of the state's trout streams and helps to put things into perspective. It can be had for $2 by writing: Pennsylvania Fish Commission, Publications Section, P.O. Box 1673, Harrisburg, PA 17105-1673.

Camping and Backpacking

As John Donne said, "No man is an island," and many anglers like, or have, to take their families along on a fishing trip. For the streams connected to or near state parks, I've included information on camping and other facilities in each park. When possible, I've also mentioned some local attractions that might amuse restless kids while Dad's on the water. Pennsylvania's state parks can provide a good, economical family vacation. Most of them are quite beautiful, and many, especially those in the wild, northern central part of the state, are uncrowded.

Backpacking is generally permitted on state forest lands—but not state game lands. A free permit is required, and can be obtained from forest offices, along with other information on backpacking. For streams flowing through, or near, state forests, I've included addresses of where to write for details on backpacking.

Float Fishing

Float fishing is almost a "Catch 22" proposition in Pennsylvania. A majority of the state's trout streams are canoeable, but only during the high water periods of early spring or winter, when the fishing is at its worst, or the season closed. Using various canoeing guides, I have noted which trout streams seem to be the most likely candidates for a float trip. Anglers can obtain further information on canoeing Pennsylvania's streams in *Keystone Canoeing* by Edward Gertler and *Canoeing Guide to Western Pennsylvania and Northern West Virginia* by the American Youth Hostels—Pittsburgh Council.

Stream Etiquette

Somebody once said that common sense is one of the most uncommon things on earth. To insure the future of quality trout fishing in Pennsylvania, however, a lot more anglers better start practicing it.

Despite the great number of streams that flow through private property, access is generally not a problem. But if fishermen continue to leave their cigarette packs, bait containers, beer cans and lunch bags, among a thousand other things, along streams, the situation could change someday. Anybody who has fished for salmon along a Lake Erie stream at the height of a good run has seen how bad things can get. Please take your garbage with you.

That little action will not only help to make sure streams remain open to fishing, but also make an outing a lot pleasanter. Nobody in their right mind wants to fish surrounded by garbage; it takes away from everything, even the size and fight of a trophy fish.

Similarly, nobody likes to fish with another angler breathing down his neck. It may be near impossible to avoid crowds early in the season, but it is still possible to show some common courtesy. Don't try to edge another angler out of his spot or walk through the center of a pool somebody else is fishing. When the pressure is off and you encounter another fisherman on a stream, ask him which way he is headed and give him plenty of room. Some of the best fish I've ever taken have come from pools I had not planned to fish, but did so because somebody else was already in the water I wanted to try.

When parking along a stream, don't block access roads to farmers' fields. And don't tear down their fences or trees, or harass their livestock. Or build fires without permission or outside of designated areas, then make sure the fire is completely out. Just exercise your common sense. It's a wonderful way to keep out of trouble and make time spent on a stream even better.

For the Future

For the future, to help insure there always is quality trout fishing in Pennsylvania, and the rest of the nation, join Trout Unlimited. Information may be had by writing: Trout Unlimited, 501 Church Street Northeast, Vienna, Virginia 22180.

Special Regulation Waters

Following are the restrictions covering the seven categories of special regulation waters found in Pennsylvania. In many cases the regulations are similar. However, there also are small differences—like a barbless hook requirement—that could land an unsuspecting angler in trouble with the Fish Commission. Remember, ignorance is no excuse. When in doubt, check the appropriate regulations.

Fly Fishing Only Projects

1. Fishing may be done with artificial flies and streamers constructed of natural or synthetic materials, so long as all flies are constructed in a normal fashion on a single hook with components wound on or about the hook. Specifically prohibited are the use of molded facsimiles or replicas of insects, earthworms, fish eggs, fish or any invertebrate or vertebrate either singly or in combination with the other materials. Likewise prohibited are other lures commonly described as spinners, spoons or plugs made of metal, plastic, wood, rubber or like substance or a combination thereof.
2. Fishing must be done with tackle limited to fly rods, fly reels and fly line with a maximum of 18 feet in leader materials or monofilament line attached. Spinning, spincast and casting rods and reels are prohibited.
3. The use or possession of any natural bait, baitfish, fishbait or the use of any other devices, natural or synthetic, capable of catching fish other than artificial flies and streamers, is prohibited.
4. Open to fishing the year-round (no closed season).
5. Fishing hours are one hour before sunrise to one hour after sunset (except opening day of the regular trout season when the starting time is 8 a.m.).
6. Minimum size of trout caught or in possession on the waters under this regulation is nine (9) inches.

7. Daily creel limit is three (3) trout—combined species—except during the period March 1 to the opening day of the regular trout season when no trout may be killed or had in possession on the waters under this regulation.

8. Taking of baitfish or fishbait is prohibited.

Delayed Harvest Fly Fishing Only

1. Fishing may be done with artificial flies and streamers constructed of natural or synthetic materials, so long as all flies are constructed in a normal fashion on a single hook with components wound on or about the hook. Specifically prohibited are the use of molded facsimiles or replicas of insects, earthworms, fish eggs, fish or any invertebrate or vertebrate either singly or in combination with the other materials. Likewise prohibited are other lures commonly described as spinners, spoons or plugs made of metal, plastic, wood, rubber or like substance or a combination thereof.

2. Fishing must be done with tackle limited to fly rods, fly reels and fly line with a maximum of 18 feet in leader materials or monofilament line attached. Spinning, spincast and casting rods and reels are prohibited.

3. The use or possession of any natural bait, baitfish, fishbait or the use of any other devices, natural or synthetic, capable of catching fish other than artificial flies and streamers is prohibited.

4. Open to fishing the year-round (no closed season).

5. Fishing hours are one hour before sunrise to one hour after sunset (except opening day of the regular trout season when the starting time is 8 a.m.).

6. Minimum size of trout caught on or in possession on the waters under this regulation is nine (9) inches from June 15 to the last day of February.

7. Daily creel limit is three (3) trout—combined species—from June 15 to the last day of February only, caught on or in possession on the waters under this regulation.

8. Taking of baitfish or fishbait is prohibited.

Tribute of the Letort.

No Harvest Fly Fishing Only

1. Fishing may be done with artificial flies and streamers constructed of natural or synthetic materials, so long as all flies are constructed in a normal fashion on a single barbless hook with components wound on or about the hook. Specifically prohibited are the use of molded facsimiles or replicas of insects, earthworms, fish eggs, fish or any invertebrate or vertebrate either singly or in combination with the other materials. Likewise prohibited are other lures commonly described as spinners, spoons or plugs made of metal, plastic, wood, rubber or like substance or a combination thereof.
2. Fishing must be done with tackle limited to fly rods, fly reels and fly line with a maximum of 18 feet in leader materials or monofilament line attached. Spinning, spincast and casting rods and reels are prohibited.
3. The use or possession of any natural bait, baitfish, fishbait or the use of barbed hooks, or any other device other than barbless hook, artificial flies or streamers is prohibited.
4. Fishing hours are one hour before sunrise to one hour after sunset.
5. No trout may be killed or had in possession.
6. No closed season.
7. Wading is permitted unless otherwise posted.
8. Taking of baitfish or fishbait is prohibited.

Catch and Release

1. Fishing may be done with artificial lures only constructed of metal, plastic, rubber or wood, or with flies or streamers constructed of natural or synthetic materials. All such lures may be used with spinning or fly fishing gear. Use of gear not described in this section is prohibited. Specifically prohibited are the use of molded facsimiles or replicas of insects, earthworms, fish eggs, fish, or any invertebrate or vertebrate either singly or in combination with the other materials. Barbed hooks are prohibited; fishing may be done with barbless hooks only.
2. The use or possession of any natural bait, baitfish or fishbait, and the use of barbed hooks or any other fishing device other than barbless hook, artificial flies or streamers is prohibited.
3. Fishing hours are one hour before sunrise to one hour after sunset.
4. No trout may be killed or had in possession.
5. Open to fishing the year-round (no closed season).
6. Wading is permitted unless otherwise posted.
7. Taking of baitfish or fishbait is prohibited.

Delayed Harvest Artificial Lures Only

1. Fishing may be done with artificial lures only constructed of metal, plastic, rubber or wood, or with flies or streamers constructed of natural or synthetic materials. All such lures may be used with spinning or fly fishing gear. Use of gear not described in this section is prohibited. Specifically prohibited are the use of molded facsimiles or replicas of insects, earthworms, fish eggs, fish, or any invertebrate or vertebrate either singly or in combination with the other materials.
2. The use or possession of any natural bait, baitfish, fishbait and the use of any other fishing device other than artificial lures, flies or streamers is prohibited.

3. Open to fishing year-round (no closed season).
4. Fishing hours are one hour before sunrise—except opening day of the trout season, which is 8 a.m.—to one hour after sunset.
5. Minimum size of trout caught on or in possession on the waters under this regulation is nine (9) inches from June 15 to the last day of February.
6. Daily creel limit is three (3) trout—combined species—from June 15 to the last day of February only, caught or in possession on the waters under this regulation.
7. Taking of baitfish or fishbait is prohibited.

Trophy Trout Project

1. Fishing may be done with artificial lures only constructed of metal, plastic, rubber or wood, or with flies or streamers constructed of natural or synthetic materials. All such lures may be used with spinning or fly fishing gear. Anything other than these items is prohibited. Specifically prohibited are the use of molded facsimiles or replicas of insects, earthworms, fish eggs, fish, or any invertebrate or vertebrate either singly or in combination with the other materials.
2. The use or possession of any natural bait, baitfish and fishbait, and the use of any other device, natural or synthetic, capable of catching fish other than artificial lures, is prohibited.
3. Open to fishing year-round (no closed season).
4. Minimum size is 14 inches, caught on or in possession on the waters under this regulation.
5. Daily creel limit is two (2) trout—combined species—except during the period March 1 to the opening day of the regular trout season when no trout may be killed or had in possession on the waters under this regulation.
6. Taking of baitfish or fishbait is prohibited.

Limestone Springs Wild Trout Waters

1. Fishing may be done with artificial flies and streamers constructed of natural or synthetic materials, so long as all flies are constructed in a normal fashion on a single barbless hook with components wound on or about the hook. Specifically prohibited are the use of molded facsimiles or replicas of insects, earthworms, fish eggs, fish or any invertebrate or vertebrate either singly or in combination with the other materials. Likewise prohibited are other lures commonly described as spinners, spoons or plugs made of metal, plastic, wood, rubber or like substance or a combination thereof.
2. Fishing must be done with tackle limited to fly rods, fly reels and fly line with a maximum of 18 feet in leader materials or monofilament line attached. Spinning, spincast and casting rods and reels are prohibited.
3. The use or possession of any natural bait, baitfish, fishbait or the use of barbed hooks, or any other device other than barbless hook, artificial flies or streamers is prohibited.
4. Fishing hours are one hour before sunrise to one hour after sunset.
5. No trout may be killed or had in possession.
6. No closed season.
7. Wading is permitted unless otherwise posted.
8. Taking of baitfish or fishbait is prohibited.

Lake Erie at the mouth of Elk Creek.

NORTHWEST

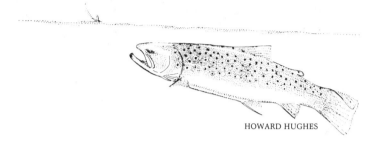

HOWARD HUGHES

Butler County
Connoquenessing Cr
Little Thorn Cr

Clarion County
Clarion River
Red Bank Cr
Maxwell Run
Toms Run

Crawford County
Conneaut Cr
Five Mile Cr
Oil Cr
Oil Cr E. Br
Sugar Cr
Sugar Cr E. Br
Thompson Run

Erie County
Conneaut Cr
Crooked Cr
Eightmile Cr
Elk Cr
Fourmile Cr
Racoon Cr
Sevenmile Cr
Sixmile Cr
Sixteenmile Cr
Twelvemile Cr
Twentymile Cr
Walnut Cr

Forest County
Allegheny River
Beaver Run
Blue Jay Cr
Maple Cr
Salmon Cr
Tionesta Cr
Tionesta Cr S. Br
Queen Cr

Jefferson County
Callen Run
Clear Cr
Clear Run N. Fork
Millstone Cr
Pekin Run
Red Bank Cr

Lawrence County
Coal Spring Run
Neshannock Cr
Sandy Cr

Venango County
Allegheny River
Little Sandy Cr
Oil Cr
Pithole Cr
Pithole Cr W. Br
Sandy Cr
Sugar Cr

Warren County
Allegheny River
Blue Eye Run
Brokenstraw Cr
Caldwell Cr
Caldwell Cr W. Br
East Hickory Cr
Farnsworth W. Br
Fourmile Run
Kinzua Tailrace
Little Brokenstraw Cr
Perry Magee Run
Pine Cr
Queen Cr
Sixmile Run
Spring Cr
Thompson Run
Tidioute Cr
Tionesta Cr E. Br
Tionesta Cr S. Br

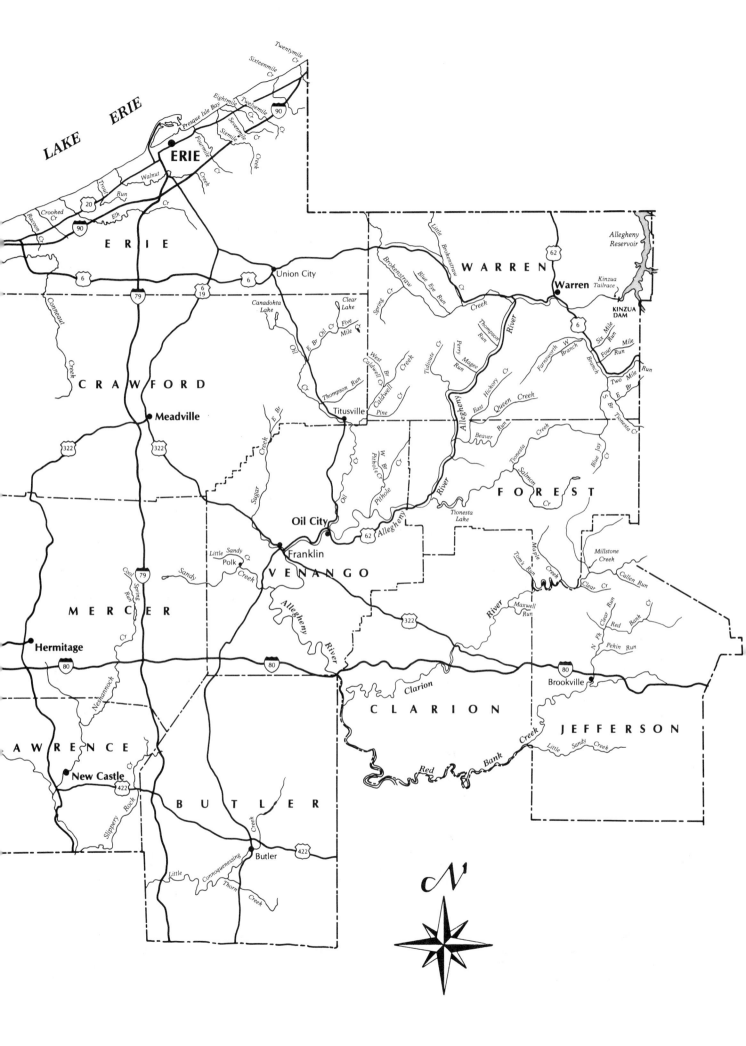

Northwest Region

Thorn Creek
Butler County

Lying like a fish hook across south central Butler County, Thorn Creek is heavily stocked with brown and rainbow trout. Its planted water runs for about eight miles, from between the villages of Renfrew and McCalmont at its mouth on the Connoquenessing Creek upstream to the village of Jefferson Center. It is one of the larger trout streams in the county, and, like most other Pennsylvania streams, under heavy pressure early in the season, but relatively empty during the summer and fall months.

Pennsylvania Route 8 cuts a path through the center of Butler County and is the central starting point for Thorn Creek. The highway actually passes over the stream in the vicinity of the village of McBride Station north of the Butler County Airport.

From the Route 8 crossing, anglers can reach Thorn Creek's lower waters by simply following the signs for Renfrew to the west. The road, accompanied by a set of railroad tracks, parallels the creek downstream, providing access at numerous spots.

Thorn Creek's upstream water can be located along a number of back roads. For anglers new to the region, however, probably the best way to reach it is to take Dodds Road east off Route 8 near Lakeview North Golf Course. Dodds Road leads to the village of Rockdale on the stream. From Rockdale, fishermen can gain further access to Thorn Creek's upper water on Reamer Road, which parallels the creek.

Reamer Road ends at its intersection with West Jefferson Road. Anglers can continue further upstream by turning east (left) on West Jefferson Road and toward Jefferson Center at the top end of the stream's stocked water. Smith Road, the first turn to the right off West Jefferson Road, also leads to some upper water at the village of Frazier Mill. Dinnerbell Road and O'Hara Road form part of a circle in the middle of Thorn Creek's bend and also give access to the stream.

The town of Butler a few miles up Route 8 from Thorn Creek was originally owned by Robert Morris of Philadelphia, best known as "the financier of the American Revolution." It was laid out in 1803, and named after Richard Butler of York County. Butler served as a lieutenant colonel with Morgan's Rifles during the Revolution, an Indian agent in Ohio and a major general in General Arthur St. Clair's expedition against the Ohio Indians in 1791, an adventure that took his life.

Saxonburg, just east of Thorn Creek upper water, was founded by German immigrants in 1832. Charles and John Roebling were sent to the New World by a group of people from the Saxony section of Germany to purchase land. The tract selected by the Roeblings covered about 16,000 acres, centering around the present site of the town. John was later to become the inventor of modern steel cable, and the builder of both the historic Smithfield Street Bridge in Pittsburgh, and the even more historic and famous Brooklyn Bridge.

For the fly fisherman venturing to Thorn Creek, possible fly choices include: Muddler Minnow, Marabou or Matuka streamers, Woolly Buggers, Muskrat, Hare's Ear, Soft Hackle Nymphs, caddis, Adams, Hendricksons, March Browns, Renegades, Gray Fox, Light Cahills, midges and terrestrials.

Slippery Rock Creek
Delayed Harvest Fly Fishing Only
Lawrence and Butler Counties

Along with being the name of a university with one of the most coveted T-shirts in the nation and a football team whose scores draw good-humored mention on national television beside the likes of Notre Dame, Michigan and USC, Slippery Rock also is the name of a town, township, oil field, oil sand and quality trout stream in northwestern Pennsylvania.

Slippery Rock Creek is a branch of Connoquenessing Creek, which flows into the Beaver River, a tributary of the Allegheny River, west of Ellwood City in southern Lawrence County. Folklore abounds about the source of the name. The most common story has it that the stream was given the name "Weschachachapochka," slippery rock, by a Delaware Indian who once slipped and fell on a slick rock along its banks. Since Slippery Rock Creek flows through Pennsylvania's oil country, and slick crude oil has seeped to the surface in various locations along the stream for thousands of years, the story is probably not too far off, especially when the Indians' habit of naming streams and rivers in a descriptive manner is taken into account.

What is said to be the original "slippery rock" is located downstream from McConnells Mill State Park near the town of Wurtemburg. It has appeared on maps of Slippery Rock Creek at least since 1874. Today, it is usually only visible during lower water periods, and can be seen from Glasser Bridge on the east bank of the creek or from the southern end of Camp Allegheny.

Like many other places in western Pennsylvania, Slippery Rock Creek—which for a time was known by European explorers as Flat Rock Creek—was visited at one time by George Washington. Traveling with Christopher Gist, one of the earliest settlers in western Pennsylvania, the first president camped near the headwaters of the stream in Mercer County on his way to Venango in 1753 and then crossed it on his return south near Wurtemberg.

Washington's mission was to warn the French at Fort Le Boeuf in Erie County that they were trespassing on land claimed by England and order them to leave. He used the Venango Path, the main trail from Fort Pitt to Erie, which crossed Slippery Rock Creek near Crolls Mills.

The stream's most evident remaining link with its past is the grist mill at McConnells Mill State Park off U.S. Route 422 north of Porterville. The first mill was built on the site in 1824 and a second in 1857. Following a fire in 1868, the present mill was rebuilt by Daniel Kennedy and sold, in 1875, to Thomas McConnell, who improved it by replacing the water wheel with turbines and the grinding stone with one of the first rolling mills in the country. Used to process oats, wheat and corn for local farmers, the mill continued to operate until 1928 when new technology made it unprofitable. It was sold to the Western Pennsylvania Conservancy in 1953, and then turned over to the state, which opened the park in 1957 and restored the mill in 1964. No camping is available.

Despite the folklore and the old mill, it is the approximately 400 feet deep, scenic Slippery Rock Gorge which draws most people to Slippery Rock Creek. Attributable to the glaciation of the area tens of thousands of years ago, the gorge marks the southernmost extent of the Wisconsin Ice Sheet which dammed up Muddy Creek and Slippery Rock Creek, creating a lake system that included, in a much larger version, Lake Arthur in nearby Moraine State Park. As the ice dam receded, Slippery Rock Gorge was cut to a depth of some 400 feet through otherwise rolling countryside. The creation of the gorge reversed the natural flow of water in the area from the St. Lawrence watershed to the Ohio River.

Kayakers and rafters who run the rapids of the gorge might view it as small and highly technical, but from the angler's point of view Slippery Rock Creek is a rather large stream when compared to most other trout streams in western Pennsylvania. While passing through the area in 1785, General William B. Irvine estimated its width as about 30 yards, a figure which is still valid today along a good deal of the roughly 20 miles of water listed as stocked by the Fish Commission.

Even though Slippery Rock Creek is both a relatively large and long trout stream, its Delayed Harvest Fly Fishing Only Project is one of the smallest special regulation projects in the state. Located on the southern end of McConnells Mill State Park, it runs for just one-half mile from Heinz Camp Road downstream to one-fourth of a mile below State Route 2022. It can be reached by taking Interstate Route 79 north from Pittsburgh or south from Erie to Porterville Exit 28 and Pennsylvania Route 488. Follow Route 488 west through Porterville for about three miles

to Heinz Camp Road. Turn left onto Heinz Camp Road and follow it for approximately 2.5 miles. At the bottom of the hill the road makes a sharp bend to the right and joins Armstrong Road; a small parking lot is located a short distance ahead on the right, immediately before the road crosses the stream on Armstrong Bridge. The Delayed Harvest Fly Fishing Only Project runs both up and downstream from the parking lot.

On the other side of the bridge, Armstrong Road becomes Center Church Road, which follows the stream for a short distance before turning and heading off to meet Pennsylvania Route 388. Just after Center Church Road turns away from the stream it is met by Mountsville Road, which leads to Harris Bridge and more fishable water upstream from the Delayed Harvest Project. Mountsville Road also runs off Route 488 about a miles and a half west of Porterville. Like Heinz Camp Road, it is clearly marked with a street sign.

Between Harris Bridge and Eckert Bridge, inside the park, lie more than two miles of water without direct contact with a road. Fishing is permitted throughout this stretch, and it is a good place for the angler to go who is looking for a little solitude. It is float-stocked by local sportsmen's clubs, and contains both rainbow and brown trout, and bass. About halfway between the two bridges is Cleland Rock, which provides a scenic vista of Slippery Rock Gorge, and can be reached by following the signs in the park, or by taking Breakneck Bridge Road off Route 488.

Primarily a caddis stream, Slippery Rock Creek can provide good action on small caddis patterns, both dries and larvae or pupae. In warmer months the fish also are susceptible to terrestrials, in particular ants and beetles. Other patterns the fly angler might try include: Adams, Hendrickson, Blue Dun, Hare's Ear, Soft Hackle Nymphs, Matuka Streamers, Woolly Buggers, March Brown, Gray Fox, Renegade, Light Cahill, Sulphurs and midges.

Outside of the park, Slippery Rock Creek can be located by taking Exit 29 off Interstate Route 79 and following Route 422 west to U.S. Route 19 north. The stream is accessible off Rock Spring Road, which runs off Route 19 between the villages of Rockville and Harlansburg, and McMurry Road, which runs off Rock Spring Road. Slippery Rock Creek also can be reached directly off Route 19 at Harlansburg.

Above Harlansburg, Pennsylvania Route 108 east follows the stream, allowing access of side roads.

Additional information on McConnells Mill State Park, including a map of the park area, may be had by writing: McConnells Mill State Park, Department of Environmental Resources, R.D. 1, Porterville, PA 16501.

Neshannock Creek
Lawrence and Mercer Counties

Trout streams which are of respectable size and cover long distances normally go through a steady progression of "civilizing" changes from their upper reaches to their mouths. The most obvious, of course, is a substantial increase in the number of people living and working along their banks. Neshannock Creek is somewhat different, however, in that the center portion of its stocked water is relatively free of the usual trappings of modern man, while its upper stretch is cornered by the borough of Mercer, and its mouth on the Shenango River by the city of

New Castle. For the trout fisherman, in this case, all the best lies in between.

Neshannock Creek is stocked with brown and rainbow trout for ten miles in Lawrence County and nine miles in Mercer County. The planted water stretches from the city of New Castle upstream toward the borough of Mercer. No single road follows the stream along its stocked length, but several bridges cross over it and different roads trail it for short pieces. And they are all within a few miles of either Interstate Route 79 or Interstate Route 80. Anglers can conveniently cover big sections of water by hopping from bridge to road to bridge.

In its lower portions, the Neshannock can be reached from a beautiful Fish Commission access point just north of New Castle. The access point opens to a scenic, if relatively short, gorge of rocks, rhododendron and overhanging trees of various species. It can be found by taking Pennsylvania Route 956 north to the village of Neshannock Falls. Route 956 touches on the stream at several places in and around the village. West of Neshannock Falls State Route 1005 (marked by a sign "New Castle 5") crosses Route 956. Follow State Route 1005 south for about three miles toward New Castle. At the first flashing yellow light turn left, or to the east, onto State Route 1002. The access point, marked by a large wooden Fish Commission sign, sits about two miles down the road just before the birdge over the creek.

Anglers can follow S.R. 1002 east across the bridge to Pennsylvania Route 168 south of the village of East Brook. Neshannock Creek's upper water can be located by taking route 168 north to Pennsylvania Route 208 in the farming village of Volant. Route 208 west crosses the stream in the village next to an old mill out of which local craftsmen now sell their goods. Up the hill from the mill, on Route 208 west, Mercer Street appears on the right and leads upstream.

More of the Neshannock's upper water may be reached by taking Route 208 east to U.S. Route 19 at the village of Leesburg, and then following Route 19 north toward the town of Mercer. The road crosses the stream near the village of Milburn. Creek Road, which appears near the bridge, also leads back to the stream. Historic Johnston's Tavern sits along Route 19 north of Leesburg. The tavern was built along what was once the Pittsburgh-Mercer Road by Arthur Johnston, an Irish immigrant, in 1831. He undoubtedly operated a log cabin on the site before the present stone house was built because he was issued a license in 1827. Johnston continued to run the tavern, known as the New Lodge Inn, until 1842, regularly serving workers from the nearby Springfield Iron Furnace. From 1836 to 1845, the Springfield post office also was located in the building, with the innkeeper as postmaster. The building was restored by Charles Stotz, under the direction of the Western Pennsylvania Conservancy, and is now administered by the Pennsylvania Historical and Museum Commission.

By the time Neshannock Creek reaches Interstate Route 80 it has lost quite a bit of size, and businesses and homes connected to the town of Mercer begin to show. The stream can be reached off bridges along Pennsylvania Route 258 and Route 58 south of Mercer. The Route 258 bridge is located near the state correctional institute.

According to Dr. George Donehoo's book, *A History of the Indian Villages and Place Names in Pennsylvania,* the stream may have been named by Delaware Indians who migrated to the region from eastern Pennsylvania and Neshaminy Creek. Donehoo also points out that some of the first European settlers along the stream were Scotch-Irish who once lived along Neshaminy Creek, and worshipped at Neshaminy Church. Both Neshannock and Neshaminy seem to be corruptions of the word Nischam-hanne,

which is translated to mean "two streams," "double streams" or "both streams."

A stem of the Kuskusky Indian Path, from Shannopin's Town (Pittsburgh) to Cussewago (Meadville), once forded Neshannock Creek near its mouth in New Kuskusky (New Castle). Some historians believe the path is the one George Washington used during his journey to Fort Le Beouf in 1753 after rain made the nearest way impassable. Washington and his party, which included the noted early western Pennsylvania explorer Christopher Gist, was on mission from Virginia's Lieutenant Governor Robert Dinwiddie to inform the French they were trespassing on land claimed by Great Britain. The French refused to abandon Fort Le Boeuf and Fort Presque Isle in Erie County, or any of the other stockades they had erected to protect their own claims on the Ohio Valley. They even moved down the Allegheny River to take Pittsburgh from the small British garrison guarding the "forks of the Ohio." The action led directly to the opening battle of the French and Indian War (known as the Seven Years War in Europe) at Fort Necessity the following years, and General Edward Braddock's defeat in the Battle of the Monongahela in 1755.

The Neshannock Potato, a choice variety of spud that was once widely known, originated on the Lawrence County farm of John Gilkey and was named after the stream. Gilkey's sister, Peggy, who grew up as an orphan in Washington County, was said to have traveled to the area in search of relatives whose address she did not know. On Christmas Eve 1804, she was caught in a blizzard and approached the door of the first cabin she found seeking shelter. It turned out to be the home of her brother, James.

Fly fishermen can try the Muddler Minnow, Woolly Buggers, Matuka Streamers, Hare's Ear, stoneflies, Adams, Blue Dun, Quill Gordon, caddis, Hendrickson, March Brown, Black Gnat, Light Cahill, Soft Hackle Nymphs, Black Gnat, midges and terrestrials.

Cool Spring Run
Mercer County
Delayed Harvest Artificial Lures Only

Grassy, bushy mud banks and a gentle, meandering nature typify Cool Spring Run, a low country stream stocked for five miles with brown and rainbow trout from its mouth on Neshannock Creek (see which) near the town of Mercer upstream to U.S. Route 62. Access to the stream's lower water is available along Pennsylvania Route 58 east and its upper water off Route 62 near Interstate Route 79 Exit 33 west toward Mercer.

Cool Spring has a 1.25 mile long Delayed Harvest Artificial Lures Only Project running from the bridge on State Route 2014 upstream to the abandoned railroad grade. It can be found by taking Dump Road (Township Road 702), which runs off East Market Street, which can be picked up off Route 58 east.

Mercer Borough near the mouth of Cool Spring Run is located around the site of an old Indian village. It was laid out in 1803 by John Hodge, who donated 200 acres from the county seat, and named in honor of Bridgadier General Hugh Mercer, a Scottish physician who lived in western Pennsylvania and played an important part in the Revolutionary War battles of Trenton and Princeton, where he was killed. The town was once a nationally known horse mart, specializing in "streeters," or horses used for drawing street cars. General Lafayette was entertained in Mercer during his 1825 tour of the United States. The town also was once famous for the Hartegig health springs.

Slippery Rock Creek.

Like several other towns in Pennsylvania, Mercer once served as a stop on the Underground Railroad, smuggling slaves up from the South in the years prior to the Civil War. The slaves were hidden in the Hanna-Small White House on South Pitt Street. The home was described in Anna Pierpont Siviter's book, *1861-1868: Recollections of War and Peace.* Mercer's other connection to the Civil War period is the birthplace of John A. Bingham. Mr. Bingham served as a judge advocate at the trial of Mary Eugene Surratt and other alleged conspirators in the assassination of Abraham Lincoln, and as counsel in the impeachment of President Andrew Johnson.

Fly patterns that should bring some success on Cool Spring Run include: Adams, Blue-Winged Olives, Blue Duns, caddis, Muddler Minnows, Woolly Buggers (olive, black or brown), Matuka Streamers, Hendricksons, Hare's Ears, Soft Hackle Nymphs, Lead-Winged Coachmen, March Browns, Black Gnat, Gray Fox, Light Cahills, Mosquito, Renegade, midges and terrestrials.

Little Sandy Creek
Jefferson County

Farmland streams are few and far between in mountainous Jefferson County. One of the best since mining operations in its watershed have dropped off is probably gravel-bottomed Little Sandy Creek.

Arising in State Game Lands 31 in the southcentral part of the county, Little Sandy Creek is stocked for 11 miles to its confluence with Redbank Creek north of Mayport in Clarion County. It can be reached off Pennsylvania Route 36 on the edge of the village of Coolspring. State Route 3018 runs off Route 36 and into the village where it becomes Coolspring Road, which leads back to Game Lands 31 and a bridge across the stream.

Downstream portions of Little Sandy Creek can be fished by following State Route 3031 off Route 36 near Coolspring and

Allegheny River.

toward the village of Worthville, a distance of three miles. S.R. 3031 touches on the stream at several points on the way to Worthville. It also offers access along side runs such as Burkett Road and Pine Run Church Road.

As Little Sandy Creek nears Worthville it grows appreciably in size until it is a fairly large trout stream. S.R. 3031 runs straight through the center of the village as it continues to follow the creek downstream to the village of Langville.

The Catawba Path, one of the most important Indian trails in North America, once crossed Little Sandy Creek at Worthville. Also known as the Great Catawba War Path, the Iroquois Path, the Iroquois Main Road, the Cherokee Path and the Tennessee Path, with connections at both ends it was once possible to travel all of the way from Canada to Florida and west into the Mississipii Valley along the path.

Aquatic life in the stream is said to be good. Fly anglers might try Hare's Ears, stoneflies, Muddler Minnows, Blue Duns, Quill Gordons, Adams, caddis, Lead-Winged Coachman, Black Gnat, Hendricksons, Soft Hackle Nymphs, Royal Coachman, March Browns, Gray Fox, Light Cahills, midges and terrestrials.

Red Bank Creek
Jefferson County
Float Trip

Big and popular are two adjectives that succinctly describe Red Bank Creek. The reasons are simple. It is first-rate brown trout water. It is accessible in several spots off two major roads, but seldom crowded by pavement. And it is an easy, often pretty float that can be broken up into three convenient stretches, right for a full day, a morning or an afternoon.

A tributary of the fabled Allegheny River, Red Bank Creek is stocked over a 15-mile length, from its beginnings at the junction of North Fork Red Bank Creek (see which) and Sandy Lick Run in Brookville, downstream to approximately the Clarion County line. Its upper water may be reached by taking Interstate Route 80 Exit 13 and following U.S. Route 322 toward Brookville. Pennsylvania Route 36 south from Brookville crosses over the stream and parallels it for roughly a mile. A railroad bed across Route 36 is another way to fish the stream, especially after the road begins to pull away from it. Anglers interested in floating the creek can start here and take out at Baxter, Summerville, Heathville or Mayport in Clarion County. The best floating period is probably May or early June, depending on how much rain has fallen through the spring.

Brookville is the county seat of Jefferson County, which was named after Thomas Jefferson, who was president when it was carved out of Lycoming County in 1804. Built on the inner slopes of three hills, it is a pleasant town of old shops and homes that reflect back to the region's past as a lumber, oil, coal and railroad center. The Catawba Path, probably the most important Indian trail in North America, followed Route 36 from Brookville through the village of Stanton. Using off-shoots, it was possible to travel the Catawba Path all the way from Canada to Florida and west into the Mississippi Valley.

Visitors walking down Brookville's quaint and colorful Main Street today will find no indication of the strange, some might say morbid, notoriety that once fell upon the town. In 1857, it was the scene of a grave-robbing that helped lead to the legalization of dissection of human cadavers by doctors and medical schools in Pennsylvania. The incident occurred when Dr. William J. McKnight, four other physicians and two other persons exhumed the body of a black man and conducted secret classes on it for days until townspeople found out and stopped the proceedings. The outcry brought a great deal of attention to the need for doctors and their students to be able to legally dissect human corpses. Government being the same throughout history, however, it was another ten years before the legislature finally passed a law legalizing dissection.

Another Brookville resident who gained an odd sort of fame was Douglas Stahlman. As a teacher at Clear Run School in 1890, Stahlman became involved in a fight with a lumberman. He received a severe head injury during the altercation and had to have a steel plate put in his head. About 1900, he fell under the influence of Dr. John A. Dowie, a faith healer from Chicago and founder of Zion, Illinois, and became a religious fanatic. With hammer and chisel in hand, Stahlman began roaming the surrounding forests, carving some 500 Biblical passages on trees and rocks, most of them along streams. Around 1920, Stahlman was committed to Dixmont Hospital in Pittsburgh. He died in 1937 and was buried in Temple Cemetery.

Some of Stahlman's carvings are said to still be visible. Two carvings near Red Bank Creek are on the south side of U.S. Route 322 just east of and across from the Pinecreek Fire Hall, and on Route 28 about a half-mile south of its junction with Route 322, east of the McCullough farm.

Route 28 south off Interstate Route 80 Exit 13 parallels Red Bank Creek downstream at varying distances all of the way to New Bethlehem in Clarion County. It first touches on the stream at Baxter and provides direct access at numerous points between there and Summerville. Boaters can put in at Baxter and float to Summerville or Mayport.

Since Route 28 is one of Jefferson County's main arteries, Red Bank Creek is an often busy affair rimmed by traffic and businesses around Baxter and Summerville. Anglers looking for something quieter and more scenic should head for the village of Heathville. It can be reached from Summerville by turning off Route 28 onto Carrier Street and then Water Street. Make a right onto Water Street, cross over the bridge in the center of town. Signs point the way to Heathville, two miles away along State Route 3007.

In Heathville, Strauser Road and Baker Trail provide direct access to Red Bank Creek. Anglers can reach the stream in plenty of other spots by walking along the railroad tracks that parallel it through the area.

Traditional patterns should produce for the fly fisherman on Red Bank Creek. These include: Adams, Blue Dun, Quill Gordon, Muddler Minnows, Woolly Buggers, Matuka Streamers, Hendrickson, caddis, March Brown, Black Gnat, Lead-Winged Coachman, Gray Fox, Light Cahill, midges and terrestrials.

(Also see Little Sandy Creek and North Fork Red Bank Creek, Jefferson County).

North Fork Red Bank Creek
Delayed Harvest Fly Fishing Only
Pekin Run, Clear Run
Jefferson County

North Fork Red Bank Creek
Special regulation waters are easily among the most popular trout fishing spots in Pennsylvania. Yet, unless the stream on which they are located flows alongside a main road, finding them

for the first time often is far from a simple task. The main reasons for this situation are a terrible lack of directional signs throughout the state, backed by frequent conflicts between local and official names for streets, routes and landmarks. The situation should become even worse in the near future, since the Pennsylvania Department of Transportation has embarked on a project to change the numbers of all its secondary roads, from legislative routes to state routes.

To every rule, however, there is an exception and North Fork Red Bank Creek is such a pleasure.

Not that the North Fork is the most unique stream in the commonwealth. Of medium size with a mixture of rocky rapids, riffles and pools, it resembles a hundred other freestone streams in every corner of the state. Even the quality of its fishing, though good, is certainly not the best available anywhere. What makes this project so refreshing is the number of signs surrounding it. Not ony is there a small, wooden Fish Commission sign pointing to the turn-off, somewhat unusual in itself, but also a large gate with a painting of an angler welcoming visitors to the project.

On top of the relative abundance of signs, the borough of Brookville also offers anglers fishing North Fork Red Bank Creek Delayed Harvest Fly Fishing Only water amenities like a parking lot and restrooms in the Dr. Walter W. Dick Memorial Park. But then such attention to the needs of visiting fishermen seems only natural for a town that took its name from the large number of "brooks" around it, and whose cash flow is greatly enhanced by the dollars of out-of-towners.

If the presence of signs and adequate parking is not enough, access to the project involves little more than taking Interstate Route 80 Exit 13 and following U.S. Route 322 south through the center of Brookville. As Route 322 starts to leave the shops and offices behind and bend down a hill, the project turn-off is immediately to the left—indicated by the Fish Commission marker, the park sign and the gate. The special water extends upstream for two miles.

Much of North Fork Red Bank Creek outside the fly fishing section is a walk-in prospect. Some of the upper stretches can be reached by continuing past the entrance to the fly fishing project to the traffic lights roughly a hundred yards away. At the lights turn left onto Richards Street (State Route 4005). Follow it to the village of Richardsville where the road crosses the stream.

Additional access to upper North Fork Red Bank Creek is available by continuing on S.R. 4005 out of Richardsville to the village of Munderf. Turn right at Munderf onto State Route 1027 leading to the village of Warsaw. The road crosses the stream on State Game Lands 54 between Munderf and Warsaw.

Although brown trout are present, brook trout are the predominant species in the stream. Fly choices include caddis patterns, Adams, Hendricksons, Soft Hackle Nymphs, Hare's Ears, Blue Quills, March Browns, Black Gnats, Light Cahills, Sulphurs, Royal Coachman and terrestrials.

Pekin Run

A tiny tributary of the North Fork with, reportedly, some good fishing for wild brook and brown trout, Pekin Run is accessible off Richard Street (S.R. 4005) below Richardsville, where a steel bridge passes over the creek. It is stocked for four miles, approximately two miles upstream and two miles downstream. Access is by walking, though Mays Road off Richard Street, just outside of Richardsville, does run down to some of the upper water.

Clear Run

A second little stocked tributary of the North Fork, Clear Run

can be found by continuing on Richard Street (by now Richardsville Road) through Richardsville to the village of Dixon Corner. In Dixon Corner, turn left onto Township Road 484, and then right onto Fire Tower Road. Follow Fire Tower Road to Clear Run Road, the third road on the left, about three miles outside of the village. Clear Run Road crosses the stream after a ride of between five and six miles.

Access to some of Clear Run's lower three miles of stocked water may be had by taking Jim Town Road, which runs off Clear Run Road to the left a short distance before it crosses the stream. Follow Jim Town Road to Township Road 359, the first right turn. T-359 (Gilbert Road) crosses the stream.

Fly fishermen can try some of the same patterns mentioned under the North Fork.

(Also see Red Bank Creek.)

Clarion River
Elk, Forest and Jefferson Counties
Float Trip

Toms Run
Clarion County

Maple Creek
Forest County

Clear Creek, Callen Run
Jefferson County

Maxwell Run
Elk County

Clarion River

"Aluminum hatches" of canoes have become the bane of most large trout streams in the eastern United States. And with two popular state parks rimmed by canoe rental operations, a state forest, state game lands, and Pennsylvania's only national forest providing almost unlimited public access, the Clarion River can match its hatch against the best of them anywhere and at anytime. For the angler who can avoid the noisy, splashing multitudes, however—a frequently hopeless task on weekends and holidays, especially when students from nearby Clarion State University surrender to the normal urges of youth—the Clarion holds some 40 miles of often fine, often scenic and easily floatable trout and smallmouth water.

But nobody should complain too much about problems with popularity. For it means clean water. And up until the mid-1970s, the Clarion River's water was anything but clean. As a major water route for the region's once powerful lumber and tanning industries, the river for decades was far too polluted for trout, or any other aquatic creatures. Old-timers along the river can still tell stories of dark brown water full of smelly foam, so thoroughly tainted by pollutants it even stained the rocks. A sad and terrible fate for a river whose clear sounding ripples, "condensed and reflected to a silvery mellowness" by the surrounding forests, led early travelers to compare it to the musical instrument.

The big change in the Clarion River came about because of both an extensive clean-up campaign and the economic hard times of the mid-1970s. The downturn in business cut deep into the industrial output of Ridgway and Johnsonburg. Paper mills, tanneries and other industrial concerns which once poured their wastes into the river's headwaters suddenly were forced to stop or cut operations way back. With the drop in production, and efforts by the state Department of Environmental Resources to treat mine drainage problems, the river was able to flush itself and by the early 1980s was well on its way back.

The Clarion River's trout water, stocked by the Fish Commission with fingerlings, runs from Ridgway in Elk County to Cook Forest State Park on the Clarion County line. It makes an easy, novice float over its entire stocked length. Anglers with canoes or rafts can customize their trip to just about any length by putting in or taking out at numerous points from Ridgway downstream all of the way to Cooksburg next to the park.

Roads closely parallel the river over much of its length, also giving fishermen without a canoe or raft countless opportunities to fish the Clarion. Pennsylvania Route 949 West parallels the river from Ridgway downstream through State Game Lands 44 to the village of Portland Mills. From Ridgway, fishermen can reach further down the river by taking Main Street west past Ridgway Recreational Park. Main Street turns into Laurel Hill Road as it approaches the Allegheny National Forest. The road turns to dirt and gravel a short distance inside the forest, and touches on the river between the villages of Beuhler Corner and Hallton. The road continues to follow the river from there all of the way downstream to the end of its trout water at Cook Forest State Park. Anglers coming from Ridgway, however, can follow the road only as far as Millstone Creek, where a closed bridge ends the trip.

Visitors interested in camping in the area can take the road leading to the right about a mile before the bridge, or a second

Clarion River.

road to the bridge. They both lead to Loleta Campground, which is operated by the U.S. Forest Service and situated on Millstone Creek. Loleta holds 32 camp sites, 40 picnic sites, vault toilets, drinking water and a swimming area, but that may be closed. Camping is on a first-come, first-served basis. No reservations are accepted. The normal operating period is Memorial Day through Labor Day.

The Clarion's lower trout water is most conveniently reached in Cook Forest State Park, which anglers coming from the east can find by taking Interstate Route 80 Exit 13 and following Pennsylvania Route 36 into the park. Fishermen coming from the west can locate it by taking Interstate 80 Exit 8 and then Pennsylvania Route 66 north to the village of Leeper where Route 36 south appears and leads into the park. Route 36 crosses over the river at the old village of Cooksburg near the park office. River Road meets Route 36 in the area of the office and closely parallels the river upstream to the village of Clarington, a distance of about six miles.

Cook Forest State Park, like Cooksburg, is named in honor of the Cook family. John Cook settled in the area in 1828 and began a lumbering business with a sawmill on Toms Run, which meets the river near the park office. According to the park's "Recreational Guide," Andrew Cook inherited the land on which the park now stands from his father in 1857. In the 1920s the Cook Forest Association was formed to help preserve the large stand of virgin white pine in the forest. The association raised money to help the state purchase the land from the A. Cook Sons Co. and establish a park in 1927.

Cook Forest State Park now covers 6,422 acres of the Cook family's land. It has a Class A campground with 226 sites opened on a year-round basis, and contains modern washhouses, hot and cold running water and showers (not open from late October to late May), a dump station and on-site hookups.

In addition to the campground, the park holds 24 family cabins available from the second Friday in April until the end of the antlerless deer season in mid-December. Reservations for the cabins can be made in advance, and most are reserved for the 14 summer weeks following Memorial Day.

For the non-fishing visitor and the off-hours, Cook Forest State Park offers hiking along 27 miles of trails, scenic views and photography opportunities, swimming at a guarded pool (Memorial Day weekend to Labor Day), 4.5 miles of bridal paths, picnicking, various environmental education programs, and, nearby, canoe rentals. The park also has a nature museum in a former sawmill near the swimming pool. Included in the museum are specimens of trees found in the park, logging and rafting tools, models and other artifacts from the region's lumbering past. Half the sawmill/museum is operated by a local craft group, the Cook Forest Sawmill Center for the Arts, that presents demonstrations of various traditional crafts throughout the summer and fall. Some of the crafts are available for purchase. For those people interested in learning a craft, classes are available for both adults and children. Details may be had by writing: Cook Forest Sawmill Center for the Arts, P.O. Box 6, Cooksburg, PA 16217.

About five miles outside of the park River Road meets Pennsylvania Route 899 south, which leads into Clarington where the road to Millstone Creek can again be found near the store.

Clear Creek State Park provides access to the south side of the Clarion River between Clarington and Millstone Creek. It can be reached off Route 949. From Clarington, follow Route 899 to its junction with Route 36, and then take Route 36 to the village of Sigel where Route 949 may be picked up.

The first public campsites at Clear Creek State Park were opened in 1922. In May 1933, the Civilian Conservation Corps moved into the area. When they left, five years later, the park included vacation cabins, a swimming area, food concession, comfort stations, trails, bridges and roads. The 1,209-acre park today has 53 Class B campsites with pit toilets and sanitary dump stations. The campground is open year-round, but access is not guaranteed in the winter. Non-fishing visitors will find 15 miles of hiking trails, swimming at a guarded beach (Memorial Day weekend to Labor Day), picnicking and an environmental education program. Canoe rentals are available from outfitters located outside the park.

Like Cook Forest State Park, Clear Creek also has family cabins available for weekly rental from the second Friday in April to the end of the antlerless deer season in mid-December. The 22 cabins include single beds, a fireplace or wood burning stove, tables, chairs, a refrigerator, modern stove and electric lights. Half-week rentals may be had during the spring and fall.

Kittanning State Forest, 10,113 acres, sits adjacent to Clear Creek State Park and offers other hiking and scenic photography opportunities.

The usual Pennsylvania fly patterns should prove successful for fly fishermen on the Clarion River. These include: Adams, Blue Dun, caddis, Quill Gordon, Muddler Minnow, Mickey Finn, stoneflies, Hare's Ear, Lead-Winged Coachman, Blue-Winged Olives, Hendrickson, Royal Coachman, March Brown, Gray Fox, Light Cahill, Soft Hackle Nymphs, Black Gnat, midges and terrestrials.

Information on the various public lands that touch on the Clarion River is available from the folowing sources:

Supervisor's Office, Allegheny National Forest, 222 Liberty St., P.O. Box 847, Warren, PA 16365. An excellent map of the forest and bordering lands may be had by including $1.00.

Cook Forest State Park, Department of Environmental Resources, P.O. Box 120, Cooksburg, PA 16217.

Clear Creek State Park, Department of Environmental Resources, R.D. 1, Box 82, Sigel, PA 15860.

Kittanning State Forest, Department of Environmental Resources, R.D. 1, Clarion, PA 16214.

Tributaries

With over 40 miles of trout water, the Clarion River has a lot of stocked tributaries for anglers to choose from when the main river is running high and discolored, or when they are just in the mood to fish something smaller. The larger and more important tributary streams are profiled in individual stories. Anglers also should see West Branch Clarion River, East Branch Clarion River, Big Mill Creek, Millstone Creek and Bear Creek in Elk County; and Spring Creek in Elk and Forest counties. Following are some of the other feeders, including Toms Run in Cook Forest State Park and Clear Creek in Clear Creek State Park. Fly fishermen can try some of the same patterns mentioned under the Clarion River.

Toms Run

Appearing at the downstream end of the Clarion's stocked water, Toms Run flows through the heart of Cook Forest State Park. John Cook started his lumber business along this little stream when he built a sawmill on it in 1828. Today, it feeds the children's fishing pond near the park office. It can be reached by following Toms Run Road off Route 36 in the park and toward the Log Cabin Inn and sawmill. The park's "Recreational

Guide," available free of charge at the office, contains a small map showing the exact lay of the stream. Its stocked water runs from its mouth upstream a couple of miles.

Maple Creek

Maple Creek enters the Clarion just before Route 899 joins River Road upstream of Cook Forest State Park. Stocking begins at the mouth and continues upstream for about four miles. Access is mainly a walk-in affair. The lower portion of the stream can be fished by hiking in off River Road. The upper water by taking Route 899 north to the village of Redclyffe and then turning onto either Coon Road, or Bear Run Road. Coon Road appears a little south of Redclyffe. It leads to a dirt and gravel road, which, in turn, crosses the stream. Bear Run Road meets Route 899 at Redclyffe and crosses Maple Creek. (It is the second stream over which the road runs. The first stream is Bearpen Run, which is not listed as an approved trout water.)

Clear Creek

Planted for approximately three miles from its mouth upstream, Clear Creek is accessible off the main road running through Clear Creek State Park. Outside of the park, its upper water can be reached by following Corbett Road across Route 949 from the entrance to the park. Silvis Trail, which runs off Corbett Road, leads to the stream's headwaters. Check Clear Creek State Park's "Recreational Guide" for a map of the park and stream.

Callen Run

Kittanning State Forest surrounds Callen Run, which empties into the Clarion near Heath Pumping Station off Route 949 between Clear Creek State Park and the village of Dutch Hill. Its stocked water covers three miles, and it can be reached by following Callen Run Road off Route 949 at Heath Pumping Station. The "Public Use Map," available free of charge, for Kittanning State Forest provides a good overview of the stream.

Maxwell Run

Running through State Game Lands 44, Maxwell Run is accessible directly off Route 949 at the Elk and Forest county line. A dirt road running off Route 949 where it crosses the stream parallels the upper portion of its five miles of stocked water. The stream's lower water can be reached by Metts Road (Township Road 483) to Township Road 308. Metts Road can be picked up off Route 949 in State Game Lands 54 between the villages of Dutch Hill and Green Briar in Jefferson County.

Tionesta Creek and
South Branch Tionesta Creek
Forest and Warren Counties

West Branch Tionesta Creek
Four Mile Run, Six Mile Run
Farnsworth Branch
Warren County
East Branch Tionesta Creek and
Two Mile Run
Warren and McKean Counties

Blue Jay Creek, Salmon Creek
The Branch
Forest County
Allegheny National Forest

Tionesta Creek
Float Trip

Meandering along the northern edge of Forest County and southeast corner of Warren County, Tionesta Creek is undoubtedly the best known trout stream in the entire Allegheny National Forest. The main stream is formed by the confluence of its West, South and East Branches just south of the town of Sheffield, Warren County. Its stocked water runs from that point downstream for about 23 miles to the village of Kellettville, Forest County.

As befits the most popular stream in the area, Tonesta Creek is easily accessible over all of its stocked length off Pennsylvania Route 666, which can be picked up off U.S. Route 62 at the village of East Hickory (also see East Hickory Creek) north of Tionesta Borough, or Pennsylvania Route 948 at the village of Barnes south of Sheffield. Anglers who enjoy float fishing can canoe the stream's planted water from the village of Lynch downstream to Kellettville, a distance of about 15 miles. According to the American Youth Hostels—Pittsburgh Council's *Canoeing Guide to Western Pennsylvania and Northern West Virginia,* the stream is canoeable for about 35 percent of the year, normally the spring. It is too low when the gauge at Sheffield measures 2.1 feet or lower. The U.S. Forest Service's Minister Creek Campground is located about 15 miles below Sheffield and is a convenient overnight spot for anglers fishing Tionesta Creek and its tributaries. However, it has only six campsites, vault toilets and a hand pump. No reservations are taken. Camping is on a first-come, first-served basis.

Kellettville marks the official end of Tionesta Creek's stocked water. But canoeists can continue downstream—picking up some smallmouth bass or even a muskie—all of the way to Tionesta Reservoir at the town of Tionesta, where the stream finally empties into the Allegheny River. Wooded and wild, especially after it turns away from Route 666, canoeists can find numerous good campsites along the lower portion of Tionesta Creek, as well as plenty of wildlife to enjoy in off moments.

With the vast majority of its land in the public domain, Forest County holds the smallest population of any county in Pennsylvania. Tionesta is the county's only full-fledged borough. It takes its name from Tionesta Creek, an Indian name that has been translated by various authors to mean "it penetrates the island," "it penetrates the forest," "home of the wolves," and "there it has fine banks." A Munsee and Delaware Indian village known as Goshgoshing, "places of hogs," stood near the present town of Tionesta for about five years from 1765 to 1770. David Zeisberger, the famous Moravian missionary and explorer of northern Pennsylvania, visited the village in 1767. Two years later, he built the first Protestant church west of the Allegheny Mountains on the site. His mission was opposed by both the Munsees and the Senecas who controlled the region. The Munsees did not like it because it interfered with their drinking; the Senecas because they feared it would lead to the construction of a fort and the English takeover of the region. Such opposition resulted in plenty of thrilling times for Zeisberger. His trials while preaching to the Indians in Forest County became the subject of a famous Moravian Society painting.

Zeisberger also was probably the first white man to record the presence of oil along the stream. In his journal he noted that the Indians used it "medicinally for toothache, rheumatism, etc. Sometimes it is taken internally. It is of a brown color and burns well and can be used in lamps."

Once the Europeans took possession of Tonesta Creek and the surrounding lands from the Indians, oil, along with lumbering and tanneries, quickly became the region's main industries. The boom years for all three industries ended around the turn of the century. On a much smaller scale, oil and lumbering still help to support the local economy. Loosely regulated drilling operations also cause a number of problems for the environment.

Like many other well-known streams in Pennsylvania, Tionesta Creek was touched by an Indian trial. The Goshgoshing Path, from West Hickory to Clearfield, passed over the stream near the present day Nebraska Access to the Tionesta Reservoir.

Tionesta Creek fly anglers can try the Adams, Blue Quill, Yellow Stonefly, Hare's Ear, Blue Dun, Black Gnat, Muddler Minnow, Black-Nosed Dace, Woolly Bugger in black, olive or brown, Lead-Winged Coachman, Black Gnat, caddis, Renegade, Professor, March Brown, Light Cahill, midges and terrestrials.

West Branch Tionestsa Creek

Sixteen miles of the little West Branch is stocked with trout and access along almost all of that distance is as easy as along the main stream. The stocked water runs from about the town of Sheffield to its headwaters west of Clarendon. U.S. Route 6 parallels the stream from Sheffield to Clarendon south of the county seat of Warren. Chapman Dam Road (State Road 2006), with signs for Chapman State Park, appear in Clarendon and provide access to the West Branch back to its headwaters at 68-acre Chapman Lake (stocked).

Anglers looking to stay in the area while fishing the West Branch or other nearby streams will find a Class B campground with 83 sites at Chapman State Park. Open year-round, the campground offers only pit toilets, water and a dump station. Non-angling campers will find picnic facilities, 16 miles of hiking trails, a playfield, swimming at a guarded beach (Memorial Day weekend to Labor Day), environmental education programs in the summer, boating (no rentals) and a snack bar.

Fly fishermen should find some success with the same patterns mentioned for Tionesta Creek. Details on Chapman State Park may be had by writing:

Chapman State Park, Department of Environmental Resources, R.D. 1, Box 1610, Clarendon, PA 16313.

Farnsworth Branch

Forest Service Road 154 runs off Chapman Dam Road on its way to Chapman State Park and gives access to Farnsworth Branch, a tributary of the West Branch Tionesta Creek that is stocked for 7.5 miles. F.S.R. 154 parallels the stream all of the way to the Farnsworth Fish Hatchery.

Six Mile Run

Only one mile of Six Mile Run is stocked with trout. This tiny tributary of Tionesta Creek can be located by taking the dirt road running to the east in the village of Tiona on U.S. Route 6 north of Sheffield.

Four Mile Run

Planted with trout for six miles from its mouth upstream, Four Mile Run can be reached from the village of Saybrook near St. Paul's Church on Route 6 north of Sheffield. Its upper water may be found by taking Forest Service Road 259 off Route 6 between Roystone and Ludlow, and following it back to Forest Service Road 365 which leads down to the stream.

Two Mile Run

Bordered by a road on one side and an old railroad bed on the other, Two Mile Run might not be as pretty as some of the other tributaries of Tionesta Creek, but its open banks should be a welcome sight to the angler who has been battling the brush on some of these other small streams. It is stocked for a total of ten miles—five in Warren County and five in McKean County—upstream from its mouth in Sheffield. Access to its entire stocked length is available off U.S. Route 6 between Sheffield and Kane. See Tionesta Creek for possible fly patterns.

South Branch Tionesta Creek

Trout are stocked for 3.5 miles along the South Branch in Warren County, and two miles in McKean County. The planted water runs from Sheffield upstream through the villages of Donaldson and Brookston along Route 948 south toward Ridgway. Access is available at numerous spots off Route 948. Fly anglers can once more try some of the patterns listed for Tionesta Creek.

Sheffield, resting at the center of fishing on Tionesta Creek and its tributaries, was founded in 1864 to service tanneries along Tionesta Creek. For a time during the 1870s and 1880s, Sheffield also was a center for the commercial slaughter of the passenger pigeon. Up to 700,000 birds were shipped from the town at a time. (Also see Kinzua Reservoir Tributaries.)

East Branch Tionesta Creek

Touched by a major road—Route 948 at Donaldson—only at its mouth the East Branch is the least accessible of all the main stems of Tionesta Creek. But it is stocked for ten miles—one mile in Warren County and nine miles in McKean County—so offers plenty of angling opportunities.

The lower portion of the East Branch can be reached by hiking upstream from Route 948 in Donaldson. Access to the upper water is available only off forest service roads, which can be difficult to locate. Anglers would do well to spend $1.00 for a Forest Service map of Allegheny National Forest. Otherwise, the East Branch may be found by taking Forest Service Road 133 from U.S. Route 6 in Ludlow. F.S.R. 133 crosses the stream and also intersects with F.S.R. 149 and F.S.R. 470, both of which provide additional access. State Route 3002, which can be picked up off Route 6 in either Wetmore or the Wildcat Recreation Site on Two Mile Creek, touches on two other forest service roads, 126 and 468, that lead to the East Branch. F.S.R. 468 joins F.S.R. 133 for additional access.

Blue Jay Creek

A tributary of the main branch of Tionesta Creek, Blue Jay Creek is stocked for five miles from near its mouth upstream. It can be reached off Blue Jay Road (State Road 1003), which runs south of Route 666 at the village of Lynch.

Salmon Creek and The Branch

Salmon Creek joins Tionesta Creek at the very end of its stocked water in Kellettville. It is stocked for six miles from its confluence with The Branch upstream. Access is available by taking F.S.R. 127 off Route 666 in Kellettville and then F.S.R. 145, which follows Salmon Creek upstream.

The Branch, also stocked for six miles, is accessible off F.S.R. 127 just outside of Kellettville. F.S.R. 361 meets 127 about 1.5 miles beyond its intersection with F.S.R. 145 and Salmon Creek to provide some access to The Branch's upper water.

Allegheny National Forest

Information on Allegheny National Forest, including details on backpacking, may be had by writing:

Supervisor's Office, Allegheny National Forest, 222 Liberty Street, P.O. Box 847, Warren, PA 16365. Enclose $1.00 for a complete map of the forest.

East Hickory Creek
Forest and Warren Counties
Delayed Harvest Artificial Lures Only

Beaver Run, Queen Creek
Forest County

East Hickory Creek

"A Land of Many Uses" is the motto of Allegheny National Forest in Pennsylvania's northwest corner. And it is a title that certainly fits. Anybody who visits the forest will find themselves surrounded by a myriad of hiking trails, wild and stocked trout streams, cross-country skiing and snowmobile roads, campgrounds, herds of deer, flocks of turkey, and one of the largest and most popular lakes in the state, Allegheny Reservoir, or, as it is more commonly known, Kinzua Dam.

Alongside this abundance of hunting, fishing, hiking and boating opportunities, the forest holds extensive reserves of oil and gas, and vast tracts of timber, all of which are exploited for profit. Many people feel these resources, especially the oil, is often obtained in a manner that harms the environment. Poorly capped old wells, hastily bulldozed roads, improperly constructed waste pools and a shortage of enforcement officers all have combined to threaten the beauty of the forest in recent years.

The reason large portions of the half-million-acre national forest are drilled and cut is because the federal government does not own mineral rights to the land. Deeds signing over the property to the public trust, beginning with Calvin Coolidge's signing of the proclamation creating the forest in 1923, have routinely preserved mineral rights for the companies or people who had previously owned it. Exceptions exist, of course, and among the chief ones is Hickory Creek Federal Wilderness.

Acquired through the efforts of the Western Pennsylvania Conservancy, Hickory Creek Wilderness is wedged between East Hickory Creek and Middle Hickory Creek. It is a roadless tract of over 9,400 acres covered with hardwood forests, meadows, bogs and beaver ponds. It is the only federal wilderness area in Pennsylvania and five neighboring states. The area was extensively lumbered by the firm of Wheeler and Dunsebury starting around 1910. The company began operations in the state in 1837. It continued for 100 years, and along the way covered what is now the Hickory Creek Wilderness Area with tram roads and railroad spurs.

Although some wild trout fishing is available in upper reaches of East Hickory Creek, through the wilderness area the stream's stocked water begins further south, below Forest Service Road 119 in Warren County. Its 1.7 mile long Delayed Harvest Artificial Lures Only water lies even further south in Forest County. The stream is planted with browns, rainbows and brookies for ten miles, about five miles in Warren County, and five in Forest County, from downstream of the village of Endeavor upstream toward F.S. 119.

Most of East Hickory Creek's stocked length can be easily reached by taking U.S. Route 62 to the village of East Hickory. In the village, turn onto Pennsylvania Route 666 and follow it to Endeavor. A dirt road, which parallels and crosses the creek, appears on the north side of Route 666 at Endeavor. The special regulation water runs from Otter Creek Bridge upstream to Queen Creek Bridge and is well marked with signs. From the village of Queen, basically a collection of hunting camps, access is mainly a walk-in affair.

Fly fishermen wondering what to try on this medium-sized mountain stream might consider such standard patterns as the Blue Dun, Adams, Blue-Winged Olive, stoneflies, Hare's Ear, Woolly Bugger, Muddler Minnow, Mickey Finn, Matuka Streamers, Hendrickson, Black Gnat, March Brown, Royal Coachman, Renegade, Light Cahill and terrestrials.

Beaver Run

Beaver Run is a small tributary of East Hickory Creek that joins with the latter at Endeavor. It is stocked for about eight winding miles from its junction with East Hickory Creek upstream into its headwaters. Access is available directly off Route 666 from Endeavor beyond Forest Service Road 209. A dirt road then follows the stream as it turns away from the highway.

Queen Creek

Queen Creek joins East Hickory Creek at the village of Queen near the upstream end of that creek's Delayed Harvest Artificial Lures Only water. Like Beaver Run, it is another small tributary that might serve the angler best when everything else in the area is running high and muddy. A dirt road running off to the right, or east, in Queen parallels the lower stream, but most of its three miles of stocked water can be reached only on foot.

Fly anglers on both Queen Creek and Beaver Run should find some success with the patterns mentioned under East Hickory Creek.

Hickory Town, or Lawunakhannek (middle stream place), Delaware and Munsee village, once stood at the mouth of East Hickory Creek on the Allegheny River. David Zeisberger, the Moravian missionary, once preached to the Indians in this town. The inhabitants, however, preferred whiskey and women to the light of religion and ran him out. Zeisberger's trials among the Indians of Forest County is the subject of a famous Moravian painting.

(Also see Tionesta Creek.)

Tideioute Creek
Perry Magee Run, Thompson Run
Warren County

In 1803, at odds with his church, the lay preacher George Rapp disposed of the property he owned in Wurtemberg, Germany, and came to America. He bought 5,000 acres of land on the Ohio River about 25 miles north of Pittsburgh. The next year about 600 of his followers arrived, and then the year after the group formed the Harmony Society, with the purpose of working hard and living simply in "harmony" with God and the earth.

Under such proven tenets, the society prospered. By 1825, after returning from a stay in Indiana, they controlled such a large volume of the trade in western Pennsylvania that some people began screaming for their dissolution. They owned tens of thousands of acres of land, a bank, several factories, coal mines, oil pipelines and oil wells. Because of the society's rule of celibacy, however, the good times were doomed to end. The rule saw more than 250 members desert the group as early as 1832, while natural attrition and a lack of new converts claimed the rest. The last two harmonists dissolved the society in 1906.

Among the numerous pieces of land the Harmony Society did own at one time was the site of Tidioute on the Allegheny River at the mouth of Tidioute Creek—translated at one time or another to mean "seeing far," "straight water," "cluster of islands" and "on the great river." The society's communal coffers were enriched by both their lumber and oil interests around the town. Like at Pithole City, Titusville, Smethport and other boom towns in Pennsylvania's oil fields, land prices multiplied almost with every new gusher.

Tidioute in the twentieth century is just another sleepy little mountain town with its best years in the past. Its remaining signs of greatness are mainly the large frame houses of the boom years that still dot its Main Street. But it still manages to come alive every year during the whitetail deer season, when hunters from across Pennsylvania, New York and Ohio take to the surrounding big woods of Allegheny National Forest and State Game Lands 86, and the state of the trout season. In between, it has a well-known fishing tournament to keep the blood flowing.

Tidioute Creek

Tidioute Creek is the first of three good trout streams anglers can reach by simply following Main Street through town and up the Allegheny River. It holds some four miles of stocked water, running from its mouth in town upstream beyond the village of Hemlock. Access can be had by following Tidioute Creek Road up the mountain alongside the stream and toward Hemlock.

Perry Magee Run

Enveloped by State Game Lands 86, Perry Magee Run has no road running alongside of it for easy access over its entire length. But it can be reached by continuing up the Allegheny to the village of Magee just inside the game lands where it enters the river. It also can be reached by following Township Road 372, the second road to head up into the mountains after Tidioute Creek Road, and then hiking in. Where the road forms the border of the game lands is where it is closest to the stream.

Thompson Run

Rated by some anglers as the best in the area, Thompson Run

can be found by continuing to drive upstream to the village of Athom. The main road will turn to gravel as it nears the stream. An unpaved dirt road follows Thompson Run from its mouth upstream over its approximately three miles of planted water.

Fly fishermen on all three streams should catch fish using the Royal Coachman, Adams, stoneflies, Quill Gordon, caddis, Hendrickson, Muddler Minnow, Woolly Buggers, Mickey Finn, Matuka and Marabou Streamers, Hare's Ear, Muskrat, March Brown, Gray Fox, Black Gnat, Light Cahill, midges and terrestrials.

The map of Allegheny National Forest published by the U.S. Forest Service contains Tidioute Creek, Perry Magee Run and Thompson Run, and should be a standard piece of equipment for anglers fishing streams in the national forest and its surroundings. It can be had for $1.00 by writing: Supervisor's Office, Allegheny National Forest, 222 Liberty Street, P.O. Box 847, Warren, PA 16365.

The map also can be purchased at the forest headquarters and any of the four ranger stations or the Kinzua Point Information Center at Kinzua Dam.

(Also see Tionesta Creek and East Hickory Creek.)

Brokenstraw Creek
Little Brokenstraw Creek
Blue Eye Run, Spring Creek
Warren County

Brokenstraw Creek

Easy access and a heavy stocking allotment of browns and rainbows make Brokenstraw Creek—sometimes referred to as the Big Brokenstraw—one of the most popular trout waters in Warren County. Running from the New York State line in the far western corner of Warren to meet the Allegheny River at Irvine, it also is the longest trout stream in the county. The stocked water extends for approximately 15 miles from the village of Spring Creek downstream to the town of Youngsville.

The name Brokenstraw appears to be a corruption of the Seneca Indian name "Kachuidagon," or "broken reed," according to *A History of the Indian Villages and Place Names in Pennsylvania*. The Delaware Indians translated the word as "Poquihhilleu," "broken," which early French explorers in the region translated as "La Paille Coupee," a phrase that in English means "broken straw."

Buckaloon, outside of Irvine, was once the site of an Indian village. It seems to be another corruption of the Delaware "Poquihhilleu." This time by Irish traders. Buckaloon, along with the village of Connewago at the present site of Warren, was destroyed by General Daniel Brodhead in a 1779 campaign against Indians sympathetic to the British during the Revolutionary War. The U.S. Forest Service now operates Allgeheny National Forest's Buckaloons Campground on the mouth of Brokenstraw Creek in the area of the old Indian village. It contains 40 campsites with flush and vault toilets and water fountains, as well as a picnic area, launch ramp for the Allegheny River and hiking trail. As with all national forest campgrounds, sites are available on a first-come, first-served basis. It is open with full services from Memorial Day to Labor Day. No reservations are accepted.

Besides making their home along Brokenstraw Creek, the Indians also used the stream in their travels. Brokenstraw Path, which ran from Buckaloon to Waterford, or Fort Le Boeuf, in Erie County, followed along the stocked portion of the stream.

Access to Brokenstraw Creek may be had by taking U.S. Route 6 west from the town of Warren. Route 6 crosses and then parallels the stream from Youngsville to Pittsfield. In Youngsville, access is available off west Main Street, but there is a lot of private property in the area.

At the town of Pittsfield, Pennsylvania Route 27 west appears. It follows Brokenstraw Creek to the village of Garland, where Pennsylvania Route 426 meets it and trails the stream over the remainder of its stocked water to the village of Spring Creek. Parking areas along the road generally denote access points. Bridges also cross the stream in a couple of places.

Little Brokenstraw Creek

Like Brokenstraw Creek, Little Brokenstraw Creek also originates in New York State and has relatively easy access. However, it is less than half the size of the Big Brokenstraw which it joins in Pittsfield.

Crossing the state line near Bear Lake, the Little Brokenstraw winds its way through the wilderness of northwestern Warren County alongside the old Erie Railroad line. It is stocked for over 11 miles from above the village of Lottsville on Pennsylvania Route 957 to its mouth in Pittsfield. Access is available off Route 6 west from Pittsfield and Pennsylvania Route 958, which runs off Route 6 a short distance before the village of Wrightsville. Both Route 6 and Route 958 cross the stream. Several other bridges from which anglers can reach the stream run off both roads.

Fly patterns for both streams might include: caddis, Quill Gordon, Hendrickson, March Brown, Adams, Hare's Ear, Muskrat, Black Gnat, Soft Hackle Nymphs, marabou streamers in black, white or yellow, Muddler Minnow, Mickey Finn and Woolly Buggers.

Blue Eye Run

Flowing through State Game Lands 143, Blue Eye Run is a nice wilderness tributary of Brokenstraw Creek. It is stocked for seven miles from its mouth upstream. Access is limited to a dirt road, which can be found running off Route 27 to the north just before its junction with Route 462 in Garland.

Spring Creek

Planted with trout for about four miles, Spring Creek is accessible off Cemetery Road, running off Route 462 east of the village of Spring Creek and toward the village of Ross Corners. The stocked water starts around Jackson Hill Road outside of Ross Corners. Cemetery Road parallels Spring Creek upstream through the villge of West Spring Creek, where Hyde Road takes over and follows it along most of the remainder of its stocked length.

Fly fishermen can try any of the patterns mentioned for Brokenstraw Creek and Little Brokenstraw Creek on these tributary streams.

Kinzua Tailrace Allegheny River
Warren County
No Closed Season

The opening of Kinzua Dam in 1966 changed a lot of things along the Allegheny River all of the way from the New York line to Pittsburgh. It impounded a lake 27 miles long which annually brings millions of tourist dollars into a two-state region known as the Alleghenies. It stopped the yearly flooding of towns and cities along the river, and likewise the periods of drought that sometimes left those same communities high and dry. It inundated historical tribal lands granted to the Seneca Indians shortly after the Revolutionary War. And it lead the Fish Commission to establish a year-round trout fishery in its tailwaters.

At just three-quarters of a mile in length, the Kinzua Dam tailrace is the shortest piece of year-round trout water in the commonwealth. But that does not mean it is a small trout fishery. The Allegheny below the dam is a full blown river, extremely big water when compared to most other trout habitat in Pennsylvania.

Despite a width that might give pause to many anglers without a boat, the tailrace is very fishable from its banks. Trout lie scattered throughout its waters, and become quite active when the temperature rises. The general rule is to move closer to the whitewater of the discharges when the river level is low, and further away when it is high. The faster water, with its higher oxygen content, also is usually a better choice for the warmer months, while the deeper, calmer stretches are more productive during colder months since they require a smaller expenditure of energy by the logey trout.

High water periods of late winter and early spring may turn off many visiting anglers, but locals maintain it is one of the best times to fish the tailrace. Water temperature during the winter months runs around 33 degrees. It starts rising in April toward the 40-degree mark. In mid-May, the upper gates of the dam are normally opened. This is another good period to fish the tailrace, as are those times when the dam's discharge is frequently changed.

The year-round portion of the Allegheny River in Warren County runs from the wire about a hundred yards downstream of Kinzua Dam to Dixon Island. It can be located by taking U.S. Route 6 east through the borough of Warren. Shortly after the road crosses the Allegheny River it will be joined on the left by Pennsylvania Route 59. The parking area for the tailrace is clearly marked on the left. Route 59 also may be picked up off U.S. Route 219 south of Bradford in McKean County.

Though a smattering of rainbows appear, most of the trout taken from the tailrace—walleyes and muskies also can be caught in the stretch—are browns. Rigged minnows account for the most fish caught from the banks. Popular lures during the peak spring period include jigs with white bucktail or plastic bodies, and small minnow-type plugs, such as Rapalas and Rebels, in gold and silver.

Due to the strength of the current during the best fishing periods, and the distances that often need to be covered, fly fishing is not the most productive of methods in the tailrace. For those anglers who favor the method, streamers and bucktails in black, yellow or white remain possibilities, as do large attractor patterns like the Woolly Bugger.

For anglers who might want to explore the area further, there is an information center, which can provide materials on the river, Allegheny Reservoir, campgrounds and other accommodations and sights, in the tailrace parking lot. Information, including an indispensable map of Allegheny National Forest (cost $1.00) also may be had prior to a visit by writing: Supervisor's Office, Allegheny National Forest, 222 Liberty St., P.O. Box 847, Warren, PA 16365.

Pennsylvania Trout & Salmon Fishing Guide

Kinzua Tailrace, Allegheny River.

Caldwell Creek
Delayed Harvest Fly Fishing Only
West Branch Caldwell Creek
Catch and Release
Warren County

Pine Creek
Warren and Crawford Counties

Caldwell Creek and West Branch Caldwell Creek

Nestled deep in the southwest corner of Warren County, far from the interstates, or even a major state highway, Caldwell Creek and West Branch Caldwell Creek are two very beautiful freestone streams that combine fine fishing with a splendid sense of isolation. Anglers who visit these waters might at times imagine they have stepped into a calendar, and should definitely leave with all the good feelings trout fishing is meant to inspire.

Caldwell Creek is a tributary of Pine Creek, which joins historic Oil Creek east of Titusville and Colonel Edwin Drake's famous oil well, the first well in the world drilled exclusively for the purpose of finding oil (see Oil Creek and Pithole Creek). The Cornplanter-Venango Indian Path, between the Indian towns of Venago (Franklin) and Cornplanter, now buried beneath the waters of Alleheny Reservoir, once passed near the stream.

Land surrounding both Caldwell Creek and West Branch Caldwell Creek, as might be expected, has been touched by the lumber and oil industries. Actually, the two streams were near the center of Pennsylvania's oil industry throughout the nineteenth century. But any damage the rush might have inflicted upon the streams is not very evident today. In fact, Pennzoil and the Hammermill Paper Co. worked with the Fish Commission and Trout Unlimited on the West Branch's Catch and Release Project.

Even though Caldwell Creek and its West Branch are off the beaten path, it is not all that difficult to reach, and dirt and gravel roads provide plenty of access.

Pennsylvania Route 27 is the starting point for both streams. It can be picked up off Pennsylvania Route 8 in Titusville for anglers coming from the south, or U.S. Route 6 at Pittsfield in the north. A short distance south of the village of Grand Valley a green road sign points to Selkirk two miles away. The road, State Road 3004, crosses the stream at Selkirk, marked by the ruins of the Valley Gun Shop and a scattering of homes. Caldwell Creek's 1.2 mile Delayed Harvest Fly Fishing Only Project begins immediately downstream of the Selkirk Bridge and continues downstream to the Dotyville Bridge. A dirt road runs straight ahead off S.R. 3004, just past the gun shop and provides access to the lower portion of the project. This road runs parallel to the stream, though a short hike is generally required to reach it. Parking is available at various locations.

West Branch Caldwell Creek's Catch and Release water may be found by turning right onto a dirt and gravel road that meets S.R. 3004 near the Selkirk Bridge. The 3.6-mile long project lies about a half-mile down the road. It is marked both by a steel bridge and a Fish Commission sign, and runs from that point upstream to Three Bridge Run.

Popular fly patterns are: Quill Gordons, Hendricksons, March Browns, Hare's Ears, Muskrats, stoneflies, caddis, Light Cahills, Black Gnat, Woolly Buggers, marabou streamers in white, yellow and black, Muddler Minnows, Mickey Finns, Matukas and terrestrials.

Pine Creek

Fed by Caldwell Creek, Pine Creek joins the East Branch Oil Creek in East Titusville to form Oil Creek. Of medium-size, it is stocked for some eight miles, from its confluence with the East Branch upstream.

Access to Pine Creek's stocked water may be had directly off Route 27 at the village of Enterprise in extreme southwestern Warren County. Its upper stocked length may be reached by taking Township Road 303 on the east side of Route 27 toward the village of Pineville. The first road on the left parallels the creek, at a distance, upstream, and meets McGraw Road (Township Road 309). Another left turn onto McGraw Road leads to the stream.

The secondary road (State Route 3002) running to the east from Route 27 in Enterprise leads to Pine Creek's downstream water and East Titusville. S.R. 3002 parallels the stream, though it is out of sight, all of the way to East Titusville. Access also is available along Mt. Hope Road, Keyes Road and Doteyville Road, all of which run off S.R. 3002.

Anglers who are fishing Caldwell Creek can gain quicker access to lower Pine Creek by simply following Dotyville Road, which parallels Caldwell Creek downstream, from Selkirk through Dotyville to its end. Fly fishermen can try some of the same patterns mentioned for Caldwell Creek and West Caldwell Creek on Pine Creek.

(Also see Oil Creek, East Branch Oil Creek.)

Oil Creek
Crawford and Venango Counties

East Branch Oil Creek
Thompson Run, Five Mile Creek
Crawford County

Oil Creek

August afternoons in Pennsylvania are normally hot and muggy, even in the mountains. And August 27, 1859 was no different. William "Uncle Billy" Smith, a native of Salina, Pennsylvania, and his men were gathering their tools together to quit work for the weekend when the drill they were operating slipped into a crevice and dropped another six inches. It had reached a depth of 69 feet. Probably thinking about their dinner, and possibly a cool drink, the crew pulled the drill from the hole and headed for their homes.

As was his habit, late the next afternoon, Sunday, Smith, along with his 15-year-old son, Samuel, stopped by the well to look it over and tinker a bit. But something was different this time. When he peered into the pipe he noticed a dark fluid floating on top of the usual water. He lowered a piece of rain spout he had fashioned into a ladle to the bottom of the derrick and dipped up a sample. It was oil. They had expected to find oil, but not until they were down several hundred feet. He could not believe it. Immediately, he sent his son running to inform the crew.

"They've struck oil! They've struck oil!" he shouted, announcing the arrival of the first well drilled specifically for oil in North America. The manager of the drilling operation, Colonel Edwin L. Drake, would find Smith and his son standing guard over the well, and a mixture of tubs and barrels brimming with oil, when he arrived for work the following morning.

Drake Well on Oil Creek.

Oil was not an unknown substance before the successful Drake/Smith well in 1859. Natural petroleum springs were known in ancient Roman times. And, according to information gathered by the Pennsylvania Historical and Museum Commission in connection with the Drake well, French missionaries in seventeenth century America are believed to have been describing an oil spring near Cuba, New York when they wrote of "thick and heavy water, which ignites like brandy and boils in bubbles of flame when fire is applied to it." The eighteenth century also saw reports of trade in oil being conducted with the Seneca Indians, which is probably why "Seneca Oil" became another term for petroleum in Colonial America.

Early settlers used crude oil mainly as a medicine. The popularity of oil lamps and an increase in machinery of various types brought a dramatic rise in demand for petroleum in the 1840s. This demand came at a time when whale oil was declining and lard was proving inadequate. It was the resulting search for an alternative source of petroleum that eventually led to a decision to try drilling a well.

Dr. Francis Brewer, a physician from Massachusetts who was a pioneer in the use of petroleum for medical purposes, moved to Titusville, Pennsylvania on the banks of Oil Creek in 1851. The purpose of his trip was to work for his father's lumber firm, but he almost immediately became interested in an old oil spring located on the Hibbard family farm near the village of Upper Mill. In the fall of 1853, Dr. Brewer carried a small bottle of oil from the spring to Hanover, New Hampshire, where it impressed Dartmouth University professors as both a medicine and chemical.

But it was the label—depicting a derrick over a salt well from which oil flowed as a by-product—that drew the attention of George Bissell, a graduate of Dartmouth and native of Hanover then practicing law in New York City. He began to wonder if the oil could be used as an illuminant, and then, along with Jonathan Eveleth, decided to form a company to possibly develop the spring and market the oil. After several trips to Titusville, Bissell and Eveleth purchased the Hibbard farm for $5,000, and then on December 30, 1854 organized the Pennsylvania Rock Oil Company of New York, the first petroleum company in the world.

Following a number of business maneuvers, the Seneca Oil Co. was given control of the Titusville land on March 23, 1858. "Colonel" Edwin L. Drake, a middle-aged, sickly railroad conductor whose chief qualification may have been the interest he showed in oil from the spring, was named general manager of the company at a salary of $1,000 a year. He arrived in Titusville in May 1858.

Throughout the summer of 1858, Drake's crews sunk several wells by the back-breaking means of pick and shovel, while drilling methods were being worked out. One of the hand-dug wells actually did strike oil, but another nearly drowned a crew member when it opened a spring that filled the shaft within a matter of minutes. The accident persuaded Drake to push ahead with drilling plans.

Lacking any practical drilling experience, Drake went looking for help. Two of the first drillers he hired never showed up, and a third was kept from the job by problems at a salt well he was working on. Then the colonel found William Smith, who had worked on salt well around Tarentum, Pennsylvania. He agreed to do the drilling fo $2.50 a day, including the services of his son and his own drilling tools. He arrived in Titusville in May 1859, and three months later earned his entrance into history.

In the years following the success of Drake's venture, northwestern Pennsylvania became the center of the oil industry in the United States. Towns like Titusville, Oil City and Franklin at-tracted fortune hunters from all over the globe and boasted their own millionaires' rows, where those who did strike it rich built their homes overlooking the oil fields. Such an untamed rush for wealth naturally destroyed the environment, especially Oil Creek, along which much of the petroleum lay buried. Photographs of the period at the Drake Well Museum reveal a dirty, festering sewer rimmed by hills of raw mud, shacks of green, unseasoned lumber and rickety oil derricks. In 1861, when the price of oil dropped to ten cents a barrel, petroleum was even dumped directly into the stream in an attempt to improve prices.

By 1875 most of the region's wells had run dry and many of the boom towns had withered. At least one, Pithole City, disappeared altogether. One man's ceiling is another man's floor, though, and with the decline of the region's petroleum industry, Oil Creek, and other local streams, slowly, over the decades, began to cleanse themselves.

Today, Oil Creek is one of the best trout streams in the region. And over 13 miles of it are protected by Oil Creek State Park. It extends from the Drake Well Museum in Titusville downstream toward the borough of Rouseville, the site of the first great oil well fire in the region. The stretch, which is accessible only off a bicycle path, is well stocked with both brown and rainbow trout. The lower section of the stream can be reached by following the signs for the park off U.S. Route 8 just north of Rouseville. Anglers who are not crazy about walking two, three or four miles to fish will be glad to know a concession in the park rents bicycles—but ony from Memorial Day to Labor Day. Before and after those holidays the middle portions of the park water belong mostly to the hardy fishermen, or those who own a bicycle, or canoe. Oil Creek is canoeable from March through June.

Although the park, which was developed to tell the story of the nation's early petroleum industry, does not contain a campground, there are a number of other things an angler's family can do while he is out on the water. Over 32 miles of hiking trails exist in the 7,007 acre park. The terrain includes steep hills, deep hollows and swamp lands. Picnicking is available, including in selected spots along the bike path. But the visitor's center, with an extensive display on the early oil boom, is the best distraction of all. In addition, a seasonal interpreter presents historic and environmental programs.

The upper reaches of the park water may be reached by following the signs for the Drake Well Museum off Pennsylvania Route 8 near Titusville. The northern end of the bicycle path appears near the entrance to the museum grounds. Anglers who would really like to learn something about the beginnings of the nation's petroleum industry should consider spending an hour or two at the museum where they can see a recreation of Drake's first well, as well as numerous other pieces of nineteenth century oil drilling equipment.

Oil Creek itself is stocked for some 27 miles, all of the way from above Riceville in northern Crawford County, to about Rouseville south of Oil Creek Park. Access to the stream outside of the park is available along Pennsylvania Route 36 between East Titusville and Titusville, and Route 8 between Titusville and the Hydetown. From Hydetown the stream can be reached only by side roads. State Route 1011 picks up the stream in Hydetown to Clappville. From Hydetown to Tyronville, Oil Creek is trailed by State Route 1020. At Tyronville, Township Road 860 parallels the creek to Centerville, where Route 8 again appears and runs alongside the stream to about Riceville.

Among the favorite fly patterns on Oil Creek are: Quill Gordons, Henricksons, March Browns, Sulphurs, Cahills, Royal Coachmen, Lead-Wing Coachmen, Soft Hackle Nymphs, Adams, caddis, Hare's Ear and terrestrials.

East Branch Oil Creek

Approximately ten miles of East Branch Oil Creek in Crawford County is stocked with trout. The planted water runs from Centerville on Route 8 where the stream empties into Oil Creek, upstream to Spartansburg on Pennsylvania Route 77.

Smaller than its larger relative, the East Branch also is less accessible. However, it can be fished off Route 8 in Centerville, Pennsylvania Route 89, between Buell Corners and Pennsylvania Route 77, where it flows along the road for a piece, as well as off Route 77 in Spartansburg. Fly fishermen can start with some of the same flies used on Oil Creek.

Thompson Run

Thompson Run meets East Branch Oil Creek at the village of Hydetown on Route 8 a short distance north of Titusville. It is stocked for 3.5 miles in two portions, from its mouth upstream to roughly Stewart Road, and then from about Route 89 upstream. It can be reached by turning east off Route 8 and onto Gilson Ridge Road in the center of Hydetown. Gilson Ridge Road crosses and follows the lower stream, the first road to the right then parallels it upstream, at a distance.

On Route 89, Thompson Run can be found at the village of Shelmadine Springs. Bethel Road parallels the creek upstream off Route 89 for a short distance.

Five Mile Creek

Five Mile Creek joins East Branch Oil Creek between the villages of Buell Corners and Merchant Corner on Route 89 north of Titusville. Its two miles of stocked water, reaching from its mouth upstream, can be found by following a dead-end secondary road which meets Patcheon Road on the east side of Route 89 about three miles south of Merchant Corners.

Both Thompson Run and Five Mile Creek are small streams, so might be good choices to try when the streams they feed are running high or discolored. Fly anglers can use the same patterns mentioned under Oil Creek.

(Also see Pithole Creek, Pine Creek in Crawford and Warren Counties, and Caldwell Creek.)

Pithole Creek
West Branch Pithole Creek
Venango County

Ghost towns are most often associated with the western United States. Their dark-eyed facades, tumbleweed strewn streets, faded saloon signs and squeaky swinging doors have been standard fare for western movies since the days of silent film. Most of them were built on gold or silver, and died as soon as the "mother lode" gave out, which in many cases was only a matter of a year or two.

Because of the image created by Hollywood, few people would think to place a ghost town east of the Mississippi River, and certainly not in a state as old and heavily populted as Pennsylvania. George Washington crossing the Delaware River to catch the British by surprise; the Continental Army freezing without shoes at Valley Forge; or the founding fathers gathering in Philadelphia to argue over a constitution are among the images most often associated with Pennsylvania. Only a relatively few people would think to connect the state with a ghost town. Yet the abandoned town of Pithole City has a history as rich and every bit as exciting as any ghost town in the West.

In the years before the Civil War the region around Pithole Creek was a wilderness. Only two small farms belonging to two brothers, Thomas and Walter Holmden, stood along its banks about five miles upstream of its mouth on the Allegheny River. Then in the spring of 1864 I.N. Frazier and James Faulkner, two employees of the Humbolt Refinery in Plumer, leased 65 acres of land from Thomas Holmden, formed the United States Petroleum Co. and set in motion plans to drill for oil.

Frazier and Faulkner's venture was a true wildcat affair. At the time, virtually all the oil produced in the world was coming from wells along either Oil Creek or the Allegheny River. The pair had no way of knowing for certain if any oil at all existed along Pithole Creek. But they formed the United States Petroleum Co and, with the aid of a witch hazel divining rod, selected a spot to start drilling in the flat land next to the creek. That first well, and several following it, turned out to be dry. As the company began drilling what was later to become known as the "Frazier Well," two local speculators, Thomas Duncan and George Prather, appeared on the scene and purchased the Holmden Farm for $25,000. The well hit, and oil started to flow at the rate of 250 barrels a day. With a barrel selling for $6, the company's stock jumped from $6.25 a share to $40. This at a time when bread could be bought for a penny or two a loaf.

News of the Frazier Well quickly spread throughout the oil region. In April, at the same time Lee was surrendering to Grant at Appomattox Court House in Virginia, a Boston company drilled a well just 100 feet beyond the boundary of the United Sttes Petroleum Co. land. Known as the Homestead Well, it too began flowing at the rate of 250 barrels—and attracted an investor, whose Dramatic Oil Co. withdrew early—by the name of John Wilkes Booth.

The end of the Civil War left the country flooded with paper currency and businessmen eager to see the good times continue. The break up of the army also left thousands of discharged soldiers in need of work. When word about the discovery of oil at Pithole Creek, a location once considered unpromising, reached both groups it set off a stampede. The rush of humanity toward the little Allegheny River tributary quickly grew beyond anything the oil region had ever seen. Roads leading to the site clogged with fortune hunters of every type. Production rose to 500 barrels a day at the Homestead Well and 1,200 barrels a day at the Frazier Well. The United States Petroleum Co. divided its property into half-acre lots and offered them to newcomers for $3,000 a piece. They sold 80 lots.

In May 1865, just five months after the Frazier Well began to flow, Pithole City was laid out in 500 lots along 22 streets on a hill above Pithole Creek. Buildings went up at a furious pace, many in as little as five days. Lots measured just 33 feet in width and could not be purchased. They had to be leased for a period of three years, after which the owner of the building could either remove it or sell it to the owner of the property. If a five-year lease was desired buildings had to be surrendered to the landowner at the end of the period. Lots rented for between $275 and $850 a year.

At the same time the 500 lots on the hillside were being filled, exciting things were happening at the wells on the flats around the Pithole Creek. On June 17 the United States Petroleum Co. sunk a well that began flowing at the rate of 800 barrels a day. Two days later another well started spewing 400 barrels a day. These "Twin Wells" alone gave the company an income of $2,000 a day.

From an ecological point of view, such incredibly rapid growth could bring nothing but disaster to the environment. On June

19th storage tanks connected to the Frazier Well burst pouring some 2,500 barrels of oil into Pithole Creek. Two boys playing along the creek about a half-mile below the tanks touched a lighted match to the crude. The resulting fire took the efforts of over 200 men to extinguish. But the "No Smoking" signs that immediately sprouted like weeds all over the flats did little good. The fire was only the first of dozens to visit the town during its boom days. PitholeCreek itself became a muddy, stinking scar.

By the end of June 1865, wells along Pithole Creek were producing 2,000 barrels of oil a day, a full one-third of the region's total output. Long processions of wagons moved back and forth from Pithole City to Titusville, Oil City and other shipping points. The heavy traffic quickly destroyed all the roads leading into the town. Near the end of July many teamsters stopped hauling oil out of Pithole. Worried merchants and shippers in Titusville hurriedly put together a fund to repair the roads. Teamsters were required to contribute $1.00 a week out of their own pockets. The price of shipping oil to the nearest railhead rose to $3.00 a barrel, or exactly the same amount for which a barrel was selling in Pithole.

The excitement on Pithole Creek reached its peak in September, nine months after the Frazier Well began to flow. Production rose to 6,000 barrels a day. The original Holmden Farm property purchased by the United States Petroleum Co. accounted for 4,000 barrels of that total. Duncan and Prather, who had sold the farm to three Titusville men in July for $1,300,000, took it back when the buyers could not meet the terms of the sale. In August it sold again for $2,000,000. This same land would be bought by Venango County in 1878 for $4.37 and sold to a private owner for $83.76 in 1886.

Like boom towns in Colorado or Wyoming, Pithole City attracted a wide, often unseemly group of citizens, and had a diverse, often rough, social life. At its height, with a population of over 15,000 people, the town had two telegraph offices, two banks, two churches, a post office, water company, fire company, daily newspaper, scores of grocery stores, hardware stores, blacksmith shops, a 1,100 seat theater and nearly 60 hotels or boarding houses. Populating it all were such characters as Ben Hogan, the "wickedest man in the world," who later became an evangelist, and French Kate, his partner and one of the most famous "upstairs" girls ever to call the town home.

"The Trinity M.E. Church was crowded last night with all that could possibly get in, a great portion of the audience standing in the aisles and the back part of the room, down to the head of the staircase.

"The meeting was opened with prayer by the Rev. Craft and Ben Hogan came forward and addressed the crowd for nearly two hours. His talk was principally of his old life (formerly proprietor of the notorious 'Floating Place' well known to oilmen as a gambling hall and den of iniquity) and his reformation and the sincerity of his repentance. He speaks of his being converted weeks before his wife 'English Jenny,' and his efforts to have her follow him. At the conclusion of his remarks, the choir sang, 'Where is my wandering boy?' " Oil City Derrick, January 26, 1880.

The decline and final abandonment of Pithole City was every bit as swift as its rise. In August 1865, the Homestead Well suddenly stopped flowing. The same month the Grant Well and others on the Holmden Farm burned. Then in October, fires destroyed $1.5 million worth of oil property on the flats along the creek, and the next month the Frazier Well quit spouting. January 1866 saw a sharp overall drop in production, February and March disastrous fires on Holmden Street and Brown Street, two major thoroughfares in the town, and April six major fires that sent a large portion of the town up in smoke.

Pithole City lived on through the remainder of 1866 and into 1867. But businesses and residents continued to drift away. By the end of its second year the town, for all intents and purposes, was dead. Only a handful of people remained on the site in 1870. A few years later there was nothing left to mark the location but empty cellar holes and odds and ends of lumber. The greatest bubble in the early history of the oil industry had burst.

Pithole City may have been a flash in the pan as far as cities go, but its legacy lives on everyday in no less a form that the Alaskan pipeline. For it was at Pithole where the world's first commercially successful crude oil pipeline was built. Although the line, which was designed by Samuel Van Syckel, consisted of two pipes measuring just two inches in diameter each and running only 5.5 miles from Pithole to the Miller Farm, where the oil could be picked up by the railroad, it completely revolutionized the oil transportation business. The cost of moving the crude from source to market fell from $3 a barrel hauled out on the muddy roads to $1. The pipeline instantly caught on, and soon lines were running from all the principal oil fields to the refineries of Titusville, Oil City and Franklin.

The streets of Pithole City are now nothing more than mowed paths along a grassy and wooded hillside. The major streets and buildings have been marked and small displays erected by the Pennsylvania Historic and Museum Commission. A museum also has been established along the top of the hill full of photographs of the way things used to be.

Pithole City may be long gone, but the creek around which all the excitement grew remains, and certainly is in much better shape than in the old days. Pithole Creek, which takes its name from the deep fissures or "pits" on its west side near the point where it empties into the Allegheny River, begins near the village of Neiltown, Forest County. It is stocked with brown trout over a distance of 10.5 miles from the Forest/Venango County line downstream to State Route 1004 east of the village of Plumer. Until it is joined by West Branch Pithole Creek near Pithole City, however, it is a small stream measuring only three or four feet across. From there downstream it rapidly grows in size until it is a relatively large stream by the time it reaches the Allegheny River opposite the village of Henrys Bend.

Access to Pithole Creek is limited and available mainly along back roads that cross it at various points or parallel it for short distances. Its lower stocked water can be found by taking Pennsylvania Route 227 to Plumer and then turning east on S.R. 1004 toward State Game Lands 235 and away from Oil Creek State Park.

North of Route 227 signs appear for Pithole City. State Route 1006 leads back to the historic site and crosses over the West Branch just upstream of its confluence with Pithole Creek proper. Township Road 614 appears on the left just before S.R. 1006 crosses the stream. It parallels the West Branch upstream for about a mile. Township Road 639 joins Route 227 on the east about 3.5 miles north of the turn-off for Pithole City also crosses the West Branch.

From the bridge near Pithole City, S.R. 1006 trails the smaller portion of Pithole Creek upstream in a rough sort of way for about two miles when it crosses over it once more at the intersection with Township Road 626. Continuing east from there Township Road 634 appears and crosses over the creek. Just on the other side of the bridge T-C34 joins the fun following the tiny stream across Pennsylvania Route 36.

Pithole Creek fly fishermen can try: Blue Quills, caddis, Quill Gordons, Adams, Hare's Ears, stoneflies, Hendricksons, Lead--Winged Coachmen, March Browns, Gray Foxes, Light Cahills, Yellow Drakes, Sulphurs, Black Gnats, midges and terrestrials.

Sugar Creek
East Branch Sugar Creek
Venango and Crawford Counties

Sugar Creek

Relatively large in size when compared to most Pennsylvania trout streams, Sugar Creek is stocked for about 17.5 miles in Venango and Crawford Counties. The stocked water runs from its mouth on historic French Creek (not an approved trout water) in Venango County upstream to the village of Cooperstown, where its main branches converge. A gap then appears between Cooperstown and the village of Bradleytown. Stocking resumes at Bradleytown and continues north into Crawford County.

Sugar Creek is a pretty stream flowing through mostly farm country with a touch of woods in its lower, larger portions from its mouth to Cooperstown, and wilder forest lands from Bradleytown into Crawford County.

Like Sandy Creek (see which) to the south, George Washington also crossed Sugar Creek on his expedition along the Venango Path to Erie County's Fort Le Boeuf in 1753. A French force had recently evicted the Englishman, John Frazier, from his trading post in Venango (Franklin) and built Fort Machault on the site. Nevertheless, when then Major Washington arrived on the scene he was received politely by the French commander who referred him to his superior at Fort Le Boeuf. After spending two days in Venango, Washington and his party again set off, on December 7, with their letter from Virginia's Lieutenant Governor Robert Dinwiddie warning the French they were trespassing on territory claimed by Britain. They probably crossed Sugar Creek near the mouth of Warden Run downstream from the village of Wyattville.

"Finding the water too deep for fording, they swam the horses, carried the baggage over on trees, and camped for the night," writes Paul A.W. Wallace in *Indian Paths of Pennsylvania*.

The next day the party proceeded northwest along French Creek, through what is now Carlton and Cochranton, then on to Meadville and Fort Le Bouef. In his journal of the trip, Washington dismissed the final five days between Venango and Fort Le Bouef in two sentences.

"7th. . .At 11 o'clock we set out for the Fort, and were prevented from arriving till the 11th by excessive Rains, Snows, and bad Traveling, through many Mires and Swamps. These we were obliged to pass, to avoid crossing the Creek (French Creek), which was impossible, either by fording or rafting, the Water was so high and rapid."

As at Fort Machault, politeness marked Major Washington's reception at Fort Le Bouef (Waterford). In reply to Lt. Governor Dinwiddie's demand they withdrew, however, the French commander said he would hold possession of the Ohio country for France until he received orders to the contrary from the Governor General of Canada. The French also unsuccessfully tried to woo the Indians in Washington's party, including the Seneca Half King Tanachariston, with guns and others presents.

Washington's return home was marked by a continuance of bad weather and hard traveling conditions, as well as his near drowning in a stream fording. His report also led to Lt. Governor Dinwiddie sending a troop of about 40 volunteers to establish a fort at the forks of the Ohio. That first English fort on the site of Pittsburgh lasted less than three months, until a force of some 500 French descended upon it by boat on the Allegheny River.

U.S. Route 322 west of Franklin today follows, and provides good access, to the lower portion of Sugar Creek from its mouth on French Creek upstream to the junction of Pennsylvania Route 427 at Wyattsville. Route 427 trails Sugar Creek from that point north beyond the junction of Pennsylvania Route 27 and the Crawford County line. Parking is available at various spots along both roads

Sugar Creek fly anglers can try, along with any of their favorites, such traditional patterns as Quill Gordon, Blue Dun, stoneflies, Hendrickson, March Brown, Gray Fox, Adams, Hare's Ear, caddis, Light Cahill, Pheasant Tail Soft Hackle, Muddler Minnows, Mickey Finns, Matukas in olive, black and gray, and Woolly Buggers in the same colors.

East Branch Sugar Creek

Although smaller than Sugar Creek, East Branch Sugar Creek still offers some good trout fishing. It is planted with fish for about five miles from the village of Wallaceville downstream to Cooperstown where it joins the main branch of Sugar Creek.

As with its bigger neighbor, access to the East Branch is available off Route 427 from U.S. Route 322. Township Road 595 appears on the right about a mile north of Cooperstown. It follows the stream back into State Game Lands 96, and, eventually, out to Pennsylvania Route 428 south of Wallaceville. Fly anglers can try some of the same patterns listed for Sugar Creek.

Sandy Creek
Mercer and Venango Counties

Little Sandy Creek
Fly Fishing Only
Venango County

Sandy Creek

In 1748 King George II of England granted a half-million acres of land in the upper Ohio region to the Ohio Land Co. composed of "gentlemen from Virginia and Maryland." The move was not a popular one with residents of Pennsylvania. Nor with the French, who also had claimed the territory. In response to the British move, the Governor General of Canada sent a force of over 1,000 men into the region to erect a series of forts. This action in turn prompted Virginia's Lieutenant Governor Robert Dinwiddie, who had been appointed proprietor of the grant, to order a 21-year-old newly commissioned officer to Fort Le Boeuf (Waterford) in Erie County with a letter to the French commander. The letter maintained, "It is so notoriously known that the Lands on the Ohio River to the West of the Colony of Virginia belong properly to the Crown of Great Britain" and "to know his Reasons for this unjustifiable Step in invading our Lands."

On Friday, November 30, 1753 the young officer, Major George Washington, whose older brothers, Lawrence and Augustine, were members of the Ohio Land Co., left the Indian town of Logstown (near Baden), 18 miles down the Ohio River from Pittsburgh, for Fort Le Boeuf. With his party of Europeans and Indians was Christopher Gist, a well-known explorer and plantation owner in colonial western Pensylvania, and the Dutch adventurer Jacob Van Braam, who was to act as an interpreter. The weather was an atrocious mix of rain, snow and sleet. Warned by the Indians that the nearest and best trail was impassable the party was forced to take what to Washington was a disagreeable route through Venango (Franklin), where the French had already established a fort.

The variation of the **Venango Path** up which Washington traveled took him over numerous streams. Probably all of them held good populations of trout back in those days, and almost certainly the party supplemented its supplies with a catch of fish. While the total catch may be a world lower nowadays, some of those same streams still offer good fishing. Among them Sandy Creek, which Washington crossed near the present village of Pecan.

Sandy Creek, sometimes also referred to as Big Sandy Creek, is stocked for over 30 miles from its source at Lake Wilhelm in Maurice K. Goddard State Park (no camping facilities) to its mouth on the Allegheny River downstream of Franklin. It is a medium-sized stream with good fly hatches and only fair accessibility from main roads.

Sandy Creek's upper water can be reached by taking Interstate Route 79 Exit 34, and following Pennsylvania Route 358 east to the village of Sandy Lake and U.S. Route 62. At Sandy Lake, Route 62 north parallels the stream at a varying distance through the village. Beyond Sandy Lake the stream begins to pull further away from the road and is hidden behind an alternating landscape of woods and farms. About a mile and a half below the village, the stream also enters a series of swamps and becomes clogged with a lot of downed trees and brush. Anglers can fish the water downstream of Sandy Lake by walking the railroad grade alongside the stream.

State Game Lands 130 offers the next good access to Sandy Creek. It can be found by continuing north on Route 62 to Reeds Furnace Road, which also is marked by a white "State Game Lands" sign, on the right. The road leads to an abandoned bridge with plenty of parking. Sandy Creek through Game Lands 130 is an often flat-bottomed affair, meandering its way through a swampy wilderness of birch and other hardwoods. State Route 3015 to the village of Raymilton joins Route 62 just past the Mercer/Venango County Line and offers access to the stream outside of Game Lands 130.

Past Raymilton, Sandy Creek once again pulls close to Route 62 and continues to hug the road into the town of Polk. State Route 3024, which appears on the east side of Polk, across from the east entrance to Polk State School, trails the stream at varying distances to State Route 3013. Access also is available at Pecan, near where Washington crossed the stream, on S.R. 3013.

Fly fishing along Sandy Creek centers around the traditional Pennsylvania hatches. These include: mid-April to late June, Blue Dun, Quill Gordon, stoneflies, Blue-Winged Olive, Hendrickson, March Brown, Gray Fox, Brown Drake, Green Drake, Sulphurs, Light Cahill, caddis and terrestrials; June, Blue-Winged Olive, Sulphurs, Light Cahill, Brown Drake, caddis, midges and terrestrials. Fly anglers also might try such impressionistic patterns as the Adams, Hare's Ear, Pheasant Tail, orange or yellow soft hackles, Black Gnat, Renegade, Muddler Minnow, Mickey Finn, Black-Nosed Dace, Woolly Bugger and Bivisible.

Although Washington was clearly the most famous person to ever travel the Venango Path (corruption of an Indian word meaning "a mink") from Pittsburgh to Erie, he was not the only individual of historical note to use that old Indian trail. For over 40 years after Wshington's journey the trail, or one of its variations around the region's swamps, was an important military road. Colonel Henry Bouquet, whose victory over the Indians at the Battle of Bushy Run in Westmoreland County during Pontiac's Rebellion of 1763 brought peace to the frontier, is known to have traveled the road, as did General "Mad Anthony" Wayne. General Wayne, who earned his nickname for his reckless actions during the War for Independence, used the road in 1794 on his way to the Battle of Fallen Timbers. His victory in that fight finally ended all threats of Indian War in western Pennsylvania.

Along with the Venango Path, the Cayahaga Path also touched in Sandy Creek. Named after the Cayahaga Region, which included the mouth of the Cuyahoga River and Cleveland, the Cayahaga Path ran from Franklin to Akron, Ohio. It more or less followed Sandy Creek from Sandy Lake to Franklin.

(Also see Sugar Creek.)

Little Sandy Creek

Smaller, a bit faster flowing and rockier than much of Sandy Creek, Little Sandy Creek also is accessible off U.S. Route 62. The highway passes over the stream on the eastern edge of Polk and the Polk State School property. A large, wooden Fish Commission sign plainly marks both the bridge and the creek.

The lower water of Little Sandy Creek's 2.5-mile long Fly Fishing Only Project can be reached at the Route 62 bridge, or by turning onto State Route 3024 across from the east entrance to Polk State School. S.R. 3024 also marks the downstream boundary of the special regulation water, only a short distance above Little Sandy's mouth on Sandy Creek.

Upper portions of Little Sandy Creek's Fly Fishing Only water can be found by entering the east drive of the beautiful Polk State School property. Walk-in fishing is permitted from the road leading to the cemetery. More of the upper water is accessible by continuing up the drive past the cemetery road. Next to a line of pine trees another, unmarked, road appears on the right. This leads back to a pump house. If the chain is up the angler will have to park at the top of the hill and again walk in to the stream. Otherwise, a small amount of parking is available at the bottom of the road. Polk State School was established in 1897. It is the second oldest and the largest mental hospital in Pennsylvania.

Fly fishermen on Little Sandy Creek can try some of the same patterns mentioned for Sandy Creek.

S O U T H W E S T

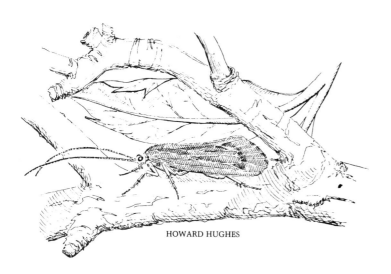

HOWARD HUGHES

Allegheny County
Allegheny River
Monogahela River
Ohio River

Armstrong County
Allegheny River
Buffalo Cr
Cherry Run
Crooked Cr Res
Kiskimenetas River
Mahoning Cr
Patterson Cr
Pine Cr N. Fk
Pine Cr S. Fk

Beaver County
Beaver River
Ohio River

Cambria County
Chest Cr
Conemaugh River

Fayette County
Big Sandy Cr
Chaney Run
Dunbar Cr
Indian Cr
Mill Run
Youghiogheny River

Greene County

Indiana County
Conemaugh River
Little Mahoning Cr
Mahoning Cr

Somerset County
Allen Cr
Blue Hole Cr
Brush Cr
Clear Run
Cub Run
Fall Cr
Glade Run
High Point Lake
Jones Mill Run
Kooser Lake
Kooser Run
Laurel Hill Cr
Little Wills Cr
McClintock Run
Shade Cr
Shafer Run
Stony Cr
Whites Cr
Wills Cr
Youghiogheny River

Washington County

Westmoreland County
Allegheny River
Conemaugh River
Four Mile Run
Kiskiminetas River
Loyalhanna Cr
Mill Cr
Youghiogheny River

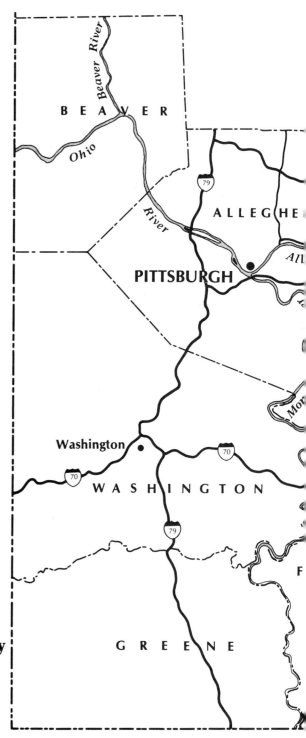

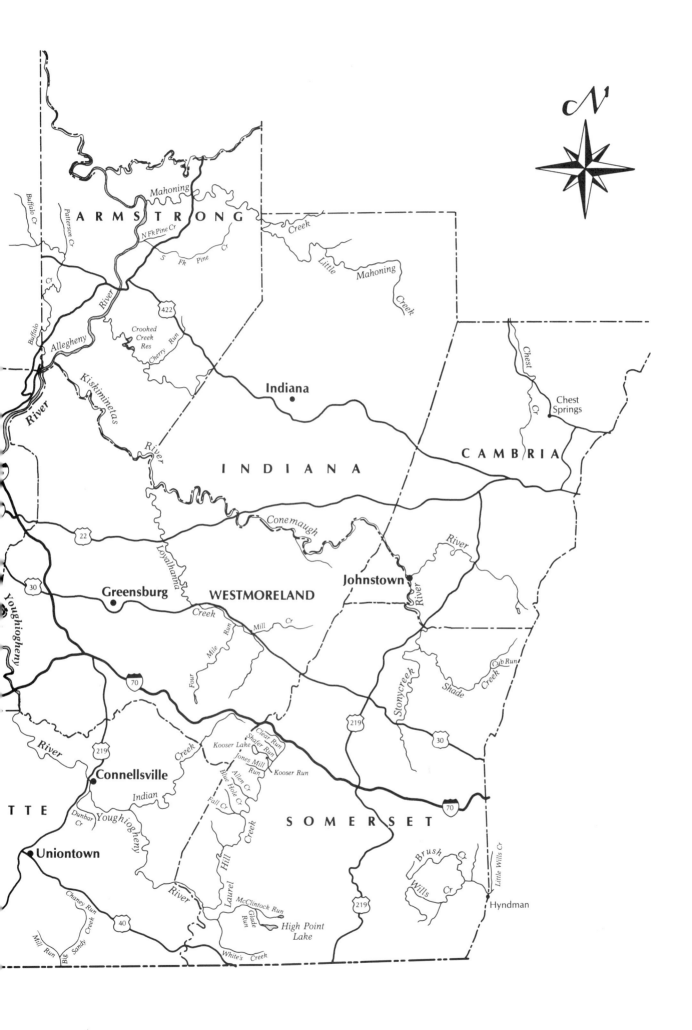

Southwest Region

Buffalo Creek
Butler and Armstrong Counties

Little Buffalo Creek
Butler County

Patterson Creek
Armstrong County

Buffalo Creek

No solid evidence exists to show that Pennsylvania ever had its own buffalo herd. The best archaeologists can do is point to strays from the main herd further west wandering into the state. This despite the fact Pennsylvania abounds with old tales about the beast and is literally covered with streams bearing the name Buffalo, including this one flowing along the Butler/Armstrong County line less than an hour away from the skyscrapers of Pittsburgh's Golden Triangle.

A pretty, surprisingly isolated stream, considering its proximity to Pittsburgh, Buffalo Creek is stocked for 7.2 miles in Butler County and 17.9 in Armstrong County. It is the heaviest stocked stream in Armstrong and among the heaviest in Butler. Browns and rainbows are its main fare, supplemented by a scattering of smallmouth bass in its lower reaches.

Access to portions of both Buffalo Creek's upper and lower water is easiest off U.S. Route 422 west of Kittanning. Route 422 crosses over the stream at the village of Buffalo Mills near Worthington. On the west side of the bridge State Route 4035 leading south to the village of Buffalo Creek provides access to some of the downstream water.

Both Township Road 314 and Township Road 300, which appear at a "Y" intersection south of Buffalo Creek, will take the angler further downstream. T-300 runs to Township Road 308 and the village of Boggsville near the downstream end of the stocked water, while T-314 actually makes a loop to touch on the stream and rejoin T-300.

Upstream of Buffalo Mills, Buffalo Creek can be reached by following S.R. 4035 to the north and toward the village of Craigsville. From Craigsville, fishermen can travel further upstream by taking Township Road 358 to the village of Nichola.

Above Nichola, the stream is accessible by following Fenelton Road to the village of Fenelton and then turning north onto the Chicora Fenelton Road. Duffyschool Road, Hilderbrand Road and Rattagan Road, all running east of Chicora Fenelton Road and the village of Chicora, lead to the stream.

Kuskusky-Kittanning Path, from Kittanning to New Castle, once crossed Buffalo Creek in about the same spot as Route 422. The path was an offshoot of the Great Shamokin Path, one of the most important Indian trails in colonial Pennsylvania. Kittanning to the east of the stream was a famous Indian town and gathering place for war parties. Colonel John Armstrong and 300 troops from Fort Shirley in Cumberland County attacked the town on September 8, 1756, killing Chief Jacobs and 42 of his braves. The attack was in revenge for an Indian attack on Fort Granville in eastern Pennsylvania. Europeans first arrived in Kittanning in 1791, but continued Indian raids kept the town from being permanently settled until 1796.

Freeport, near the mouth of Buffalo Creek, was laid out by David Todd in 1796 and originally called Todds Town. The western division of the Pennsylvania Canal crossed the Allegheny River at Freeport on a large aqueduct and lower Buffalo Creek on a second aqueduct. The area at the mouth of Buffalo Creek also was a general gathering place for militia guarding the frontier against Indians in the 1970s.

Buffalo Creek fly fishermen might start with Quill Gordons, Adams, stoneflies, Hendricksons, caddis, Soft Hackle Nymphs, Muskrats, Hare's Ears, Renegades, Black Gnats, Muddler Minnows, Matuka Streamers, Woolly Buggers, March Browns, Light Cahills, midges and terrestrials.

Little Buffalo Creek

Nearly three miles of stocked brown and rainbow trout water await the angler who decides to leave Buffalo Creek for Little Buffalo Creek. The stream is tiny and slow-moving with deep holes and a good share of holdover fish. It can be reached by State Route 1019 north off Route 422 and through the village of Coylesville to Fenelton. Fenelton Road crosses L.R. 10036 in the village and parallels Little Buffalo Creek both upstream and downstream. Dalmagro Road, which runs off Fenelton Road above the village, also leads to the stream. Fly fishermen should give some of the same patterns mentioned under Buffalo Creek a try.

Patterson Creek

Buffalo Creek's only other stocked tributary is Patterson Creek. It is planted from its mouth near Craigsville upstream for about five miles. Access to the stream may be had by taking State Route 4035 off Route 422 at Buffalo Mills and to Craigsville. In the village turn north toward the village of Foster Mills and State Game Lands 259. After crossing the stream continue to Township Road 362, which parallels the creek. Again, fly fishermen might try the same patterns listed under Buffalo Creek.

South Fork Pine Creek
North Fork Pine Creek
Armstrong County

South Fork Pine Creek

Forested valleys and a lack of development make South Fork Pine Creek probably the most scenic trout stream in all of Armstrong County. Over nine miles of this beautiful little waterway are stocked with brook and brown trout, extending from its confluence with North Fork Pine Creek near the Allegheny River upstream to the village of Echo.

Despite its wildness, access to the South Fork is good. Anglers can reach both its upper and lower waters by taking Pennsylvania Route 66 to Pine Furnace Road between the villages of Spaces Corners and Slabtown north of Kittanning. Where Route 66 crosses the stream, Pine Furnace Road appears on the east. It parallels the stream through the villages of Pine Furnace Station and Pine Furnace.

Above Pine Furnace, the road ends on Township Route 628. Further upstream access to the South Fork may be had by following T-628 south across the stream and then continuing on to the villages of Oscar and Echo at the upper end of the planted water.

Lower South Fork Pine Creek can be located by taking Township Road 529 on the west side of Route 66 just north of Pine Furnace Road. T-529 follows the South Fork to the end of its stocked water.

Fly fishing on the South Fork is said to be good into the middle of summer. Anglers might try such patterns as the Hare's Ear, stoneflies, Muskrat, Adams, Quill Gordon, caddis, Muddler Minnow, Woolly Buggers, Hendrickson, March Brown, Black Gnat, Renegade, Light Cahill, Sulphurs, midges and terrestrials.

North Fork Pine Creek

North Fork Pine Creek joins the South Fork to form Pine Creek proper just above the Allegheny River. It is stocked only on the west side of Route 66. Access is available by turning west onto State Route 1029 and following it to State Route 1032 which parallels the stream. Fly fishermen can try some of the same patterns listed under the South Fork, as well as any personal favorites.

Lone angler on Pine Creek.

Cherry Run
Armstrong County

A small feeder stream for the U.S. Army Corps of Engineers Crooked Creek Lake, Cherry Run is heavily stocked with brown and brook trout over a distance of about five miles from U.S. Route 422, downstream to the lake.

Route 422 provides the first access to Cherry Run when it crosses it roughly two miles east of the village of Whitesburg. At Cherry Run bridge, State Route 2005 to the south provides good downstream access to Cherry Run until the Corps of Engineers's property, when fishing becomes a walk-in affair.

Crooked Creek Lake is a warmwater fishery built by the Corps of Engineers to help keep Pittsburgh above water. The park bordering the lake, however, contains a campground and swimming area for anglers interested in staying nearby. Details may be had by writing: Crooked Creek Lake, R.D. 3, Ford City, PA 16226, or Public Affairs Office, Pittsburgh District, U.S. Army Corps of Engineers, 1000 Liberty Avenue, Pittsburgh, PA 15222.

Frankstown Path, from Harrisburg to Kittanning, once crossed over Cherry Run at about the same spot as Route 422. Called the most important Indian trail over Pennsylvania's mountains, at its western end, the path was also sometimes called the Kittanning Path. Colonel John Armstrong used it in 1756 during his expedition to the Indian town of Kittanning. Armstrong's action was in retaliation for an Indian attack on Fort Granville in eastern Pennsylvania. Captives from that fight were force-marched to Kittaning and several were tortured. Armstrong managed to free 11 of them during his assault.

Cherry Run fly anglers might try such traditional patterns as the Blue Dun, Muskrat, Adams, Hendrickson, March Brown, caddis, stoneflies, Muddler Minnows, Woolly Buggers, Hare's Ears, Soft Hackle Nymphs, Black Gnat, Light Cahill, Sulphurs, midges and terrestrials.

Little Mahoning Creek
Delayed Harvest Fly Fishing Only
Indiana County

Rain, some anglers say just the threat of a shower, can turn Little Mahoning Creek from a sparkling, pleasant up-country stream into a muddy drainage ditch. The reason for such a dramatic change is the presence of numerous strip mines near the creek's headwaters. When the weather forecast is favorable, however, this medium-sized tributary of Mahoning Creek and the Allegheny River is among the very best trout waters, at least from the fly fisherman's point of view, in the Fish Commission's Southwest Region. For it contains some of the best mayfly hatches to be found in the region, including the spectacular Green Drake.

Altogether, some 20 miles of Little Mahoning Creek is stocked—from its headwaters around the village of Deckers Point downstream beyond Pennsylvania Route 210 and the village of Georgeville—making it the largest trout stream in Indiana County. Besides stocked fish, several sections of the stream are said to hold a good population of carry-over browns.

Little Mahoning's four-mile long Delayed Harvest Fly Fishing Only water reaches from S.R. 1034 at the village of Rochester Mills upstream to Cesna Run. It can be found by taking U.S. Route 119 to Pennsylvania Route 236 near the Route 119 bridge over Little Mahoning Creek north of Marion Center and following it back toward Rochester Mills. State Route 10380 appears on

the right a short distance beyond the white church in the village. It parallels the creek upstream all of the way beyond the project water. The Fly Fishing Only stretch also can be reached in Rochester Mills by turning right at the church.

Downstream portions of Little Mahoning Creek can be found along S.R. 4020 about a quarter of a mile upstream of the Route 119 bridge (posted). From the Route 119 bridge Route 236 trails the creek downstream through the valley to Route 210, providing access at various points along the way.

Upper sections of Little Mahoning Creek resemble a mountain stream with high banks covered by rhododendron and hemlocks. Four small dams appear in the Rochester Mills area to slow the water down and begin its change into more of a farm country stream. Below Route 119 the creek becomes a winding, meandering affair bordered by numerous willow trees.

Little Mahoning Creek concentration.

Mahoning is a common Indian word which appears throughout Pennsylvania as the name of numerous creeks and runs, villages and even towns. It is reportedly a corruption of "Mahoni," meaning "a lick," having a reference to the mineral licks frequented by deer, elk and other animals.

The Great Shamokin Indian Path once crossed Little Mahoning Creek at the present village of Smicksburg. The trail ran from Shamokin (Sunbury), said to be the most important Indian town in colonial Pennsylvania, to Kittanning, a gathering place for war parties on the Allegheny River, and the largest Indian town in the state until it was attacked by Colonel John Armstrong in 1756. Moravian Bishop John Ettwein used the path, even camping east of the creek, when he led 200 of his Indian converts from Friedenshutten "Tents of Peace" at Wyalusing on the Susquehanna River. The mission Indians were forced to leave the area after the Iroquois sold it to the Europeans at the Treaty of Fork Stanwix in 1768. They used the path to travel to the Beaver River.

Along with its Green Drake hatch in late May and early June, Little Mahoning Creek also has hatches of Brown Drakes and Sulphurs about the same time. A Light Cahill hatch appears later in June. Early season flies to try include: Quill Gordon, Hendrickson and stonefly nymphs. March Brown, Grey Fox and caddis are other good choices as the spring days warm. Summer angling centers around terrestrials and midges on fine leaders.

Chest Creek
Cambria and Clearfield Counties

Not only is Chest Creek one of the biggest trout streams in both Cambria and Clearfield Counties, but also one of the most accessible. Pennsylvania Route 36 parallels the stream from its mouth on the West Branch Susquehanna River at the village of Mahaffey along U.S. Route 219 in Clearfield County, all of the way upstream to Patton in Cambria County.

From Patton, Chest Creek can be reached by taking Township Road 464 near the bridge crossing the creek and following it upstream. T-464 joins State Route 1009, which crosses the creek upstream.

About a two-mile section of Chest Creek, starting at the Thomas Mill Bridge on State Route 4024 (which can be picked up off Route 36 just south of St. Boniface) is stocked upstream by railroad car and access is by walking only. The stocked water begins at Bradley Junction, on State Route 1007, which can be picked up off U.S. Route 219 north of Ebensburg or Pennsylvania Route 53 in Lorretto

Tiny and usually placid in its farmland headwaters, Chest Creek turns swift and rocky around the Thomas Mill Bridge, then calms again near the town of Westover. North of Westover, it sets a somewhat steadier, winding pace bracketed by mud banks. Because of both past and present mining operations, Chest Creek's scenery is nothing outstanding. Although some places are almost pretty, others are fairly ugly.

Anglers who enjoy fly fishing might try the Quill Gordon, Adams, Hendrickson, March Brown, caddis, Hare's Ear, Renegade, stoneflies, Light Cahills, Sulphurs, Black Gnats, midges and terrestrials.

Frankstown Path, the major Indian trail between Harrisburg and Kittanning, once crossed Chest Creek at Eckenrode Mill northwest of the village of Chest Springs. According to Paul A. W. Wallace's *Indian Paths of Pennsylvania,* traces of the trail may still be seen just beyond Chest Creek on a small plot of rising ground that the Cambria County Historical Society has preserved as a memorial of old trading days.

No state park touches on Chest Creek, but Prince Gallitzin State Park lies a few miles east of Patton. It has a 437-site Class A campground open on a first-come, first served basis from the second Friday in April to the end of the antlerless deer season in mid-December. There are 109 sites available on a reservations basis from the Wednesday preceding Memorial Day through Labor Day. Park facilities include a store, laundromat, guarded swimming beach, hot showers, flush toilets and sanitary dump stations. In addition, non-fishing visitors will find boat rentals on 1,600-acre Lake Glendale, nine miles of hiking trails, a bridle path and environmental education programs.

Prince Gallitzin State Park is named for Demetrius Augustine Gallitzin (1770-1840), a Russian nobleman, and the first ordained priest to receive all of his orders in the United States. He eventually earned the title "Missionary of the Alleghenies" and founded the nearby town of Loretto. Land for the park was acquired in 1957 and the first recreational facilities opened in 1965. The park can be reached by following the signs from Route 36 at Patton on State Route 1021.

Information on the park may be had by writing: Prince Gallitzin State Park Department of Environmental Resources, R.D. 1, Box 79, Patton, PA 16668.

Loyalhanna Creek
Delayed Harvest Artificial Lures Only
Mill Creek, Four Mile Run
Westmoreland County

Loyalhanna Creek

Loyalhanna Creek in the Delaware Indian language means "middle stream" or "at the middle stream." It gets its name from being located midway between the waters of the Juniata River and the Ohio River on the Raystown Path from Raystown (Bedford) to Shannopins Town (Pittsburgh). It unites with the Conemaugh River at Saltsburg to form the Kiskiminetas River, which enters the Allegheny River near Freeport.

A village at the present site of Ligonier was probably established by the Delaware Indians soon after their migration from the Susquehanna Valley in 1727. Fort Ligonier, named after Sir John Ligonier, Viscount of Enniskillen, was erected on the site of the village in the late summer of 1758. As the western most outpost of the British army, it was to be used as a jumping off point for the capture of Fort Duquesne (Pittsburgh) from the French by General John Forbes.

While waiting for General Forbes to arrive on the scene and assume command of his army at the fort, Major James Grant decided to lead an expedition of his own against Fort Duquesne. With a force of 37 officers and 805 enlisted men, he advanced as far as what is known as "Grant's Hill" in the city of Pittsburgh. There he was attacked by a group of French and Indians out of Fort Duquesne, and lost nearly 275 men.

Emboldened by their victory, the French gathered together a force of about 1,200 men and launched their own attack against Fort Ligonier. Under the command of Colonel James Burd the fort withstood the attack, and was waiting when General Forbes arrived.

During Pontiac's Conspiracy, Fort Ligonier came under attack once more and, with Fort Pitt, became the only fort west of the mountains not to fall to the hostile Indians. Lt. Archibald Blane was in command of the fort in early May 1763 when the Indians cut all communication between it and Fort Pitt. Colonel Henry

Bouquet, who was in Philadelphia at the time, was ordered to the relief of Fort Pitt. When he reached Carlisle, he sent a force of 30 Highlanders ahead to aid Fort Ligonier. They helped to hold the fort until August 2 when Colonel Bouquet and his army arrived.

Three days after reaching Fort Ligonier, Colonel Bouquet met the Indians at the Battle of Bushy Run near Jeannette. That two-day fight broke the back of Pontiac's Conspiracy and ended much of the hostilities along the frontier.

"We continued on our way along the Old Trading Path, which kept for 10 or 12 Miles, for the most part along the low grounds of the Loyal hannon, tho, its sometimes turned of the River and Crossed some Ridges and the Points of hills," Lt. Colby Chew wrote of his reconnaissance mission out of Ligonier for the Forbes expedition. "The high Land is well Timbered. The Ridges not high, the Low grounds of the River and in General of all the Creeks very thick and Bushey."

Thanks to purchases made by the Western Pennsylvania Conservancy, the hills around Loyalhanna Creek's trout water still hold timber and its banks brush. Which is not a small accomplishment, since the stream lies at the end of an almost unbroken chain of towns, shopping malls, fast food restaurants and car lots extending for almost 50 miles from Pittsburgh through Westmoreland County. It is stocked with browns and rainbows for about seven miles from Kingston Dam upstream to the town of Ligonier. All of its trout water lies next to U.S. Route 30, so it is very accessible.

Because of its proximity to so many people and location tight against a major highway, the Loyalhanna always has attracted more than its share of fishermen. It is not unusual to see "anglers" completely circling its pools on weekends early in the season. But things are getting better. The outlook for the stream as a quality place to fish has improved dramatically since the establishment of its Delayed Harvest Artificial Lures Only Project. The special regulation water has brought a more serious and conscientious type of fisherman to the stream, as well as a new feeling of pride in the resource.

Like the rest of the stream's trout water, access to the Loyalhanna's Delayed Harvest Project involves little more effort than finding a place to pull off Route 30. The project runs from the Pennsylvania Route 711 bridge, directly across Route 30 from recreated Fort Ligonier, downstream 1.5 miles to State Route 2045, or Duggan's Bridge. At its most remote, it is no more than about a hundred yards off the highway.

Fly hatches on Loyalhanna Creek are sporadic and unreliable. The absence of good hatches, however, means the stream's trout are generally willing to take what they can get. Successful fly patterns include: caddis, Blue Dun, Quill Gordon, Hare's Ear, Muddler Minnow, Matuka Streamers, Woolly Buggers, Adams, Hendrickson, Renegade, March Brown, Gray Fox, Black Gnat, Light Cahill, midges and terrestrials.

Mill Creek

A medium-sized tributary of the Loyalhanna, Mill Creek is stocked with brown and rainbow trout over a distance of about 6.5 miles from its mouth upstream beyond the village of Waterford. Access is available along Route 711 north of Ligonier and off Pennsylvania Route 217 to Waterford.

General Arthur St. Clair once built his home, Hermitage, along what is now Route 711, a couple of miles north of Ligonier. General St. Clair was the grandson of the Earl of Roslyn. He served with British forces in the Battle of Quebec. During the Revolution, he switched sides to fight against his former comrades, distinguishing himself at the Battle of Trenton and Battle of Philadelphia.

Following the war, St. Clair became a delegate to the Continental Congress, serving as its president during 1787, the year when the constitution was adopted. Two years later he served as the first governor of the Northwest Territories. In 1791, St. Clair led an expedition against the Ohio Indians during which he suffered his greatest defeat.

Financial defeat soon followed St. Clair's military defeat. In 1792, he resigned his army commission, despite being exonerated by Congress. Ten years later, President Jefferson removed him from the governorship of the Northwest Territory. Forced out of Hermitage, he lived the remaining years of his life in a crude cabin on Chestnut Ridge to the west of Ligonier and Mill Creek. He died there in 1818 and is buried in St. Clair Park in Greensburg.

The water quality of Mill Creek is better than that of Loyalhanna Creek. As a result, aquatic life is more abundant and hatches better, though still not great. Fly anglers can try some of the same patterns mentioned for the Loyalhanna.

Four Mile Run

With about 12 miles of stocked water, reaching from its source in Lake Donegal all of the way to its mouth on Loyalhanna Creek, Four Mile Run is the longest trout stream in Westmoreland County. As might be expected, it also holds the greatest variety of water types. There are quiet stretches of big woods and crowded portions of summer cottages; deep, slow pools and fast shallow riffles; mud banks and sheer mountain cliffs running down to its edge; places where it is wider than the stream it feeds and others where an angler can almost jump across.

As with the Loyalhanna, Route 30 is the main artery leading to Four Mile Run. State Route 2043 runs off Route 30 to the south immediately before Long Bridge and Idlewild Park. It follows the stream, providing access at different points, through the villages of Buttermilk Falls and Darlington, and to State Route 2037, which appears on the right just before the main road starts up a hill away from the stream. S.R. 2037 parallels and crosses Four Mile Run for the next few miles.

Although access to the stream is easy, anglers should be careful of private property. A lot of summer cottages and hunting camps occupy its banks for several miles upstream of Route 30. Fly anglers can again try some of the patterns recommended for Loyalhanna Creek.

Indian Creek
Westmoreland and Fayette Counties

Plateau streams are well known to have a split personality. On top of the mountains they are usually meandering, sluggish affairs of long pools, mud banks, gentle riffles and few rocks. Dropping down off the high ground, they change completely into rocky, whitewater torrents, especially early in the season when the snows are still melting and April showers are in full swing.

Flowing across the Allegheny Plateau along the western side of Laurel Hill, Indian Creek is clearly a plateau stream. But it is also somewhat different. Where the normal plateau creek does not metamorphosis until it plunges down off the mountains, Indian Creek changes character within a relatively short distance, and while still near the top of Laurel Hill. The upper portion of its stocked water from State Route 1058 in the village of Champion upstream above Pennsylvania Route 31 resembles a meadow stream of mostly low, mud banks and slow, deep pools decorated by the occasional dairy cow. Below Champion, almost from the exact point where Roaring Run adds its flow, Indian Creek becomes more of a mountain stream, surrounded by rhododendrons and hardwoods, and full of fast, rocky water. Yet there has been no unusual drop in elevation. Pennsylvania Route 711 parallels the stream with only some insignificant rises and dips.

As far as accessibility goes, Indian Creek has to be one of the easiest to reach trout streams in the state. Anglers can find it by taking Pennsylvania Turnpike Exit 9 at Donegal and following Route 31/711 east toward Somerset. Route 711 splits off Route 31 at Jones Mill and parallels the stream, at varying distances, all of the way to the downstream end of its stocked water in the village of Melcroft.

Route 31 follows the stream through Jones Mill. On the eastern edge of the village, immediately before Route 31 crosses the stream and starts up Laurel Hill, Pennsylvania Route 381 appears. It leads back to the village of Kregar and provides access to the upper portion of Indian Creek's stocked water, only about a mile above Route 31.

The area around Indian Creek was once a prosperous lumbering and mining area. Both industries are still active, and strip mining has caused some problem, but nowhere near those of days gone by. Jones Mill took its name from a mill built along the stream by the Jones family in about 1800. Jones Mill, Indian Head, Melcroft, Normalville and other villages along the stream carry the look of former "company towns'" of square, frame duplex homes.

Anglers who enjoy fishing with a fly should find success with a variety of patterns on Indian Creek, including: Adams, Blue Dun, Muddler Minnow, Soft Hackle Nymphs, stoneflies, Hendrickson, caddis, Hare's Ear, March Brown, Gray Fox, Blue-Winged Olives, Black Gnat, Lead-Winged Coachman, Light Cahill, midges and terrestrials.

Clear Shade Creek
Fly Fishing Only
Cub Run
Somerset County

So well aware was the great American philosopher and naturalist Henry David Thoreau of man's need to escape "civilization" he chose the single word "Solitude" for the title of a chapter in his classic work *Walden*. Yet, as all of those who crave it from inside offices and factories understand, solitude is something that every year becomes more elusive, especially in combination with good fishing in a state as heavily populated as Pennsylvania. Clear Shade Creek in northerwestern Somerset County is a pleasant exception.

Located less than 10 miles from the coal mines and factories of Johnstown, within an hour's drive of Greensburg, Somerset, Altoona and Bedford, and about two hours from Pittsburgh, Clear Shade is a true oasis of quiet and beauty in a region that has long suffered the ravages and consequences of industrialization.

Clear Shade's one mile long Fly Fishing Only Project is one of the most splendidly isolated special regulation waters in the state. The only road leading back to it is a cinder-surfaced affair belonging to the Windbar Area Authority. It is used to service the small dam (closed to fishing) the authority operates along the stream and is barred to private vehicles by a steel gate. Anglers who wish to test their skills on the project face a two-mile hike either upstream or down.

The upstream trail to Fly Fishing Only water starts off Pennsylvnia Route 160 about three miles north of Central City. Approximately 100 yards north of where Route 160 crosses the stream, above its confluence with the polluted Shade Creek, is the

Clear Shade Creek.

WAA access road. While the road is closed to vehicles, walkers and bicyclers are permitted to use it. Fishermen who own a bicycle and can transport it to the stream are advised to do so. Using them to reach the project, as well as other parts of the stream, lengthens an angler's fishing time and generally makes for a more pleasant day.

Downstream access to the Fly Fishing Only water can be had by taking Verla Drive off Pennsylvania Route 56 in Gallitzin State Forest between the villages of Ogletown and Rummel and toward the village of New Ashtola. From the crossroads in New Ashtola turn left onto Crumb Road and follow it roughly four miles down to the stream.

Because of its isolation, the Fly Fishing Only project offers some of the best angling to be found anywhere along the stream However, anglers should not overlook the portions of stream both above and below the special regulation water. Clear Shade's headwaters are easily accessible off Route 56 in Ogletown, or by taking Crescent Road to Hollow Road, which follows the creek upstream. Wild brookies are available in the upper reaches, but the stream is narrow and choked tight with brush, so not exactly a joy to fish.

Downstream of Crumb Road, Clear Shade Creek widens considerably into a series of deep pools and rocky runs. Stocked and hold-over browns and rainbows are more common here than in the headwaters or other, less accessible, stretches.

Upstream of the Route 160 bridge, Clear Shade runs very rocky with a lot of pocket water and very high banks that make the stream impossible to reach in a lot of places. The abundance of rocks and lack of vegetation along the banks at times can leave an angler with a feeling of desolation, but the fishing can still be quite good. And privacy easy to find.

Insect life along Clear Shade Creek is varied and fairly abundant. There are respectable caddis and mayfly hatches over most of the stream, and the grassy banks that line much of the creek above the WAA dam provide a steady supply of terrestrials, such as ants, crickets, beetles and grasshoppers. Fly fishermen should find success with Adams, Quill Gordon, Hendrickson, caddis, stoneflies, March Brown, Renegade, Light Cahill and midges.

Since Clear Shade Creek's upper waters, from Ogletown to the bridge of Crumb Road, flows through Gallitzin State Forest backpacking is a possibility for anglers who really want to experience the area. Both the 22-mile Lost Turkey Trail and the J.P. Saylor Trail run through the area. Details on both trails, as well as a free "Public Use Map" of the forest that shows the stream, may be had by writing: District Forester, Gallitzin State Forest, 131 Hillcrest Drive, Ebensburg, PA 15931.

Cub Run

The only stocked tributary of Clear Shade Creek, Cub Run, can be reached by following Cub Run Road, off the bridge over the main stream at Cumb Road. Its planted water runs for two miles.

Willis Creek and Brush Creek
Somerset County

Little Wills Creek
Bedford County

Wills Creek and Brush Creek

July is normally a very dry month in Pennsylvania. It is a time when many freestone streams drop to their lowest levels and turn too warm for fishing. By the end of the month the thoughts of trout anglers across the state have begun to revolve around the cold, even flows of the famous limestone waters. The days of the White Fly are approaching on Yellow Breeches Creek and the Tricorythodes on Falling Springs.

For the Wills Creek basin in southeastern Somerset County, however, July 1984 was a different story altogether. Unexpectedly heavy rains had already brought the stream well up over its usual level and left the ground saturated when the storm struck. It was a once in a lifetime storm. A storm of legend. Within the space of just two hours it dumped a full five inches on the valley. By the time it passed, the railroad tracks and several roads touching on Wills Creek were gone, and the village of Fairhope and town of Hyndman devastated.

Since that apocalyptic day, Wills Creek has changed quite a bit, at least along the lower portion of its stocked water around Fairhope and Hyndman. In hopes of avoiding a repeat performance, bulldozers have channelized the stream, moved boulders that once nurtured pools, reconstructed banks and generally sterilize the stream. Only time will tell how successful the changes have been in taming Wills Creek. But if history holds true, Mother Nature will do what she pleases, the best efforts of man and his machines notwithstanding, and re-mold the stream into the image she desires.

Despite the alterations, a lot of pleasant fishing still can be found along Wills Creek. Its roughly 20 miles of stocked water extends from Hyndman on Little Wills Creek in Bedford County, upstream to about the village of Mance and its headwaters in State Game Lands 82. The stream's lower water may be reached by following State Route 3004 (which turns into State Route 2019) east from Hyndman on Pennsylvania Route 96 and toward Fairhope.

About a mile after crossing the bridge in Fairhope, S.R. 2019 runs to the left. The bridge passes over Brush Creek, a stocked tributary of Wills Creek. Anglers can gain further access to Brush Creek by continuing past this first bridge to a second one near a set of waterfalls. Township Road 407 appears on the other side of this second bridge. More of Brush Creek can be reached by following it for about two miles to the first road on the right and then following that down to the water.

Brush Creek is a beautiful little wilderness trout stream, flowing through a scenic gorge of rock cliffs, gravel bars, hemlocks and rhododendron, and a good place to try when Wills Creek is running high.

Wills Creek's upper water can be found by taking the first bridge off S.R. 2019 over Brush Creek, and then following State Route 2020 to State Route 2015, which leads to the village of Glencoe. More of Wills Creek's upper water can be located by following the first right in the center of Glencoe and then a tenth of a mile beyond turning left. Follow this rough, dirt road (Township Road 377) for 2.5 miles upstream to a house, another road on the right, a small creek and then a trail on the left. The trail runs down to the stream about a hundred yards away. Anglers can continue on T-377 all of the way out to Pennsylvania Route 160.

Fishermen coming from the western part of Pennsylvania can reach Wills Creek's upper water by following the signs for Glencoe and Fairhope off Route 160 and then along S.R. 2020 and T-754. Much of Wills Creek, particularly in its upper reaches, is isolated, but the scenery is of questionable merit, marred especially by an active set of railroad tracks and the usual garbage that finds its way to backwoods streams.

Wills Creek also is an oddity of sorts for western Pennsylvania in that it belongs to the Potomac River watershed, emptying into the North Branch Potomac River at Cumberland, Maryland. It is named after Will, an Indian who lived along its mouth before 1755. The Indian name for the stream was Caiuctecuc or Cucucbetuc, the translation of which has been lost. Several Shawnee tribes occupied sites along the lower stream, but left the area for Ohio before European settlers began to move up the valley.

The stocked portion of Wills Creek has always occupied an out-of-the-way sort of place. But Fort Cumberland at Wills Town on its mouth played an important role in colonial affairs of the mid-eighteenth century. It was the jumping off point for the expedition that ended in George Washington being driven out of Fort Necessity in 1754 and General Edward Braddock's defeat in the Battle of the Monongahela the following year. It also served as a refuge for the remainder of Braddock's army in the retreat lead by Colonel Thomas Dunbar.

The story of all three incidents begins in the spring of 1754 when Virginia's Lieutenant Governor Robert Dinwiddie decided to send a detachments of troops into the Ohio Valley to force the French out of Fort Duquesne (Pittsburgh). British claims to the land were based on the Treaty of Utrecht signed in 1713, and the Treaty of Chapelle, signed in 1748. French claims went back further to La Salle's expedition around the Great Lakes in 1682. Nothing much was made of either case until King George II granted a half million acres of land in the upper Ohio region to the Ohio Land Co. in 1748. To protect their claims and keep communications open between their settlements in Canada and Louisiana, the French built Fort Presque Isle and Fort Le Boeuf in Erie County in 1753, then in 1754 drove the small British garrison away from the "forks of the Ohio" (Pittsburgh).

Colonel Joshua Fry was put in command of the troops sent by Lt. Governor Dinwiddie to drive the French out of Fort Duquesne in the spring of 1754. But he was fatally injured at Wills Creek (Fort Cumberland) and the expedition taken over by his aide, 22-year-old Major George Washington, who the year before had traveled to Fort Le Boeuf to inform the French they were trespassing on land claimed by Great Britain. With his original force of 150 men, and another 150 volunteers from South Carolina, Washington pushed up the Warriors Path along Wills Creek and toward Redstone (Brownsville), the proposed base for an attack on Fort Duquesne. At Great Meadows, near the plantation of Christopher Gist, who had traveled with Washington to Fort Le Boeuf the previous year, the force stopped to throw up breastworks and plan their next move.

On May 28, Washington's troops surprised a party of French near their camp. In the short skirmish that followed, more than 30 of the French were killed or captured, including their leader Coulon de Jumonville. News of Nobleman de Jumonville's death rocked both Paris and London. The covert operations of both countries in distant outposts suddenly spilled out into the open. The fighting—known as the French and Indian War in this country and the Seven Years War in Europe—would end with England's domination of what was to become the eastern United States.

"The volley fired by a young Virginian in the backwoods of America set the world on fire," the English author Horace Walpole would later write of the engagement in the wilds of Pennsylvania.

When word reached Washington on June 29 that the French were advancing on his position with a large force, he ordered his troops to begin work on a stockade. Christened "Fort Necessity," the stockade was in trouble from the start. Rain slowed construction, supplies ran low, expected reinforcements did not arrive, a number of the soldiers fell ill and morale sank.

Scouting parties were driven back on July 3 before work on the fort was completed, and then shortly before noon that day, Coulon de Villiers, the half-brother of de Jumonville, appeared with a force of over 1,000 men and the Battle of Fort Necessity was underway.

"We continued this unequal fight, with an enemy sheltered behind the trees, ourselves without shelter, in trenches full of water, in a settled rain, and the enemy galling us on all sides incessantly from the woods, 'til 8 o'clock at night, when the French called to parley," Washington would later write for the *Carolina Gazette,* "sent Captain Van Braam, and Mr. Peyronee, to receive their proposals, and about midnight we agreed, that each side should retire without molestation. That we should march away with all the honours of war, and with all our stores, effects and baggage. Accordingly the next morning, with our drums beating, and our colors flying, we began our march in good order. . .."

Washington's retreat from Fort Necessity helped lead to the naming of General Edward Braddock as the commander and chief of all British forces in America, and his arrival in Virginia in February 1755. A one-time officer of the legendary Coldstream Guards, General Braddock was a gentleman soldier trained to fight on the well-ordered battlefields of Europe. The guerrilla warfare tactics employed by the French and their Indian allies were laughable to him. By May he had gathered a force of some 1,400 regulars and 700 colonial troops as Fort Cumberland on the banks of Wills Creek and begun laying a military road toward Fort Duquesne.

Although Fort Duquesne was well-built and easily capable of withstanding an infantry attack, Beaujeu, the commander, feared Braddock's artillery. And so, with a force of just 70 French regulars, 150 Canadians and 600 Indians, he elected to attack the superior British force at the crossing of the Monongahela River near the mouth of Turtle Creek.

After a preliminary engagement on July 9 near the present borough of Braddock just outside of Pittsburgh, the French and their allies unleashed a full-fledged assault on Braddock's advanced guard. The colonial troops, including Washington and a wagon driver named Daniel Boone, quickly took over and began fighting back from behind trees and other cover. Some British troops followed their lead, but the sight of regular troops fighting from behind rocks and trees so disturbed Braddock that he ordered his troops to form ranks in the middle of the fight. The result was 184 men and 63 officers either dead or wounded. The general himself was wounded, some say by a colonial soldier named Thomas Faucett, whose brother Braddock had struck with his sword to drive him out of cover.

The remnants of Braddock's army, with the general in the back of a supply wagon, beat a disorganized retreat back to the rear guard camp of Colonel Thomas Dunbar (see Dunbar Creek). Confronted with the sight of so many defeated troops, Dunbar then panicked, burying his supplies and beating a hasty retreat to Fort Cumberland. He did this despite the fact the army still totaled some 1,500 men.

The site of Braddock's defeat is today the location of a run-down, grimy milltown. Dunbar's camp likewise holds an old coal mining town whose best days are long past. Only Washington's tiny Fort Necessity remains as an historic artifact of the expeditions that started on the banks of Wills Creek, and the war which left us all speaking English instead of French. The recreated fort and its surrounding grounds now are under the care of the National Park Service. It can be found along U.S. Route 40 just west of the village of Farmington and southwest of Ohiopyle State Park.

Fort Duquesne was eventually captured by General John

Forbes with an army that was formed in Lancaster and traveled a more northern route. Wills Town, or Fort Cumberland, regained some of the importance it lost after General Forbes constructed his road through Raystown (Bedford) in 1806 when congress authorized construction of the first National Road, what is now U.S. Route 40. Wills Creek became a thriving way station along the route.

Aquatic insect life in Wills Creek and Brush Creek is said to be fairly good. Fly fishermen should find success with such standard patterns as the Adams, Blue Dun, Hare's Ear, stoneflies, Quill Gordon, Soft Hackle Nymphs, Hendrickson, Muddler Minnow, Matuka Streamers, Mickey Finn, Woolly Buggers, caddis, March Brown, Black Gnat, Light Cahill, Gray Fox, Renegade, midges and terrestrials.

Little Wills Creek

Like Wills Creek, Little Wills Creek draws most of its flow off the Allegheny Plateau. It is a small, busy stream of rocky rapids and gravel bars surrounded by farmland and mountainsides. Its proximity to Route 96, however, results in more trash and other eyesores, though it is far from an ugly stream.

Little Wills Creek's stocked water extends from just north of Hyndman and its junction with Wills Creek to about the village of Madley, a distance of approximately 6.5 miles. Access is available directly off Route 96 and at two bridges, one at the village of Fossilville, the other roughly a mile upstream. Fly fishermen can try some of the same patterns mentioned under Wills Creek.

While no state parks are located in the immediate area of Wills Creek and Little Wills Creek, Shawnee State Park with its 300 Class A campsites, electrical hookups, dump station, hot showers and flush toilets and is only about 20 miles north of Hyndman on Route 96. The campground is open from the second Friday in April to mid-December. Swimming at a guarded beach and boat rentals are available on 451-acre Shawnee Lake. The park also contains 12 miles of hiking trails (see Raystown Branch Juniata River).

Information on the park may be had by writing: Shawnee State Park, Department of Environmental Resources, P.O. Box 67, Schellsburg, PA 15559.

McClintock Run
Glade Run, Whites Creek
Somerset County

McClintock Run
Glade Run

An isolated, wild tributary of the polluted, but nevertheless often scenic, Casselman River, McClintock Run holds about 4.5 miles of stocked water from its mouth upstream to its source in Deep Valley Lake. It can be found by taking Pennsylvania Route 281 south from Somerset through the villages of New Lexington, Kingwood and Paddytown. At Paddytown bear left off Route 281 onto State Route 3001 toward the village of Fort Hill, one mile away.

Follow S.R. 3001 through a narrow railroad tunnel and across the Casselman. After the road crosses the river bear to the left on the paved road and follow it up the side of the mountain. Access to McClintock Run's lower water is available by turning right onto a dirt road a short distance before the Fort Hill Union Church,

a small, white country chapel. S.R. 3001 also crosses the stream just below the church.

Glade Run is a tributary of McClintock Run. It takes its source from High Point Lake in the shadow of Mount Davis, at 3,213 feet the highest mountain in Pennsylvania.

Although a dirt road runs back along McClintock Run near the church and to Glade Run, it is private and posted against trespassing. So, the only access to its lower water is by hiking up McClintock from the S.R. 3001 bridge at the Fort Hill church.

Glade Run's upper reaches may be found by continuing over the S.R. 3001 bridge and up the hill approximately two miles to Township Road 330, or the first road to the left. T-330 runs back to High Point Lake, where anglers can reach the start of the stream by following a little side road along the western end of the lake.

Mount Davis is part of Negro Mountain running down into Maryland. It is named after an early settler. Negro Mountain itself is named for a black man who, in the early eighteenth century, sacrificed his own life by holding off an attacking party of Indians while his white traveling companions escaped. The incident may have occurred further south in Maryland.

Two other stories with hints of legend touch on the Mount Davis area. One day in either the spring or early summer of 1830, 10-year-old Lydia Shultz, who was living on the slopes of the mountain, was sent out to bring home the cows and became lost. When she didn't return, her family and neighbors went searching for her, but never found her. Months went by and the family grew to accept the loss of the child. Then one day she was found in the woods. She had become quite wild, living on berries and anything else she came across, and even hiding from the searchers.

Baughman's Rocks take their name from the body of a possible murder victim that was never found. Henry Baughman was an ill-tempered man, who was one day out looking for some stray cattle with his two sons. Becoming angry because his youngest son, August, was slowing the search, Henry struck him with a stick, knocking him unconscious. Thinking August dead by the blow, Henry took his body and laid it between some rocks. Returning to the site later, he could not find the body. On the testimony of his other son, he was found guilty of second degree murder and given a prison sentence. What happened to August remains a mystery to this day.

Fort Hill Path, from Fort Hill to Winding Ridge, once paralleled McClintock Run over Negro Mountain. It is believed to have been an offshoot of the Turkeyfoot Path. Fort Hill itself was the site of a fortified Indian village.

Fly fishermen on McClintock Run and Glade Run should find some success with stoneflies, Hare's Ears, Adams, Hendricksons, caddis, March Browns, Royal Coachman, Renegade, Light Cahill and terrestrials.

Since Forbes State Forest surrounds both streams, anglers should obtain a free "Public Use Map" from the forest office to help them find their way around. One may be had by writing: District Forester, Forbes State Forest, Route 30, Laughlintown, PA 15655.

Whites Creek

Another little tributary of the Casselman River, Whites Creek can be found by continuing on Route 281 to its junction with Pennsylvania Route 523 in Confluence, and then taking Route 523 east toward the villages of Harnedsville, Dumas and Beachy. The stream's stocked water starts around Dumas. It is accessible off Route 523 from there upstream to Listonburg. In Listonburg, take State Route 3004 toward the village of Unamis. That road follows Whites Creek along the remainder of its 4.5 miles of planted water.

The Turkey Foot Path, joining Cumberland, Maryland with Confluence and eventually Pittsburgh, once crossed Whites Creek at Dumas. Turkeyfoot was the original name for Confluence, gaining that title from the fact the Youghiogheny River, the Casselman River and Laurel Hill Creek meet at the town, forming a sort of "turkey foot." A road was ordered built along the path by the Ohio Company in 1751.

"Resolved that it is necessary to have a Road cleared from the mouth of Wills Creek to the three forks of the Youghogane and the Col. Cresap be empowered to agree with any person or persons willing to undertake the same so that the expence thereof does not exceed twenty-five pounds Virginia currency."

Too bad the Ohio Company is not in charge of PennDOT's road building budget. Twenty-five dollars for a 40-mile long road!

(Also see Youghiogheny River and Laurel Hill Creek.)

Laurel Hill Creek
Delayed Harvest Artificial Lures Only
Shafer Run, Kooser Run
Jones Mill Run, Allen Creek
Blue Hole Creek, Fall Creek
Somerset County

Laurel Hill Creek

Stretching for some 30 miles through the heart of southwestern Pennsylvania's Laurel Highlands, Laurel Hill Creek is the second longest tributary (tied with the much further north and polluted Sewickley Creek) of the Youghiogheny River. When it, and the 53-mile-long Casselman River, join the "Yough" in the southern Somerset County town of Confluence, the famous whitewater river's flow literally doubles in volume.

Besides being one of the longest tributaries of the Youghiogheny, Laurel Hill Creek also is among the cleanest to enter the river inside Pennsylvania. Although its flow is less than half that of the Casselman River, its alkaline water works as a buffer against the acid mine drainage of the Casselman, enabling the middle Youghiogheny to thrive—at least when the canoeists are gone—as a trout fishery.

Laurel Hill Creek travels through a lot of picturesque areas, but some of its very best fishing water is in Laurel Hill State Park. Started back in the mid-1930s by members of President Franklin D. Roosevelt's Works Progress Administration and Civilian Conservation Corps, the park is one of the largest in western Pennsylvania, covering more than 3,935 acres. When it opened, it was one of five federal demonstration parks—Raccoon, Blue Knob, Hickory Run and French Creek being the others—in the state. The federal government turned it over to Pennsylvania with the stipulation it always be used for recreation, on October 25, 1945.

In addition to being one of the largest and first state parks in western Pennsylvania, Laurel Hill Park also is interesting in that some 1,000 of its acres, including mineral rights, were donated by the Bethlehem Steel Corp. So it serves as a good example of big business as conservationist.

No significant historical events are attached to the park or the stream. However, George Washington's troops did camp within its boundaries in 1794 on their way west to Washington County to put down the "Whiskey Rebellion." That fight, which threatened to tear the young republic apart, arose when local farmers decided they did not care for a new tax placed on their product and no longer wanted to be part of the Union.

Off the main road through the park there once stood an inn, near what is now Group Camp No. 8, and below it a grist mill for grinding the local wheat and rye. At the head of 65-acre Laurel Hill Lake there also once stood a pottery factory and iron forge.

For the angler, Laurel Hill State Park is especially important because it contains the entire 2.2 miles of Laurel Hill Creek's Delayed Harvest Artificial Lures Only Project. From Pennsylvania Turnpike Exit 10 in Somerset, the park can be reached by driving west on Pennsylvania Route 31 then turning left on State Route 3037, which is plainly marked with a "Laurel Hill State Park" sign. The park also can be reached from Turnpike Exit 9 in Donegal by traveling east on Route 31 through the village of Jones Mill and past Kooser State Park to S.R. 3037, and another directional sign.

Laurel Hill Creek's Delayed Harvest Project begins on the park boundary with the Conestoga, Buck Run Camp of the Boy Scouts of America, and continues downstream to where the main road through the park crosses the stream just above the boat launch for the lake.

Access to its lower reaches is available by simply following the park road to where it crosses the stream. A small parking area is provided near the bridge and parking also is permitted along the road. The middle and upper sections of the project can be reached by taking the road to the Boy Scout camp, which is marked with a brown sign and meets Route 31 approximately 150 yards west of S.R. 3037 or by following the main road through the park to the gravel road leading back to "Group Camp No. 4 & No. 6."

For those anglers who might want to stay in the area, Laurel Hill State Park has a Class A family campground of 270 tent or trailer sites with flush toilets, hot water showers, sanitary dumping stations and drinking water. It is open from the second Friday in April until mid-October. A limited number of sites remain open until the end of the antlerless deer season in mid-December. For those off-hours, or family members who don't care to fish, Laurel Hill Park offers hiking on a variety of trails, boating on 65-acre Laurel Hill Lake (no rentals), swimming at a guarded sand beach from Memorial Day weekend to Labor Day and picnicking.

Outside the park, Laurel Hill Creek offers an abundance of fishing opportunities all of the way down to the town of Confluence and the Youghiogheny River.

The stream's headwaters on the north side of Route 31 in the village of Bakersville can be reached by taking State Route 4001 off Route 31 at the "Y" intersection just west of the turn-off for Laurel Hill Park. A small convenience store and gas station sits in the middle of the "Y." In Bakersville, S.R. 4001 makes a turn to the north. It parallels the stream from that point into its headwaters, but at a distance that keeps the water well out of sight. A Fish Commission access site at the Somerset Water Plant runs down to the stream and a small dam.

Anglers who are interested in covered bridges can follow the main park road south past the dam and large white house which serves as a contact station to its junction with State Route 3029. At the "T" intersection make a left across the bridge and then a quick right onto State Route 3033 running toward the village of Scullton. Follow S.R. 3033 for about four miles past McKeesport YMCA's Camp Soles and a large trailer park to where it joins Pennsylvania Route 653. Make a right onto Route 653 and continue downhill less than a mile to Kings Mountain Bridge. A dirt and gravel road next to the bridge provides parking and also leads over the mountain to another fishing spot at Whipkey Dam, a small mill dam.

A second covered bridge can be reached by taking the first right past Kings Mountain Bridge, across from an old half-demolished brick farm house, and following State Route 3035 for about a mile to the village of Barronvale. Caddis are plentiful in both the Kings Mountain and Barronvale areas. The water, however, tends to warm faster than in the Delayed Harvest Project, where there is plenty of shade.

Another popular fishing area can be reached by making a left where S.R. 3033 meets Route 653 near Scottyland and following it to its junction with Pennsylvania Route 281 in New Lexington. From that point make a right and following Route 281 south for approximately three miles to the village of Kingwood. Bear right in Kingwood onto State Route 3007 past the Kingwood Church of God. S.R. 3007 parallels Laurel Hill Creek at a great distance and then meets with it again roughly four miles from Kingwood at the village of Humbert.

S.R. 3007 rejoins Route 281 about two miles downstream from Humbert. A right at this juncture leads to the village of Ursina and then Confluence. Laurel Hill Creek is wide and frequently very shallow in this area. Trophy trout are sometimes stocked in it by local businesses.

No specific hatch captures the attention of anglers along Laurel Hill Creek, though, stoneflies, caddisflies, mayflies, midges and terrestrials are all present in fairly good numbers. As in most freestone streams, the fish tend to be opportunistic, taking whatever comes their way, within reason, of course, and if it is presented properly. Pattern choices include: Adams, Quill Gordon, Hendrickson, caddis, Hare's Ear, Soft Hackle Nymphs, stonefly nymphs, March Brown, Gray Fox, Renegade, Light Cahill, Sulphurs, Black Gnat, midges and terrestrials.

Further information on Laurel Hill State Park may be had by writing: Laurel Hill State Park, Department of Environmental Resources, RD 4, Box 130, Somerset, PA 15501.

Forbes State Forest touches on Laurel Hill Park and its "Public Use Map," available free of charge, provides a great overview of the stream and its tributaries, including roads leading to them. It may be picked up at the park office, or by writing: District Forester, Forbes State Forest, Route 30, Laughlintown, PA 15635.

Shafer Run

Shafer Run is the first stocked tributary of Laurel Hill Creek. It is a tiny little feeder stream that joins Laurel Hill on the north side of Route 31 upstream of the Fish Commission access area and Somerset water plant. Anglers who might want to try it when the main stream is running high or discolored can find Shafer Run by taking S.R. 4001 off Route 31 and through Bakersville, the same as if they were headed for Laurel Hill's upper water.

Township Road 394 is the first turn to the left off S.R. 4001 beyond the Laurel Hill access. Shafer Run flows along the right side of the road, which parallels the creek along its approximately 2.5 miles of planted trout water.

Kooser Run

Named after an early settler, Kooser Run cuts through the heart of Kooser State Park and is easily accessible off the park road, both above and below Kooser Lake (stocked). Kooser Park is located along Route 31 roughly midway between the Donegal and Somerset exits of the Turnpike. The park's "Recreational Guide" contains a map that anglers can use to pick out the more remote locations of Kooser Run's three miles of stocked water.

Although only 170 acres in size, Kooser State Park is a pretty little facility holding both a 60-site campground and nine family cabins. The campground is rated Class B, meaning amenities are limited to water, pit toilets, a dump station and tables. But it is open year-round.

Niceties in the family cabins are likewise limited. The minimal furnishings include beds, chairs, tables, a stove, refrigerator and electric lights. Firewood is provided, when available, for wood-burning stoves and fireplaces to heat the cabins. The rental season begins in the spring and ends in the fall. Reservations are assigned by a lottery. Applications are mailed directly to the park, and must include a stamped, self-addressed envelope. Only one application per year is accepted. Cabins are rented only by the week in the summer.

Along with camping, Kooser Park offers opportunities to hike, swim at a guarded beach (Memorial Day weekend to Labor Day), picnic, a playfield for the children and a snack bar during the summer months.

Further details on the park, including reservation forms for a cabin, may be had by writing: Kooser State Park, Department of Environmental Resources, R.D. 4, Box 256, Somerset, PA 15501.

Jones Mill Run

Located in Laurel Hill State Park, tiny Jones Mill Run is easily accessible off the main road running through the park, as well as the Tram Road Trail. Signs clearly mark both the stream's location along the road and Tram Road Trail. Stocked for 3.5 miles, Jones Mill Run also holds a picturesque old CCC dam.

Allen Creek

Second homes, hunting camps and a road that almost falls into the stream at places, makes Allen Creek less than a gem to look at, but it still is a possible alternative to a rampaging Laurel Hill Creek.

Allen Creek is stocked for about two miles from its mouth upstream. It can be reached by taking the main road through the park downstream past Laurel Hill Lake to the "T" intersection with S.R. 3029. Make a left onto S.R. 3029 and then the next right, immediately after the bridge over Laurel Hill Creek, onto S.R. 3033. Follow S.R. 3033 for about a quarter of a mile to State Route 3039, which appears on the right next to a stand of pine trees. Turn right onto S.R. 3039 and follow it back along and then over Laurel Hill Creek to Allen Creek.

Blue Hole Creek

Blue Hole Creek meets Laurel Hill Creek near the covered bridge in Barronvale. Surrounded by Forbes State Forest, it is a pretty little feeder stream, more isolated than some other Laurel Hill tributaries. It can be reached by taking S.R. 3035 off Route 653 at the Kings Mountain Bridge and following it back to a "T" intersection with State Route 3014 in Barronvale. At the intersection turn right onto S.R. 3014 and then left at the first road (Township Road 493) just before the bridge over Laurel Hill Creek and the Barronvale covered bridge. Blue Hole Creek flows along the right side of the road, which leads back to Blue Hole Road in the state forest. Blue Hole Creek is stocked for three miles from its mouth upstream.

Fall Creek

A tributary of Blue Hole Creek, Fall Creek and its three miles of stocked water can be found by continuing straight past the sign for Blue Hole Road. Township Road 338 appears there and trails Fall Creek, flowing on the right, upstream.

(Also see Youghiogheny River.)

Youghiogheny River

Fayette County
No Closed Season/Float Trip

Mention the Youghiogheny River, meaning "a stream flowing in a contrary direction," or "in a roundabout course," to outdoor enthusiasts in the eastern United States and more likely than not the first subject to arise will be whitewater rafting. And with good reason. Since the "Yough" is one of the finest whitewater rivers in the East. The popularity of the river is immediately evident during a stroll through the falls parking lot at Ohiopyle State Park. On any given day of the year it is possible to find cars, trucks, vans, and some others vehicles in categories all their own, bearing license plates from Ohio, West Virginia, Maryland, Virginia, New York, New Jersey, Michigan, Illinois, Tennessee and half a dozen other states.

What makes the Youghiogheny so popular a whitewater river is first of all the U.S. Army Corps of Engineers Dam at Confluence. The flood-control service it has provided since 1943 makes the river runnable by rafters and canoeists 24 hours a day, 365 days a year. Secondly, Mother Nature has arranged the river into accessible lengths of varying difficulty that are suitable for either novice, intermediate or advanced rafters and canoeists. Thirdly, it is centrally located to all those different license plates in the parking lot, and, finally, it is protected. Fourteen miles of the first 27 miles of the Yough in Pennsylvania, the most popular area, flows through Ohiopyle State Park, and the rest through a lightly populated valley without roads.

With so many attributes working in its favor, it is not surprising that the Yough receives more visitors than probably any other river in the country. About 45,000 people regularly float the "Middle Yough," or the stretch of water between the town of Confluence and Ohiopyle, and over 150,000 the section of the lower Yough from Ohiopyle to Bruner Run. Add to those figures the more than 1.5 million others who annually visit the area to hike, swim, bicycle or just look, and it is easy to see why Ohiopyle State Park is said to be the only state park in Pennsylvania that earns a profit.

Beyond the whitewater and the scenery that attracts the vast majority of visitors to the river, the Youghiogheny also exists as an excellent big-water trout fishery, one that is actually getting better all of the time and still wonderfully under utilized.

Of the approximately 73 miles of the Youghiogheny River flowing through Pennsylvania, only the first 27 miles, from the tailrace of the Corps of Engineers dam in Confluence to the dam at South Connellsville is managed by the Fish Commission as a cold water fishery. Of that total, only about the first mile, from the dam downstream to the Casselman River, is planted with adult trout. The remainder of the trout water has been frequently stocked with fingerlings, hundreds of thousands of them, which make the Yough the next best thing to a true wild trout angling experience.

Because it is the only area that is stocked with adult trout by the Fish Commission (other areas almost all of the way to the river's end in McKeesport receive some adult fish from sportsmen's clubs), the section from the dam downstream to the Casselman receives the most fishing pressure of probably any stretch of the river. But there are still times when an angler can have nearly all of it to himself. The best spots in this area are directly below the outflow pipes of the dam, and the islands and riffle downstream from the Pennsylvania Route 281 bridge leading into Confluence. Access is available by following Route 281 north off U.S. Route 40 east of Uniontown, or by taking Route 281 south from Somerset.

Immediately below the stocked waters is the first floatable section of the river. Known as the "Middle Yough," because it marks the exact center of the 132-mile long river, this is the second most popular stretch of the river among rafters and canoeists. While anglers can no longer expect to spend a day in quiet solitude along the Middle Yough, the competition from other fishermen is still next to nothing. Noisy rafters and canoeists are the greater threat to the fishing.

"We also found other places where the water was rapid but not so deep, and the current smoother; we easily passed over them, but afterwards we found little or scarce any bottom. There were mountains on both sides of the river. We went down the river about ten miles."

George Washington wrote these lines about the Middle Youghiogheny River back in 1754 while exploring it as a possible water route to supply an attack on Fort Duquesne (Pittsburgh). He gave up on the idea once he reached the falls in Ohiopyle and turned back. What else the first president might have had to say about the middle river and its surroundings on his return trip nobody will ever know for certain. For when he was defeated at nearby Fort Necessity a short time later, the French translator who was handed his journal complained it contained nothing but a description of the land. He saw no reason to provide an exact interpretation and allowed the journal to disappear forever.

Even with the construction of the dam at Confluence the approximately 11-mile long Middle Yough has not changed much from Wasington's time. It is still a place where the water is rapid but shallow, the pools smooth and deep, and mountains tower above. "The Singing River" as Tim Palmer calls it in his book *Youghiogheny Appalachian River*.

According to geologists, the Youghiogheny is an "antecedent" river, meaning it predated the mountains surrouding it and was already flowing in its northwestern direction when they were being formed some 300 million years ago.

Altogether, the river cuts through four ridges in the Allegheny Mountain section of the Appalachians. Two of them—Laurel Hill, below Confluence, and Chestnut Ridge, downstream from Ohiopyle—in Pennsylvania. The gaps it has carved through these ridges range from about one mile to just 150 yards. The wooded slopes rise some 1,700 feet at 45-degree angles to hold the morning mist and cast the river in early shadows. Where the water flows over hard sandstone, the angler will find the rapids for which the Youghiogheny is famous.

For the trout angler, the Middle Yough offers a good variety of water types. Along with rapids, which provide a frisky break from what would be a very ordinary float trip, there are long, deep flats, rocky pools, shallow riffles and fast chutes. Something to suit just about every fishing taste.

Access, at least legal access, to some of the Middle Yough's best water for years meant a long hike, either upstream from Ohiopyle or downstream from Confluence, along the old Western Maryland Railroad right-of-way. In the late 1970s, however, the Western Pennsylvania Conservancy purchased a 26-mile long portion of the right-of-way from the Chessie System, which took over the Western Maryland Railroad, and resold the section in Ohiopyle State Park to the commonwealth. Today, the old right-of-way is a beautiful bicycle path running all of the way from the borough of Ohiopyle to the Ramcat Falls, the first rapids below Confluence, where it connects with a paced road which continues on to the tailrace of the Corps of Engineers Dam.

Besides making it easier for the angler to fish the Middle Yough, the completion of the bicycle path also has brought a lot more people into the area. Where once a fisherman could stand in the fading light and hear only the rush of the water over the rocks, he is now just as likely to hear the laughter and occasional shouts of the cyclists on the path. But that is only a minor distraction. For chances are still very good no other anglers will be in sight, and if one does materialize he will probably be so far away as to qualify as a mirage.

A sign near the bridge at Ohiopyle points the way to the start of the bicycle path in that town. The upper end of the path at Ramcat Falls may be reached by taking Ramcat Hollow Road, the paved road next to the Route 281 bridge on the opposite side of the river from Ohiopyle. The start of the bike path is about two miles away. Plenty of parking is provided at both ends.

Along with providing parking for the bicycle trail, the lots at Ohiopyle and Ramcat Falls also mark the put-in and take-out spots for anglers floating the middle river.

Nearby deposits of coal and the plentiful lumber of the surrounding mountains may have been the mainstays of Ohiopyle—meaning "water whitened by froth"—in its early years, but the town has been a summer tourist attraction since the late Victorian period. The area was so popular as an outing site, especially the Ferncliff Peninsula, that the Baltimore & Ohio Railroad actually ran regular Sunday excursions, round-trip cost one dollar, to the town from Pittsburgh. The Ohiopyle of those days contained several hotels and boarding houses. The most famous of them all was Ferncliff Hotel, with its tennis courts, a bowling alley, fountains and dining room capable of seating 150, not to mention a hot spring for the health conscious. Workmen tearing down the hotel were later to discover the source of the "spring" in the hotel's boiler room.

Land for Ohiopyle State Park was acquired in the mid-1960s with the aid of the Western Pennsylvania Conservancy, and money from the Mellon family, Edgar Kaufmann, owner of the Kaufmann Department Stores in Pittsburgh, and the West Penn Power Co. The first phase of construction in the park was completed in 1970 with the development of the falls area at Ohiopyle.

While there are plenty of fish in the Youghiogheny around Ohiopyle, it is not really a place for any serious angler to spend much time. It is simply too thick with rafters, hikers, picnickers, strollers, photographers, lovers, haters, waders, campers, sunbathers, and just plain sightseers. For those who still want to try the area, it can be reached by a couple of different trails, and the best approach is probably to stop at either the park office or the information center near the falls and pick up a recreational guide to the park.

Below the Bruner Run take-out, the river returns to sanity. In fact, from there to South Connellsville, where the Fish Commission stops maintaining the river as a trout fishery, the

Youghiogheny River.

Youghiogheny is, for the most part, undeveloped and deserted. The main reason being its inaccessibility. Anglers who want to fish here either have to begin hiking along the abandoned Western Maryland Railroad right-of-way, or take to a raft or canoe. No road touches on the river throughout this entire nine-mile stretch.

Anglers who plan on float fishing the Bruner Run to South Connellsville water should be aware of a series of Class II and Class III rapids extending for about two miles below the put-in. This whitewater can be portaged if necessary. After that the river settles down to a series of long pools and shallow riffles over a rocky bottom. The Bruner Run Access can be reached by taking State Route 2019 off Route 381 toward the park's campground and then following the signs to Bruner Run.

The popularity of the lower Yough at Ohiopyle has forced park authorities to establish a strict quota system for boaters floating the river between the town and Bruner Run. As a result of this quota—960 commercial, guided rafters, and 960 private, unguided—access to the Bruner Run take-out is limited to shuttle buses. Therefore, anglers interested in floating the Bruner Run to South Connellsville stretch, which has no quota, must contact the park office "two or three days" prior to their planned trip—unless, of course, they do not mind a 1.5 mile walk with a canoe or raft—to make arrangements to have the gate barring access to Bruner Run opened.

The take-out for the run may be reached by taking Route 381 from Ohiopyle to Normalville and then Pennsylvania Route 711 north through South Connellsville. Turn right on Pittsburgh Street in South Connellsville and follow it for about two miles until the road dead ends. Turn right at the dead end and curve down toward the river on another dirt road. Parking is available at an industrial parking lot along the road—but don't block the gate. Canoes or rafts must be carried up a hill and across the railroad tracks to the gate.

No detailed information is readily available on aquatic insect hatches along the Youghiogheny. The river does have a very good population of caddisflies which can be successfully imitated by such impressionistic patterns as the Elk Hair Caddis, Humpies and Henryville Special on the surface, and soft hackles below it. Large stonefly nymphs, as well as such old favorites as the Hare's Ear, Muskrat and Tellico also produce well at times. The river contains a large number of crayfish, so anglers might try those, too. Mayfly activity is very sporadic. Many anglers who are very familiar with the Yough have never encountered a good hatch of any species.

Ohiopyle State Park offers a campground with 223 Class A sites. It includes washhouses with hot showers, flush toilets, a dump station, a contact station to secure permits and park information, four children's playgrounds, as well as tent, trailer and walk-in sites. The campground is open year-round. Because of all the boaters, advance reservations are required to insure campsite availability throughout the year. Reservations are accepted any time within the calendar year.

Besides the campground, limited accommodations also are available at the Ohiopyle Youth Hostel. Reservations are suggested. Details may be had by contacting the Pittsburgh Council, American Youth Hostels, Inc., 6300 Fifth Ave., Pittsburgh, PA 15232.

Further information on the park is available by writing: Ohiopyle State Park, Dept. of Environmental Resources, P.O. Box 105, Ohiopyle, PA 15470.

Fallingwater

Frank Lloyd Wright's world famous Fallingwater, perhaps the most praised and written about private home of the twentieth century, stands only about five miles north of Ohiopyle State Park

along Route 381. Any angler who decides to fish the Youghiogheny River and does not take a couple of hours off to visit this cantilevered wonder over Bear Run Falls is missing an extraordinary opportunity. Donated to the Western Pennsylvania Conservancy by the Kaufman family in 1963, the home is open to the public on a regular basis through the warmer months.

(Also see Laurel Hill Creek.)

Big Sandy Creek
Chaney Run, Mill Run
Fayette County

Big Sandy Creek • Chaney Run

Whitewater rafters south of the Mason and Dixon Line are probably more familiar with Big Sandy Creek than trout fishermen. Down in West Virginia, the Big Sandy is known as a highly technical whitewater run, some people even compare it to the upper Youghiogheny River in western Maryland, one of the premier whitewater runs in the United States.

A tributary of West Virginia's famous Cheat River, entering that waterway near the end of its most rafted section, Pennsylvania's portion of Big Sandy Creek is stocked for eight miles from its confluence with Mill Run upstream. The village of Elliotsville sets at about the center of the stock water, leading to excellent access upstream and fair downstream.

Fishermen can reach Elliotsville by taking Route 381 south off U.S. Route 40, the National Pike, at the village of Farmington. In Elliotsville, the Big Sandy, which does not really live up to its name in Pennsylvania, can be reached by taking Wharton Furnace Road, State Route 2003, north toward the village of Wharton Furnace.

Wharton Furnace Road also picks up Chaney Run just outside of Forbes State Forest and parallels upstream into the forest and the village of Wharton Furnace. Chaney Run holds three miles of stocked water and is a possible alternative to a high and discolored Big Sandy Creek. Wharton Furnace Road also can be picked up directly off Route 40 west of the villages of Chalkhill and Wiggins. Follow the signs for Wharton Furnace, site of one of the last active iron furnaces in Fayette County.

Below Elliotsville, Big Sandy Creek can be reached either by walking, or by continuing on Route 381 south toward West Virginia. On the right, just before Route 381's intersection with Township Road 311, a dirt and gravel road appears and leads back to the stream and the Quebec Wild Area of Forbes State Forest.

Big Sandy and Chaney Run fly fishermen might try stoneflies, Adams, Blue Dun, Quill Gordon, caddis, Hendrickson, March Brown, Muddler Minnow, Royal Coachman, Renegade, Light Cahill, Sulphurs, midges and terrestrials.

Mill Run

Big Sandy's other stocked tributary is Mill Run. It is planted for couple of miles in its headwaters in Forbes State Forest. It can be reached by taking T.R. 345 off Wharton Furnace Road at Elliotsville, and then the first road to the right. Mill Run lies about three miles away and is paralleled for a short distance by the road.

A good overview of Big Sandy, Chaney Run and Mill Run may be had by obtaining a copy of the "Public Use Map" for Forbes State Forest. It is available free of charge by writing: District Forester, Forbes State Forest, Route 30, Laughlintown, PA 15655.

Dunbar Creek
Fayette County
Fly Fishing Only

When a geographic entity bears the name of a person, it is usually that of a hero, or at least someone who was once considered a hero, such as Mt. McKinley, Mt. Kennedy, the Jefferson River or the Madison River. Fayette County's Dunbar Creek is the exact opposite, however. It carries the name of the officer who was in command of the reserve regiment of British General Edward Braddock's army during its march to capture Fort Duquesne (Pittsburgh) from the French and Indians in 1755; a man who, after learning of the general's defeat, decided it was time to lead his own troops into winter quarters—only it was the middle of July.

Colonel Thomas Dunbar was a career officer from a respected family who might have made a good soldier on the well organized battlefields of Europe, but, like Braddock himself, was hopelessly out of his element in the backwoods of colonial Pennsylvania. Confronted with the sight of defeated troops, Colonel Dunbar beat a hasty retreat from his camp near the creek and town which now bear his name to Fort Cumberland (see Wills Creek) in what is now Maryland. He did this despite the fact his command of nearly 1,500 able-bodied men outnumbered the French and Indians who controlled Fort Duquesne by approximately three to one.

"I have little of news to add since my father's last letter to you, inclosing copies of his orders to Colonel Dunbar, whose retreat is thought by many here to be a greater misfortune than the late General Braddock's unhappy defeat," wrote Captain William Shirley, Braddock's secretary, to Deputy Governor Robert Morris. "What dishonor is thereby reflected upon the British Army. Mr. Dunbar has ever been esteemed an exceedingly good officer, but nobody here can yet guess the reason of his retreat in the circumstances he was in. . . In the meantime it is a most mortifying and shocking consideration that so fine an army should be beat and entirely drove out not only of the field, but so far from it by about 500 Indians and French. . ."

Dunbar's retreat to first Fort Cumberland, and then Philadelphia, left the frontier wide open and revealed to the French the extent of the victory they had won. It also put the Indians, who had been wavering until that point, solidly behind the French and sent them on a reign of terror through Pennsylvania, Maryland, Virginia and even parts of the Carolinas.

"It is supposed that near one hundred persons have been murdered or carried away prisoners by these barbarians who have burnt the houses and ravaged all the plantations in that part of the country," wrote Captain Dagworthy, who was sent with a relief column to Fort Cumberland in October of 1755. "Parties of the enemy appear within sight of Fort Cumberland every day, and frequently in greater numbers than the garrison consists of."

Although Dunbar Creek itself has remained clean enough to sustain a quality fishing project since the 1950s, the area surrounding it is a far cry from what Colonel Dunbar's troops once knew. Situated deep within the legendary bituminous coal fields of southwestern Pennsylvania, the mountains, valleys and towns of the area have been ravaged by America's rush to industrialize in the late nineteenth century and early days of the twentieth. The hunger of the now disappearing steel mills which once promoted H.L. Mencken to label Pittsburgh "hell with the lid off" has left its mark in the form of ruined coke ovens, black piles of slag and abandoned railroad grades.

The borough of Dunbar itself, with its empty store fronts and old, frame "company" homes, has dwindled to just over 1,300 souls and holds the dubious distinction of being the only Pennsylvania town on a tributary of the Youghiogheny River not to have a sewage treatment plant. The town's sewage lines discharge raw waste directly into the lower reaches of Dunbar Creek and eventually the river.

While the roads leading up to Dunbar Creek may not be the most scenic in Pennsylvania, the area surrounding most of the stream is pleasant. Hemlock, birch, oak and laurel drop down to rocky, worn pools and runs bordered by ferns and mosses, making it an almost classic Eastern mountain stream.

No particular insect seems to dominate Dunbar Creek. The trout are usually ready to take whatever they can get. Old hands on the stream report success on caddis larvae and pupae, terrestrials, especially the inch worm, beetle and ant, as well as some of the more traditional dry flies, including the Adams, Blue Dun, Hendrickson, March Brown, Light Cahill and Sulphurs. Bright, attractor patterns such as the Royal Coachman and marabou streamers also work well on the stream's brook trout.

Dunbar Creek's Fly Fishing Only Project begins at its confluence with Glade Run and continues 4.1 miles downstream to the stone quarry along State Route 1053. It can be reached by taking U.S. Route 119 north from the West Virginia border and Uniontown or south from Connellsville and Pennsylvania Turnpike Exit 8 in New Stanton. A directional sign pointing the way to the town of Dunbar is situated along Route 119 approximately three miles south of Connellsville.

After turning off Route 119, follow S.R. 1053 through the town, bearing to the right where it meets the edge of the old business district, and then left at the T intersection across the bridge. Continue on along the stream and up the hill where S.R. 1053 parallels the first couple miles of the project. Parking spots are available in numerous places next to the stream. At the Game Commission Headquarters Building S.R. 1053 starts up a hill and a dirt and gravel road continues on along the stream for about another half mile. There is a parking lot at the end of this road.

The water near the town of Dunbar also is popular with anglers. This area, however, has none of the charm or wildness of upstream stretches. But it is open to all-comers, so frequently draws crowds, especially early in the season.

Jack Dam on Dunbar Creek.

NORTH CENTRAL

Cameron County

Brooks Run
Clear Cr
Cowley Cr
Driftwood Br
Elk Fork
Hicks Run E. Br
Hicks Run W. Br
Mix Run
North Cr
Portage Cr
West Cr

Center County

Bald Eagle Cr
Black Bear Run
Black Moshannon Cr
Elk Cr
Little Fishing Cr
Logan Br Spring Cr
Moshannon Cr W. Br
Penns Cr
Pine Cr
Poe Cr
Sinking Cr
Spring Cr

Clearfield County

Chest Cr
Clearfield Cr
Little Clearfield Cr
Susquehanna River W. Br
Trout Run

Clinton County

Beaverdam Run
Big Fishing Cr
Hyner Run
Hyner Run Left Br
Hyner Run Right Br
Kettle Cr
Little Fishing Cr
Susquehanna River
Trout Run
Young Womans Cr L. Br
Young Womans Cr R. Br

Elk County

Bear Cr
Bennett Br
Big Mill Cr
Clarion River
Clarion River E. Br
Clarion River W. Br
Crooked Cr
East Fork Cr
Hoffman Run
Middle Fork Cr
Rocky Run
Straight Cr
West Cr
Wilson Run

Lycoming County

Grays Run
Hoaglands Run
Larrys Cr
Little Bear Cr

Little Pine Block House Cr
Loyalsock Cr
Pine Cr
Pleasant Stream
Rock Run
Slate Run
Susquehanna River
Trout Run
Upper Pine Bottom

McKean County

Allegheny Reservoir
Allegheny River
Brewer Run
Chappel Cr
Kinzua Cr
Kinzua Cr S. Br
Marvin Cr
Meade Run
Potato Cr W. Br
Sugar Run N. Br
Willow Cr

Potter County

Allegheny River
Bailey Run
Big Moores Run
Cross Fork
Dingman Run
Fishing Cr W. Br
Freemans Run
Genesee River
Genesee River Mid Br
Genesee River W. Br
Germania Br Kettle Cr
Kettle Cr
Little Kettle Cr
Lyman Run
Oswayo Cr
Sinnemahoning River
Sinnemahoning E. Fork
South Woods Br Sinnemahoning

Snyder County

Kern Run
Middle Cr
Middle Cr S. Br
Swift Run

Tioga County

Babb Cr
Cedar Run
Mill Cr W
Pine Cr
Pine Cr W. Br
Roaring Br Lycoming Cr
Slate Run
Stoney Fork

Union County

Bear Run
Buffalo Cr
Buffalo Cr N. Br
Laurel Run
Little Buffalo Cr
Penns Cr
Rapid Cr
Weikert Run

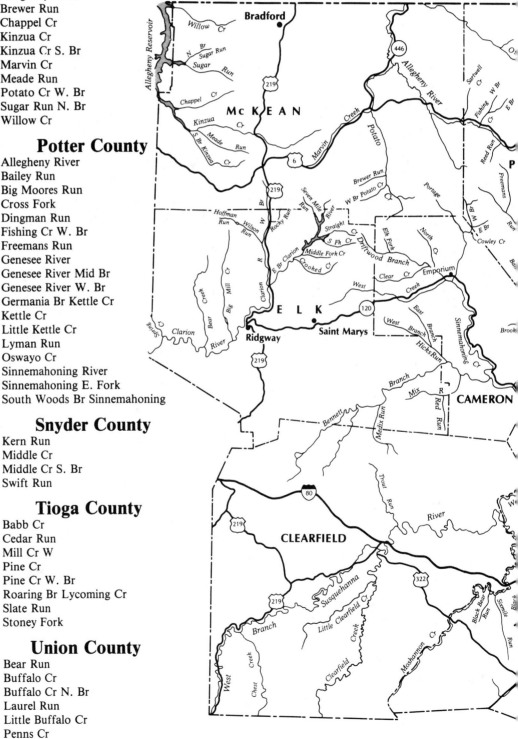

North Central Region

Little Clearfield Creek
Clearfield County

Clearfield County's early industries were coal mining, iron making and lumbering. At one time there were more than 400 sawmills operating within its boundaries. Coal, building stones and clay continue to be taken from its hills in quantity. Tanning—Clearfield Furs are famous throughout the state—tile and brick manufacturing also are important ingredients in the local economy.

The effects of all this heavy industry, both past and present, understandably has been extremely hard on the environment. Mining scars dot Interstate Route 80 during its passage through the county, and its two longest streams, West Branch Susquehanna River and Clearfield Creek, for which the county was named, offer only very limited angling opportunities. There waters actually take on the tint of a heavily chlorinated swimming pool in places.

Despite all of this abuse, however, Clearfield County still offers a scattering of decent trout streams. Chief among these is probably Little Clearfield Creek.

Stocked with rainbows and browns for 12 miles between the village of Kerrmoor on Pennsylvania Route 729 upstream almost to its mouth on Clearfield Creek, Little Clearfield Creek is a slow moving, bottomland stream of medium width with brushy banks. It is the most popular stream in the county, and so naturally crowded. Anyone looking to fish in solitude should not visit this stream until later in the season, when many fishermen have moved on to walleye, pike, muskies and bass.

Little Clearfield Creek is cut by two state routes and tracked by several minor roads that provide access in numerous locations. It can be reached by taking Interstate Route 80 Exit 19 and following Pennsylvania Route 879 west past the town of Clearfield and Hyde. At Curwensville, take Pennsylvania Route 453 south to the village of Olanta where it crosses the stream.

Before reaching the village of Olanta, after the village of Bloomington, a green road sign will point the way, on the right, to New Millport where access to some of Little Clearfield's upper water is available off State Route 3007.

In Olanta, a good portion of the stream's lower water may be reached by turning left, at the sign for Glen Richey, onto State Route 2022. Little Clearfield Creek begins to widen near the village of O'Shanter on S.R. 2022. Access is available at the bridge in the village, and by an old railroad grade which parallels the stream for about two miles.

Standard fly patterns such as the Adams, March Brown, Hendrickson, Hare's Ear, Light Cahill, caddis and terrestrials are possible starting points for the fly fisherman.

Trout Run
Fly Fishing Only
Clearfield County

Thick hemlock and rhododendron kept the path to the stream cool even in the middle of August. Three deer appeared on my left, stared until I took another step and then were off, their tails waving in alarm. They were the first whitetails I had seen along a stream that week. I wondered if they were plentiful in the area and made a mental note to possibly include them in the story on Trout Run. They would make for a nice bit of color.

When I reached the stream, it was a pleasant surprise. Overhung with more rhododendron and surrounded by a flat plain of second-growth hardwoods, it reminded me of some of the best placed I had hunted deer in Pennsylvania. The shallow, green pools and splashing, little rapids fit the scene perfectly. Even the two summer homes along its banks did not detract from the setting. Well-kept and sturdy, they would have served any landscape artist's need for perspective. I was still congratulating myself on the find, thinking how I would have to come back again soon and try it, when I saw the man walking up behind me. Since the road leading to the stream led straight through the middle of a barnyard, I had half expected company, someone looking to see what I was up to. We exchanged greetings.

"Thought I'd take a ride back to see what the fly project looks like," I said then. "Pretty stream. How's the fishing?"

He shook his head.

"They don't stock this anymore," he said.

I looked at him, wondering what kind of line he was going to feed me to maintain his privacy.

"It's listed in the book you get with your license," I pointed out.

"Oh, I don't know about that," he said. "But they haven't stocked this the last two years."

"Is there some kind of problem?" I asked.

"They say it's acid rain," he shrugged.

I glanced at the Fish Commission posters labeling the area as Fly Fishing Only. They were weathered to the point where I could barely read even the heading. I knew the Fish Commission replaces worn signs every season. They have enough trouble with people sneaking into such projects with bait without giving the offenders the excuse they didn't see any signs.

When I got back to my car, I immediately checked my "Summary of Fishing Regulations and Laws." There was Trout Run under the Fly Fishing Only Projects—"1.5 miles; From one mile above Rt. 879 upstream to and including the Trout Run Corp. property." But when I turned to the back, to the "Approved Trout Waters" section, Trout Run was missing from the list. It was missing from the list the year before that, too, I discovered when I got home. And from "Trout Fishing in Pennsylvania," the Fish Commission's guide to the state's trout streams.

Pennsylvania stands at the very center of the acid rain controversy. It is downwind from the four states which contribute most to acid precipitation, and is the second biggest producer itself. Studies have shown the pH of Pennsylvania's rainfall to average between 4.0 and 4.1—1,000 times the acidity of neutral water.

The geology of the state's valleys, its famous limestone, is an excellent buffer against acid rain, or else the story would be far worse than it is already. The mountains are quite another matter, however. The sandstone and shale of our ridges have little or no buffering capabilities. Runoff from them is the straight stuff, making over 30 percent of the state's 5,000 miles of stocked trout streams vulnerable to acid precipitation and 45 percent of its 9,000 miles of unstocked, native trout waters, according to the Fish Commission.

"And the impacts of acid rain are cumulative," writes Water Resources Coordinator Fred Johnson in the Fish Commission publication "Acid Precipitation." "As a watershed is continually stressed by acid rain, its ability to buffer the low pH water is gradually reduced. When the watershed's buffering capacity is used up and it is pushed over the edge to the acid side of the balance sheet, it may 'never' recover."

Unless there is a significant reduction in sulfur and nitrogen oxide emissions in the near future, Fish Commission scientists estimate that at least half of the present vulnerable streams, or about 3,000 miles of trout water, could be lost by 1991. Add to the stream loss another several thousand acres of lakes, and the economic loss could total some 75 million dollars annualy.

Isn't it time to get involved?

Bennett Branch Sinnemahoning Creek
Clearfield County

Stretching from north of DuBois in Clearfield County across the panhandle of Elk County into Cameron County, Bennett Branch Sinnemahoning Creek covers roughly 50 miles. It is well known to many anglers and deer hunters from southwestern Pennsylvania who travel up Pennsylvania Route 255 and Penn-

sylvania Route 555 to Potter County and surrounding lands in pursuit of their sport.

Even though Bennett Branch is a huge stream, acid mine drainage problems limit its stocking to approximately a four-mile length, from the village of Penfield upstream to its headwaters in State Game Lands 93, between Route 255 and Pennsylvania Route 153. It is a smaller, brushier stream in this stocked portion, maybe half the size of what the legions of deer hunters see. Nevertheless, it is said to produce some big brown and brook trout on occasion.

Anglers can find Bennett Branch's stocked water by taking Interstate Route 80 Exit 17 and following Route 255 north to Penfield. Route 255 passes over the stream at two points outside of Penfield. Access is available at both of those spots. Immediately after the second Route 255 bridge, secondary roads run to the right and left. Both provide access to the stream. Fishermen should keep in mind that neither Route 255 bridge is very large, and not go speeding over them.

Although Bennett Branch is not planted with trout downstream of Penfield, it does hold some interesting history. Tyler Hotel, located on the northern edge of the village of Hollywood, is reputed to have played host to President Ulysses S. Grant shortly after his election in 1868. Philip P. Bliss, a noted evangelist, singer and hymn composer of the late nineteenth century, was born nearby in 1838 and worked in the region as a lumberman during his youth. He published four collections of songs: "The Charm" (1871), "The Song Tree" (1872), "The Joy" (1873) and "Gospel Songs" (1874). His most popular song was "Hold the Fort," inspired by a message signaled by General William T. Sherman during the Civil War. Bliss and his wife died in a train wreck in 1876.

Further down Bennett Branch, the famous cowboy movie star Tom Mix was born near where Mix Run (see which) enters the stream.

Fly fishermen on the Bennett Branch can try such traditional patterns as the Adams, Hendrickson, Hare's Ear, Muskrat, Royal Coachman, Soft Hackle Nymphs, Black Gnat, Light Cahill, caddis and terrestrials.

Black Moshannon Creek
Six Mile Run, Black Bear Run
Centre County

Black Moshannon Creek

Abandoned coal mines, eroded slag piles, crumpling quarries and rundown logging towns often make it easier for a person traveling around Pennsylvania to imagine the state in the midst of the Industrial Revolution than as a virgin wilderness full of elk, bison, moose, mountain lions, eagles and wolves. But all of those creatures once did occur in fair numbers within the state—transplanted elk and bald eagles still can be seen in a couple of small areas thanks to the work of the Game Commission, and reports of a mountain lion occasionally surface. Beyond those cases, though, almost the only proof left of the others are some local folktales and the names of a few mountains and streams. Among these is Black Moshannon Creek, or "Moose Stream."

Anglers visiting Black Moshannon Creek today may be more likely to find a wood nymph or satyr—in only the broadest sense of their meanings, of course—than a moose. But with roughly its first six miles protected by Black Moshannon State Park and Moshannon State Forest, this amber-stained, little rocky stream is still a pleasure with excellent scenery and good fishing.

Adding to the scenery and the fishing is the fact that access to most of Black Moshannon's upper water is walk-in only. No roads encroach on the stream from just below the park to Interstate Route 80, though the drone of traffic on the highway becomes apparent long before the pavement itself is in sight.

Black Moshannon State Park may be reached from the east by taking Interstate Route 80 Exit 26, U.S. Route 220 south to Pennsylvania Route 504 in Unionville. From the west or southwest, the park can be found by taking Route 220 to its junction with U.S. Route 322 at Port Matilda and following that north to Philipsburg, or by taking Interstate 80 Exit 18, Route 322 south toward Philipsburg and Route 504 which cuts through the center of the park.

Prior to the development of Black Moshannon State Park by workers of the Civilian Conservation Corps in the 1930s, the site held the small lumbering town of Antes. Located on the old Erie Turnpike between Erie and Philadelphia, the town also served as a stage stop. It had a hotel, the "Antes House," a Post Office, store, blacksmith shop, a school and bowling alley.

According to the park's "Recreational Guide," the present dam, which forms Black Moshannon Lake, occupies the site of a beaver dam. The first man-made dam was built on the site by a lumber company that also built a sawmill next to it. The area around the park was so heavily timbered that at one point more than a million meters of logs were stored in the lake. Many of the white pine trees felled by the loggers' axes ranged from three to six feet in diameter.

As part of the Allegheny Front, the underlying rock formations carry bituminous coal, some of which is still being mined near the park. The region also was once mined for clay.

Fish on. Driftwood Branch Sinnemahoning Creek.

Access to the stream may be had by following Black Moshannon Road, a dirt road, running off Route 504 near the dam. The road parallels the stream out of the park into Moshannon State Forest. Anglers should be careful not to follow it past the "Short Trail" snowmobile trail. At that point the road is moving away from Black Moshannon Creek and back out toward Route 504.

The lower reaches of the stream's stocked water is accessible by taking Interstate Route 80 Exit 22 and following Pennsylvania Route 144 to the village of Moshannon. Pick up Township Road 325 in the village near the junction of Route 144 and Route 53, and take it down to the stream. An approximately five-mile long stretch of the stream runs along Interstate Route 80 in this lower reach, and there is a large piece of clear-cut forest, so it is not nearly as pleasant an experience as the upper water.

Regular hatches along the stream include: Hendricksons in early May and Brown Drakes in late May. Other flies anglers might try are: Adams, Hendricksons, Renegade, Blue Quills, Soft Hackle Nymphs, Light Cahills, Hare's Ears, Sulphurs, caddis and stoneflies.

Camping anglers will find 80 Class A sites with flush toilets, showers, laundry tubs and a sanitary dump station in 3,481-acre Black Moshannon State Park. They also will find 13 family cabins with a stove, refrigerator, electric lights, fireplace and minimal furnishings. Both the campground and the cabins are open from the second Friday in April to the end of the antlerless deer season in late December. The cabins are available for weekly rental throughout the period, as well as half weeks in the spring and fall.

Swimming is not permitted in Black Moshannon Lake. However, non-fishing members of the family can still picnic and

hike, or take in a program—from Memorial Day weekend to Labor Day weekend—at the park's Environmental Education Center.

Further information on the park may be had by contacting: Black Moshannon State Park, Department of Environmental Resources, R.D. 1, Box 183, Philipsburg, PA 16866.

Six Mile Run

Like its neighbor Black Moshannon Creek, Six Mile Run is a tributary of polluted Moshannon Creek, joining the larger water downstream of the village of Winburne. It is a small mountain stream full of very cold water, and dotted with beaver dams and a man-made impoundment. The cold properties of its water make it fishable through most of the summer and provide it with a surprisingly good Yellow Drake hatch, starting in mid-June and continuing through July.

Six Mile Run may be reached by taking Route 504 west from the dam in Black Moshannon State Park toward Philipsburg. About a half-mile past Airport Road a dirt road will join Route 504 on the left. This is Six Mile Run Road. It parallels the stream to Clay Mine Road, which then picks up the creek and follows it to its headwaters.

Six Mile Run's lower stocked water may be reached by taking Munson Road (next to the bridge) out of the park and toward Kylertown. Munson Road passes over Six Mile Run at its mouth.

Besides the Yellow Drake hatch, anglers also can try the fly patterns mentioned for Black Moshannon Creek.

Black Bear Creek

Originating in Moshannon State Forest, Black Bear Creek is another little tributary of Moshannon Creek right next door of Six Mile Run. It is stocked for two miles, from its mouth upstream, and, like lower Six Mile Run, can be reached by taking Munson Road out of Black Moshannon Park and toward Kylertown. Six Mile Run is the first stream Munson Road passes over when it reaches Moshannon Creek, Black Bear Creek the second.

Fly fishermen can again try patterns listed under Black Moshannon Creek, as well as any other proven patterns in their fly box.

Author's Note: *Central Pennsylvania's Bald Eagle Valley contains two Bald Eagle Creeks. They both begin in the same swampy area southwest of Port Matilda; however, one, the far longer of the two, flows northeast to form Foster Joseph Sayers Lake in Bald Eagle State Park, Centre County, and eventually drains into the West Branch of the Susquehanna River near Lock Haven. The other, shorter one, flows southwest into the Little Juniata River near Tyrone, Blair County.*

Bald Eagle Creek (East)
Centre County

"There are a number of streams in Pennsylvania that contain trout over the 24-inch mark," former Penn State University fly fishing instructor George Harvey once wrote back in the 1960s. "But if you want to fish a stream that has a lot of them, try Bald Eagle Creek in Centre County."

While Harvey's words about big trout still hold somewhat true, his other remarks about Bald Eagle being only a marginal stream over four-fifths of its length for most of the trout season, and full of miles upon miles of nearly barren water also bear repeating. For except in the spring when the water level is up and the temperature down, Bald Eagle Creek contains only one good, productive stretch of trout water. This is the approximately

3.5-mile section between the town of Milesburg, where Spring Creek adds it cold, fertile flow, downstream to the village of Curtin. This out of a total length of more than 50 miles of water, almost 27 of which are listed as being stocked by the Fish Commission.

Spring Creek's rejuvenating flow dissipates by the time Bald Eagle reaches Curtin, but that really does not mean much, since just downstream of the village it enters Bald Eagle State Park and is captured to form 1,730-acre Foster Joseph Sayers Lake, named after a local Medical of Honor winner.

Bald Eagle Creek—like Bald Eagle State Park, Bald Eagle State Forest, Bald Eagle Mountain, Bald Eagle Valley and everything else named Bald Eagle in Centre County and surrounding areas—is named after the Munsee Indian Chief "Woapalanne," translation Bald Eagle. (That is according to Dr. George Donehoo's *A History of the Indian Villages and Places Names in Pennsylvania*. According to the official recreation guide to Bald Eagle State Park, Chief Bald Eagle was a member of the LeniLenape tribes and his named "Wapelanewack.")

In his history, Dr. Donehoo says Chief Bald Eagle once lived on the flat at the junction of Spring Creek and Bald Eagle Creek, the present site of Mileburg. He is believed to have led many Indian raids on settlers and American soldiers during the Revolutionary War. Among these raids was one on April 11, 1779 when Captain John Brady was killed and another on August 8, 1779 during which James Brady was killed with a group of soldiers on Loyalcock Creek in Lycoming County (see which).

Captain Samuel Brady, John's son, blamed Bald Eagle for both killings and, following a series of raids by the chief in Westmoreland County, set off up the Allegheny River in pursuit of the raiders. He finally caught up to them at the mouth of Red Bank Creek in Jefferson County (see which), about 15 miles north of Kittaning, at what is now known as Brady's Bend. The Indians were attacked by Brady's party and, according to family tradition, Chief Bald Eagle was killed in the fight.

Following the Revolutionary War, the area around "Bald Eagle's Nest," or home, in Centre County, became a sort of resort for the Indians. Milesburg, laid out by Colonel Samuel Miles, replaced it in 1793.

Access to Bald Eagle involves nothing more than getting on Pennsylvania Route 220. As Bald Eagle Mountain parallels the stream to the south, Route 220 parallels it to the north. Nowhere is the stream more than a five minute walk from the road. Those anglers wishing to try the stream's best stretch between Milesburg and Curtin can turn off Route 220 onto Pennsylvania Route 144 at Milesburg. Immediately across the bridge, Iddings Road runs off to the left and provides access to the upstream end of the good water. Downstream, Bald Eagle Creek's best stretch can be reached by turning at the brown "Pennsylvania Historical & Museum Commission" sign and following Township Road 219 back through Curtin Village and along the stream.

Curtin Village is a recreation of an early Pennsylvania ironmaking village. In 1810, Roland Curtin, a Scotch-Irish immigrant, in partnership with Moses Boggs, started Eagle Forge on the site. Shortly after Boggs retired in 1815, Curtin constructed Eagle Furnace, using the adjacent Bald Eagle Creek to transport his product to the Susquehanna River at Lock Haven. Roland Curtin's sons took over the business in 1842, constructing Pleasant Furnace, the now restored furnace, which operated all of the way into the 1920s, gaining the distinction of being the last cold-blast charcoal iron furnace to operate in the United States.

Along with the furnace, the mansion which Roland Curtin built near the furnace in 1831, has been restored and is now part of Curtin Village. Guided tours are available May through October.

Bald Eagle Creek, even in its best stretch, is not much of a fly fishing stream when compared to others in the area. Its hatches are sporadic and of varying quality, but include: early season, mid-April to late May, Blue Quills, Quill Gordons, Black Quills, Hendricksons and Gray Fox; mid-season, June and July, Pale Evening Duns, Light Cahills, Isonychia and Yellow Drakes; late season, August, Tricorythodes. Large wet flies and nymphs also can produce on Bald Eagle, but it is the bait and spin fisherman who generally does the best.

Bald Eagle State Park sets along Pennsylvania Route 150, and can be reached by following Route 220 to Route 150. It has camping sites for 35 tents and 25 recreational vehicles. The tent sites are all of the walk-in type and approximately 150 feet off the road. A sanitary dump station is available for use by camping vehicles. The campground is open from the second Friday in April to the third Saturday in October.

Further information on Bald Eagle Park may be had by writing: Bald Eagle State Prk, R.D. 1, Box 54, Howard, PA 16841.

Details on Curtin Village are available by contacting: Roland Curtin Foundation, P.O. Box 312, Ballefonte, PA 16823.

Spring Creek
(Fisherman's Paradise)
No Harvest Fly Fishing Only
Centre County

Back in 1954, Centre County's Spring Creek was rated one of the top 100 trout streams in the United States. Its reputation was greater even than that of the Letort, and much older, going back at least to the turn of the century. Well-known anglers from all over the nation made it a point to travel to the town of Bellefonte to test their skills on Spring Creek's waters. Among the famous who have wet a line in the stream were Theodore Gordon, the godfather of American fly fishing, and Ray Bergman, whose book *Trout* was for years referred to as the Trout Fisherman's Bible.

Bergman, in fact, was so impressed by his experienced on one particular day he spent along Spring Creek that he wrote about it in detail in his book. He uses the day to point out how trout fishermen must not approach a stream with any preconceived notions, but instead always be ready to experiment and adapt to the changing situation.

In Bergman's own case, when the fish didn't react to his gently cast fly, he found they would take one slapped hard on the surface. After they stopped taking his surface offerings altogether, he turned to nymphs fished dead-drift upstream and again was successful. Then when they stopped taking his upstream offerings, he put on a piece of split shot and began working the nymphs with a hand-twist retrieve, quickly catching his three largest fish of the day.

"Do you wonder that I stress the importance of knowing many methods of using flies and lures?" he writes. "One must do so in order to get even fair results, especially in these days of concentrated fishing when the fish are becoming wiser every season."

After watching Fish Commission personnel feeding some of Spring Creek's trout and the ensuing frenzy, which resulted in fish taking flies they had previously refused, Bergman ends his musing on the stream by wondering aloud if several anglers working together might not trigger a similar response by continuously casting over a school of fish.

"It is quite likely that the fish would not be fooled by the con-

centrated attack at all," he concludes. "It is almost certain that the reason they hit the artificials floating down in company with the prepared food was because they knew that in order to get their share of "easy pickings" they had to grab anything they saw quickly and did not wait to investigate its quality or genuineness. . .One thing is sure: fish definitely know the difference between the real thing and an imitation. Sometimes they are momentarily fooled by the artificials, but it doesn't take them long to get wise."

By 1957, just three years after it was rated one of the nation's best trout streams, the miracle which was Spring Creek ended. It died, or at least a big part of it did, gasping for breath when a sewage treatment plant on an upper branch became overloaded and pumped a large quantity of untreated sewage into the water, drastically lowering the oxygen content and killing most of the aquatic life.

In the years since the sewage accident, Spring Creek also has seen gasoline and chemical spills, and just about every other abuse modern, industrial man can inflict on his environment. Somehow though, it has never completely succumbed. The heavy Green Drake hatches for which it was once known are today long gone, but the situation is not a complete loss. Actually, Spring Creek has come back to the point where many people think it now holds more (and larger) fish than when it was stocked by the Fish Commission, and hatches of Blue Quills, Slate-Winged Olives, Sulphurs, Tricorythodes, Light Cahills and various caddis have been reported. Because of continued problems with pollution, however, no fish at all may be killed or taken from its waters from the bridge in Oak Hall, downstream to its mouth in Bellefonte.

With all of the abuse Spring Creek has suffered, it is somewhat incongruous, even sad, that its No Harvest Fly Fishing Only Project should be called "Fisherman's Paradise." But the name is a leftover from the good old days of 1933 when the project was opened as the first special regulation water in Pennsylvania.

Fisherman's Paradise was started with the support of the famous conservationist and governor of Pennsylvania, Gifford Pinchot, and former Fish Commissioner Ollie Deibler. It was established both to promote the concept of catch-and-release, and as a showplace for modern fish management techniques. The original limit was two fish per day over 15 inches. In the 1950s, through the efforts of University of Michigan fisheries biologist Dr. Albert Hazzard, however, Fisherman's Paradise was turned into no-kill water. Since the problems with pollution arose to taint the stream's fish, all of Spring Creek from the bridge at Oak Hall above the Neidig Brothers' Limestone Co. to the mouth has been declared a no-kill zone by the Fish Commission, making it illegal to possess any trout from it at all.

Surrounded by gravel parking areas and picnic tables, flowing along concrete walls and over numerous stream-improvement devices, Fisherman's Paradise is a far cry from a native brook trout stream. But it was never meant to emulate one. Instead, it is a place where Dad can take the family, even if they do not fish, and let them picnic in the sun, enjoy a walk along the water or look at the trout and exhibits at the Bellefonte Hatchery just across the bridge, while he is busy flailing away at some of the smartest trout in creation.

Spring Creek's Fisherman's Paradise No Harvest Fly Fishing Only area can be reached by taking Pennsylvania Route 26 north from State College to the Nittany Mall and then bearing left on Pennsylvania Route 150. Continue on Route 150 for 3.5 miles until a green sign marked "Fisherman's Paradise 1" appears. Turn left immediately after the sign and follow the road to a "T" intersection with Spring Creek Road (State Route 3001). At the intersection make another left. Fisherman's Paradise is straight ahead.

Although Fisherman's Paradise is easily the best known stretch of Spring Creek, it is not the only one to offer good fishing. Fine, and less crowded, water exists both up and downstream of the project.

Upstream, angling opportunities exist all of the way to the village of Oak Hall, though a large limestone quarry makes some areas far from scenic or quiet. The upper waters are accessible by again taking Route 26 north from State College and turning right at the sign marked "Lemont 1." At the traffic light in Lemont follow Boalsburg Road toward Oak Hall. The road parallels the stream, though it is usually out of sight. Parking spots are available at various locations, but be sure to ask permission if private property is involved.

Houserville Road also runs off Route 26 north out of State College and parallels the stream, including a small stretch owned by the Spring Creek Chapter of Trout Unlimited. It is marked on the left with a green street sign. The better water is above the village of Houserville.

Bearing left once more off Route 26 onto Route 150 at the Nittany Mall, Rockview State Penitentiary allows fishing on its property, accessible by turning left on Shiloh Road next to a small, white church and past (fittingly enough) the state police barracks. Anglers going onto prison property are required to be out by dark, or they could be locked in by a gate that bars the road. Those who do venture into the area may not find the best fishing Spring Creek has to offer, but they certainly will see it at its wildest and most beautiful, enveloped by a shallow gorge.

Reaching water downstream of Fisherman's Paradise simply involves following Spring Creek Road out of the special project section and along the stream. Spring Creek Road continues on to join Pennsylvania Route 550 near Bellefonte, which in turn picks up Route 150 (for a short period Route 144/150) and follows the stream, now much wider and bordered by various garages, machine shops and so forth, on to Milesburg where it finally flows into ald Eagle Creek (see which).

Spring Creek hatches include: early season, mid April to June, Blue Quill, Yellow Cranefly, black, brown and tan caddis; mid season, June and July, Sulphurs, Light Cahill, Slate-Winged Olives, Blue-Winged Olives; late season, August and on, Light Cahill, Tricorythodes, ants and white midges. Cress bug patterns, such as the Muskrat and Otter also are popular. Anglers should check local sources for more complete details.

(Also see Logan Branch Spring Creek.)

Logan Branch Spring Creek
Centre County

Only four miles long and barely more than a trickle, headed by a hatchery and bordered by homes, small businesses and a busy road, on appearances alone Logan Branch hardly seems worthy of mention alongside Pennsylvania's best trout streams.

Add to its surroundings enough anxious anglers to tax the capacities of streams twice its size, and the only redeeming feature left Logan Branch is the incredible number of monster trout it produces every year; many more than any of its famous neighbors. Electroshock surveys conducted in conjunction with Operation FUTURE have revealed a solid population of fish in

the 20-inch and up range, including one 29½-inch brown weighing in at just under 11 pounds. This despite the fact the stream is not heavily stocked by the Fish Commission.

Why so many big trout choose to call Logan Branch home nobody can say for certain. It has a bountiful supply of sow bugs and sculpins, a fairly good mix of hatches, a constant limestone flow and steady temperature readings, but so do a lot of other streams in Centre County. It is a fascinating situation. One deserving of a stream that bears the name of Chief Logan of the Mingoes, a man whose eloquence and spirit once inspired Thomas Jefferson to compare him to Cicero and Demosthenes and even include "Logan's Lament" in his "Notes on Virginia."

Born at Auburn, New York in 1725, Logan, whose Indian name was Tah-gah-jute, "his lashes stick out," was the second son of Shikellay, vice-regent of the Six Nations of the Iroquois Confederacy. He was named Logan in honor of William Penn's secretary James Logan, a man who his father greatly admired.

Throughout his life Chief Logan was a great friend of the white colonists, continually arguing with the Indians for peace and restraint in their dealings with them. As so often before and after, however, Chief Logan's attitude only led to the whites' taking advantage of his people and, in the end, the massacre of his entire family. It was the slaughter of Chief Logan's family that, after he had taken his revenge, caused him to make the speech which caught Jefferson's attention.

"I appeal to any white man to say if ever he entered Logan's cabin hungry, and I gave him not meat; if ever he came cold or naked, and I gave him not clothing.

"During the course of the last long and bloody war, Logan remained in his tent, an advocate for peace. Nay, such was my love for the whites, that those of my own country pointed at me as they passed, and said, 'Logan is the friend of the white man.' I had even thought to live with you, but for the injuries of one man, Colonel Cresap the last spring, in cold blood, and unprovoked, cut off all the relatives of Logan; not sparing even my women and children. There runs not a drop of my blood in the veins of any human creature. This called on me for revenge. I have sought it. I have killed many. I have fully glutted my vengeance. For my country, I rejoice at the beams of peace. Yet, do not harbor the thought that mine is the joy of fear. Logan never felt fear. He will not turn on his heel to save his life. Who is there to mourn Logan. Not one."

During the last few years of his life, Chief Logan wandered from tribe to tribe, a broken man drowning his sorrows in whiskey and rum the whites were all too happy to supply. He was finally killed in a quarrel with his nephew near Detroit.

Logan Branch flows along Pennsylvania Route 144 between Bellefonte and Pleasant Gap. Access to it involves little more than finding a parking spot and not trespassing on posted property.

Among the fly hatches occurring along the streams are: early season, mid-April to late May, Blue-Winged Olives, Yellow Cranefly, caddis and Sulphurs; mid-season, June and July, Light Cahill, Sulphurs, Blue-Winged Olives, midges and Yellow Cranefly; late season, August, Light Cahill, Blue-Winged Olives and Yellow Cranefly. Sow bug and sculpin imitations also take fish.

Because Logan Branch is so small and under heavy fishing pressure, its big trout are very shy and skitterish. The best chance to catch a trophy here is after dark. And avoid wading.

(Also see Spring Creek.)

Penns Creek
Catch and Release
Centre, Mifflin and Union Counties

Sinking Creek, Elk Creek
Pine Creek, Poe Creek
Centre County

Weikert Run, Laurel Run
Union County

Penns Creek

From Penns Cave where it emerges in full flow under the gaze of Centre County's famous Nittany Mountain, to the town of Selinsgrove in Snyder County, near where it empties into the Susquehanna River, Penns Creek covers a distance of some 60 miles, making it the longest of all Pennsylvania limestone streams. It is very productive trout water along roughly its first 20 miles throughout the season, a good early-season trout fishery in its middle 20 miles, and home to smallmouth bass in its final 20 miles. Excellent mayfly hatches occur on it all season long, including the Green Drake, Yellow Drake, Blue Quill, Cahill and "Trico." And when there is no hatch it offers fine terrestrial fishing to ants, beetles, grasshoppers and crickets.

Despite all it has to offer, however, Penns Creek remains relatively unhonored when compared to its sisters to the south. If the Letort has added volumes to the annals of trout angling in American, and Falling Spring, Big Spring and the Yellow Breeches chapters, then Penns Creek has done no better than a scattering of pages. And not always entirely flattering pages either.

"If trout streams can be classified by gender," ends one article by Ray Elliott entitled "The Truth About Penns Creek," "then I am quite sure that Penns Creek comes under the feminine category. And believe me, she is a bitch!"

Although it is just as true at times, it is impossible to imagine anybody writing something like that about the "legendary" Letort or "gorgeous" Falling Spring.

The main problem with Penns Creek's image seems to be its size. The Letort, Falling Spring and even the Yellow Breeches are tiny in comparison. Their fish are concentrated and much easier to locate, if not always to catch. Penns Creek, on the other hand, is not only the longest limestone stream in the state, but also one of the widest, large enough to draw the attention of canoeists and rafters. Its size means its fish are spread over a much larger area than on those other limestone waters, and catching them involves a lot more fruitless time spent watching and searching, especially if no hatch is coming off and the angler is new to the stream.

Besides its size, Penns Creek is different than the classic limestone waters to the south in other ways, too. Instead of gliding flats surrounded by weedbeds of elodea and watercress, most of it flows in a succession of shallow, gravel-bottomed riffles and pools more reminiscent of a freestone than a limestone stream. Only where it emerges from its upper water near the village of Spring Mills does it contain some of the cress beds and flats so typical of Pennsylvania's limestone waters.

Appearance aside, Penns Creek is without a doubt a productive limestone stream with plenty of nymphs, crayfish and other aquatic food that trout savor. It is famous for a heavy Green

Drake hatch in late May or early June, followed by the Yellow Drake two or three weeks later, and then Blue Quills and Tricorythodes in late summer. Because of this abundance of food Penns Creek's trout tend to be selective in their feeding. Couple that with its large size and a generally unpredictable nature, and it is easy to understand why so many anglers leave the stream frustrated and cursing.

If Penns Creek has a distinct reputation among fishermen, its place in early Pennsylvania history is no less colorful.

The original Iroquois name for Penns Creek was Kayarondinhagh, the meaning of which has been lost to history. For a time it also was known as Mahoning Creek or Big Mahanoy Creek, meaning "lick" or "at the lick" in reference to the mineral deposits elk and deer regularly visited.

Understandably, most people seem to think Penns Creek was named after William Penn, the founder of Pennsylvania. However, it actually carries the name in honor of John Penn, William's grandson, who served as governor of the Pennsylvania colony from 1746 to 1776, and under whose administration the stream and the lands around it were obtained from the Indians.

The lands north of the Kittatinny Mountains were purchased from the Iroquois at the Treaty of Albany in 1754. The Penns paid some 400 pounds for the land, but its sale was very distasteful to the Delaware and Shawnee who also frequented the area. Because of this displeasure, the two tribes quickly joined the French after General Edward Braddock's defeat at the Battle of Monogahela in 1755, and the first Indian massacre following the battle occurred along Penns Creek. The massacre, during which 25 European settlers were either killed or carried off, led to the building of a string of forts throughout the area and a move to bar the Quakers, whose pacifist philosophy made them reluctant to avenge the attack, from membership in the General Assembly.

The killing of 10 Indians, all of them peaceful and about half of them women and children, on Penns Creek by Frederick Stump and his servant, John Ironcutter, almost resulted in another general Indian war in Pennsylvania during 1768.

Stump was living in the Penns Creek area in 1766 when the Indians complained to Governor Penn about his presence. In hopes of averting trouble, the governor ordered Stump to move. He never did, but his hatred of the Indians probably started at that time.

After the killings, Governor Penn placed a 200 pound price on Stump's head. He and Ironcutter were captured by Captain William Patterson on Penns Creek and taken to jail in Carlisle. The pair was freed a short time later, however, when about 75 white settlers who sympathized with them raided the jail. Following the raid, the pair was hidden for a time by friends and then escaped to Virginia. Neither was ever punished for the murders.

From State College, Penns Creek's Catch and Release Project can be reached by taking U.S. Route 322 about 15 miles east past Potter Mills. Turn left at the brown sign marked "Poe Valley State Park" and follow the road, a winding sometimes dirt and gravel, sometimes black top affair, for approximately 10 miles past Poe Valley Park and its dam to the Poe Paddy State Forest Picnic Area. Turn left at the campground sign in Poe Paddy and continue on to where the road widens and bends to the left and is met by a smaller dirt road, really an old railroad bed, on the right. Park along the side of the road and follow the old railroad bed to a former trestle and across the creek. On the other side of the stream continue straight through an old railroad tunnel to the 3.9-mile long Catch and Release project.

Poe Valley and Poe Paddy also may be reached by taking Pennsylvania Route 45 for 1.5 miles west from the Town of Millheim, and then following the signs for 12 miles.

Both Poe Valley State Park—which is named after an early set-

Penns Creek.

tler of the area who is thought to have been a cousin of the famous author of horror tales Edgar Allen Poe—and Poe Paddy State Forest Picnic Area offer camping facilities for anglers, or anybody else, who wishes to stay near the stream. Poe Paddy, once the site of a town of more than 400 people, has 45 Class B tent and trailer sites right on Penns Creek at the junction of Poe Creek, while Poe Valley has 75 Class B sites. Both campgrounds are open from the second Friday in April to the end of the antlerless deer season in mid December. Sites are handed out on a first-come, first-served basis, and they fill quickly during peak fishing times, such as the Green Drake hatch. No convenience hookups are available at Class B campgrounds. Facilities are limited to a drinking water supply, pit toilets and a sanitary dump station.

Along with camping, Poe Valley Park also holds a number of trails running off into Bald Eagle State Forest, boating on 25-acre Poe Lake, swimming at a guarded beach from Memorial Day weekend to Labor Day, picnicking and environmental programs. There also is a concession stand, selling ice, charcoal and other camping items, that operates from Memorial Day weekend through Labor Day.

Penns Creek's upper water can be located by following Route 45 east from State College to the town of Spring Mills. The stream flows directly through the center of town and cannot be missed. Follow either Fire Hall Road or Water Street through town to Penns Creek Road (State Road 2012), which parallels the stream

all of the way to the village of Coburn where it is joined by Elk Creek and Pine Creek. Much of Penns Creek's upper water is posted, so anglers should be careful they are not trespassing on private property. The area directly downstream form Coburn is one section that is open and popular.

The bottom portion of Penns Creek's stocked water is accessible by taking Pennsylvania Route 235 to the village of Glen Iron. State Route 3004 appears near the bridge in Glen Iron and parallels the creek upstream to the village of Pardee. State Route 3002, which meets Route 235 in the village of Laurelton, leads to the villages of Weikert and Cherry Run, and further upstream access.

Penns Creek hatches include: early season, mid-April to June, Blue-Winged Olives, Grannom, Black Quill, Hendrickson, Black caddis, Sulphurs, Tan Caddis, March Brown, Gray Fox, Green Drake; mid-season, June and July, Light Cahill, Isonychia, Yellow Drake and Tricorythodes. Some of the hatches, such as the Tricorythodes and Light Cahill, can continue into early fall. Anglers should check local sources for more complete information.

Further details on both Poe Valley State Park and Poe Paddy State Forest may be had by writing: Poe Valley State Park, Department of Environmental Resouces, R.D. 1, Box 276A, Milroy, PA 17063.

Information on Bald Eagle State Forest, including a free

"Public Use Map" showing Penns Creek and its tributaries, is available by contacting: District Forester, Bald Eagle State Forest, P.O. Box 111, Mifflinburg, PA 17844.

Sinking Creek

Sinking Creek is a common name for streams in limestone country. On many of the streams, the name is derived from the fact the creek actually disappears underground, into a cave formed by acid rain eating through the limestone beneath the earth's surface. Nothing so dramatic occurs on this tributary of Penns Creek, but who knows what might happen in the future.

Access to this Sinking Creek, and its approximately eight miles of stocked trout water, is available off Sinking Creek Road, near the bridge across Penns Creek in Spring Mill. Egg Hill Road, which meets Sinking Creek Road about three miles upstream, provides further upstream access and leads to Route 144, where Sinking Creek can be found between the villages of Potters Mills and Centre Hill. Red Mill Road, running off Route 144 near where it crosses the stream, also continues upstream.

Sinking Creek's source in Colyer Lake can be found by following the sign for the lake off U.S. Route 322 west of the village of Tusseyville. Dogtown Road can be found near the lake and follows the creek downstream. Fly fishermen can try some of the same patterns mentioned under Penns Creek.

Elk Creek

Any stream capable of supporting a population of wild trout minus special regulations in a region as famous and attractive to trout fishermen as central Pennsylvania has to be something extraordinary. Elk Creek and its wild browns is a prize. Publicity literature for the Federation of Fly Fishermen's 1986 Conclave even rated it as "one of the best fly streams." This in an area with such well known trout waters as Spring Creek, Penns Creek and Fishing Creek.

What enables Elk Creek to survive as a quality trout fishery is neither its remoteness, much of it flows along a busy road, nor its size, by any standards it is small, but rather the simple wryly toughness of its fish. Do not travel to this little limestone stream with thoughts of easy fishing since it is not stocked. But do go there with expectations of solitude and an angling challenge. Ed Sutryn, the inventor of the McMurray Ant, chose Elk Creek as the first testing ground for his fly because of the difficulty of its fish (see Fishing Creek, Clinton County). He took "only two or three fish" that day back in 1965, but lost another of 18 or 19 inches.

Elk Creek's fishable water stretches for some 16 miles through Brush Valley between Brush and Shriner mountains into Penns Valley where it joins first Pine Creek and then, a short piece later, Penns Creek just above Coburn. Along the way its character changes from a riffly brook in the lovely, intensely farmed Amish country above the hamlet of Smulton to a swift, rock garden of a mountain stream in the "narrows" between the mountains back to a quiet farm-country water below the town of Millheim.

The presence of Millheim, population about 800, adds a historic touch of sorts to Elk Creek. A 72-acre section of the town—including outhouses, smokehouses and backyard barns—has been added to the National Register of Historic Places because of its importance in the early settlement, industrial development, transportation growth and architecture of Penns Valley.

The town, whose name means "home of the Mills," was settled in the early 1770s and established as a milling center for much of the region by 1786. It continued to enjoy a steady industrial, commercial and residential growth through the last half of the nineteenth century. Pomeroy's Atlas Map of 1874 shows it with 13 stores and 14 major industries, including a planing mill, sawmill, woolen mill, dye house, two foundries and machine shops, two flour mills, two tanneries, a limestone quarry, marble works, a chair factory, and several cement works and lime kilns.

Architecturally, the town reflects a Victorian flavor with some of the most richly decorated "gingerbread" homes in all of Centre County. The borough's commercial district has more of a turn-of-the-century look to it than some of the side streets because of two fires which destroyed many of the original structures in the late nineteenth century.

Although Elk Creek parallels Pennsylvania Route 192 all of the way through Brush Valley from Livonia to Spring Bank on Pennsylvania Route 445, it never actually comes in sight of the roadway. To reach its upper water, anglers should take Route 192 to Rebersburg and then turn at the sign for Smulton, where a bridge crosses the stream and joins Elk Creek Road (State Route 1012), which follows the stream toward Spring Bank. Elk Creek is little more than a brook in this area.

From Smulton downstream to Spring Bank, Elk Creek can be reached by taking Route 192 to Route 445 and then picking up Elk Creek Road, marked by a green street sign on the left, just above Millheim Narrows, also marked by the same street sign.

The start of the narrows marks the beginning of probably the most productive water on the stream. Access to the entire "narrows" stretch is available off Route 445. Parking is available at various spots all of the way down to Millheim.

Below Millheim, Elk Creek is accessible in several locations by following Township Road 837 to the town of Coburn where the stream meets Pine Creek.

Elk Creek hatches include: early season, April to late May, Blue-Winged Olives, Blue Quills, March Browns, Pale Evening Duns, Light Cahills and Green Drakes; mid-season, June and July, Slate-Winged Olives, Blue-Winged Olives, Light Cahills, terrestrials and Tricorythodes; late season, August, Blue-Winged Olives, Tricorythodes and terrestrials. Other fishermen do well with minnows, worms and spinners.

Pine Creek

Pine Creek's lower trout water, about two miles worth, can be found by turning off T-387 and onto State Route 2018 between Millheim and Coburn. S.R. 2018 appears on the left just before the bridge leading into Coburn and parallels Pine Creek upstream to the village of Woodward.

At Woodward, Pine Creek is stocked upstream for about four miles. It can be reached off Route 45 in the village, or by following Township Road 887, which appears near the bridge, to a "T" intersection where Pine Creek Road (Township Road 515) runs to the right and further upstream. Fly anglers can try some of the same patterns mentioned under Penns Creek and Elk Creek.

Weikert Run

Holding about three miles of stocked trout water, Weikert Run can be found by following the bridge across Penns Creek at Weikert and then turning right onto a dirt road. Further upstream access is available by continuing straight on the paved road to a cross roads and then turning right onto Weikert Run Road.

Laurel Run

Laurel Run feeds Penns Creek along Route 235 between the villages of Laurelton and Laurel Park. Its stocked water covers about six miles from its mouth upstream to the Union/Centre County line. It can be reached off Route 45 from near the county line downstream to the junction of Route 235, which then parallels the stream to its end. Several side roads also provide access.

Middle Creek
North Branch Middle Creek
South Branch Middle Creek
Kern Run, Swift Run
Snyder County

Middle Creek

Aided by a touch of limestone and a good size, Middle Creek is the best trout stream in Snyder County. It is stocked for some 25 miles, from the village of Middle Creek downstream to the town of Middleburg, and big water between Beavertown and Middleburg, where anglers can find the stocked fish supplemented with a number of holdovers.

Flowing through the center of rolling and ridge-lined Snyder County, Middle Creek also is a pleasant stream to fish. Its upper reaches are often surrounded by deep woods of hemlock that gradually give way to scenic farms and bottomlands of wooded buffs. Second homes and hunting camps are at a minimum, especially compared to Penns Creek, which parallels it to the north. Only at the downstream end of its stocked water in Middleburg is it defaced by trash and other trappings of the modern world.

Access to Middle Creek's bigger water is readily available along several side roads running off U.S. Route 522 between Middleburg and the village of Beaver Springs. These include: Furnace Road just west of Middleburg, State Route 3007 a short distance beyond and State Route 3009 toward the village of Paxtonville. On the south side of the stream, a secondary road also follows the creek from above Paxtonville down to Middleburg.

Near the Route 522 bridge over Middle Creek, Creek Road appears on the north bank and parallels the stream up to Pennsylvania Route 235. Covered Bridge Road and Pine Swamp Road both run off Creek Road and back to Route 522. Access also is available off the Route 235 bridge, upstream of which is a small dam.

At Beaver Springs, Middle Creek begins a bend to the north. Anglers can reach some of its upper water by going north of Route 235 toward the villages of Benfer and Troxelville. After passing the lake formed by the dam, Route 235 crosses the stream again. Township Road 463 appears at the bridge. It offers access to the stream at different points on its way back to Township Road 570, which leads into the village of Middle Creek and the end of the stocked water.

Tuscarora Path, from North Carolina to Sunbury, once crossed Middle Creek near the village of Kantz. The trail took its name from the Tuscarora tribe, which used it in 1713 to escape attacks from settlers in their homelands in the Carolinas and seek protection under the Iroquois. Many of those refugees settled along the Great Bend of the Susquehanna in northeastern Pennsylvania and New York. Others, however, scattered throughout Pennsylvania, as evident by the numerous streams and hills named after the tribe.

Selingrove near Middle Creek's confluence with Penns Creek and the Susquehanna River, was laid in 1790 by Anthony Selin, a Swiss soldier of fortune who accompanied Lafayette to America. Governor Simon Snyder, Pennsylvania's third governor under the constitution of 1790, built his home in the town at 121 Market Street. He served as governor from 1808 to 1817.

Isle of Que, French for "tail island," along which Middle Creek joins Penns Creek and the Susquehanna River, is a long peninsula of land that was once owned by Chief Shikellemy, who deeded it to Conrad Weiser, the colonial ambassador to the Indians, in 1754. According to legend, the chief had a dream in which Weiser presented him with a beautiful rifle. Indian custom required Weiser to hand over his weapon. A few days later, Weiser then told the chief, "I dreamed that Shikellemy presented me with the large and beautiful island situated in the Susquehanna River." As Shikellemy gave the land to Weiser, he is reputed to have said, "Tarachawagon (Weiser), let us never dream again."

Middle Creek is said to have fairly abundant aquatic life. Fly fishermen should find success on the main stream and its tributaries with such traditional patterns as the Quill Gordon, Adams, Hendrickson, Soft Hackle Nymphs, Muskrat, Hare's Ear, Matuka Streamers, Woolly Buggers, March Brown, Light Cahill, Sulphurs, Black Gnat, midges and terrestrials.

Portions of Bald Eagle State Forest lie both north and south of Middle Creek and touch on at least two of its tributary streams. Anglers can get a great overview of the stream by obtaining a free "Public Use Map" of the forest. They are available at the forest offices, or by writing: District Forester, Bald Eagle State Forest, P.O. Box 111, Mifflinburg, PA 17844.

North Branch Middle Creek

Flowing out of Walker Lake, the North Branch is stocked with browns and rainbows for about six miles from the lake downstream to its mouth. Access is available along Route 235 about midway between the lake and Route 522. Creek Road, running to the east off Route 235 at Benfer, also crosses the stream.

South Branch Middle Creek

Surprisingly wide for a tributary stream, Middle Creek's South Branch holds eight miles of stocked water running from its mouth upstream. It can be found by taking Ridge Road near the Route 522 bridge over Middle Creek in Beaver Springs (site of a covered bridge). Ridge Road parallels the South Branch at a distance, giving access off several side roads, including, Township Road 568, Township Road 560 (which leads to another secondary road following the stream along its north side), Township Road 461 leading to the village of Lowell.

Kern Run

Winding north off Shade Mountain and through Beavertown, Kern Run is stocked for three miles from its mouth on Middle Creek upstream. Both the upper and lower water of this little mountain brook can be reached by following Township Road 588 off Route 522 on the west side of Beavertown, where it goes underground for a period.

Swift Run

Brook trout fishing is reported to be very good along Swift Run, another pleasant, little mountain tributary of Middle Creek. Its eight miles of planted water extend from its mouth upstream past the forest headquarters office of Bald Eagle State Forest. State Route 4012, which runs off Route 235 just above the Benfer bridge, leads to the stream's lower water. Its upper water can be found by continuing north of Route 235 to Troxelville. In the village, turn left where Route 235 bends to the east and follow the road toward the forest headquarters.

Fishing Creek
Trophy Trout
Clinton County

65

Little Fishing Creek
Centre and Clinton Counties

Fishing Creek

"Fishing Creek is Fishing Creek is Fishing Creek," Pittsburgh born Gertrude Stein might have written while instructing Ernest Hemingway back in the Paris of the 1920s. And she certainly would have been correct. Actually, she could have repeated the name three or four dozen more times and still not have touched every stream named Fishing Creek, Big Fishing Creek or Little Fishing Creek in Pennsylvania. For one or another stream bearing those names seems to flow through almost every county in the commonwealth. Only two, however, are worthy of mention beyond their immediate areas. And one of these is this tributary of Bald Eagle Creek in Clinton County.

How good is Fishing Creek can probably best be answered by pointing out that it surrendered the Pennsylvania record brown trout, some 15 pounds, 4 ounces, to angling author and Penn State fly fishing instructor Joe Humphreys back in 1977. Before, and since, it has entertained more fishermen with two and three pound trout than possibly any other stream in the state. Na-mee-si-ponk, "it tastes fishy," as the Delaware Indians said.

Clinton County's Fishing Creek—which sometimes also is referred to as Big Fishing Creek since it has a tributary known as Little Fishing Creek (the confusion can be endless) arises in the Loganton region of Sugar Valley and flows for about 34 miles through a mixture of gentle farm country and rugged mountains to join Bald Eagle Creek near the village of Flemington.

Although the many brush-clogged channels, swift runs, and rocky bottom and banks of its Trophy Trout Project make it resemble a mountain freestone stream, Fishing Creek is a true limestone water. Along its upper length, about Loganton to Tyersville, it flows through what is called Karst Topography, a sort of lumpy landscape whose shape is determined by a labyrinth of limestone caves. Anglers who choose to explore these upper waters will find side valleys dead-ending in ridges, sink holes and places where streams completely disappear underground. Near Cedar Run, Fishing Creek itself goes underground in several places during the summer months.

Around Tylersville, the gentle southwest flowing waters of upper Fishing Creek start a 180-degree turn through gaps in Big Kettle Mountain and then Big Mountain, which eventually leave it running in a northeast direction. Known as the "Narrows," this is the location of the stream's five-mile-long Trophy Trout Project and its most productive stretch. The narrows also mark a dramatic change in the appearance of the stream. Gone are its low banks and scenic farms. In their place now begin to appear the giant boulders, heavy rapids and undercut banks of Pennsylvania's wild mountain country.

At the village of Clintondale, where Fishing Creek finishes its turn through the mountains, the stream once again begins to take on a gentler appearance. More development also starts to appear in the form of homes and farms. But the views are still appealing. At Mill Hall, however, a dredged and leveed channel makes Fishing Creek look more like a drainage ditch than a quality trout stream. The final passage through Bald Eagle Valley is once more pleasant as the stream passes in a smooth path through a floodplain forest.

Fishing Creek's Trophy Trout Project—daily creel limit two trout, minimum size 14 inches—is the most productive stretch of the stream. It can be reached by taking Pennsylvania Route 64 east from State College or west from Lock Haven to the village of Lamar. Turn onto State Route 2002 at the "Federal Fish Hat-chery" sign and follow it back to the Lamar Fish Hatchery. The project starts just upstream of the hatchery and continues, with S.R. 2002 paralleling it, to the Tylersville Fish Hatchery. Anglers going to the project shoud be aware of a "No Sunday Fishing" rule in some areas. The rule was enacted to appease landowners. So don't ruin a good thing.

Above Tylersville Pennsylvania Route 880 follow the stream at varying distances to Loganton. It offers access at State Route 2007, State Route 2009, Stover Road (Township Road 350) and Pennsylvania Route 477.

Below the Trophy Trout water, Fishing Creek is probably most productive from Mackeyville downstream for a couple of miles. State Route 2004, which can be picked up off State Route 2004 at the Lamar Hatchery, as well as in Clintondale and Mackeyville, follows the stream providing access in a number of places.

As far as hatches are concerned, Fishing Creek has just about everything. Early season, mid-April through late May, sees the appearance of Blue-Winged Olives, Blue Quills, Quill Gordons, Black Quills, Hendricksons, Yellow Cranefly, Sulphurs, March Browns and Gray Foxes. With the mid-season, approximately June and July, arrive the Green Drakes, Light Cahills, Isonychia, Sulphurs, Yellow Drakes, Blue-Winged Olives and Tricorythodes.

Along with mayflies, Fishing Creek's trout also can be taken on caddis patterns, ginger and white midges, and terrestrials, especially ants. The stream, in fact, was the scene of an incident which led to the invention of the "McMurray Ant," those extraordinarily effective balsa wood-bodied ant imitations that swept the fly fishing world in the early 1980s. It occurred back in the mid-1960s, when retired U.S. Postal Service mechanic Ed Sutryn of McMurray, Pennsylvania, decided to take a break from an unsuccessful day on the water. Leaning back against an oak tree, watching the fish which had refused everything he had tossed at them continue to rise, Sutryn felt ants falling on his shoulder. Brushing them off, he did not think anything of it at the time. But later, at home, he remembered them and a trout he had once taken from a small spring pond on a live grasshopper. When he cut that fish open it had been packed full of ants. Then he recalled the pond, like Fishing Creek, had been surrounded by large, overhanging trees.

"I just put two and two together after that," he said.

Knowing what food those trout were feeding on did not mark the end of the problem, however. For Sutryn that was just the beginning. The only ant patterns in general use back in the 1960s were either made of silk thread or fur. They were difficult to see when they were on the water and often sank.

Because Sutryn was dissatisfied with the visual qualities and floating properties of the traditional ant patterns, and because he had always had an unconventional bent when it came to fly tying—as well as the mechanical penchant for tinkering—he began thinking about different materials he might use for an ant.

His first choice of material was cork. It floated well and was hard, exactly like the body of a natural. His next step was to whittle a body out of a small piece. The resulting design looked good, but he knew it would not stand up to more than a single fish.

"The idea struck me then, why not just string it on a piece of nylon?" Sutryn remembers.

Running a short length of monofilament through the two tiny bits of cork not only strengthened the fly, but also gave it the distinctive thin-waisted appearance of a live ant.

To test his new design, Sutryn decided to pay a visit to Centre County's Elk Creek (see which). He knew the stream had a good population of wild brook trout. And they were tough. For he had fished it without any real luck more times than he cared to recall.

"That was the first really serious workout I gave them," he said, and then added, "The thing that got me about the ant was that they came up nice and easy and took it almost like they were licking their lips. They weren't a bit afraid of it."

For the record, Sutryn took "only two or three fish" that day back in 1965, but also lost one of 18 or 19 inches. And proved to himself the pattern worked.

Little Fishing Creek

A pretty little meadow stream with good access directly off Route 64, Little Fishing Creek meets Fishing Creek near Lamar. It is stocked from the village of Hublersburg downstream to its confluence with Fishing Creek. Access is directly off Route 64 and several side roads. Fly anglers can try some of the same patterns as on Fishing Creek.

Rapid Run, Buffalo Creek
North Branch Buffalo Creek
Union County

Rapid Run

As its name clearly states, Rapid Run is a swift-flowing little freestone trout stream characterized by deep pocket water and heavy riffles. Under changes enacted by the Fish Commission's Operation FUTURE, it also is one of the heaviest stocked trout streams in Union County, receiving thousands of brown and brook trout both before and during the season. But such a heavy stocking schedule does not mean Rapid Run is loaded only with hatchery pets. It also contains a few holdovers of bragging proportions, as well as some natives in its more inaccessible reaches.

Fishing Creek in Clinton County.

Rapid Run begins in a swampy area of Bald Eagle State Forest, roughly two miles southwest of Raymond B. Winter State Park. It combines with Halfway Run in the park to form Halfway Lake, a seven-acre impoundment formed by the first stone dam ever built by the Civilian Conservation Corps. The best fishing is reportedly from the park downstream for approximately 11 miles to where it joins Buffalo Creek at the village of Cowen. Pennsylvania Route 192 parallels the stream, at varying distances, from its headwaters all of the way to its mouth. So access to Rapid Run involves little more than finding a place to park the car.

One of the most interesting features of Rapid Run is Rapid Run Gorge just south of Halfway Lake. The gorge offers a clear look at all five of the rock formations—starting with the Reedsville and continuing up through the Bald Eagle, Juniata, Tuscarora and Rose Hill—of which the surrounding mountains are made. In addition, it also contains a slope of white quartzite boulders, some of them more than six feet in diameter. This "scree slope," or "boulder field," is a relic of the Ice Age, formed between 10,000 and 15,000 years ago by the extreme cold of a glacier which stopped about 30 miles to the northeast of Williamsport.

According to "Pennsylvania Trail of Geology Park Guide 19," "At this particular spot, the thick quartzitic Tuscarora sandstone beds were split into loose angular boulders that gradually moved down the mountainside under the influence of gravity. At the end of this last glacial episode, virtually all of the mountain slopes of Pennsylvania were covered by this natural blanket of broken stone. As the climate warmed, vegetation and shallow soil reclaimed the barren mountainsides, leaving only patches of bouldery terrain here and there . . ."

Mother Nature was not the only one to treat the lands surrounding Rapid Run harshly. Starting back in the 1870s, the lumber industry did its very best to completely clear the mountains of their forests, and almost succeeded. By the turn of the century the industry's careless logging methods, aided by fire, had damaged the resource to the point where the land was no longer of any use to it and the state was able, in 1905, to purchase the site of R.B. Winter State Park. Even today, nothing is left in many places but bare rocks, while in the Pine Swamp area of the forest the rotting stumps of white pine trees 200 feet high and six feet in diameter, big enough to build an entire home, can still be seen.

R.B. Winter State Park was originally opened back in the 1930s as Halfway State Forest Park. It was named Halfway because it marked the halfway point through Brush Valley on Narrows Road, the present Route 192. Its name was changed in 1955 to honor Raymond B. Winter, a forester who worked in the area for 45 years. A tavern, barn and sawmill all once stood on the site.

For anglers who wish to stay in the area, R.B. Winter State Park, which is listed among "The Thirty Best Kept Secrets of Pennsylvania's State Parks," has a 60-site campground opened from the second Friday in April to the end of the antlerless deer season in mid-December. It offers latrines, hand washing facilities, a sanitary dump station, drinking water, shaded sites and a playfield. Small food and supply concessions also operate on a seasonal basis.

Bait fishermen generally do well on Rapid Run. No reliable information is available on fly hatches along the stream. Impressionistic patterns such as the Adams, Irresistible, Elk Hair Caddis, Hare's Ear, Muskrat and so forth should produce, however. Further information on the park is available by writing: R.B. Winter State Park, Department of Environmental Resources, R.D. 2, Box 377, Mifflinburg, PA 17844.

Details on Bald Eagle State Forest, including a public-use map outline of roads and trails, may be had by contacting: District Forester, Bald Eagle State Forest, P.O. Box 111, Mifflinburg, PA 17844. (Also see White Deer Creek.)

Buffalo Creek

Like Fishing Creeks, Mill Creeks and Spring Creeks, there is no shortage of Buffalo Creeks in Pennsylvania. This one is a pleasant little meadow stream that meets Rapid Run in the village of Cowan before continuing on to the West Branch Susquehanna River at Lewisburg.

Access to Buffalo Creek begins right at Cowan on Route 192, the downstream end of its planted water. Buffalo Creek Road (Township Road 306) appears next to the bridge over the stream and leads upstream. Further upstream access is available off Strickler Road (Township Road 347), which runs off Buffalo Creek Road shortly before it reaches Pennsylvania Route 45.

Off Route 45, Buffalo Creek can be reached along Buffalo Road and Fourth Street at Mifflinburg, where a .85-mile section of the stream has been set aside for youngsters 12 years of age and younger, and physically handicapped persons.

Above Mifflinburg, Buffalo Creek can be reached off Route 45 by taking Hoover Road, Schuck Road and Kaiser Run Road. All three roads also lead to State Route 3003, which parallels the stream on its north side. Aikey Road, running off S.R. 3003 west of Kaiser Road, marks the approximate end of the stream's stocked water.

North Branch Buffalo Creek

Another little meadow/farm country stream, North Branch Buffalo Creek is stocked from its mouth upstream though the village of Red Bank. It can be reached by turning west off Buffalo Road at both the villages of Johnstown and Red Bank. Johnstown Road parallels the North Branch on its west side and eventually leads to Reber Road, which trails the stream to the upper end of its stocked water.

Fly fishermen on Buffalo Creek and North Branch Buffalo Creek can try some of the same patterns mentioned under Rapid Run.

White Deer Creek
Delayed Harvest Fly Fishing Only
Union County

Though Interstate 80 is just over the hill, a visitor to White Deer Creek's 2.5-mile Delayed Harvest Fly Fishing Only Project would be hard-pressed to know it without looking at a map. For almost all of its length this gem of a little mountain freestone stream flows through the public lands of Bald Eagle State Forest where development has been held down to some gravel roads and a scattering of hunting camps. No fast food restaurants or gas stations along this stream, only forests of oak, hemlock and mountain laurel populated by whitetail deer, bear, squirrels, wild turkey, woodcock and grouse.

Arising in Brush Valley on the Centre County/Clinton County line, tiny "Woap'tuchanna," or White Deer Creek (probably named by an Indian who once spotted an albino deer along its banks) cuts straight across Union County to enter the West Branch of the Susquehanna River at the village of White Deer opposite Watsonville.

While today White Deer Creek is as picturesque a little trout stream as anyone might want to see, it was a far different story at the turn of the century. Back then the biggest logging industry in the United States was busy consuming thousands upon thousands of acres of surrounding forest. Trees 200 feet high and six feet in diameter, enough wood to build a home, fell with impunity to the lumberman's ax. Even now, nothing but bare rocks and mineral remain in many places within the surrounding forest where the Industrial Revolution treaded.

McCall Dam State Forest Picnic Area, located just upstream of White Deer's special regulation water, occupies the former site of McCall Dam. Originally built by settler John McCall in the 1850s to power one of the largest sawmill/shingle mills of the time, the dam was enlarged to help float white pine logs down the creek to the mills of Watsonville. All that remains of the dam now is a semi-open area with a few picnic tables, a pump, an organized group tent camping area and a comfort station.

White Deer Creek's Delayed Harvest Fly Fishing Only water runs from the Union County/Centre County line downstream to Cooper Mill Road. It can be reached by taking Pennsylvania Route 192 east from Centre Hall outside of State College, or west from Lewisburg and into Raymond B. Winter State Park. At the west entrance to the park turn onto McCall Dam Road (well marked by a wood sign) and follow it for three miles to the picnic area. White Deer Creek Road joins McCall Dam Road on the right just above the picnic grounds and parallels the entire project, though the stream is usually out of sight.

A total of 19 miles of White Deer Creek, approximately half of it in Bald Eagle State Forest, flows through Union County, and there are many other good, isolated, lovely stretches of water to fish besides the special regulation water.

White Deer Creek Road runs along the stream, crossing it twice, for roughly another four miles below the Delayed Harvest Project. It then joins Sugar Valley Narrows Road (State Route 1010), which continues on paralleling the creek all of the way to White Deer. Sugar Valley Narrows Road and White Deer Creek Road also may be reached by taking Exit 29 off Interstate 80. Except for the last few miles of its length White Deer remains peaceful and free of dense development.

White Deer Creek.

Immediately upstream from McCall Dam Picnic Area, the fisherman who does not mind walking a bit can pick up White Deer Creek Trail and follow it on to more angling opportunities.

Further upstream, White Deer Creek's headwaters may be reached by taking Black Gap Road off McCall Dam Road between R.B. Winter State Park and the McCall Dam Picnic Area, and then continuing on west along Engle Road. Both roads are gravel and dirt, and not the easiest going, but clearly marked by wooden signs. Kemmerer Trail off Engle Road will take the angler even further back into the headwaters.

Although White Deer Creek is a very picturesque, and heavily stocked, water, it may not be to everyone's liking because it is small and its banks usually lined with heavy brush and trees. On top of those obstacles, it frequently breaks up into several channels that make the fishing all the more tight.

Fly hatches on White Deer Creek include, mid-April through mid-May, Hendricksons; mid-May to early June, Green Drakes; and early June into September, Isonychia or Slate Drake. Caddis and terrestrial patterns also can be productive at times. Other patterns that should produce include: Adams, Hare's Ear, March Brown, Gray Fox, Soft Hackle Nymphs, Royal Coachman and Light Cahill.

Camping is available at 695-acre R.B. Winter State Park (see Rapid Run) from the second Friday in April until after the antlerless deer season in mid-December. The park, which is listed under the 30 least used state parks in Pennsylvania, contains 60 campsites for tents, trailers or motor homes. Latrines, hand washing facilities, drinking water and a sanitary dump station are provided. All sites are completely shaded and near a playfield and Halfway Lake, a seven-acre dam stocked with trout. The park also has a food and supply concession which is open on a seasonal basis.

Details on the park are available by writing: R.B. Winter State Park, Department of Environmental Resources, R.D. 2, Box 377, Mifflinburg, PA 17844.

Information, including a public-use map, on Bald Eagle State Forest, may be had by contacting the District Forester, Bald Eagle State Forest, P.O. Box 111, Mifflingburg, PA 17844.

(Also see Rapid Run.)

Lycoming Creek
Hoaglands Run
Grays Run
Fly Fishing Only
Pleasant Stream, Rock Run
Lycoming County
Roaring Branch
Lycoming and Tioga Counties
West Mill Creek
Tioga County

Lycoming Creek

Excellent access is available to practically the entire length of Lycoming Creek off U.S. Route 15 and Pennsylvania Route 14 north of Williamsport. The creek, whose name is a corruption of "Legaui-hanne" meaning "sandy stream," is the smallest of Lycoming County's three major trout waters—Pine Creek and Loyalsock Creek being the other two—but by no means a tiny stream. It is well-stocked over a distance of about 25 miles from

Cogan Station upstream to the Tioga County line. But, as is typical of most Pennsylvania freestone streams, it is best fished in the spring and fall.

In the Indian Deed of 1768, Lycoming Creek was referred to as Tiadaghton Creek, the Indian name for Pine Creek, the translation of which has been lost. The confusion in names lasted until 1784 when state officials, who were preparing to make another land purchase from the Indians, asked the Iroquois to clarify the boundary of the previous deed. The Indians answered:

"With regard to the Creek called Teadaghton mentioned in your Deed of 1768, we have already answered you and again repeat it, it is the same you call Pine Creek, being the largest emptying into the West Branch of the Susquehanna."

Squatters who ignored the question over the names and settled in the territory west of Lycoming Creek called themselves the "Fair Play Men" and set up their own court to settle problems arising between them. Decisions of the court were enforced by expelling offenders from the region.

French Margaret's Town, or French Town, was an Indian village at the mouth of Lycoming Creek and is now a suburb of Williamsport. French Margaret was of mixed French and Indian blood, and a celebrated Indian personality of the mid-eighteenth century. She was the first person to put into effect the "Local Option Law" on alcohol, forbidding the use of rum in her town. French Margaret's daughter, Queen Esther, gained a notorious fame during the Wyoming Massacre in 1778. Immediately following the battle, Queen Esther ordered 16 captured settlers placed around a rock with their head against it. She then climbed atop the stone, and to avenge the death of her only son in the battle, smashed the head of all but two of the captives who escaped by a sudden dash to the Susquehanna River. The incident earned her the title "Fiend of Wyoming."

Seshequin Path, also sometimes called Lycoming Path, was an important Indian trail that followed Lycoming Creek from Williamsport to Ulster. It was used by both early missionaries and Colonel Thomas Hartley when he destroyed Queen Esther's Town near present day Athens, Bradford County, a few weeks after the Battle of Wyoming. Hartley's expedition, along with proving an Indian trail could be used to move troops, set the stage for General John Sullivan's march into the Indian lands of New York in 1779. Sullivan's expedition is the first example of "scorched earth" warfare on record.

Williamsport, which grew up around the mouth of Lycoming Creek and French Margaret's Town, during the latter half of the nineteenth century was one of the greatest lumbering centers in the world, and a major stop on the Underground Railroad for slaves from the South seeking to escape to Canada. Today, it is best known as the home of the Little League World Series.

Although Lycoming Creek's stocked water begins at Cogan Station, its lower water is generally hemmed in by a busy highway and plenty of clinging population. The water from the village of Trout Run, where towering, wooded mountainsides replace the billboards and trailers, is far more scenic. Access is available directly off Pennsylvania Routes 15 and 14, as well as numerous villages.

Good fly patterns for Lycoming Creek—and its tributaries—include the Hare's Ear, Quill Gordon, March Brown, Adams, Hendrickson, stoneflies, Brown Drake, Soft Hackle Nymphs, Blue-Winged Olive, caddis, Light Cahill, Sulphurs, Muddler Minnow, Woolly Buggers (black, brown and olive), midges and terrestrials.

Hoaglands Run

Traveling north from Williamsport, Hoaglands Run is the first stocked tributary of Lycoming Creek. A small, coldwater stream, it is stocked for six miles from about the village of Perrysville upstream.

Anglers can reach Hoaglands Run by taking Pennsylvania Route 973 off Route 15 in Cogan Station and following it toward the village of Quiggleville. The stream parallels Route 973. Above Quiggleville a dirt and gravel road parallels the stream north to Cogan House. Like Lycoming Creek, Hoaglands Run is best mainly in the spring and fall.

Grays Run

Trout are plentiful throughout Grays Run's Fly Fishing Only Project, and often ready to cooperate with the angler. But the stream's small size and the surrounding brush can make for some frustrating casting.

Both Lower Grays Run Road and Upper Grays Run Road run off Route 14 about two miles into Tiadaghton State Forest and provide access to the stream's special regulation water. They are marked by blue street signs. The fly fishing only water runs from the concrete bridge at the old Civilian Conservation Corps Camp upstream 2.5 miles to the Grays Run Hunting Club property. Parking is available at the bridge, as well as various spots upstream. Grays Run Road follows the stream all of the way to its headwaters.

Lower Grays Run Road also offers access to Grays Run below the special regulation water, where a good population of holdover fish often exist.

Grays Run, both in and out of the project, is a lovely, peaceful Pennsylvania mountain stream, and readily available to the public since it flows through Tiadaghton State Forest. Backpacking is even an option for anglers who would like to spend a couple of days on it. Fly fishermen can try the same patterns suggested for Lycoming Creek.

Pleasant Stream

A deep gap in the boundary of Tiadaghton State Forest puts most of Pleasant Stream's lower water on private property. Nevertheless, access is good for this little stram, which is stocked from its mouth upstream about 10 miles. Another spring and fall trout stream, Pleasant Stream can be reached by turning east off Route 14 at the village of Marsh Hill and onto Pleasant Stream Road, which parallels all of its stocked water.

Rock Run

Blessed with numerous waterfalls, rugged canyons and deep picturesque pools cut into solid rock, Rock Run may be the most beautiful trout stream in the state. Even the Department of Environmental Resources is high on its beauty, both mentioning the stream and using a photograph of it in the "Tiadaghton State Forest Public Use Map."

Rock Run flows along the southern border of the forest's McIntyre Wild Area, a 7,498-acre preserve within Tiadaghton. It can be found by again turning east off Route 14 and crossing Lycoming Creek at the village of Ralston, then continuing on into the woods. Rock Run Road bears to the right where the dirt and gravel road splits and parallels the stream. As is typical of such backcountry roads, parking places usually designate access points to the stream. Rock Run maintains a good flow throughout the year and is fishable even at the height of summer.

Roaring Branch

Cascading Roaring Branch is the last tributary of Lycoming Creek in Lycoming County. It is stocked over a distance of three miles from its mouth upstream, and primarily an early season stream good into June and then again in the fall. Access is available off Route 14 just across the Tioga County line at the village of Roaring Branch along a dirt and gravel road that parallels the stream off to the west.

West Mill Creek

The final stocked branch of Lycoming Creek is West Mill Creek. It is another small stream stocked for three miles from its mouth upstream. Access is available along State Route 2017 on the north side of the village of Roaring Branch.

TIADAGHTON STATE FOREST

Anglers planning on fishing Lycoming Creek and its tributaries should consider obtaining a "Tiadaghton State Forest Public Use Map." The publication is available free of charge and will help put everything into perspective. It may be had by writing: District Forester, Tiadaghton State Forest, 423 E. Central Ave., Williamsport, PA 17701.

Larrys Creek
Lycoming County

State Game Lands 114 is an almost rectangular chunk of public real estate lying exactly midway between Lycoming Creek and Pine Creek. Because no main roads touch on it, the angler who follows Larrys Creek into this remote area will be in for as real a wilderness fishing experience as is possible in Pennsylvania.

Larrys Creek is stocked for seven miles from Salladasburg on Pennsylvania Routes 287 and 973 upstream into the game lands. In the upper portions of the stocked water above Route 973 Larrys Creek is a small, swift flowing stream of braided channels cutting a scenic path through a narrow V-shaped canyon of steep, rocky slopes. From Route 973 downstream to Salladasburg the addition of more tributaries, including Second Fork Larrys Creek, adds some size to the stream. The surrounding valley also widens below Salladasburg, running off to a set of piney hills, and a scattering of houses.

Access to Larrys Creek may be had by taking Route 287 north from U.S. Route 220 at the village of Larrys Creek between Jersey Shore and Williamsport. Route 973 joins Route 287 at Salladasburg. Route 973 east parallels the stream for a couple of miles, offering access at different points. About a half mile after Route 973 crosses Larrys Creek, a dirt and gravel road appears to the left, just as the highway begins to turn away from stream. This road leads part of the way back to Game Lands 114. A hiking trail follows the creek the remainder of the way.

For nearly 75 years after the signing of a treaty with Chief Widaagh in 1700, Larrys Creek was at the center of a land controversy between the European settlers and the Indians. Strangely, it was the settlers in this instance who were cheating themselves. The treaty set the western boundary of the lands the Indians were selling at Tiadaghton Creek. The settlers believed this stream was Lycoming Creek, while the Indians maintained it was the further west Pine Creek. The difference gave the whites hundreds of thousands of acres more than they would have had if the boundary had been Lycoming Creek.

Until confusion over the land was settled for once and all by the second Treaty of Fort Stanwix in 1784, settlement of the territory between Lycoming Creek and Pine Creek, including Larrys Creek, was forbidden. As in other dealings with the Indians, however, the law meant nothing to some Europeans, and squatters' homes eventually dotted the region. Because these settlers were beyond the normal court system they dubbed themselves the "Fair Play Men" and set up their own tribunal to handle disputes among themselves, punishing offenders by banishing them from

the region. According to legend, they also gathered to declare their independence from Great Britain under an elm near Pine Creek on July 4, 1776.

Before settlers moved into the area, the Great Shamokin Path crossed Larrys Creek near its mouth. The path ran from Shamokin (Sunbury) on the Susquehanna River, probably the most important Indian town in colonial Pennsylvania, to Kittaning, a gathering spot for war parties on the Allegheny River. It was an important link in the Indian trail system and was used by Bishop John Ettwein when he led 200 Christian Indians from Wyalusing on the upper Susquehanna to the Beaver River following the sale of their land by the Iroquois in 1768.

Among the possible fly patterns to try on Larrys Creek are: Quill Gordon, Blue Dun, Blue-Winged Olive, Adams, Hendrickson, stoneflies, March Brown, Gray Fox, caddis, Light Cahill, midges, terrestrials, Renegade, Muddler Minnow, Mickey Finn, Woolly Bugger, Hare's Ear, Black Gnat and Soft Hackle Nymphs in pheasant tail, yellow, olive and orange.

Pine Creek
Float Trip
Potter, Tioga and Lycoming Counties
West Branch Pine Creek
Potter County
Stony Fork
Tioga County
Cedar Run
Trophy Trout
Tioga and Lycoming Counties
Slate Run
Fly Fishing Only
Tioga and Lycoming Counties
Francis Branch
Fly Fishing Only
Tioga County
Trout Run, Upper Pine Bottom
Little Pine Creek, Blockhouse Run
Lycoming County

Pine Creek

Pennsylvania has a hundred trout streams with scenery worthy of any landscape artist's brush. It has a hundred others whose scenic beauty has been marred by development, but whose fishing remains the equal of any in the eastern United States. It is doubtful there is any single stream in the state, however, that offers such a dazzling mixture of trout fishing and scenery as Pine Creek, from its headwaters in northeastern Potter County, through Tioga County to its mouth on the West Branch Susquehanna River near Jersey Shore in southern Lycoming, Pine Creek has it all. On the water, there are long, deep pools, rapids filled with huge boulders, swift chutes and shallow riffles out of which 20-inch browns are taken every year. Around the creek, there are gently sloping mountains, wide valleys, rocky cliffs, big woods of pine and hemlock, and, of course, the 1,000-foot deep gorge known as the "Grand Canyon" of Pennsylvania.

Before the glaciers of the last Ice Age moved into north central Pennsylvania, Pine Creek, also sometimes referred to as Big Pine Creek, flowed in a northeasterly direction toward New York. The gravel, sand and clay the glaciers pushed ahead of them formed a natural dam that reversed the stream's flow and forced its waters to cut a new path, and the magnificent Grand Canyon, across the mountains to the south. Officially known as Pine Creek Gorge, a 12-mile section of the Grand Canyon was preserved for future generations in 1968 when it was designated a National Natural Landmark by the National Park Service. Today, the area is one of the most famous, and popular, outdoor recreation sites in Pennsylvania. Canoeists and rafters, campers and hikers, fishermen and hunters all flock to it by the thousands.

At its start, the trout fisherman's Pine Creek is a far different stream from what visitors to the Grand Canyon see. It begins around the village of Walton on U.S. Route 6 in Potter County. Here the rough and tumble waters of the gorge run as a small creek full of surging rapids, tight bends, braided channels and fallen trees. It is designated Wild Trout Water, meaning it is not stocked. Pine Creek's planted water does not begin until the Genesee Fork enters the stream east of Walton. It continues from there south all of the way to Waterville and Little Pine Creek in Lycoming County.

Along with marking the beginning of Pine Creek's stocked water, Genesee Fork also adds some welcome size and balance. The swift mountain brook begins to show some longer, cobble-lined runs, a few pools and sloping ledges as it makes its way through a wide, pleasant, mostly undeveloped valley all of the way to Galeton.

The town of Galeton has for decades marked the gateway to Potter County's "Black Forest" for thousands of deer hunters. For Pine Creek it marks another increase in size by the addition of West Branch Pine Creek. This first major tributary of Pine Creek enters the main stream just above Pennsylvania Route 144 and a large dam. Galeton also sees the wide valley through which the stream has been flowing begin to narrow. But it still leaves enough room for the thick forests and gently sloped mountains to keep the stream tucked out of sight of the highway.

U.S. Route 6, Pennsylvania's longest road, is the main access route to Pine Creek all of the way from Walton in Potter County downstream to Ansonia, where the stream takes an abrupt turn to the south. Bridges that provide further access to the stream appear at Walton, Genesee Fork, just above and below Galeton, at Watrous, east of Gaines and Pennsylvania Route 349, and at Rexford and Ansonia. A two-mile section of the stream south of Ansonia can be reached by taking Colton Point Road toward Colton Point State Park, and then turning onto Owassee Road, or the first road to the left. Owasee Road parallels the stream, offering access at different points. Anglers who park at the end of the road and continue to hike along the stream will see the 1,000 feet high walls of the canyon begin to rise, and have a chance to fish some of the best, least pressured water on the creek.

The heart of Pine Creek appears below Ansonia. From there until the village of Blackwell the stream is at its most remote, most impressive and most popular. Access is limited to rafts and canoes, or a long, steep hike. The stream holds enough water to be floated from the early spring to about the middle of June. Much of that time, though, especially early in the season, the stream may be too high and discolored for good fishing. Other times anglers may have to vie with both commercial rafters and private canoeists for use of the stream. For those fishermen who decided to float Pine Creek over the approximately 17 miles between Ansonia and Blackwell, a campground has been established roughly about halfway through the run. It contains pit toilets, picnic tables, water and fireplaces.

Leonard Harrison State Park and Colton Point State Park set astride Pine Creek downstream of Ansonia, and both offer access to hikers. Colton Point Park, one of "The Thirty Best Kept Secrets of Pennsylvania's State Parks," may be reached by following the sign off Route 6 near Ansonia. Leonard Harrison Park can be found by following the signs off Pennsylvania Route 660 west of the Tioga County seat of Wellsboro. Colton Point Park was developed by members of the Civilian Conservation Corps in the mid-1930s. It was established on state forest lands purchased around the turn of the century and named for Henry Colton, a nineteenth century lumberman from the area. Leonard Harrison State Park honors Leonard Harrison, a civic-minded Wellsboro businessman of the late nineteenth and early twentieth centuries. Mr. Harrison owned and developed "The Lookout" area of the park as a public picnic ground. He gave it to the state in 1922. Like Colton Point, Leonard Harrison Park was developed by the CCC through the mid-1930s.

Fishermen who want to camp in the area will find 25 Class B campsites at Colton Point Park and 30 Class B sites at Leonard Harrison. They are both open from the second Friday in April to the third Sunday in October. Amenities are limited to pit toilets, picnic tables, water and a sanitary dump station. Turkey Path Trail allows access to Pine Creek from both parks. It is roughly a one-mile hike from the developed portions of both parks to the stream. Access to the stream both upstream and downstream of the path is available by hiking along the Conrail tracks which parallel the water.

From Blackwell almost all of the way down to the West Branch Susquehanna River, Pine Creek is again tied into a road. Pennsylvania Route 414 follows it so closely at many points that reaching the water frequently means nothing more than climbing down a bank or walking across a short flood plain. Two other campsites for canoeists and rafters similar to the one located in the gorge below the parks can be found just downstream of the villages of Slate Run and Waterville.

Except for the latter half of the nineteenth century, when Pennsylvania's lumber industry was probably the greatest in the world and its waters were needed to transport the logs to market, Pine Creek's rugged terrain has generally kept it out of history's limelight. However, Pine Creek Path did run along the stream from Jersey Shore to Genesee, New York. War parties and other groups of Indians regularly traveled the route, but it never made a successful wagon road. Paul A.W. Wallace in *Indian Paths of Pennsylvania,* tells the story of John Peet who used the path to bring a team of oxen and a wagon to Jersey Shore from Potter County in 1811. "Crossed the Pine Creek eighty times going to and and eighty times coming from mill," he would later write, "was gone eighteen days; broke two axle-trees to my wagon, upset twice, and one wheel came off in crossing the creek."

Fly hatches along Pine Creek include: mid-April through late May, Quill Gordon, caddis, Hendrickson, March Brown, Gray Fox, Green Drake and Light Cahill; June, Light Cahills, Brown Drake, Blue-Winged Olives, midges and terrestrials. Other flies that produce on Pine Creek are: stoneflies, Hare's Ears, Adams, Woolly Buggers and Muddler Minnows.

Information on both Leonard Harrison and Colton Point State Parks may be had by writing: Leonard Harrison State Park, Department of Environmental Resources, R.D. 6, Box 199, Wellsboro, PA 16901.

West Branch Pine Creek

Stocked for more than 12 miles upstream from Galeton, West Branch Pine Creek is very similar to the upper reaches of Pine Creek from Walton to Galeton. It is loaded with tight bends, undercut banks, fallen trees and cobbly rapids. The fairly narrow valley through which it flows includes a patchwork of woods, pastures and abandoned or rundown farms.

The West Branch can be reached by taking State Route 2002 off Route 6 in Galeton toward Germania Station and Lyman Run State Park (see Lyman Run). The road parallels the stream to provide access to all of the stocked water in numerous places, including a bridge at Germania Station.

Fly anglers can try some of the same patterns mentioned for Pine Creek.

Stony Fork

Technically speaking, Stony Fork is not a tributary of Pine Creek. It is a tributary of Babbs Creek, which joins Pine Creek at the village of Blackwell on the Tioga and Lycoming County line. But it is such a pretty little wilderness stream and the access so good it would be a shame not to include it.

Besides its fishing, what makes Stony Fork particularly interesting is sandstone. It is everywhere. it comes in the form of memorable ledges, boulder studded banks and a gravel-filled streambed. All of it in easy reach of a dirt and gravel road.

Stony Fork lies about three miles west of the village of Morris on Pennsylvania Route 414. A bridge, the only one between Morris and Blackwell, appears on the right at the mouth of the stream. It leads to Stony Fork Road (Township Route 462), which in turn follows the creek upstream to the villages of Draper and Stony Fork. Because of a feeder stream tainted by acid mine drainage approximtely the lower two miles of Stony Fork are not stocked. The planted water begins above the orange waters of the feeder. Fly anglers might try some of the traditional patterns recommended for Pine Creek—as well as those mentioned under other streams in this section.

Cedar Run

Only two streams in Pennsylvania hold Trophy Trout Projects. Fishing Creek in Clinton County (see which) is one, Cedar Run, Pine Creek's second outstanding tributary, and its first in Lycoming County, is the other.

Cedar Run, like its better known neighbor Slate Run, is the type of trout stream the complete angler might expect to find as his final reward in heaven. Enshrined in a steep, narrow canyon its sparkling waters are a picture-perfect array of deep green pools, cascading whitewater, rocky riffles and waterfalls plunging down from sidestreams. Towering overhead is a wilderness of second growth hemlock and pine, beach and ash, maple and black cherry. In its up reaches beaver also add their presence to the scene, occasionally providing an amusing interlude for a lucky fisherman.

Practically all of Cedar Run is protected by Trophy Trout Project regulations. This means fishing is limited to flies and artificial lures only. The project extends for 7.2 miles from Cedar Run's mouth on Pine Creek, upstream to its confluence with Buck Run beyond the village of Leetonia. The entire section is well-marked with Fish Commission posters.

On Route 414, Cedar Run lies approximately six miles south of Blackwell and five miles north of the village of Slate Run. Its lower water is accessible directly off Route 414 at the bridge which crosses its mouth opposite the "village" of Cedar Run, once a thriving logging town with several thousand people, now essentially an inn and general store.

The stream's upper stretches can be reached on State Route 4009, a side road marked by a yellow "Y" traffic sign, on the rise just south of the same bridge, which also marks the point where, for the angler traveling from the south, Route 414 first changes for asphalt to dirt and gravel. It is an easy to overlook road. So go

slow. Anglers who plan to use the road early in the season also should know it quickly turns from asphalt to dirt and gravel, and is often muddy or icy in the spring. It can be dangerous at times and probably should not be attempted in bad weather without a four-wheel drive vehicle. The road crosses the creek at five points before Leetonia, another former logging settlement that is now nothing more than a name on the map.

Being surrounded by the public lands of Tiadaghton and Tioga State Forests, Cedar Run is a possible choice for anglers who enjoy backpacking. Camping is generally permitted on state forest property after obtaining a free permit from a local district forest office or ranger.

Fly hatches on Cedar Run include: mid-April to the end of May, Blue-Winged Olives, Blue Quills, Quill Gordons, Hendricksons, March Browns, Gray Fox and Green Drakes; June, Green Drakes, Light Cahills, Lead-Winged Coachman, Blue-Winged Olives; summer, terrestrials and midges. Other fly patterns an angler might try during the year are: Adams, Hare's Ear, stoneflies, Muddler Minnow and Woolly Bugger.

Slate Run

Slate Run may be the "premier" Pennsylvania mountain freestone stream. At least that is what a lot of anglers believe. Some other old-timers, though, say it has changed and is "not what it used to be." But then what is, or for that matter ever was, the way it "used to be?"

What is known for certain about Slate Run is that the Fish Commission has designated it a Class A stream, with "an outstanding population of wild trout," under its Operation FUTURE management program. It also has placed all nine miles of it under the protection of special regulations. From its source at the junction of Francis Branch and Cushman Branch deep in Tiadaghton State Forest, to its mouth on Pine Creek at the village of Slate Run, angling is limited to Fly Fishing Only. Hatches include: mid-April to late May, Blue-Winged Olives, Quill Gordons, Blue Quills, Hendricksons, March Browns, Yellow Stoneflies, Light Cahills, Gray Fox, Green Drakes and Sulphurs; June, Light Cahills, Green Drakes, Sulphurs, Lead-Winged Coachman and Slate-Winged Olives; summer, Tricorythodes, midges and terrestrials.

Nourishing this profusion of hatches and the wild trout that rise to them is a crystalline little stream full of green pools, winding rapids and hidden waterfalls. Surrounding it is an equally stunning, often humbling, setting of sheer mountains, dark, mystical stands of pine and hemlock, rocky bluffs and silent glens. As with Cedar Run, it may be the closest thing to perfect harmony man can find on earth.

Even though many stretches of Slate Run are gloriously isolated, in reality a road is never very far off. The steepness of the valley through which the stream flows simply makes it impossible for all but a mountain goat or big horn sheep to reach it in most places. What access there is starts by turning off Route 414 and crossing Pine Creek at the village of Slate Run. A wooden sign points out Slate Run Road to the right. Access to the mouth of the stream is available behind the Slate Run Hotel. Slate Run Road climbs up the mountain past the hotel and follows the stream, with some wild switchbacks, all of the way back to the junction of Francis Branch and Cushman Branch. Points from which the stream can be reached off the road are either marked by signs or parking areas.

Since Slate Run cuts a path through Tiadaghton State Forest backpacking anglers may enjoy a stay along it—after obtaining a free permit from a local forester. Algerine Wild Area borders the stream on the north and holds the Black Forest Trail.

Francis Branch

It takes the Francis Branch and the Cushman Branch to form Slate Run. Since Slate Run is only about 15 feet wide in most places anglers can imagine the size of Francis Branch—roughly half that of Slate Run.

But fishermen who enjoy tiny mountain brooks should like Francis Branch. Like Slate Run it is a wild trout fishery and passes through two counties. Its headwaters are in Potter County, but its most fishable water, including its Fly Fishing Only Project, is in Tioga County.

Francis Branch's two miles of Fly Fishing Only water extend from its mouth and the Francis-Cushman Hole upstream to Kramer Hollow. Access means following Slate Run Road from Route 414 and the villge of Slate Run the entire nine-mile length of Slate Run. Francis Road appears to the left at the end of Slate Run Road and is marked by a wooden sign. Fly fishermen can try some of the same fly patterns mentioned for Slate Run.

Trout Run

Five miles of Trout Run is stocked with trout beginning at its mouth across from the village of Cammal on Pine Creek upstream toward Lycoming and Clinton County line.

Although Trout Run is not far from Slate Run and Cedar Run, unlike those two streams it cannot be reached off Route 414. No bridge crosses Pine Creek in the area. So, access must come from Pennsylvania Route 44 west at Waterville. Narrow Gage Road is the second dirt road to the right following the village of Lucullus and leads back to Trout Run Road which gives access to Trout Run both upstream and downstream.

Also, unlike Cedar Run and Slate Run where fish can be caught year-round, Trout Run is a spring and fall mountain stream. Fly anglers can try some of the same patterns mentioned for Pine Creek, Slate Run and Cedar Run.

Upper Pine Bottom

Another small mountain brook feeding Pine Creek, Upper Pine Bottom is stocked for four miles from its mouth upstream. Like Trout Run, Upper Pine Bottom is basically a spring/fall water. Despite its easy access—all of its stocked water can be reached off Route 44, starting from the point where it splits off from Route 414—Upper Pine Bottom continues to maintain something of a wilderness feel. It should appeal to fishermen with children or those who have a difficult time getting around.

Employees of Little Pine State Park maintain a day-area along the creek for anglers and other visitors. It contains picnic tables, water and a comfort station.

Little Pine Creek and Blockhouse Run

Cutting into Pine Creek gorge at Waterville, Little Pine Creek is a scaled-down version of Pine Creek, but with generally faster water. Blockhouse Run is essentially the headwaters of Little Pine Creek and an even faster flowing bit of stream.

Little Pine Creek can be reached by turning right off Route 44 onto State Route 4001 immediately after crossing the bridge in Waterville. S.R. 4001 parallels the stream through Little Pine State Park to the village of English Center and the junction of Pennsylvania Route 287 and 284. Above English Center Route 284 follows Little Pine Creek to its origin at the meeting of Blockhouse Run and Black Creek. Access is available at numerous points.

From its mouth upstream to its source, Little Pine Creek flows through a beautiful, narrow valley of summer cabins that turns, near its end, into a canyon wide enough only for the stream and a set of railroad tracks. Like Pine Creek, Little Pine Creek also flowed north, as a tributary of the Tioga River, until the move-

ment of glaciers into north central Pennsylvania. Sandstone outcrops and precipitous cliffs reaching up to 1,000 feet bear witness to the creek's fight with the glacier and the changing of its course toward the south.

Little Pine Creek is stocked from its mouth upstream to English Center. A two-mile stretch of private club land stops the stocking, and the public fishing, between Little Pine and Blockhouse Run in the Texas Creek/Blacks Creek area. Above the posted water the stocking of Blockhouse Run starts and continues upstream beyond busy U.S. Route 15. The prettiest section of Blockhouse Run is paralleled by Route 284 between Blacks Creek and U.S. Route 15. The valley through which it flows is mostly empty, its scenery marred only by an ugly powerline.

Fly action along Little Pine Creek is similar to Pine Creek. Anglers can try: mid-April through late May, Quill Gordon, caddis, Hendrickson, March Brown, Gray Fox, Green Drake, Light Cahill; June, Light Cahill, Brown Drake, Blue-Winged Olives, midges and terrestrials. Other flies the angler might use on both Little Pine and Blockhouse Run include: stoneflies, Hare's Ears, Adams, Woolly Buggers and Muddler Minnows.

Camping and other diversions are available at Little Pine Creek State Park for fishermen not only working Little Pine Creek and Blockhouse Run, but also lower Pine Creek, Upper Pine Bottom, Trout Run, Slate Run and even Cedar Run. The park, which like Leonard Harrison and Colton Point, was built by the Civilian Conservation Corps in the mid-1930s, has 100 Class B campsites open year-round. Amenities include a dump station, flush toilets, water, fire rings and picnic tables. Non-fishing visitors will find nearly 23 miles of hiking trails, swimming and boating (no rentals) at 94-acre Little Pine Lake, picnicking and environmental education programs. Like Colton Point State Park, it is listed as one of "The Thirty Best Kept Secrets of Pennsylvania's State Parks," so should not be crowded.

Information on the park is available by writing: Little Pine State Park, Department of Environmental Resources, Waterville, PA 17776.

SUSQUEHANNOCK, TIOGA AND TIADAGHTON STATE FORESTS

Anglers planning on fishing Pine Creek, or one of its tributaries, should consider obtaining a "Public Use Map" of Tioga, Susquehannock and/or Tiadaghton State Forest. The maps show roads, trails and other points of interest through the forest. Susquehannock State Forest, named after an Indian tribe, touches on the upper reaches of the stream and the West Branch; Tioga, "at the forks," covers the middle section, including Pine Creek Gorge; and Tiadaghton, meaning unknown, the lower portions. Maps may be had by writing:

District Forester, Susquehannock State Forest, Department of Environmental Resources, 8 East Seventh Street, Coudersport, PA 16915.

District Forester, Tioga State Forest, Department of Environmental Resuorces, 96 West Avenue, Wellsboro, PA 16901.

District Forester, Tiadaghton State Forest, 423 E. Central Avenue, Williamsport, PA 17701.

Lyman Run
Fly Fishing Only
Potter County

Rain and runoff at one time or another make every freestone stream in Pennsylvania unfishable during the early part of the trout season. For some, like Little Mahoning Creek in Indiana

County, it seems as if all that's required is the passing of a thunderhead for their waters to turn coffee-brown.

Though no freestone stream in the commonwealth is totally immune to the fickle weather of a Keystone State spring, some stand up to it better than others. Among these is Lyman Run through its four-mile long Fly Fishing Only Project.

Like most other streams that hold up well to the rigors of the early season, Lyman Run has its location and size to thank for this blessing. Flowing across east central Potter County, it is far from the main roads and drainage pipes which channel water toward streams nearer the beaten path. The land around it also is heavy with woods and mossy soil that tends to hold water longer and release it in a gradual fashion. On top of that, upper Lyman Run is a small, tributary stream, so when it does get dirty it quickly flushes itself.

All of these qualities which make Lyman Run a good stream to turn to when everything else in the area is running high and muddy, also help to make it tough fishing. Along with stocked fish, its water holds an abundance of native brookies, as well as some browns. Those wild fish can become very skitterish and really stir things up in the clear water and tight quarters, which is the reason the stream is seldom crowded.

Even though Lyman Run's Fly Fishing Only water is in an out of the way location, finding it is not difficult since it is situated in 595-acre Lyman Run State Park, one of "The Thirty Best Kept Secrets of Pennsylvania's State Parks," and literally surrounded—at a discreet distance, of couse—by three of Potter County's major arteries. It can be reached by following the park signs for about six miles off state Route 144 at Galeton; or for six miles on Lyman Road (State Route 2004) from state Route 44 near Cherry Springs; or for five miles on Rock Run Road from U.S. Route 6 near the Denton Hill Ski Area.

In the park, Lyman Run Road, running downstream past Lyman Lake (stocked), parallels the project water. Anglers also can fish the stream below the dam all of the way to its junction with West Branch Pine Creek off Lyman Run Road. Fly patterns to try include the Adams, Royal Coachman, Renegade, caddis, Cahills, Blue Quills, Hare's Ears, Soft Hackle Nymphs, March Browns, Hendricksons, terrestrials and Sulphurs.

Like many other parks in Pennsylvania, Lyman Run State Park once served as a camp for Franklin D. Roosevelt's Civilian Conservation Corps. Prior to the establishment of the CCC camp in the 1930s, the land on which the park stands was practicaly denuded of trees during northcentral Pennsylvania's lumbering boom years of the late nineteenth and early twentieth centuries. Lyman Lake was completed in 1951, and construction of park facilities began shortly afterwards.

Today, for anglers who might want to spend a few days on Lyman Run and neighboring streams, the park offers a campground with 50 Class B sites with drinking water and comfort stations, as well as a sanitary dump station for recreational vehicles. Non-fishing members of a family also will find opportunities for hiking, swimming and picnicking.

Fishermen who would like to learn more about the region's lumbering past might consider a midday visit to the Pennsylvania Lumber Museum. It is located on Route 6 about five miles north on Rock Run Road which starts near the dam spillway. Operated by the Pennsylvania Historical and Museum Commission, the museum contains a full-scale recreation of a logging camp complete with sawmill, steam locomotive, blacksmith shop and bunkhouse, as well as numerous exhibits in a modern museum building. The extensive CCC exhibit is a special favorite with older visitors who might have spent some time in the "corps."

In addition to its permanent displays, the lumber museum also sponsors annual attractions such as a "Bark Peelers Convention," featuring contests in bark peeling, frog jumping, tobacco spitting, checkers and birling, and a "Woodhick Weekend," during which a stay in a logging camp is recreated and workshops are conducted in such things as orienteering, dried flowers, dulcimer making and woodcarving.

Further information on Lyman Run Park may be had by writing: Lyman Run State Park, Department of Environmental Resources, P.O. Box 204, Galeton, PA 16922.

Information on the lumber museum may be had by writing: Pennsylvania Lumber Museum, P.O. Box K, Galeton, PA 16922. (Also see Pine Creek.)

Hyner Run
Right Branch Hyner Run
Left Branch Hyner Run
Clinton County

Tucked between Pennsylvania Route 120 and Pennsylvania Route 44 in the northeast corner of Clinton County, Hyner Run is a pleasant mountain brook that—along with its Right Branch and Left Branch—is stocked over a distance of seven miles. Portions of its upper waters also hold some wild trout.

Of Hyner Run's entire length, only about the last mile before it empties into the West Branch Susquehanna River flows through private land. The remainder of the stream is protected by either Hyner Run State Park or 276,764-acre Sproul State Forest, so the angler who chooses to try this stream is free to roam without fear of violating anybody's privacy, and even do some backpacking.

Hyner Run is located six miles east of the town of Renovo on Route 120 at the village of Hyner. It is immediately identifiable by an old cast iron marker bearing its name. Hyner Mountain Road (State Route 1014) joins Route 120 near the bridge. It is marked by a sign for Hyner Run State Park and parallels the stream to the park. Hyner Run Road joins Hyner Mountain Road on the left at the entrance to the park. Anglers can follow it past the park office and swimming pool to gain access to the stream's upper reaches.

Outside the park's boundary the road turns to dirt and gravel. A short distance beyond Abes Fork Road in Sproul State Forest, it also splits. Right Branch Hyner Run appears on the right just before the split. The road to the right (Hyner Road) follows the Right Branch, the road to the left tracks the Left Branch Hyner Run.

Hyner Run State Park, part of which was once occupied by a Civilian Conservation Corps camp, offers 30 Class B campsites with level pad, picnic table and fire ring. Water, handwashing facilities and a dump station are centrally located. It is open from the second Friday in April to the end of the antlerless deer season in mid-December.

For the off hours and family members not particularly interested in fishing, the park has a large swimming pool—open Memorial Day weekend to Labor Day—a children's playground and picnic area. Hyner View Picnic Area is adjacent to the park and provides a beautiful view of the West Branch Susquehanna. The area was the original site of the "Flaming Fall Foliage Festival," an annual event in Renovo.

Fly fishermen might try Adams, Hendricksons, March Browns, Hare's Ears, Soft Hackle Nymphs, Blue Quills, Sulphurs, Light Cahills, wet and dry caddis patterns, and, in the warmer months, terrestrials.

Further information on the park is available by writing: Hyner Run State Park, Department of Environmental Resources, Box 46, Hyner, PA 17738. (Also see Young Womans Creek.)

Young Womans Creek Right Branch
Fly Fishing Only
Young Womans Creek Left Branch
Clinton County

Young Womans Creek Right Branch

Founded by people as tolerant as the Quakers, it is not surprising Pennsylvaia has a rich racial, ethnic and religious heritage. The mixture has provided the state with many benefits in every phase of human endeavor, not to mention a wide variety of unusual stream names. Like Young Womans Creek.

The original Indian name for this tributary of the West Branch Susquehanna River was "Maunquay" or "Mianaquaunk." According to Dr. George Donehoo's *A History of the Indian Villages and Place Names in Pennsylvania,* the name may be a corruption of "Minqua," for "Conestoga," a tribe which once lived in northern Clinton County. However, he also points out, the suffix "qua" or "quay" is a usual female designation in compound words. So the Indian name could have been translated to mean Young Woman.

Whatever the story behind its name—Donehoo also suggests the names "Maunquay" or "Mianaquaunk" might mean "place of meeting"—Young Womans Creek today presents anglers with almost 11 miles of medium size, freestone trout water. This includes a 5.9 mile long Fly Fishing Only Project with wild trout, and stocked stretches both above and below it.

Surrounded by Sproul State Forest, and the first piece of state forest land purchased by Pennsylvania back in 1898, the scenery around Young Womans Creek matches its fine fishing. The stream's clear waters cut an often swift, rocky path through a narrow mountain valley marred only by a scattering of hunting cabins and a gravel road. Suggested fly patterns include: Blue Quills, Adams, Soft Hackle Nymphs, Hendricksons, March Browns, Green Drakes, Renegade, Light Cahills, caddis, both wet and dry, Sulphurs and terrestrials.

Young Womans Creek may be found by taking Interstate Route 80 Exit 26 and following Pennsylvania Route 220 toward Lock Haven. At Lock Haven pick up Pennsylvania Route 120 and continue on that past the villages of Glen Union, Ritchie and Hyner to North Bend, formerly Young Womans Town. Near the bridge crossing Young Womans Creek and the Fish Commission's North Access to the West Branch Susquehanna turn right onto State Route 4005. Follow S.R. 4005 through the center of the village past the post office and hotel. The road splits a short distance beyond. Take the road to the left. It parallels the stream. The Fly Fishing Only water, which is on the creek's Right Branch, begins three miles upstream near the state forest property, and is plainly marked.

Young Womans Creek Left Branch

A smaller version of the Right Branch, Young Womans Creek Left Branch offers about 8.5 miles of fishing for both stocked and wild fish. Flies similar to those suggested for the Right Branch also are possible choices here.

The Left Branch may be reached by again taking S.R. 4005 through North Bend and bearing to the left where the road splits apart. As S.R. 4005 descends to cross Young Womans Creek, two wooden signs pointing to the Left Branch and the Right Branch will be evident on a stump to the left. Follow the road to the left.

Anglers looking to stay in the area can camp at nearby Hyner Run State Park. Located a few miles south on Route 120 near the village of Hyner, the 180 acre park offers 30 Class B campsites with water and toilets on a year-round basis. For non-fishing members of the family it has picnic areas, a visitors center, playground, hiking trails and a swimming pool, open from Memorial Day weekend to Labor Day. Anglers who choose to camp in the park can fish Hyner Run, too (see which).

Details on the park are available by writing: Hyner Run State Park, Box 46, Hyner, PA 17738.

Kettle Creek
Catch and Release
Tioga, Potter and Clinton Counties
Germania Branch, Little Kettle Creek
Cross Fork Creek
Fly Fishing Only
Potter County
Trout Run, Beaverdam Run
Clinton County

Kettle Creek
Germania Branch

Beginning near 2,440-foot high Cedar Mountain a few miles west of famous Pine Creek Gorge in Tioga County, Kettle Creek flows for roughly 50 miles through one of the most scenic valleys in all of Pennsylvania before it empties into the West Branch Susquehanna River near Westport. It is a wild, dark land still populated by more animals than humans; home to the whitetail deer, black bear, wild turkey, ruffed grouse and mysterious raven. The Forbidden Land as it was known to the various Indian tribes, or the Black Forest as it was called by the Germans who settled there after the Indians were gone.

Like the mountains surrounding it, the origin of the name Kettle Creek is shrouded in folklore and mystery. One of the most frequently repeated stories has the stream being named Kettle Creek by Europeans coming up the West Branch who found a brass kettle in it left by Indians who had raided a settlement. Another story has the name coming from an Indian, known as Black Kettle to the settlers, who lived near the mouth of the creek. A third story reports the stream was named Kettle Creek after a large rock on the West Branch near the mouth of the stream. The rock had three potholes in which the Indians used to boil their food by filling them with water and tossing in hot rocks.

The topography of the stream itself may have had something to do with its name. Below Weed Run in Clinton County, in an area known as "The Bunk" (one of the Outstanding Scenic Geological Features in Pennsylvania) it makes a strange, tight turn, flowing first south around Oxbow Bend and then directly north toward Trout Run. From the air, or a map, the bend forms the outline of what might be a huge kettle.

As one of the finest brook trout fisheries in all the United States through the latter half of the nineteenth century, Kettle Creek regularly drew the rich and powerful from the cities of the east coast. Among them President Ulysses S. Grant.

It was through a friend, Colonel A.C. Noyles, a successful lumberman and merchant from Clinton County, that President Grant became acquainted with Kettle Creek. Invited to stay at the colonel's home at Westport for a vacation, the President would ride north up the stream to Cross Fork and then begin fishing his way back. In the process he also lived up to his reputation as a drinker by stopping off in every tavern along the trail, usually supplying free drinks for any veteran of the Civil War he found inside.

In his book, *Forbidden Land,* Robert S. Lyman, Sr., relates a tale from an old resident of the area which also shows the savior of the Union to have been a lady's man of sorts. According to the story, the President came across a small log schoolhouse near Beaverdam Run while on one of his fishing excursions. Deciding he should make his presence known, he stopped and knocked on the door. A pretty schoolmarm opened it. As soon as he saw her he kissed her, and then as she stood there in amazement and embarrassment began to laugh.

"You have just been kissed by the President of the United States," he told her, and then continued on his way.

Although Kettle Creek is no longer the brook trout stream it once was, it still offers a good variety of angling opportunities. Native brookies continue to exist in its headwaters, while stocked browns and rainbows are available in the reaches around Ole Bull State Park, and downstream into Kettle Creek State Park.

Under Operation FUTURE, Kettle Creek's 1.7-mile Catch and Release Project is no longer stocked with hatchery fish, though some, naturally, find their way there, and relies on natural reproduction to maintain its fish population. As a result, it offers anglers a chance to fish over some crafty streambred browns. The lower sections of Kettle Creek, below the Alvin R. Bush Dam at Kettle Creek State Park, turn quite warm and are not stocked with trout. Those stretches also suffer somewhat from acid mine drainage pollution. However, some areas do contain smallmouth bass that can be a lot of fun in the summer.

A number of different fly hatches occur along Kettle Creek throughout the season. They include: April to mid-May, Blue-Winged Olives, Blue Quill, Quill Gordon, Hendrickson, caddis, Sulphurs and March Browns; mid-May through June, Sulphurs, March Brown, Gray Fox, Yellow Stonefly, Green Drake, caddis, Brown Drake, Isonychia, Blue-Winged Olive and Tricorythodes. Terrestrials and such all-round patterns as the Adams, Royal Coachman, Renegade, Soft Hackle Nymphs, Hare's Ear, Woolly Buggers and streamers also produce on the stream.

Kettle Creek's upper waters may be reached by following Pennsylvania Route 144 to the village of Olena and then turning east onto Pennsylvania Route 44. Follow Route 44, which parallels the stream for over a mile, to Rauch Road (S.R. 2001), or the first road to the left. Continue straight on Rauch Road, past Randall Road, which splits off to the right shortly before Rauch Road makes an almost 90-degree bend to the left and becomes Township Road 433. (Confused yet?) T -433 leads down to first Kettle Creek and then up Germania Branch, which is stocked from its mouth upstream for two miles.

Anglers can gain further upstream access to Kettle Creek by taking Randall Road off Rauch Road and following it to Butternut Hollow, the first road to the left. Butternut Hollow leads down to Slider Road, which parallels Kettle Creek into Tioga County and its headwaters. Bear to the left where Butternut Hollow Road meets another secondary road about a mile and a half off Randall Road.

Kettle Creek.

Access to Kettle Creek improves dramatically at Oleana. From that point all of the way downstream of Cross Fork, the stream can be reached off Route 144. Parking is available at the bridge in Oleana, where Little Kettle Creek adds its flow, and only a couple of miles downstream is Ole Bull State Park, with all of its facilities.

Ole Bull State Park is named after Ole Bornemann Bull, a famous nineteenth century Norwegian violinist who became very fond of Potter County and the Kettle Creek area while touring the United States in the mid-1840s. During a second visit in 1852 he established a colony, "New Norway," of his countrymen in the area. New Norway was an outgrowth of the Young Norway movement which sought to revive the culture of Norway and free it from the influences of Sweden and Denmark. The famous Norwegian playwright Henrick Ibsen also was a member of the movement with Bull, and many people believe one of his most famous characters, Peer Gynt, is based on Bull.

The New Norway colony was meant to give ambitious Norwegians accustomed to scratching a meager living from their country's stony soil a fresh start toward prosperity. Bull purchased an 11,144-acre tract of Potter County land for the colony from Williamsport businessman John Cowan for $10,388. In a fast move, however, Cowan retained 658 of the most tillable land for himself, a fact Bull did not realize until much later and that, after a year of extreme hardship for the 105 Norwegians who moved to the area, ended the experiment.

New Norway actually consisted of four settlements: New Bergen, New Norway, Valhalla, named after the mythical home of Odin, Norse god of poetry who was said to receive warriors slain in battle, and Oleana, which Bull named after himself and his mother. Bull built his own home on a shelf of mountain he named "Nordjenskald" near Valhalla on the present site of the park. Known as Ole Bull's "castle," in reality the home was only a large two-story frame house with a commanding view of the surrounding country. It was never completed and eventually sold to a doctor who Bull persuaded to move to the area, and who used the wood to build his own home, "The State House" on the east side of Kettle Creek. It remained until a fire gutted it in 1923.

In 1920, the commonwealth purchased the land on which Ole Bull State Park now stands, and in 1925 opened a simple picnic area on it. The Civilian Conservation Corps enlarged the park to its present size of 117 acres during the 1930s. The park today offers a variety of recreational opportunities including: swimming (from Memorial Day weekend to Labory Day), picnicking, hiking and sightseeing. The park's water holds brown, rainbow and brook trout. A restricted area for children ages 12 and under, and handicapped persons is available from below the small concrete dam to the upstream side of the concrete fordway crossing the stream.

For those fishermen who like to camp, Ole Bull State Park offers 81 Class B campsites in two places along Kettle Creek. Year-round camping is available, although winter access is restricted to Area Two next to the park office. All sites include a picnic table, fire ring and level gravel pad. Water, pit toilets and a sanitary dump station also are nearby.

In addition to the improved campgrounds in the park, free camping is available in Susquehannock State Forest, surrounding the park and creek. This is primitive camping without any amenities whatsoever. A permit is required and may be had at the park office and the Forest Warden office in Cross Fork.

Downstream of Ole Bull State Park, Kettle Creek flows through a few miles of private lands, followed by its No Harvest Fly Fishing Only Project. Access to the project is available by parking along Route 144 and walking through the fields which often separate the stream from the road, and at the Route 144

bridge above Cross Fork. The project runs from about 500 feet below the bridge upstream for 1.7 miles.

Route 144 continues to follow Kettle Creek for roughly eight miles downstream of Cross Fork. Where Route 144 turns to cross the stream and head toward Renovo, fishermen can gain further access to Kettle Creek's lower waters by driving straight ahead on Kettle Creek Road to Kettle Creek State Park, one of "The Thirty Best Kept Secrets of Pennsylvania's State Parks, translation uncrowded. They also can reach the lower water by following the signs for the park off Pennsylvania Route 120 at Westport.

Camping is available at the park in two Class B campgrounds holding about 40 sites each. The lower campground is open from early April through the end of the antlerless deer season in mid-December. The upper campground is open from the start of the trout season early in April to mid-October. For the off-hours, or for family members who do not fish, there is swimming, from Memorial Day to Labor Day, picnicking, hiking, sightseeing from some beautiful nearby vistas and boating opportunities on 160-acre Bush Dam (Kettle Creek Reservoir) and seven-acre Kettle Creek Lake.

Details on Kettle Creek State Park and Ole Bull State Park are available by writing: Kettle Creek State Park, Department of Environmental Resources, Star Route, Renovo, PA 17764.

Ole Bull State Park, Department of Environmental Resources, R.D. 1, Cross Fork, PA 17729.

Susquehannock State Forest touches on upper Kettle Creek, while Sproul State Forest surrounds a good portion of the lower stream. Information on these public lands, including an invaluable Public Use Map that provides a great overview of the stream and its tributaries, may be had, free of charge, by writing: District Forester, Susquehannock State Forest, 8 East Seventh Street, Coudersport, PA 16915.

District Forester, Sproul State Forest, Star Route, Shintown, Renovo, PA 177120.

Little Kettle Creek

Because nobody knows what Mother Nature might do next, it is always a good idea for anglers to keep their opinions open when heading toward a large stream, especially early in the season when major streams are often high and muddy. And certainly if they have to travel several hours to reach their goal. Kettle Creek has a number of smaller, feeder streams that might be good alternatives when things are going wrong, starting with Little Kettle Creek.

Stocked for about three miles from its confluence with Kettle Creek at Oleana upstream toward the village of Carter Camp, Little Kettle Creek is easily accessible off Route 44/144 between those two settlements. Hungry Hollow Road runs off Route 44/144 near the top end of the stocked water and provides further access. Fly fishermen can use some of the same patterns listed under Kettle Creek.

Cross Fork Creek

Northern Pennsylvania is dotted with hundreds of tiny villages, some little more than crossroads, that during the logging boom at the turn of the century were robust towns of several thousand people. They came complete with rows of saloons and bawdy house, shops of every type imaginable, fancy hotels and restaurants, and even theaters and railroad lines.

With most of the forests clear-cut and the mountains bear scares by World War I, all of these towns lost their reason for being. Gradually, the hotels and restaurants closed their doors, the banks failed and the railroads were sold off. The people who had come to call the towns home and raised their families in them were forced to move on to the cities. Thousands no doubt ended up in the steel towns of the south, which in the early 1980s found themselves in the same position as the logging towns, with their mills closing and people drifting away.

Cross Fork on the Potter/Clinton County line was one of those boom towns. At its peak it was home to over 2,500 individuals. It could even boast of providing the first stage for George "Gabby" Hayes. As a runaway teenager from Wellsville, New York, the man who was to gain fame in over 200 movies as the lovable, old sidekick to Roy Rogers and John Wayne made his acting debut in Cross Fork.

Now left with a couple of hotels, restaurant/bars and gas stations, a tackle shop, fire hall and mixture of hunting/fishing camps and homes, one of the main bits of recreation—aside from the Christmas in July party—in Cross Fork today is a stroll across the bridge to check on Kettle Creek.

But Kettle Creek is not the only quality trout stream flowing near the village. Only a hundred yards or so downstream from the bridge, Cross Fork Creek comes tumbling out of a narrow, heavily wooded valley to join Kettle Creek on its way to the West Branch Susquehanna River and eventually the Chesapeake Bay.

Since the Fish Commission's new management plan, Operation FUTURE, reclassified Cross Fork Creek as a wild trout fishery in the early 1980s, it has not been stocked with hatchery fish. The absence of easily fooled fish, consequently, has led to a corresponding drop in anglers. So fishermen hoping to get away from the crowds on Kettle Creek might consider trying this tributary. A good population of wild brown trout and brookies is said to exist both in, and above, the stream's Fly Fishing Only Project, which runs for 5.4 miles from Bear Trap Lodge downstream to the Weed property along its mouth.

Access to Cross Fork Creek's lower water is available directly off Route 144 near Cross Fork, or by turning right on the dirt road across from the Cross Fork Sportsmen's Club Cooperative Nursery. The upper stretches can be reached by turning onto Township Road 416, another dirt and gravel road down the road from Cross Fork.

Hatches include: April through mid-May, Blue Quills, Quill Gordons, Hendricksons; mid-May into June, March Browns, Gray Fox, Sulphurs, Green Drakes, Light Cahills, Isonychia, Brown Drakes; summer, Blue-Winged Olives and Tricorythodes. Stoneflies and terrestrials also should work.

Trout Run

Four miles of stocked water await the angler who chooses to stop at Trout Run. This tributary of Kettle Creek is accessible off Trout Run Road, which meets Kettle Creek Road near The Bunk above Kettle Creek State Park. It is the first road running to the north below Kettle Creek Road's junction with Route 144.

Beaverdam Run

Beaverdam Run, and its three miles of stocked water, lie just outside the upstream boundary of Kettle Creek State Park. An old tram road running off to the west provides access off Kettle Creek Road a short distance above the backwaters of Bush Dam. Fly anglers can try some of the same patterns mentioned under Kettle Creek and Cross Fork Creek.

First Fork Sinnemahoning Creek
Potter and Cameron Counties
Big Moore Run, South Woods Branch

Freemans Run,
East Fork Sinnemahoning Creek
Bailey Run
Potter County
Brooks Run
Cameron County

First Fork Sinnemahoning Creek

Typical of many streams in the "Big Woods Country" of north central Pennsylvania, First Fork Sinnemahoning Creek passes through three distinct phases as a trout water. In its headwaters near tiny Prouty Place State Park in south central Potter County, it is home to the tiny and colorful native brook trout. Around the village of Costello, it holds a population of shy and clever wild browns, while along Pennsylvania Route 872 below Costello, and through Sinnemahoning State Park it offers stocked browns, rainbows and brookies.

As the First Fork's trout population changes, so does its size and makeup. For its first six miles downstream to Costello, the stream is a diminutive bit of crystal clear water hurrying along a narrow and beautiful valley of steep, forested slopes and old pasture land where deer appear during the evenings. Rhododendron, hemlock and hardwoods shade its way and present plenty of opportunities for the unwary angler to hook his fly or lure. A collection of hunting and fishing camps also make it a must for fishermen to keep their eyes open for posted land.

At Costello, the First Fork is swelled by the addition of Freeman Run, and then at the village of Wharton by the waters of East Fork Sinnemahoning Creek. Where development is concerned, something different happens, too. It lessens. The hunting camps grow fewer and grassy meadows more abundant. With the exception of Wharton, this relative absence of people lasts for over 15 miles to Sinnemahoning State Park.

Another eight miles of stocked trout water, big stocked trout water, exists between the park and the First Fork's mouth on Sinnemahoning Creek at the village of Sinnemahoning Creek. Altogether, the stream contains some 20 miles of stocked water spiced by the wild browns and brookies in its upper stretches.

When Europeans began moving into the lands around Sinnemahoning Creek and its tributaries in 1784, the region's forests of hemlock and pine already were between two and three centuries old. The first settlers saw the vasts stands of timber more as obstacles to travel and farming than a resource. Then, around 1840, the axes began to fly. Sawmills and towns sprang up along local rivers and streams, the highways of the industry into the twentieth century. Now a sedate little mountain village whose liveliest days revolved around the arrival of trout fishermen and deer hunters from Philadelphia and Pittsburgh, Sinnemahoning, translation "stony lick," was among the wildest of those lumbering boom towns. A bit of nineteenth century verse reflects some of the town's character when it was the scene of frequent drunken battles between loggers and raftsmen.

There is a place called Sinnemahone
Of which little good is known;
For sinning, ill must be its fame,
Since Sin begins its very name.
So well indeed its fame is known
That people think they should begin
To drop the useless word Mahone,
And call the country simply Sin.

Route 872, which can be picked up off Pennsylvania Route 120 at Sinnemahoning, gives access to the First Fork all of the way from its mouth to Costello. State Route 3003 then appears in Costello just before the Route 872 bridge over the stream, and follows the creek up into its headwaters.

Sinnemahoning State Park, one of "The Thirty Best Kept Secrets of Pennsylvania's State Parks," was opened three years after the completion of the George B. Stevenson Dam in 1955. It is named after a Clinton County state senator who led the drive for the project, which is designed to alleviate flooding in the Susquehanna River basin. The park holds a Class B campground with 40 sites. Amenities are limited to pit toilets, a dump station, water, picnic tables and fire ring. A play cabin, swing set and sandbox are available for younger visitors. The campground is open from the second Friday in April through the end of the antlerless deer season in mid-December.

Along with the campground, Sinnemahoning State Park's 1,190 acres offer boating, fishing and swimming (Memorial Day weekend to Labor Day) on First Fork Sinnemahoning Lake, hiking and picnicking.

Although only five acres in size, Prouty Place State Park, another of "The Thirty Best Kept Secrets of Pennsylvania's State Parks" (meaning hardly anybody visits it), the First Fork's headwaters also contains a campground. Like the one in Sinnemahoning Park, it is rated Class B with the same minimum of facilities and season—the second Friday in April to mid-December. Hiking and picnicking also are available.

Elk State Forest, Sproul State Forest and Susquehannock State Forest are other public grounds that touch on the stream, and possible places to backpack. Details on the park and the forests, including free "Public Use Maps," may be had by writing:

Sinnemahoning State Park, Department of Environmental Resources, R.D. 1, Box 172, Austin, PA 16720.

Prouty Place State Park c/o Lyman Run State Park, Department of Environmental Resources, P.O. Box 204, Galeton, PA 16922.

District Forester, Elk State Forest, R.D. 1, Route 155, Emporium, PA 15834.

District Forester, Sproul State Forest, Star Route, Shintown, Renovo, PA 17764.

District Forester, Susquehannock State Forest, 8 East Seventh Street, Oswego, PA 16915.

First Fork has a variety of caddis and mayfly hatches. These include: mid-April through mid-May, Blue-Winged Olives, stoneflies, Quill Gordons, caddis, Hendricksons, Sulphurs, March Browns and Gray Fox; mid-May to mid-June, caddis, Sulphurs, March Browns, Gray Fox, Green Drake, Light Cahills, Brown Drake and Lead-Winged Coachman, midges and terrestrials. Anglers also should not overlook such impressionistic patterns as the Adams, Muddler Minnow, Mickey Finn, Hare's Ear, Black Gnat, Renegade, Soft Hackle Nymphs and Royal Coachman.

Big Moore Run

The First Fork's first stocked tributary, Big Moore Run, meets the larger stream below Prouty Place State Park near the Fox Fire Trail. It can be reached off Township Road 304, the second dirt and gravel road after Costello and just before Fox Fire Trail. Both the lower portion of Big Moore and its headwaters are designated Wild Trout Water, meaning they are not stocked. The stream's approximately one mile of planted water lies in its middle. Anglers should bear to the right where the road splits apart (the left road follows Little Moore Run, which is not stocked), and continue upstream a short distance to insure they are in the stocked section. Big Moore is a possible choice when the larger streams are running high and muddy.

South Woods Branch

Another good choice during bad weather is South Woods Branch. It is stocked from its mouth upstream roughly three miles into its headwaters. Access is available off South Woods Road (Township Road 302), the first road after Costello.

Freemans Run

North of Costello, on Route 872, lies Freeman Run, the first major tributary of the First Fork. It is a small creek, meandering its way through the old bottomlands of another narrow Potter County valley, and stocked over a stretch of seven miles from Costello upstream to where Route 872 turns away from the water. Access over its entire length is available directly off Route 872.

Freeman Run is interesting for more than its trout fishing. About a mile and a half above the village of Austin lies some of

White pine covered bank.

the ghostliest ruins to be found anywhere in Pennsylvania. They are of the once quarter-mile long Austin Dam. Built in 1909 by one of the many lumber companies which once operated in the region, its purpose was to carry logs and supply power for the sawmill and papermill in Austin, then a sizeable town of a few thousand people.

For two years the dam, which measured 15 feet thick and 75 feet high, did its job without any problems, holding back the waters of Freeman Run and helping to bring prosperity to the town. Then the rains of 1911 came, pushing the water behind the dam to ever higher levels. Finally, on Primary Election Day, the cement could hold no longer. At 2:30 p.m. it burst. The subsequent deluge wiped out most of Austin and killed 87 people. The death toll would have been much higher if it were not for the extra phone operators on duty to report the election results. They were able to warn the vast majority of the people living in the water's path. Chunks of concrete measuring 100 feet across still lie along Freemans Run near the base of the old dam. Others, some of them as big as houses, are scattered more than 100 feet downstream of the dam site.

Prior to the lumber industry's takeover of the region, Costello (Canoe Place) sat at the head of Little Portage Path, which joined the Susquehanna River watershed with the Ohio River watershed through the Allegheny River. Although rougher, Little Portage Path was frequently used as an alternative to the Big Portage Path, from Emporium to Port Allegheny, because it was almost five miles shorter (see Driftwood Branch Sinnemahoning Creek) and the First Fork was generally navigable over a longer distance than the Driftwood Branch. Little Portage Path met with Big Portage Path at Keating Summit, from which point the two trails continued down Portage Creek to Port Allegheny.

Freemans Run fly fishermen can try some of the same flies mentioned for the First Fork.

East Fork Sinnemahoning Creek

Clear flowing and tiny, hugging a steep, wooded mountain on one side and flat bottomlands of hunting camps on the other, the East Fork closely resembles the upper reaches of the First Fork, which it joins at Wharton.

It is stocked with brown, rainbow and brook trout for more than 12 miles from its mouth upstream through the village of Conrad. A portion of the creek around Conrad also is classified as Wild Trout Water, meaning it is suitable to sustain a population of wild fish, but that does not necessarily mean it holds a lot of streambred trout.

The East Fork can be found by taking Route 872 to Wharton. Turn off Route 872 where it crosses the stream, drive past the hotel and up East Fork Road (State Route 3001) to reach the stream. East Fork Road parallels the creek upstream.

Hatch activity on the East Fork is similar to the First Fork.

Bailey Run

Accessible off Bailey Run Road, the last dirt and gravel road running to the east off Route 872 just before Wharton, Bailey Run is another tiny tributary fishermen might want to try during periods of bad weather, or early in the season. It is stocked from its mouth on the First Fork upstream about 1.5 miles.

Brooks Run

The last stocked tributary of the First Fork, tiny Brooks Run can be reached on Brooks Run Road off Route 872, opposite the entrance to Sinnemahoning State Park. It is stocked from its mouth upstream for about three miles, and another foul weather possibility.

Allegheny River
Potter and McKean Counties
Dingman Run, Reed Run
Fishing Creek, Startwell Creek
Potter County

Allegheny River

Thanks to the Steelers' domination of the National Football League during the 1970s, millions of people across the nation have heard of the Allegheny River. They have glimpsed it reflecting the lights of downtown Pittsburgh on Monday nights and watched pleasure craft cruise it on bright Sunday afternoons. A few times, they may even have seen it choked with ice during a January playoff game. And almost always they were told by Howard Cosell or Frank Gifford how the Allegheny flows together with the Monongahela to form the Ohio River right outside of Three Rivers Stadium—this usually while a camerman in the Goodyear blimp shot an overall view of the city.

Of all the millions of people who have seen the Allegheny River on television, or cross it every week on the way to and from their jobs in Pittsburgh, only a comparatively few are aware it is a quality trout stream. But that is understandable when it is considered the river's prime trout water lies about 150 miles to the northeast in two counties with a population probably less than than a sellout crowd at a Steelers' game.

Although three-quarters of a mile of the river below Kinzua Dam in Warren County (see which) is stocked, the Allegheny's main trout water is further upstream. It runs for about 24 miles, from upstream of the village of Colesburg in Potter County, downstream to the town of Port Allegany in McKean County. Access is off two main roads, Pennsylvania Route 49 from Colesburg to Coudersport, and U.S. Route 6 from Coudersport to Port Allegany.

Office workers in Pittsburgh who are accustomed to viewing the wide, green waters of the lower river would not recognize the upper Allegheny. Born as a meadow brook of pools and gravel-bottomed riffles in the rolling hill country of the Allegheny Plateau, the river in its headwaters above Coudersport averages only six to eight feet in width, and is actually small enough to jump in some places. Several tributaries and springs swell it to between 10 and 15 feet in width around Coudersport, a size it maintains throughout the remainder of its stocked length.

Size and the number of people living along its banks aside, the Allegheny is two different rivers in another sense. The upper section, from its source to Salmanaca, New York, is an ancient river. It has been following the same path for millions of years. The river from Salmanaca to Pittsburgh is new, just a blink of an eye in geological time. It has been cutting its path south since the Wisconsin Glacier turned it away from the Great Lakes only about 20,000 years ago.

Allegheny has been translated to mean "fair or beautiful river," but most likely means "stream of the Alligewi," according to *A History of the Indian Villages and Place Names in Pennsylvania* by Dr. George Donehoo. The Alligewi was a tribe of Indians who lived in the region east of the Mississippi River drained by the Ohio and its tributaries long before the arrival of the Europeans. They were frequently at war with the Delaware and the Iroquois, who finally drove them south away from the river.

Coudersport, the county seat of Potter County, and well-known gathering place for deer hunters, was founded by John Keating, an Irish soldier of fortune who managed some 300,000 acres of land in the area for the Ceres Land Co. (See Marvin and Potatoe Creeks.) Keating gave 50-acre homesteads to each of the first 50 settlers. He also suggested the town be named Coudersport for Jean Samuel Couderc, a member of the Amsterdam banking firm that held the money of the aristocratic refugees from the French Revolution who invested in the Ceres Land Co.

The Moravian missionary David Zeisberger (1721-1808) was one of the first white men in the region and camped at the site of Coudersport in 1767. He remains a great store of knowledge about the Indians in early Pennsylvania. Along with the journal he kept on his travels among the Indians, he also wrote, or edited, *A Delaware and English Spelling Book* and *A Collection of Hymns for the Christian Indians*. He is remembered today by a monument in Coudersport.

The village of Roulette, about nine miles downstream of Coudersport, was another settlement named after a member of the Ceres Land Co., Jean Roulette, when it was established in 1816. For almost 70 years, until the last hemlock in the region was cut in 1912, lumbering was Roulette's chief industry.

Port Allegany, at the end of the river's stocked water, was a major lumbering center between 1830 and 1840. Logs harvested around it were shipped down the Allegheny River to Pittsburgh by raftsmen who then walked back to the town to start the trip all over again. Many of them made 20 or more such trips a year. Later, after the region began producing oil, rafts were used to transport crude down the river. Raftsmen from across the United States journeyed to Port Allegany to work, in the process turning it into a real boom town. The "Camp Barber's Song" explains why most of them wore thick beards.

> *In Port Allegany, not far from this spot,*
> *A barber he opened a neat little shop,*
> *He bought a razor full of notches and rust,*
> *To shave the poor devils who came there for trust.''*

Like many other towns on a canoe portage, Port Allegany was originally known as Canoe Place. It stood on the Big Portage Path linking the Allegheny River to Driftwood Branch Sinnemahoning Creek (see which) at Emporium. After the Fort Stanwix Treaty of 1784, vast tracts of land around the town were sold or disposed of by lotteries. Samuel Stanton purchased 1,000 acres of ground on which the town stands. His son Daniel joined him in 1824 and, along with some partners, built a sawmill around which the town grew.

Fly anglers can tempt the river's brooks and browns with: Quill Gordons, Blue Duns, Hare's Ear, Muddler Minnows, Gray Ghost, Mickey Finn, Hendricksons Blue Quills, March Browns, caddis, Black Gnat, Royal Coachman, Soft Hackle Nymphs, Renegades, Light Cahills, Sulphurs, midges and terrestrials.

* * *

Four of the upper Allegheny River's tributaries are stocked with trout. Anglers might want to keep them in mind during bad weather when the river is running high or discolored. Fly fishermen can try the same patterns mentioned for the Allegheny River.

Dingman Run

A little brook trout stream, Dingman Run is the first stocked tributary of the Allegheny River. It is stocked for 2.5 miles from its mouth upstream. It can be found by turning north on State Route 4007 off Route 6 about a mile west of Coudersport and heading toward the village of Hebron. The stream parallels the creek.

Reed Run

Two miles of stocked water is available along tiny Reed Run. It can be reached along State Route 3009, which meets Route 6 on its south side about a mile west of the village of Mina.

Fishing Creek

Probably the best upper Allegheny River tributary, Fishing Creek can be found by turning north off Route 6 along Fishing Creek Road (State Route 4005) across from Roulette. Its main branch is stocked for two miles, its East Branch for 2.5 and its West Branch for three miles. The East Branch can be reached by continuing toward Hebron on Fishing Creek Road, the West Branch by bearing to the left on State Route 4003 at the "Y" in the road.

Startwell Creek

On the border of Potter and McKean counties, Startwell Creek is the last stocked upper Allegheny River tributary. It has 3.5 miles of stocked water reaching upstream from its mouth. Access is available off State Route 4001, which meets Route 6 at the village of Burtville and parallels the creek over its entire distance toward the village of Willston.

Genesee River
(East Branch, Middle Branch
West Branch)
Potter County

There is something about divides, those rough, irregular boundaries separating watersheds, that seems to intrigue the human mind. Many of us feel a certain mysticism in the idea of standing upon a single spot of land and, at least theoretically, watching a cup of water poured from our left hand drain into, say, the Gulf of Mexico, while a second cup poured from our right finds its way into maybe the Great Lakes. Every year thousands of us stop along the Continental Divide in the western United States to have our photographs taken on that great demarcation line between the Atlantic and Pacific oceans. Probably half of us who stop on the Continental Divide also find time to relieve ourselves on both sides of the line, and so, theoretically, spread our scent over two oceans.

In Pennsylvania there are ten major watersheds: the Delaware, North Branch Susquehanna, West Branch Susquehanna, Susquehanna, Allegheny, Monongahela, Ohio, Potomac, Erie and Onatrio. Through them the state's runoff water is funneled to the Atlantic Ocean, the Gulf of Mexico, the Cheasapeake Bay and the Great Lakes. And among them is probably one of the most extraordinary junctions to be found anywhere in North America. It is located just southeast of the tiny village of Raymond in Potter County. From that vague point, it is possible to enter, with only a few steps, either the watershed of the Chesapeake Bay, the Gulf of Mexico or the Great Lakes. A young, healthy person, with a good pair of boots and a knowledge of the mountains, might even drink from the headwaters of all three watersheds within a single hour—provided they have a purifying unit along.

The streams at the heads of the three watersheds are the Allegheny River, Pine Creek and the Genesee River. Of them, the Allegheny is easily the most famous because it joins the Monongahela River in Pittsburgh to form the Ohio. Pine Creek also is very well-known as a destination for thousands of canoeists and sightseers to the "Grand Canyon of Pennsylvania," or Pine Creek Gorge. Only the Genesee River lacks a real identity in Pennsylvania. The Genesee may be a historic waterway in New York, where the great bulk of it lies, but in Pennsylvania the name is more recognizable as a beer than a river.

What makes the Genesee River, whose three branches and their tributaries form the whole of the Ontario Watershed in Pennsylvania, relatively unknown when compared to its neighbors is, of course, its size. The river's three tiny branches hold 17 miles of stocked trout water, essentially its entire length in Pennsylvania. The Allegheny River and Pine Creek, on the other hand, cover well over a hundred miles, and have figured prominently in the state's history.

Location is another problem when it comes to Pennsylvania's portion of the Genesee. It is, as the saying goes, out in the middle of nowhere. There are no towns or highways of any size near it in either Pennsylvania or New York. It's position along the top of the Allegheny Plateau also robs it of dramatic scenery. There are no deep gorges or striking vistas to charm visitors.

Nevertheless, trout fishing on the Genesee can be good. And access to all three branches is easy. The Middle Branch is reachable along Pennsylvania Route 449 all of the way from the start of its stocked water near the village of Harmontown downstream to the New York line. The West Branch can be found along Pennsylvania Route 244, which parallels the stream from the beginning of its stocked water at the village of Eillsburg downstream to Genesee.

Access to the East Branch is somewhat more difficult than either the Middle Branch or West Branch. Probably the easiest way to find it is to go to the village of Genesee and turn east off Route 449/244 onto State Route 1010 and then State Route 1011, which parallels the East Branch from Genesee, through Hickox, past a landing field to the start of its stocked water beyond the village of West Bingham.

All three branches of the Genesee River meet at the village of Genesee, as well as all three access roads.

Pennsylvania's Genesee River may now occupy a wilderness backwater, but it once was the meeting place for three Indian trails: The Pine Creek Path, from Jersey Shore to Genesee; the Oswayo Path, from Genesee to Singlehouse; and the Forbidden Path, from Athens to Olean. The Forbidden Path was particularly interesting because it guarded the rear of the Seneca Nation and, for security reasons, was forbidden to all white men.

Who was the first European to break the rules and travel on the path is open to debate, according to Paul A.W. Wallace in his book *Indian Paths of Pennsylvania*. Some historians believe that Champlain's emissary Etienne Brule made the journey to try to enlist Indian allies in 1615. However, no documentary evidence exists to support a European presence on the path prior to Moravian missionary David Zeisberger's journey through the region in 1767. In 1779, General John Sullivan used a portion of the path to the east on his expedition against the Indians allied with the British in New York. Sullivan's expedition was to revenge Indian raids on settlements in northeastern Pennsylvania.

Fly anglers along the three branches of the Genesee River might try the Adams, Blue-Winged Olive, caddis, Muddler Minnow, Hare's Ear, Woolly Bugger, Hendrickson, Renegade, Royal Coachman, March Brown, Sulphurs, Black Gnat, Lead-Winged Coachman, Light Cahill, midges and terrestrials.

(Also see Oswayo Creek.)

Oswayo Creek
Potter and McKean Counties

Up until the decimation of the region during the logging boom of the latter half of the nineteenth century, northern Potter and McKean counties held the largest virgin stand of white pine in all of Pennsylvania. Not only was the tree plentiful, but pine timber

from the area was considered to be of the very best quality. Early lumbermen looked upon it as the finest available anywhere in the United States. And they were not the first people impressed by the resource. The Indians who occupied the land before them were so taken with the dark forests, they named the stream flowing through it Oswayo Creek, or "Pine Forest."

"Here, to my great delight, I saw for the first time a pine forest in America. . .the wildest and densest woods imaginable," wrote David Zeisberger, a Moravian missionary, who was the first European to record a visit to the region in 1767.

While the heavy stands of "Oswayo white pine" may be long gone from the scene, and even many of the farms that replaced them abandoned, the little stream at the heart of it continues to distinguish the area. It does it with the renowned quality of its trout fishing; running from wild, streamborn fish in its upper reaches through a mixture of stocked and holdover fish downstream to the village of Sharon Center.

Beginning in the shallow farm valleys between the villages of Oswayo and Andrews Settlement, Oswayo Creek sculpts a meandering path of long, deep pools and gentle riffles across the Allegheny Plateau to empty into the fabled Allegheny River below the town of Portville, New York. Access to practically the entire stream is a simple matter off main roads. The upper, wild trout stretch, follows Pennsylvania Route 244, which can be picked up off Pennylvania Route 44 north of Coudersport, the county seat of Potter County. Route 44 itself meets Oswayo Creek at the village of Conesville and continues on along and over it all of the way into New York. Parking areas along both roads usually denote access points.

As on other Pennsylvania freestone streams, fishing along Oswayo Creek is generally best during the spring and early summer. Productive flies include: Cahills, Sulphurs, Adams, Hendricksons, March Browns, Black Gnat, Blue Quills and various caddis imitations in both wet and dry forms.

Anglers might also note that downstream of Sharon Center the Fish Commission stocks muskies. Trout, as well as smallmouth bass, still frequent the water, but finding them may become a bit difficult after the water warms a bit and the big predators go on the prowl.

History buffs may be interested to know too that Oswayo Creek, from Singlehouse downstream, was once followed by the "Forbidden Path." This path, which ran from Athens, Tioga County, to the upper Allegheny River in New York, traversed the southern border of the Iroquois Confederacy. Its location made it a sort of backdoor to the Indian nation, and so travel on it was forbidden to all white men, thus the name "Forbidden Path."

Although it is possible a member of Champlain's expedition up the St. Lawrence may have visited the area as early as 1615, the Moravian missionary Zeisberger remains the first white man to document his trip along the path. Full of missionary zeal, he undertook his trip in 1767 despite threats from the Indians. Because of their displeasure, however, he found the Senecas "not at all friendly to the cause of the Gospel."

The first European settlement along the stream was eventually established at Ceres on the New York line. Francis King founded the town in 1779 after traveling up the West Branch Susquehanna River and then down the Allegheny River to its junction with Oswayo Creek.

(Also see Genesee River.)

Driftwood Branch Sinnemahoning Creek
Delayed Harvest Fly Fishing Only
(Float Trip)

West Creek
Elk and Cameron Counties
Elk Fork, Clear Creek
Portage Creek, North Creek
Cameron County
East Branch Cowley Run
West Branch Cowley Run
Cameron and Potter Counties

Travel by canoe in Pennsylvania was more difficult for early settlers than in either Canada or the New England states. It was tough, first, because of the lay of the mountains and, second, because of the lack of canoe birch in the forests. Unlike in Canada, where the land was mostly flat, and New England, where the rivers pierced the mountains, Pennsylvania's rivers and streams flowed alongside the mountains, leaving them insurmountable barriers in many places.

The lack of canoe birch in the forests caused the Indians and early settlers to use dugouts, or canoes constructed of elm bark. These were both clumsy and heavy crafts when compared to birch canoes, next to impossible to portage over the mountains. River travelers normally chose to abandon their crafts near the headwaters of one stream, walk across the mountain to the headwaters of the next and then build another craft. This portage problem led to many early settlements being called "Canoe Place," because they marked the start, or end, of a canoe route.

Among the most important settlements known as Canoe Place in the state was Emporium along Driftwood Branch Sinnemahoning Creek, translation "stony lick," in Cameron County. Called Shippen by early settlers, in recognition of Edward Shippen who owned the land on which it sat, and then later Emporium because

of its prominence as a commercial center for the region, the town occupies the southern end of one of the most unique portages, along Big Portage Indian Path, in the world. With only one carry from Emporium up the Driftwood Branch tributary of Portage Creek, across Keating Summit and then down the Allegheny River tributary of Portage Creek to Port Allegheny (another Canoe Place), a distance of just 23 miles, it is possible to travel by canoe all of the way from the Chesapeake Bay to the Gulf of Mexico, or Yellowstone National Park. The route runs from the Chesapeake, up the Susquehanna River, up the West Branch Susquehanna River, up Sinnemahoning Creek and then the Driftwood Branch, along Portage Creek and over Keating Summit then down Portage Creek, down the Allegheny to the Ohio River in Pittsburgh. From the Ohio River, the traveler can continue down the Mississippi River to New Orleans and the Gulf of Mexico, or up the Missouri River from the Mississippi and then the Yellowstone or Madison Rivers into Yellowstone National Park. Settlers in the early years of the nineteenth century actually made extensive use of the route (also see First Fork). Some people, such as Benjamin Burd, who came to the region in 1810, even made their living off the traffic on the route.

"I soon had plenty of work," he once wrote, "as settlers commenced to come up the Susquehanna River to Shippen, now Emporium, with flat boats, and pack their goods across the Portage to Canoe Place, where they made canoes and floated down the Ohio River. I had a lot of work making these canoes out of white pine logs."

The end of the nineteenth century and first half of the twentieth century saw Emporium gain notoriety for other things rather than its location. When the Climax Powder Co. opened up shop in the town in 1890 it became known as "Powder City." Dynamite used in the building of the Panama Canal was manufactured in the town. General Joseph T. McNarney, deputy chief of staff of the U.S. Army and commander of the American forces in the Mediterranean Theater during World War II was born in the town. And flagstone from the hills around the town was used for

A good idea.

the walk at the Tomb of the Unknown Soldier in Arlington National Cemetery.

Surrounded by a half-dozen quality trout streams and state forest lands full of game, Emporium today is a natural gathering place for the throngs of hunters and fishermen who regularly migrate to north central Pennsylvania.

Driftwood Branch Sinnemahoning Creek

One of the three main branches of Sinnemahoning Creek (also see First Fork and Bennetts Branch), Driftwood Branch is the largest. It is stocked with brook, brown and rainbow trout over a distance of almost 40 miles from the village of Driftwood upstream to its headwaters in Elk County.

As might be expected with so many miles of trout water, Driftwood Branch offers a wide variety of angling opportunities. Fishermen who venture into its headwaters on the divide between the Susquehanna and Allegheny watersheds will find a small brook trout stream overhung by hemlock and rhododendron. With the addition of tributaries like Elk Fork, Bobby Run, Cooks Run, Johns Run, North Creek and Clear Creek, however, the stream rapidly grows to respectable size. Below Emporium, where West Creek and Portage Creek add their considerable flows, Driftwood Branch nears the size of a river, and probably would be classified as such if it were in the western United States.

Along with size, Driftwood Branch also quickly encounters civilization as it nears Emporium. But until it is on the very outskirts of the town, most of the development is limited to some camps and well-kept homes. High banks and vegetation help by shielding much of the stream from direct view of the road.

Downstream of Emporium, Driftwood Branch wanders off into a deep, narrow valley dominated by the steep, wooded slopes of Bucktail State Park. Only the lightly traveled Pennsylvania Route 120 and a set of railroad tracks intrude on the serenity of the stream.

Bucktail State Park is one of the more unusual state parks in Pennsylvania. Named in honor of the Bucktail Regiment, it stretches for about 75 miles from just south of Emporium through Renovo to Lock Haven. Access is along Route 120, which follows the old Sinnemahoning Indian Path from Lock Haven to Port Allegheny. Facilities in the undeveloped park are limited to some picnic sites and hiking trails leading off into Elk State Forest and Sproul State Forest.

The ''Bucktail Regiment,'' sometimes called the ''Bucktail Rangers,'' for which the park was established back in 1933 was a group of Civil War volunteers from McKean, Elk and Cameron counties. The Bucktails answered a call by General Thomas Kane, founder of the town of Kane in McKean County, to ''Save The Union'' on April 17, 1861. Because of the marksmanship abilities of these mountain boys, they were used to form the nucleus of the Kane Rifles or Thirteenth Pennsylvania Reserve. The north mountains are full of stories about farmers abandoning their land and loggers their jobs so fast upon hearing Kane's summons that scythes were left hanging or leaning against fence posts and axes in trees.

The group's name comes from the bucktails they chose as their symbol and wore on their hats. Their ties to the Driftwood Branch and Sinnemahoning Creek comes from the fact they used those two streams, along with the West Branch Susquehanna River and Susquehanna River, to float on rafts to Camp Curtin near Harrisburg. The ''Bucktail Monument'' at the village of Driftwood commemorates the spot where the regiment gathered for its trip. As recent as the late 1970s the oak tree to which the rafts were tied was said to be still standing along the creek. The regiment distinguished itself in numerous battles during the Civil War, including the Battle Gettysburg, where they took part in the defense of Little Round Top.

The upper portion of Driftwood Branch's stocked water may be reached by following Route 120 through Emporium to its junction with Pennsylvania Route 46. The stream's one mile long Delayed Harvest Fly Fishing Only Project lies along Route 46 and is clearly marked by a wooden Fish Commission sign. Fishermen can park at the Cameron County Fairgrounds.

Rich Valley Road (State Route 4004) joins Route 46 on the left at the village of Lockwood. It parallels the Driftwood Branch upstream through the village of Rich Valley to Elk Fork, where it joins a dirt and gravel road which follows the stream to its headwater in Elk County.

Route 120 closely parallels the creek downstream of Emporium. Because of its steep banks, however, access is limited in many places. The Driftwood Branch from Emporium to Driftwood, a stretch that, along with trout, also holds good populations of smallmouth bass and panfish, makes a good float trip for anglers with a canoe or rubber raft.

Driftwood Branch's rocky bottom, deep pools and shallow riffles are home to a healthy variety of aquatic life. From mid-April to mid-May, action can be had with Blue-Winged Olives, Quill Gordons, stoneflies, Muddler Minnows, Hare's Ears, caddis, Hendricksons and Sulphurs; mid-May to mid-June, March Browns, Sulphurs, Gray Fox, Black Gnat, Green Drake, Brown Drake, Light Cahill, midges and terrestrials.

Elk Fork

The first stocked tributary of the Driftwood Branch, tiny Elk Fork also marks the point where the Fish Commission begins stocking rainbows and browns in the Driftwood. Upstream of Elk Fork, stocking is limited to brook trout.

Access to Elk Fork may be had by following Rich Valley Road off Route 46. The stream sets at the point where the road turns from asphalt to dirt. An old tram road parallels the creek upstream over the four miles of its stocked length, but is barred to vehicles by a gate.

Clear Creek

Clear Creek adds its flow to the Driftwood just upstream of Lockwood. Another gushing little stream, Clear Creek can be reached along State Route 4003 about a half-mile up Rich Valley Road from Route 46 on the left. The stream is stocked for six miles. The road follows it upstream along its entire distance, but access is barred by a gate about three miles along the route.

North Creek

Joining the Driftwood Branch at Lockwood, North Creek is accessible over its entire six miles of stocked water off Route 46 north. It is another small stream flowing through narrow valley.

West Creek

Flowing right along a commercial stretch of Route 120 from Emporium to the village of Truman, anglers might expect West Creek to be a noisy, even ugly stream. A mountain on one side, however, keeps a wilderness atmosphere alive, while trees and other foliage screen the water from the road, and a railroad bed. All in all, it is not too bad.

Medium-sized West Creek's stocked water runs from its mouth upstream into Elk County. State Road 4002 runs off Route 120 in Truman and provides access to the stream's upper reaches. Some water quality problems have been reported along the upper portion of the stream, so anglers may be better off limiting themselves to the stretch between Truman and Emporium.

Portage Creek

Like West Creek, historic Portage Creek also flows through a heavily developed area and close to a roadway. High banks, however, hide a lot of the stream from Route 155 and surrounding homes. This rather flat creek is stocked from its mouth upstream to Sizerville State Park. Anglers can get an idea of what early pioneers along Big Portage Path faced by continuing up Route 155 to Keating Summit and Port Allegheny.

Sizerville State Park has a Class B campground with 30 sites open from the second Friday in April to the end of the antlerless deer season in mid-December. Facilities include flush toilets, a dump station, picnic tables and fire rings. Non-fishing visitors will find a guarded swimming pool open from Memorial Day weekend to Labor Day, picnic areas, nature programs conducted by a park naturalist and hiking along four miles of trails. The park also serves as a trailhead for the Bucktail Path Trail, part of an extensive trail system running across Pennsylvania's north central counties.

Opened to the public in 1924, 156-acre Sizerville State Park is named after Sizerville, a logging boom town that once stood on the site. Sizerville itself was named for the Sizers, one of the first families to move into the region.

Further information on the park is available by writing: Sizerville State Park, Department of Environmental Resources, R.D. 1, Box 238-A, Emporium, PA 15834.

West Branch Cowley Creek

Another tiny trout water draining a narrow, isolated valley, West Branch Cowley Creek parallels Route 155 from Sizerville State Park north toward Keating Summit. Its stocked water extends for about 2.5 miles from its confluence with the East Branch upstream.

East Branch Cowley Run

Accessible off East Cowley Run Road in Sizerville State Park, East Branch Cowley Run is stocked with rainbow, brook and brown trout for over three miles from its confluence with the West Branch upstream into Potter County. It is a tiny mountain stream of rhododendron, white pine and hemlock. A small pond also is located on the stream inside of the park.

East Branch Cowley Run is much more famous in the annals of game management in Pennsylvania than trout fishing. Although Pennsylvania was once home to hundreds of thousands of beavers, greed, lack of management, the destruction of the forests and several other factors combined during the turn of the century to drive the animal to extinction in the state. In 1917, a pair of beavers was obtained by the Pennsylvania Game Commission from the state of Wisconsin and released along the East Branch. From that first pair, and others, the state's beaver population has grown to the point where they are regularly trapped and even a problem in some areas.

ELK STATE FOREST

A good portion of Cameron County and the streams mentioned here are touched by Elk State Forest, and so open to backpacking. This public land was named in honor of the large herds of elk which once roamed the region. The herd was driven into extinction in Pennsylvania in 1867 when the last animal was shot near Ridgway, Elk County. Between 1913 and 1926, the Game Commission undertook an elk restoration program by importing 177 of the animals from Yellowstone Park. The population has varied in the years since then, but is presently holding at between 100 and 125 individuals. Their range is limited to southwestern Cameron County and southeastern Elk County.

A Public Use Map of the forest would be a good addition to any angler's collection of material about the region. It outlines roads, streams and towns, and provides other information about the forest. It is available by writing: District Forester, Elk State Forest, R.D. 1, Route 155, Emporium, PA 15834.

Medix Run
Clearfield and Elk Counties
Hicks Run
East Branch Hicks Run
West Branch Hicks Run
Mix Run, Red Run
Cameron and Elk Counties

Pennsylvania Route 555 is a rolling, bending road that hugs the Bennett Branch Sinnemahoning Creek between the villages of Weedville in Elk County and Driftwood in Cameron County. Along the way it offers access to some typical mountain trout fishing in a half dozen streams, most of which flow through state forest, and so are open to backpacking. Route 555 may be reached by taking Interstate Route 80 Exit 17 and following Pennsylvania Route 255 north to Weedville.

Brown and brook trout are the predominant species in all of the streams. Anglers should do well with such standard patterns as the Adams, Light Cahill, Royal Coachman, Gray Fox, Blue Quill, Black Gnat, Renegade, Sulphurs, Hare's Ear, stoneflies, terrestrials and various impressionistic caddis imitations.

Medix Run

A small stream protected by Moshannon State Forest, Medix Run begins in Clearfield County and flows north to join the Bennett Branch at the village of Medix Run in Elk County. It is stocked over an eight-mile stretch extending upstream from its mouth, and also holds some wild fish.

Access to the stream is available by turning off Route 555 onto the Quehanna Highway (State Route 2004) at the village of Medix Run, driving across the Bennett Branch and heading toward Piper and Karthaus. The lower end of the stream, through the village, is paralleled by the Quehanna Highway. A short distance beyond the sign announcing Moshannon State Forest, about a mile off Route 555, the highway bends to the left, while a dirt and gravel road splits to the right. This forest service road is marked by a wooden sign with Medix Grade Road and Miner Road written on it, and provides access to the creek's upper water.

Hicks Run • East Branch Hicks Run • West Branch Hicks Run

Marked by a large wooden Fish Commission sign, Hicks Run is the easiest of the Route 555 streams to spot. Of medium size, it is stocked for more than three miles through Elk State Forest from its mouth at the village of Hicks Run upstream to the junction of the East Branch and West Branch.

In 1976, the Hicks Run watershed was the site of an extensive stream improvement project financed by the federal Manpower CEDA program through the U.S. Soil Conservation Service, and the Elk and Cameron County Conservation Districts. The project, along with improving streams in the watershed, also was designed to alleviate high unemployment in the area. It involved seven months of work on nine miles of stream. Consequently, anglers visiting Hicks Run and its tributaries today will see more than 600 jack dams, channel blocks and deflectors creating a better habitat for trout.

Hicks Run and East Branch Hicks Run, which is stocked for over seven miles, can be fished by turning onto a dirt forest service road near the bridge on Route 555. The road leads to the Hicks Run Ranger Station, indicated by a small sign, and runs along the main stream up onto the East Branch.

The lower portion of West Branch Hicks Run also may be reached, with some walking, off the forest service road. It is stocked from its mouth on Hicks Run upstream to State Game Lands 14. The West Branch's upper water has been designated wild trout water. Access to this stretch, however, involves a hike of about three miles.

Mix Run

Averaging less than 15 feet in width, swift and rocky, Mix Run may not appeal to some fishermen. Flowing through the Quehanna Wild Area of Moshannon State Forest, though, it is a place where an angler can get away from it all and fish for both stocked and wild trout enveloped by ferns and hemlock instead of automobiles and exhaust fumes.

Besides its beautiful wilderness surroundings and pleasant fishing, Mix Run is worthy of note for another reason, too. Near where it empties into the Bennet Branch Sinnemahoning Creek legendary cowboy star Tom Mix was born in 1880.

Early Hollywood publicity touted Mix as the son of a calvary officer who was educated at the Virginia Military Institute. It had him fighting in the Spanish-American War, the Philippine Insurrection, the Boxer Rebellion and the Boer War, as well as serving as a deputy marshall in Oklahoma and a Texas Ranger. An incredible life to say the least. But a bit to the left of the the truth. For a later biography, documented by a close relative of the actor, reveals Mix to have been the son of a poor Pennsylvania lumberman who dropped out of school after the fourth grade and, although he was a career sergeant in the artillery during all of the wars mentioned by the press agents, never saw combat and was declared a deserter in 1902.

An accomplished horseback rider from childhood, Mix did briefly serve as a Texas Ranger before joining the Miller Brothers 101 Ranch Wild West Show in 1906. He won the national riding and rodeo championship while performing with the show in 1909.

Following his winning of the national championship, Mix took a job with a different wild west troupe. Coming to the attention of the Selig Polyscope Co. shortly afterwards, he was hired to round up cattle for the 1910 silent film *Ranch Life in the Great Southwest* and immediately earned a supporting actor's role.

Remaining with Selig, Mix worked in a supporting capacity in over 100 shorter films between 1911 and 1917. Often also filling in as producer and director, Mix rarely used doubles in his roles and suffered numerous injuries while performing stunts in these action pictures.

When the Selig company closed its doors in 1917, Mix joined Fox pictures where he rapidly became the silent screen's most popular cowboy star, making over 60 full-length features, including Zane Grey's *Riders of the Purple Sage*. According to *The Film Encyclopedia* by Ephraim Katz, Mix's films were carefully packaged affairs that attracted the top directors and cameramen of the period, and spawned a wealth of imitators. Much as Clint Eastwood's movies did in the 1960s.

Mix stayed with Fox until 1928 when he joined the F.B.O. film company to make his last silent films. The following year, he joined the Ringling Brothers Circus with his famous horse, Tony. He returned to the screen in 1932 to make a few "talkies," and then

retired in 1934. *The Tom Mix Show* started a 17-year run on radio in 1933, outlasting the actor himself, who died in an auto accident in 1940, by ten years.

Tom Mix today is annually honored by a festival in the town of Dubois, southwest of the headwaters of Bennetts Branch where he once fished and swam. The remains of his birthplace—a foundation, well, walk, stump of an apple tree and collection of signs pointing out the lie of the homestead—still sit on the creek about a quarter of a mile from the mouth of the stream that bears his name.

The village of Mix Run lies between Hicks Run and Driftwood. The stream may be found by following the brown signs pointing the way to the Tom Mix birthplace, a drive of about four miles over first an asphalt road and then a dirt road along the south side of Bennetts Branch. A brown sign welcomes visitors to the homesite where a few picnic tables are available. Continuing down the road, Mix Run will be on the left. It starts in Elk County and makes a bend to meet Bennett Branch in Cameron County. Observe any fish refuge areas here and on the other streams.

Red Run

Sounding like the title to a Tom Mix movie, Red Run is another small stream lying in Elk County that joins Mix Run about halfway in its rush to Bennett Branch. It also holds both stocked and wild fish. It is accessible off Red Run Road, marked by a wooden sign near the Mix Run bridge, and by fishing upstream on Mix Run.

Since most of the land surrounding Red Run, like Mix Run, is part of Moshannon State Forest, the area is remarkably free of all but a few hunting camps. What is left is one of the closest things to true wilderness fishing obtainable in Pennsylvania.

(Also see Driftwood Branch Sinnemahoning Creek, First Fork Sinnemahoning Creek and Bennett Branch Sinnemahoning Creek.)

Marvin Creek
Delayed Harvest Fly Fishing Only
Potatoe Creek
West Branch Potatoe Creek, Brewer Run
McKean County

U.S. Route 6, "The Grand Army of the Republic Highway," has to be the most beautiful and interesting drive in all of Pennsylvania. Cutting a crooked path across the northern tier counties all of the way from New Jersey to Ohio, its setting ranges from the swamplands of the Pocono Region; to the mountains of "God's Country;" to the vast public lands of Allegheny National Forest; and, finally, the vineyard-lined shores of Lake Erie. Its history includes the state's anthracite coal fields, its legendary lumber country and the first oil fields in the world. To travel Route 6 is to bear witness not only to Pennsylvania's wild beauty and colorful past, but also the industrial development of the United States and, sadly, some of its remaining scars.

For the angler, Route 6 offers access to enough fishing to keep a person busy for ten years without duplicating an experience. Between the Delaware River and Lake Erie it leads to such diverse waters as Lake Wallenpaupack, the Susquehanna River, Loyalsock Creek, the "Grand Canyon of Pennsylvania," the Allegheny River, Kinzua Dam, Pymatuning Reservoir and a hundred other streams and lakes, among them Marvin Creek and Potatoe Creek in McKean County.

Marvin Creek

Meandering through a wide, flat valley of old pasture and scrub brush atop the Allegheny Plateau, Marvin Creek contains some ten miles of pleasant fishing for brown, rainbow and brook trout. Its stocked water runs from the stream's mouth on Potatoe Creek at Smethport upstream to about the village of Hazel Hurst, and all of it is directly accessible off Route 6. A Delayed Harvest Fly Fishing Only Project extends from the high voltage line about three miles south of Smethport downstream .9 miles, and is clearly marked by a large, wooden Fish Commission sign.

With a history dating far back into colonial days, Pennsylvania has been home to a large number of idealistic communities and religious sects. One of these groups, the Pennsylvania Dutch, has even come to represent the state in many people's eyes. Hundreds of others, however, have fallen victim to time, like "Teutonia," near the village of Marvindale on Marvin Creek.

Teutonia was established in March 1843 by Henry Ginal, a agent for the Society of Industry, a German cooperative group. It was founded, according to a newspaper interview given by Ginal shortly after the group arrived, "on the principle of community of property, money and furniture excepted, and is sustained by the cooperative of its members; an equal distribution of the profits being made half-yearly."

The society's tract comprised about 40,000 acres. It attracted approximately 450 people that first year. They built about 75 log cabins, a store, schoolhouse, sawmill and large tannery. A second settlement, Ginalsburg, also was built about four miles east of Teutonia during the first year. It contained a stone schoolhouse, several frame homes, another sawmill, a pottery and about 100 inhabitants. Nothing remains of either community today.

Fly fishermen along Marvin Creek might try the Adams, Renegade, Blue Dun, caddis, Muddler Minnow, Black-Nosed Dace, Mickey Finn, Hare's Ear, Woolly Bugger, Matuka Streamers, Blue-Winged Olives, Black Gnat, Royal Coachman, March Brown, Lead-Winged Coachman, Gray Fox, Light Cahill, midges and terrestrials.

Potatoe Creek

Farms carved up the sides of heavily forested mountains provide an odd sort of patchwork setting for Potatoe Creek. Oil and gas wells, not corn fields and diary herds, are Mckean County's usual crops.

One of the upper Allegheny River's largest tributaries, Potatoe Creek is stocked with browns and brookies for a distance of almost 16 miles from Crossmeyers Crossing just north of Smethport, downstream to the village of Betula. Access to the entire length may be had off Pennsylvania Route 46, though the stream is often out of sight. Township Road 362 also parallels the stream and can be reached by several bridges running off Route 46.

Smethport, around which fishing action on Potatoe Creek revolves, is the county seat of McKean County. It was laid out in 1807 and named in honor of Dutch bankers Raymond and Theodore de Smeth, but its story began even earlier with the arrival of John Keating, a young Irish soldier, in Philadelphia in 1792.

A captain in the Irish Brigade of the French Army, Keating came to Philadelphia on leave with letters of introduction to George Washington, and quickly became the agent for the Ceres Land Co. Financed by members of the French aristocracy who had fled their homeland at the outbreak of the French Revolution in 1789, the company purchased some 300,000 acres of land in north central Pennsylvania. Because the investors were exiles, they enlisted the services of two Dutch banking houses in Amsterdam. One of the firms belonged to the de Smeths, whose clients

included a number of princes and kings, among them Catherine the Great of Russia to whom they once lent 17 million francs.

Under the guidance of Keating and the de Smeths, the Ceres Land Co. prospered, and when it was decided to lay out a new town in 1807, Keating suggested it be named Smethport for the bankers. Keating himself was recognized when Keating Summit in nearby Potter County was given his name.

In later years, Smethport was an oil and gas producing center of considerable note. The 1860s saw wells drilled to a depth of over 1,000 feet, including some in the back yards of residents. Banker J.P. Morgan was reputedly drawn to the town by its oil. Many residents sold their homes for extraordinary sums in the speculative rush that grew around the oil and gas fields, and then, after the bubble burst, bought them back for a pittance. Smethport also claims to be the site of the first "Christmas Store" ever opened in the United States.

Potatoe Creek has a reputation as a fine night fishing stream for big brown trout. Patterns mentioned for Marvin should produce well for the fly fisherman who chooses to try Potatoe Creek.

Brewer Run

The first of Potatoe Creek's two stocked tributaries, Brewer Run can be reached along a dirt and gravel road off T-362, the secondary road running along the other side of Potatoe Creek from Route 46, roughly a mile south of Pennsylvania Route 146. Township Road 373 crosses the stream at Brewer Run, and is the last bridge before Betula. The stream is small and stocked for three miles, but could provide an alternative when Potatoe Creek is running high and discolored.

West Branch Potatoe Creek

Betula marks the entry of the West Branch into Potatoe Creek. Stocked for seven miles, this little stream is accessible off State Route 2002 in Betula. The access road follows the creek upstream over only part of its stocked length. After that walking is the only ticket.

East Branch Clarion River
Crooked Creek, Middle Fork Creek
Straight Creek
South Fork Straight Creek
Elk County
Seven Mile Creek
Elk and McKean Counties

East Branch Clarion River

Dams have ruined hundreds of miles of good trout water all across the United States. They have done it by burying swift, free water under placid depths and calling it "progress" or "the public welfare," two terms which at bottom often are only covers for greed and ambition.

In a few cases, however, dams also have improved a trout fishery. Most noticeably among these perhaps is Montana's Big Horn River. Before the construction of the Yellow Tail Dam, the Big Horn was little more than a sluggish ditch winding a path through the high plains under the eternal gaze of General Custer and his Seventh Cavalry. Now, fed by the icy water at the bottom of the dam, it is one of the premier brown trout rivers in the nation.

While by no stretch of the imagination in the same league as the Big Horn, central Elk County's East Branch Clarion River is another stream that has been aided by a dam. It is the 1,160-acre East Branch Dam whose depths keep it flowing cold and full long after most Pennsylvania freestone streams have been reduced to a scattering of pools connected by quiet trickles. If it was not for a problem with acid mine drainage, this little river could be one of the finer trout streams in the state.

As it stands, the East Branch is stocked with brook trout over a distance of seven miles downstream from the East Branch Dam in Elk State Park. It can be found by taking U.S. Route 219 to the town of Johnsburg, and then following the signs for Bendigo State Park along State Route 1004, which also parallels the stream.

Bendigo State Park holds a good looking stretch of the East Branch, including a small dam. It was named after the town of Bendigo, which was settled by Alfred Truman in 1895 when he established a sawmill on the land where the park now sits.

The town of Bendigo itself was named by the Pennsylvania Railroad after a famous English boxer, William Thompson, of the last century. Bendigo was Thompson's fighting name, a corruption of Abendigo of Shadrach, Meshach and Abendigo, the three Babylonian friends of Daniel in the Old Testament who were thrown into the furnace by King Nebuchadnezzar and survived.

Thompson lost only one fight during his career, but since boxing was illegal in mid-nineteenth century Britain he was arrested some 28 times. While in prison, his religious bend was encouraged by various chaplains and he eventually became a Methodist evangelist. He died in 1880 and, according to the park's "Recreational Guide," a monument to him was erected in Nottingham, England in 1891.

Bendigo Park was started by the citizens of Johnsonburg, a paper manufacturing center, as a community project back in the 1920s. Improvements were made by the Works Progress Administration through the 1930s, and the park deeded over to the state in 1949.

Only 100 acres in size, Bendigo State Park does not contain a campground. But it does have a large swimming pool, and a pleasant picnic area. It also is listed in "The Thirty Best Kept Secrets of Pennsylvania's State Parks," meaning that it is under-utilized.

Camping is available for anglers who wish to stay in the area at nearby Elk State Park, another one of "The Thirty Best Kept Secrets of Pennsylvania's State Parks." It can be found by continuing through Bendigo Park on S.R. 1004 to the village of Glen Hazel and then following the signs for the park and the East Branch Dam. Elk Park's campground has 75 Class B sites with flush toilets, water and a dump station, as well as picnic areas and two miles of hiking trails.

Glen Hazel, on the road between the two parks, was once known as "New Flanders." It was originally settled by a group of Belgian glass blowers, but lasted only a few years before the members of the community realized they could not make a living at their craft. Renamed Glen Hazel, the settlement then became a prosperous lumbering community.

In the nearby area of Jones Township a spot known as the "Uplands" also is of some historic interest. It was the home of Civil War General Thomas Kane, founder of the town of Kane. President Ulysses S. Grant was known to stay at Kane's home in Uplands during hunting and fishing trips to the region. State Game Lands 25, which borders Bendigo State Park, is the first

Decision on East Branch Clarion River.

piece of land purchased by the Game Commission with proceeds from hunting license sales back in 1920.

Among the flies an angler might try on the East Branch are the Royal Coachman, Adams, caddis, Hare's Ear, Mickey Finn, Lead-Winged Coachman, Soft Hackle Nymphs, Black Gnat, midges and terrestrials.

Information on both Bendigo State Park and Elk State Park is available by writing: Bendigo State Park, Department of Environmental Resources, P.O. Box A, Johnsonburg, PA 15845.

Crooked Creek

The East Branch's first stocked tributary, Crooked Creek, can be found by taking S.R. 1004 from Bendigo State Park to Glen Hazel. S.R. 1004 crosses Crooked Creek at Glen Hazel, where Glen Hazel Road (State Route 1001), leading to St. Marys, appears on the right and parallels the creek upstream through its three miles of stocked water.

Middle Fork Creek

Another little tributary of the East Branch, Middle Fork Creek, like Crooked Creek, is stocked for three miles from its mouth upstream. Located just downstream of the Corps of Engineers East Branch Dam, it can be located by following S.R. 1004 to Glen Hazel and then turning left on S.R. 1001. The first road to the right leads to the stream.

Seven Mile Run

Feeding the East Branch Dam, Seven Mile Run is stocked with trout for four miles from its mouth upstream. It can be found by following the signs along the dam for Elk State Park. From the park area, take the Wilcox Clermont Road (State Route 2001) toward Clermont. The road crosses the stream at the village of Williamsville, where a dirt jeep road appears and follows it upstream.

Straight Creek

Straight Creek is located on the east side of the East Branch Dam and accessible only off very secondary roads. Anglers can find its three miles of stocked water by following the Wilcox Clermont Road (S.R. 2001) from Elk State Park toward Clermont. A short distance before the village of Clermont, a road will appear on the right leading to the village of Straight Creek. At the village, anglers can pick up Straight Creek Road, on the right, which parallels the creek downstream toward its mouth.

South Fork Straight Creek

Like its sister stream to the north, South Fork Straight Creek is stocked for three miles. It can be found by following Straight Creek Road along Straight Creek to its junction with Naval Hollow Road, a sharp turn to the left. Continue on Naval Hollow Road to Briggs Hollow Road, the first dirt and gravel road to the right, and then follow that to the South Fork.

West Branch Clarion River
Delayed Harvest Fly Fishing Only
Elk and McKean Counties
Wilson Run, Hoffman Run, Rocky Run
Elk County

West Branch Clarion River

No solid archaeological evidence has ever been found to support contentions the American bison was once a native species of Pennsylvania. Even the accounts of early explorers and missionaries fail to mention sightings of the animal in the province. The stories about the animal that abound in the Keystone State are most likely the product of roaming bands which broke off from the main herds further west.

Despite the fact Pennsylvania probably never had a buffalo herd of its own, it still, sadly enough, managed to play an important role in the mass slaughter of the animal during the latter half of the nineteenth century. It was a role that revolved around its tanneries, one of the last stops before the hides reached the fashionable shops of New York and other East Coast cities. Elk Tannery at the town of Wilcox on the West Branch Clarion River in Elk County was once the largest tannery in the world. Established in 1865, at the peak of its production, it had branches in both Bedford and Warren counties, and between 1866 and 1875 turned out more than 1,000,000 buffalo hides.

While the leather industry continues to play a part in Elk County's economy, thankfully, it is no longer fed by an animal being hunted to extinction. And the West Branch Clarion River no longer is stained a dirty red with its blood and waste, but is now one of the finest trout streams in either Elk or McKean counties.

The West Branch is stocked with brook and brown trout for about ten miles in Elk County and approximately five miles in McKean County. The McKean water starts north of the village of Burning Well. The Elk water runs from the McKean line south to the town of Johnsonburg, a paper producing center. All of its stocked water is readily accessible off U.S. Route 219.

The West Branch's Delayed Harvest Fly Fishing Only Project is located south of Wilcox near the village of Tambine. It covers .5 miles from the intersection of Route 219 and State Route 4003 upstream to the Texas Gulf Sulphur property. It is most easily found by looking for the road sign pointing four miles to Montmorenci. A Fish Commission sign announces the project on the road to Montmorenci. Fishing is permitted only from the east bank.

Fly fishermen might try Quill Gordons, Adams, Hare's Ears, Hendricksons, March Browns, Soft Hackle Nymphs, Light Cahills, Sulphurs, caddis, midges and terrestrials.

North of Wilcox, on the Wilcox Clermont Road (S.R. 2001) in Jones Township a little over a half mile from the McKean County line, visiting anglers will find "Upland" or "Uplands." Built by W. P. Wilcox, whose family gave their name to the town, in about 1828, Uplands became the home of Thomas Kane, a Civil War general and founder of Kane, Pennsylvania, in 1856, and, in 1866, Captain Anthony A. Clay, another local Civil War hero. President Ulysses S. Grant and Simon Cameron, a Pennsylvania native, Abraham Lincoln's Secretary of War, and the man for whom neighboring Cameron was named, stayed at the home in about 1868, and President Theodore Roosevelt around 1906.

Wilson Run

The main tributary of the West Branch, Wilson Run meets the river at the town of Wilcox. It can be found by taking Pennsylvania Route 321 from Wilcox toward Kane. Route 321 parallels the stream over its entire stocked length of six miles from its mouth upstream along the edge of Allegheny National Forest.

Hoffman Run

Flowing through Allegheny National Forest, little Hoffman Run is stocked with trout for three miles. It is a tributary of

Wilson Run, joining that stream at the village of Dahoga on Route 321. Access to its upper water is available off Forest Service Road 191 at Dahoga.

The U.S. Forest Service's Twin Lakes Campground lies near the top of Hoffmans Run on Forest Service Road 290. Built by the Civilian Conservation Corps back in the 1930s, the campground holds 48 sites available on a first-come, first-served basis. No reservations are accepted. It is open from Memorial Day through Labor Day.

Along with campsites, Twin Lakes has a hiking trail, interpretive trail, adjacent spring-fed swimming and picnic area, sandy beach, trailer dump station, flush and pit toilets, and piped water. Showers are available at the beach.

Rocky Run

Entering the West Branch north of Wilcox, Rocky Run can be found by taking the first secondary road (Township Road 368) to the right off Route 219 about three miles above Wilcox. It is stocked for four miles from its mouth upstream.

Fly fishermen can try any of the patterns mentioned under the West Branch on these tributary streams.

Big Mill Creek
Fly Fishing Only
Elk County

Anglers who enjoy fishing for brook trout can find plenty of action along Big Mill Creek, a pleasant mountain stream that hugs the southeastern edge of Allegheny National Forest in Elk County. It is stocked over a distance of 12 miles from its mouth on the Clarion River north past the town of Ridgway to the vicinity of Pennsylvania Route 948. In addition to the stocked trout, it also contains some holdovers and native fish.

Although Big Mill Creek is a big woods stream, enveloped by the wilds of the national forest, good access is available over most of its length. Its upper water may be reached taking Forest Service Road 143 off Route 948 between the villages of Montmerci and Highland Corners. F.S. 143, a dirt and gravel road, parallels Big Mill Creek from Route 948 almost to the Ridgway Reservoir. The stocked water starts below the intersection with Forest Service Road 170.

Big Mill Creek's Fly Fishing Only Project runs for one mile from Nagle Bridge on Forest Service Road 135 downstream to the headwaters of the reservoir and is clearly marked with the usual Fish Commission signs. The special regulation water also may be found by taking Grant Road (S.R. 4001) off west Main Street in Ridgway. About two miles up Grant Road, past the Ridgway Gun Club and immediately after a stand of pine trees, an unmarked road appears on the left that leads down to the project. Ridgway Reservoir at the bottom of the Fly Fishing Only water also is heavily stocked with brookies, and so a sort of bonus for the angler who sometimes enjoys fishing for trout in still water.

The lower reaches of Big Mill Creek may be fished by following Main Street west out of Ridgway. Outside of the borough Main Street turns into Laurel Hill Road and heads up over a mountain to the national forest. Soon after entering the forest it crosses over the stream, providing access at that point.

Like a number of other streams across the state, Big Mill Creek is something of a victim of the "name game." The "Summary of Fishing Regulations and Laws" provided with every Pennsylvania fishing license lists the stream as "Mill Creek" in its special regulation waters section, while at the back of the booklet, under

"Approved Trout Waters" portion, it is called "Big Mill Creek." Maps also refer to it as "Big Mill Creek."

Fly selections include: Adams, Royal Coachman, March Brown, Mickey Finn, caddis, Sulphurs, Light Cahill, stoneflies, Renegade, Hare's Ear, Black Gnat, Soft Hackle Nymphs, Leadwing Coachman, midges and terrestrials.

An excellent map of Allegheny National Forest, listing Big Mill Creek and all the surrounding streams, may be purchased for $1 at all ranger stations in the forest, including the one in Ridgway on Montmorenci Road. Anglers can also write:

Ridgway Ranger District, R.D. 1, Box 28A, Ridgway, PA 15853.

Supervisor's Office, Allegheny National Forest, 222 Liberty Street, P.O. Box 847, Warren, PA 16365.

Spring Creek
Forest and Elk Counties
Bear Creek
Elk County

Spring Creek

Streams named Spring Creek can be found in practically every county in Pennsylvania. They may even be more numerous than Mill Creeks and Fishing Creeks. Only a few of them, however, are really exceptional trout streams. Centre County's Spring Creek near State College and Penn State University's Main Campus is undisputably the most famous of them all. Before it became polluted by a sewage treatment plant in 1957, it had earned a national reputation as a trout fishery. Some anglers even felt it was the best trout water in the country.

After Centre County's gem (although it remains polluted the fishing often is fantastic) one of the best Spring Creeks in Pennsylvania is probably the one flowing through Forest and Elk counties. And certainly this tributary of the Clarion River is one of the more picturesque, draining a valley through the southeastern portion of Allegheny National Forest and State Game Lands 28 where the only signs of civilization are hunting camps.

Spring Creek is stocked with brook and brown trout over a distance of 15 miles from the village of Duhring to the village of Hallton. Its lower waters can be reached by following Main Street west through Ridgway, the county seat of Elk County, and past Ridgway Recreational Park. Main Street turns into Laurel Hill Road (S.R. 3002) as it heads up over the mountain and into Allegheny National Forest. In the forest the road turns to dirt and gravel, and continues on through the village of Cross Run and Beuhler Corners. A short distance outside of Beuhler Corners it meets the Clarion River and then, in Hallton, Forest Service Road 130, which follows Spring Creek upstream through Game Lands 28.

The upper reaches of Spring Creek are accessible by following Forest Service Road 130 to Forest Service Road 131 in the village of Lamonaville. Forest Service Road 131 runs past the Kelly Pines Recreation Area to meet Spring Creek south of Duhring. Forest Service Road 227 joins Forest Service Road 130 near the village of Parrish and provides some downstream access.

More of Spring Creek's upper waters also may be reached by taking Forest Service Road 124 off Pennsylvania Route 948 in the village of Pigeon. Forest Service Road 131 meets Forest Service Road 124 just north of Duhring and leads to the stocked water.

Being well-shaded and away from main roads, fly fishing on Spring Creek is said to be good through the summer. Among the flies an angler might start with include: stoneflies, Adams, Hendricksons, Hare's Ear, Muskrat, Royal Coachman, Renegades, caddis, March Browns, Gray Fox, Black Gnat, Light Cahills, Sulphurs, midges and terrestrials.

Bear Creek

Anglers traveling to Spring Creek from Ridgway also might consider a stop at Bear Creek, another tributary of the Clarion River.

Of medium size, Bear Creek is stocked over 12 miles with brook trout. In addition, it holds some native fish which, though usually small, often provide a lot more excitement with their dancing battles across the stream's hemlock shaded pools.

Like Spring Creek, Bear Creek can be found by following Main Street west through Ridgway and then Laurel Hill Road over the mountain and into the national forest. The road crosses the stream at the village of Cross Run. Immediately before the bridge a dirt and gravel road will run off to the right. It leads back to a collection of camps and provides access for a short distance upstream.

Some of Bear Creek's upper water can be found by continuing through Cross Run to Beuhler Corners and then turning right on Forest Service Road 135. At the village of Owls Nest, Forest Service Road 135 bends to the right and leads back to the stream, as well as Forest Service Road 129, which touches on Bear Creek.

Between Cross Run and the intersection of Forest Service Roads 135 and 129, Bear Creek is a walk-in proposition that backpackers might be interested in trying. Possible fly patterns are the same as Spring Creek.

(Also see Clarion River, Big Mill Creek and Millstone Creek.)

Millstone Creek
East Branch Millstone Creek
Elk County
West Branch Millstone Creek
Elk and Forest Counties
(Northwest Map)

Millstone Creek • East Branch Millstone Creek

Finding a large trout stream in a real wilderness setting, but with easy access and some trappings of civilization nearby, is a big order in relatively small and heavily populated Pennsylvania, with 264 people per square mile. Plenty of fine streams of good size flow through state parks where they are easy to reach and visiting anglers can find campgrounds and playgrounds, swimming pools and restrooms. But wilderness is not exactly a word that can be applied to a park stream. On the other hand, streams of substantial size which dot the state's wilder regions seldom offer any creature comforts beyond a level clearing in the woods.

Millstone Creek, a Clarion River tributary located in the far western corner of Elk County, is one large stream that breaks the mold. Completely surrounded by the wilds of Allegheny National Forest, it is nevertheless easily accessible over its entire length by a forest service road, and, along its East Branch, even holds a U.S. Forest Service campground.

Access to Millstone Creek may be had by taking Pennsylvania Route 66 either north from U.S. Route 322 near Clarion, or south from U.S. Route 6 in Kane, to the town of Marienville. State Route 2005 meets Route 66 in the center of Marienville and leads to Loleta Campground (indicated by a sign).

Situated on the East Branch Millstone Creek, Loleta Campground contains approximately two dozen secluded sites, vault toilets, piped water, a picnic area and a swimming pool. The campground normally operates between Memorial Day and Labor Day. If it is open beyond that period, it will be with reduced services, which means no water, garbage pickup or snowplowing. In season, campsites are available on a first-come, first-served basis. No reservations are accepted, no more than two vehicles and eight people are allowed at any one site. There is a 14-day limit on stays.

From the campground Forest Service Road 131 traces the path of East Branch Millstone Creek upstream toward its headwaters. It is stocked with brook trout over a distance of six miles. Forest Service Road 284 follows the East Branch downstream and leads to Millstone Creek proper, which is stocked with brook trout for three miles. Both roads are marked with small wooden signs.

Possible flies include: Royal Coachman, Mickey Finn, Adams, Light Cahill, March Brown, Hendrickson, caddis, Hare's Ear, stoneflies, Renegades and Leadwing Coachman.

Catawba Path, from Olean, New York to Morgantown, West Virginia and beyond, crossed Millstone Creek near its mouth on the Clarion River. The path was one of the most important Indian trails in North America. Used extensively for both trade and war, the trail also was known at different times as the Great Catawba War Path, the Iroquois Path, the Iroquois Main Road, the Cherokee Path and the Tennessee Path. Connects made it possible to travel the path all of the way from Canada to Florida and west into the Mississippi Valley.

West Branch Millstone Creek

Most of West Branch Millstone Creek is accessible only by walking, so it is a possible choice for someone interested in backpacking. The Fish Commission lists it as being stocked from northeast of Marienville to its mouth.

Two places where the stream can be reached by road is off State Route 2005—the road to Loleta Campground—just outside of Marienville, near the entrance to the national forest. It also can be found off Forest Service Road 284—which parallels the East Branch downstream from the campground—at the West Branch's junction with the East Branch.

(Also see Clarion River, Big Mill Creek, Bear Creek, Spring Creek in Elk County.)

Allegheny Reservoir Feeder Streams
Kinzua Creek
South Branch Kinzua Creek
Meade Run, Chappel Fork
Sugar Run, North Branch Sugar Run
Willow Creek
McKean County

Kinzua Creek

Turkey hunters from across Pennsylvania look to the wilds of Allegheny National Forest to provide them with some quality sport in both the fall and spring. It is an old tradition. Possibly as old as man's presence in the area. That is if the name Kinzua, "they gobble," is any indication.

But wild turkeys were not the only gamebird for which the region around Kinzua Creek was once famous. For centuries before the last one passed into extinction around World War I, the forests from Kinzua Creek southwest toward the town of Sheffield and the village of Pigeon was a spectacular nesting ground for the Passenger Pigeon. So vast were the bird's numbers in the area the Seneca Indians actually cut a path through the wilderness whose main purpose was for hunting the birds. Known as "Pigeon Path," it ran from Cornplanter's Town—now under the waters of Allegheny Reservoir—near Cornplanter Run south through Dunkle Corners, on what was then still part of Kinzua Creek, through the village of Ludlow to Sheffield.

Even though Passenger Pigeon hunts were a major annual event for the Indians, who particularly favored the squabs, the size of the flocks were never endangered by them since they were careful not to pressure the breeding population. The same, however, cannot be said for the white man when he moved into the area. Paul A.W. Wallace in his book *Indian Paths of Pennsylvania,* notes one incident of the slaughter. On March 7, 1878 a flock of Passenger Pigeons were spotted over the town of Warren. By April 30 the Warren "Mail" was reporting 500,000 birds killed, and on June 11 over 700,000 shipped from Sheffield and 200,000 from Kane, with another 24,000 awaiting shipment.

Kinzua Creek today may be poorer for the absence of the Passenger Pigeon in the surrounding forests, but it is still a solid choice for the trout hunter. It is planted with fish from Mt. Jewett near Kinzua Bridge State Park to Kinzua Bay on the Allegheny Reservoir, making it the second longest stocked trout stream in McKean County. In addition, it offers fishing for native brook trout in its more remote sections, as well as an opportunity to tie into a big brown or rainbow moving out of the reservoir (where

Atlantic salmon also were stocked in 1986) to spawn during the fall. Spawning runs occur in Kinzua Creek, along South Branch Kinzua, Chappel Fork, Sugar Creek and Willow Creek at different times in October and early November. Unless an angler lives nearby, though, hitting a run is more a matter of luck than anything else.

Along with offering a good mixture of trout fishing, Kinzua Creek is generous when it comes to access. Either a paved or gravel road follows it through Allegheny National Forest nearly all of the way from its headwaters to its mouth.

The lower portion of the stream may be reached by following U.S. Route 6 west through the borough of Kane to its junction with Pennsylvania Route 321, or Hacker Street, and taking it north to the Big Rock Overflow/Red Bridge area of Kinzua Bay. Forest Service Road 122 appears to the right after crossing the bridge at the overflow. It parallels the stream all of the way to the village of Westline where it joins with a paved stretch of road that trails the stream to the village of Tallyho and U.S. Route 219 which crosses the stream at that point.

East of Tallyho, along Route 6 in Mt. Jewett, is Kinzua Bridge State Park. Only 316 acres in size, it does not contain a campground or swimming pool, but does hold picnic facilities, water and the Kinzua Viaduct. When it was built over Kinzua Creek back in 1882, the viaduct was the highest railroad bridge in the world. It was listed in the National Register of Historic Places in 1977.

Flies favored by local anglers include: the Blue Dun, Black Gnat, Hare's Ear, Yellow Stonefly, Blue Quill, Adams, Gray Fox Variant and Light Cahill.

Trout Unlimited stocking.

South Branch Kinzua Creek

Stocked from about two miles north of Kane to its mouth at the Big Rock Overflow of Kinzua Bay, South Branch Kinzua Creek is considered by many anglers to be the best trout stream in McKean County. One of the main reasons for its high standing is that, unlike most Pennsylvania freestone streams, it maintains a cool temperature even through the Dog Days of July and August. Most of the water is well-shaded and there are a number of springs scattered along its length.

Complimenting its cool temperatures are a large number of stocked fish, as well as solid populations of streambred brookies and browns, and some of the best fly hatches in the county. Early-season, mid-April through May, action is provided by Quill Gordons, Hendricksons, Black Quills, Sulphurs, Light Cahills, Gray Fox, Slate Drake, Brown Drakes, Green Drakes and caddis; mid-season, June and July, Sulphurs, Blue Quills, Light Cahills, Yellow Drake, Blue-Winged Olives and Slate Drake. Terrestrials also are good choices through the summer months.

Like Kinzua Creek, the stream it feeds, South Branch can be reached by following Route 6 west through Kane to its junction with Route 321 and taking that north. Though it is out of sight most of the time, the stream parallels Route 321 all of the way to its mouth. Parking areas along the road can generally be considered access points. Anglers should keep an eye open for ''Fish Refuge'' sections along the South Branch, and other streams in the area. Fishing is prohibited in these wired-off sections, but they are generally short and no problem to avoid. And obeying them is insurance of having plenty of fish in the future.

Meade Run

A small tributary of Kinzua Creek, Meade Run is stocked from its mouth upstream for roughly two miles. It also holds some native fish. It can be reached by taking Forest Service Road 150 running off Forest Service Road 122, which parallels Kinzua Creek. FS Road 150 meets FS Road 122 about a mile off Route 321.

Chappel Fork

Picture a perfect brook trout stream and chances are good Chappel Fork will compare favorably with it. Stocked for approximately eight miles from its mouth upstream to the vicinity of Marshburg, Chappel Fork is a sparkling beauty of a Pennsylvania mountain stream.

Anglers interested in trying Chappel Fork can reach it by taking Route 321 out of Kane past Kinzua Creek to the area of Dunkle Corners Fishing Bank on the reservoir at Chappel Bay. As the road turns away from the reservoir it parallels the stream for about two miles, though it is out of sight most of the time. The upper waters of Chappel Fork are accessible by continuing on Route 321 to its junction with Pennsylvania Route 59 and following it to Marshburg. Forest Service Road 455 runs off Route 321 on the right just before its intersection with Pennsylvania Route 770. About a mile off Route 321 another Forest Service Road (not numbered) runs off F.S. Road 455 to the right and touches on the stream.

Fly patterns listed for Kinzua Creek also should take some fish on Chappel Fork. Bright colored patterns such as the Royal Coachman and Mickey Finn are other choices to tempt the stream's brook trout.

Fishermen who would like to stay near Kinzua Creek, South Branch Kinzua Creek and Chappel Fork can find camping accommodations at the U.S. Forest Service Red Bridge Campground on Route 321 near the junction of Kinzua Creek and South Branch

Kinzua Creek. It is clearly marked by signs, and contains more than 50 sites, as well as a dump station, hot showers, vault and flush toilets.

A number of Forest Service campgrounds in Allegheny National Forest are open year-round with reduced services; i.e., no water, garbage pickup or snowplowing. The normal operating season for all campgrounds with full services is Memorial Day to Labor Day. In season, campsites are available on a first-come, first-served basis. No reservations are accepted. Backpacking also is permitted in the foret.

Sugar Run

Another typical little mountain stream, Sugar Run contains a mixture of stocked and streamborn trout, as well as a spawning run of browns and rainbows in its lower reaches. It is paralleled and crossed by Route 321 north off Route 59 between Marshburg and the Bradford Ranger Station.

Besides being accessible off Route 321, Sugar Run may be reached by Forest Service Roads 176 and 137. Both roads are used by oil drilling trucks, so anglers should be careful where they park along them.

Fly fishermen once more can start out with patterns suggested for Kinzua, South Branch and Chappel Fork. Keep an eye open, and obey, wired fish refuge sections.

North Branch Sugar Run

Stocked for approximately five miles from its mouth at Sugar Bay upstream, this tributary of Sugar Run is accessible along Forest Service Road 271, which runs off Route 321 north near the mouth of Sugar Run. Keep an eye open for oil drilling trucks.

Willow Creek

Lying east of Bradford, past the Bradford Water Co. property and just below the New York line, Willow Creek is the last stocked Allegheny Reservoir feeder stream in Pennsylvania. Sections of its upper water are on private property, but the bottom reaches flow mostly through national forest land and are loaded with a good supply of trout, both stocked and wild.

Intertwined with State Route 346 along its entire length, access to Willow Creek is simply a matter of finding a place to park off the highway and avoiding any private property. The stream also can be reached by following Route 321 north from Sugar Run.

Besides its fishing, Willow Creek also offers traveling anglers a place to pitch their tents. Willow Bay Campground is a 72 site Forest Service facility at the mouth of the stream. The campground has vault toilets, water fountains and a disposal station. A portion of it is open from the start of the trout season in mid-April to the end of the deer season in mid-December. As at Red Bridge near Kinzua Creek and South Branch Kinzua Creek, Willow Bay Campground is in full service from Memorial Day through Labor Day. The same first-come, first-served, no reservation rules apply.

GENERAL INFORMATION

Further details on the areas mentioned here, including maps, are available by writing:

Supervisor's Office, Allegheny National Forest, 222 Liberty St., P.O. Box 847, Warren, PA 16365.

Bradford Ranger District, Kinzua Heights, Bradford, PA 16701.

A full map of the forest is currently available for $1. But check for any price changes before ordering one.

Adams County
Conewago Cr
Little Marsh Cr
Marsh Cr
Middle Cr
Opossum Cr
Toms Cr

Bedford County
Beaver Cr
Beaverdam Cr
Bobs Cr
Cove Cr
Potter Cr
Raystown Br Juniata River
Three Springs River
Town Cr
Yellow Cr

Blair County
Bald Eagle Cr
Canoe Cr
Clover Cr
Frankstown Br Juniata River
Little Juniata River
Piney Cr
Poplar Run
Poplar Run S. Br

Cumberland County
Big Spring Cr
Conodoquinet Cr
Green Spring Cr
Letort Spring Cr
Mountain Cr
Old Town Run
Yellow Breeches Cr

Dauphin County
Armstrong Cr
Clark Cr
Conewago Cr
Mahantango Cr
Powell Cr
Stony Cr
Wisonisco Cr

Franklin County
Conococheague Cr
Conococheague Cr W. Br
Conodoquinet Cr
Falling Spring
Little Antietam Cr E. Br
Little Antietam Cr N. Br

Fulton County
Big Cove Cr
Little Aughwick Cr
Roaring Run
Sideling Hill Cr
Spring Run

Huntington County
Juniata River
Laurel Run
Spruce Cr
Standing Stone Cr
Standing Stone Cr E. Br

Juniata County
Juniata River

Mifflin County
Honey Cr
Juniata River
Kishocoquillas Cr

Perez County
Juniata River
Sherman Cr

York County
Bald Eagle Cr
Condorus Cr
Conewago Cr
Muddy Cr
Muddy Cr N. Br
Muddy Cr S. Br
Toms Run

HOWARD HUGHES

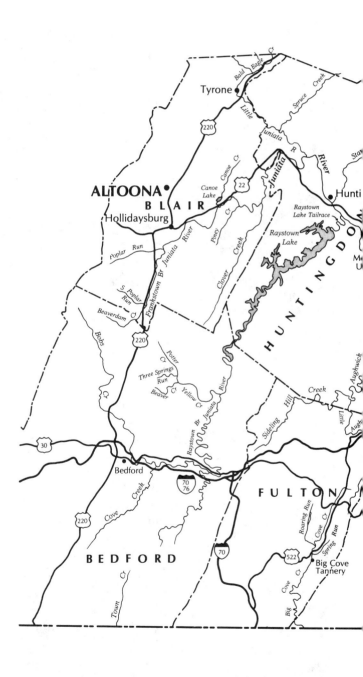

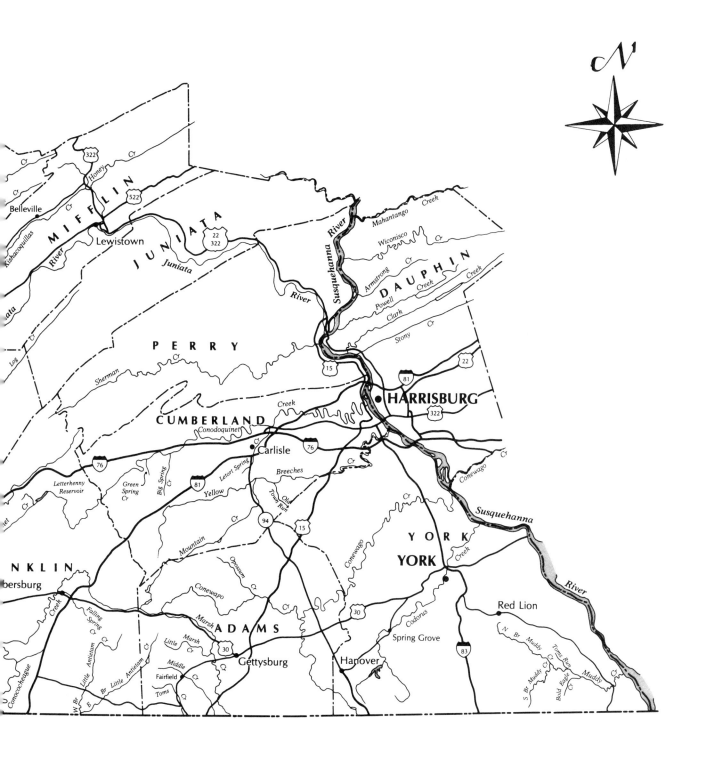

Southcentral Region

Stony Creek
Clarks Creek
Delayed Harvest Fly Fishing Only
Powell Creek, Armstrong Creek
Wiconisco Creek, Mahantango Creek
Dauphin County

Stony Creek

Eight and a half miles up the Susquehanna River from the state capital of Harrisburg, and light years above the political infighting and blustering pronouncements of that city, lies Stony Creek, the first of a series of Susquehanna tributaries that drain the narrow, wooded valleys of northern Dauphin County and offer a load of fine trout fishing.

Even though Stony Creek is the closest of the tributaries to Harrisburg, rush hour traffic can clog the streets around its mouth, it actually is the most isolated. Of its approximately 16 miles of stocked water, from its mouth upstream into Lebanon County, 11 are fully protected by State Game Lands 211 and reachable only by foot. Anglers who wish to fish its upper waters must either stumble their way along its rugged banks, or follow an old railroad bed upstream.

The Stony's medium size, deep holes, long flats with sandy bottoms interspaced by swift, rocky riffles make the stream ideal habitat for a wide variety of aquatic life. Mayflies, stoneflies, caddis and minnows all abound to attract and nourish its brooks, browns and rainbows. The combination is so good, some anglers feel Stony Creek may be the best trout stream in the county.

All of the interstate highways that feed Harrisburg also provide access to Stony Creek, as well as the other Susquehanna River tributaries to the city's north. But the easiest way to reach The Stony is by taking the Route 22/322 Exit of Interstate Route 81 toward the town of Dauphin on the east bank of the Susquehanna. In Dauphin turn onto Pennsylvania Route 225. The stream flows under Route 225 where Susquehanna Avenue appears and leads to Stony Creek Road, which parallels the creek upstream through the villages of Ellendale Forge and White Spring.

Paxtang Path, from Washington Borough to Sunbury, once crossed Stony Creek, as well as the streams north of it, in roughly the same area as Route 225 and Route 147. A gristmill also was in operation along the stream at Dauphin as early as 1770. The Appalachian Trail crosses both Stony Creek and Clarks Creek to the north in Game Lands 211.

Fly fishermen on Stony Creek find success with a number of traditional patterns, including: Royal Coachman, Adams, Blue Dun, stoneflies, streamers, Lead-Winged Coachman, Hendricksons, March Brown, caddis, Gray Fox, Light Cahill, Sulphurs, midges and terrestrials.

Clarks Creek

Many streams across Pennsylvania are famous for their heavy Green Drake hatches, others are well known for the blizzard of Tricorythodes flies they produce, and still others for the excellent caddisfly action they offer. But only one stream is recognized for its inchworm "hatch." That's Clarks Creek.

Of course, the term "hatch" is used only as a figure of angling speech when referring to Clarks Creek's inchworm fishing. For the species is certainly a terrestrial insect with a lifecycle wedded to dry land.

Actually, there is no such species as an inchworm. According to the *Merriam-Webster Dictionary,* the word is a sort of generic term for "loopers," a wide range of "rather small hairless moth caterpillars that move with a looping movement." The category includes such common pests as "bagworms" or "tent caterpillars," with their prominent silk-like bag webs, and the notorious gypsy moth, whose hunger has destroyed millions of acres of forests in the eastern United States.

Like ants, crickets, grasshoppers and beetles, the only time the inchworm is available as food for trout is when it falls from trees and brush overhanging a stream. While such an occurrence is nothing unusual and happens to one degree or another on every stream, Clarks Creek is special because of the regularity and intensity of its inchworm fall. For a period of approximately three weeks in late May and early June, the stream sees such numbers of the insects dropping to the water that its trout begin feeding selectively on them. And anglers without a proper imitation can forget about taking anything but the odd fish.

Why Clarks Creek is such a good stream for inchworm fishing apparently has to do with both its location in a part of Pennsylvania that has seen a heavy gypsy moth infestation, as well as the thick, dark stands of fir, elm, birch and maple which overhang its water along practically its entire length, providing plenty of opportunities for the insect to fall to the water. Along with inchworms, other terrestrial insects, especially black ants and beetles in smaller sizes, are productive.

Where aquatic insects are concerned, Clarks Creek is not an exceptional stream. It is primarily caddis water. Mayfly hatches do occur on occasion, but they are said to be sporadic and more the exception than the rule. Standard impressionistic patterns such as the Adams, Elk Hair Caddis and Henryville Special all produce fish, as will some of the classic streamers and nymphs like the Hare's Ear, Muskrat and Soft Hackle Nymphs.

Flowing out of Dehart Reservoir, the source of Harrisburg's water supply, in a series of long, clear flats, lower Clarks Creek runs for about 14 miles through a narrow shoestring of a valley between Third Mountain and Peters Mountain, to meet the Susquehanna River north of Dauphin. It is heavily stocked and, like most other trout streams in Pennsylvania, under considerable pressure during the early part of the season. Because of Dehart Dam, though, the stream remains relatively cool throughout the summer, and, as a result, anglers can have plenty of good fishing to themselves later in the season.

Pennsylvania Route 325 parallels Clarks Creek for its entire length, so access is simply a matter of finding a parking spot. Route 325 may be reached off Route 225 north of Dauphin.

Like Stony Creek, a good portion of Clarks Creek also is protected by State Game Lands 211. Above Dehart Dam, Game Lands 210 also appears and, although it does not often encompass the stream's banks, it helps to keep the hills around it from being overrun by second homes and trailers.

Clarks Creek's Delayed Harvest Fly Fishing Only Project starts about eight miles up Route 325 from Dauphin. It extends for two miles from the old iron furnace on the edge of Game Lands 211 upstream to the Game Commission parking lot on Route 325.

Powell Creek

No public lands protect the main branch of little Powell Creek from the encroachment of man, but the well-kept farms and accompanying woodlands do not make for unpleasant viewing. In its final miles, rocky bluffs and hemlock groves add to the setting.

Powell Creek also is different from Stony Creek and Clarks Creek in that it is stocked in two sections, from its mouth at the village of Ingelnook upstream above Route 225 and the village of Powells Valley, and downstream from its headwaters at the junction of the North Branch and South Branch Powell Creek. Its lower stocked water can be reached off Route 147 at its mouth and Route 225 about five miles upstream. Township Road 547 appears just north of the Route 147 bridge. It parallels Powell Creek upstream, leads to a bridge and Township Road 549 which continues along the creek upstream to Route 225.

Above Route 225, Powell Creek can be found by taking Camp Hebron Road (Township Road 551), which meets the highway just after it crosses the stream. By continuing on Back Road, the angler can gain access to the stream's upper waters. Sheetz Road, Lebo Road, Rodel Road, Rummel Road, Township Roads 535, 557 and 540 all run off Back Road to both the main stream and the North Fork.

Caddis imitations are reported to work best on Powell Creek in

April and May. Later in the season mayflies and streamers are the ticket. Anglers can try some of the same patterns mentioned for Stony Creek and Clarks Creek.

Armstrong Creek

Meandering through another agricultural valley, but with a few more homes than Powell Creek, tiny Armstrong Creek may be a good stream to try when others in the area are running high and dirty. It offers 15 miles of stocked water, running from its mouth at Halifax upstream. Access may be had off Route 225 just east of Halifax and Route 147 just north of the town.

Township Road 565 appears immediately after the Route 225 bridge. It loops down to a bridge and then back up to the highway. A short distance above it, Enders Road joins Route 225. It leads down to two bridges. The second one joins Township Road 571 on the left, which parallels the creek and provides access to still another bridge near the village of Fisherville, where Creek Drive picks up the stream.

Clemson Island in the Susquehanna River opposite Halifax was once the site of an Indian burial mound. Archaeologists began exploring the site back in 1929 and have turned up numerous relics believed to have been of Algonquin origin. Fort Halifax, one in the series of stockades erected to protect early settlers from Indian raids, also once stood across the river along U.S. Route 15. Fly anglers can try some of the same patterns mentioned for the other stream.

Wiconisco Creek

"Wet and dry camp" is the translation of Wiconisco Creek. It is big water of forested bluffs and bottoms, pastures and distant mountains that carve a crooked path over 40 miles across northern Dauphin County into Schulkill County. Its stocked water covers only about eight miles from its mouth upstream to Rife Road.

Access to Wiconisco Creek is available off Route 147 at a park in Millersburg, but anglers who enjoy a more aesthetic setting should move further upstream. U.S. Route 209 parallels the creek upstream from Millersburg. Landis Drive (Township Road 460) and Rife Road (Township Road 466) both run off Route 209 within the Fish Commission's stocked section. Route 209 also crosses the creek above Rife Road.

Adams, Blue Quill, March Browns, Sulphurs and Light Cahills are said to be especially productive fly patterns, but anglers should not overlook the flies mentioned under Stony, Clarks, Powell and Armstrong Creeks.

Mahantango Creek

Lying about 30 miles above Harrisburg, Mahantango Creek is the last Susquehanna River tributary in Dauphin County. Actually, it is the last stream of any type in Dauphin County, since it forms the Dauphin/Northumberland County Line. It is stocked with trout over its entire Dauphin County length, a distance of about 15 miles from the village of Klingerstown on the edge of Schuylkill County downstream.

Although secondary roads parallel Mahantango Creek, they do it at a distance, so access is essentially a bridge jumping affair. Route 147 crosses the stream below the village of Malta. On the north side of the stream Mahantango Creek Road (S.R. 3024) appears and leads to Malta where there is another bridge. Approximately 2.5 miles above Malta a third bridge is located and less than a mile upstream of it a fourth (closed). The third bridge leads to Deiblers Dam Road, which parallels the creek for a short distance on its south side.

Mahantango Creek Road joins Route 225 at the bridge leading

into the village of Pillow. On the upstream side of Pillow another bridge makes its appearance and leads to State Route 3018 and Klingerstown. Another Mahantango Creek Road (Township Road 317) runs off S.R. 3018 about three miles above Pillow and provides access to the stream. S.R. 3018 ends at Klingerstown, a small village resting at the forks of Mahantango Creek and Pine Creek.

Tulpehocken Path, from Sunbury to Womelsdorf, once crossed Mahantango Creek at Klingerstown. Because the path was a main link between Philadelphia and Shamokin (Sunbury), one of the most important Indian towns in Pennsylvania, it was frequently used by traders. Isaac Taylor was operating a trading post near the mouth of the creek as early as 1727. A number of well-known early explorers of Pennsylvania used the trail at different times, including Conrad Weiser, who often served as an emissary between the provincial authorities and the Indians, and Count Nicholas Ludwig von Zinzendorf, patron of the Moravian Church. On his journey over the stream, Count von Zinzendorf even renamed it, calling it Benegina's Creek in honor of his daughter.

The word Mahantango has been interpreted to mean "where we had plenty of meat to eat" and "where we kill deer." Isolated by rugged Mahantango Mountain to the south, Mahantango Valley today is a pleasant agricultural setting with plenty of deer and other game, and only a minimal amount of reactional development. The main problem with the area is unsightly garbage that touches the stream's long, gliding pools in too many places.

Yellow Breeches Creek
Catch and Release
Cumberland and York Counties
Mountain Creek, Old Town Run
Cumberland County

Yellow Breeches Creek

Local legend has it that Yellow Breeches Creek was given its name by British soldiers who had their white breeches turn yellow after washing them in the mineral-rich stream. But that's folklore. Serious historians believe the name is a corruption of Yellow Beeches because a large number of those trees once grew along the stream. Early records also call the stream Shawnee Creek, probably after the tribe which once lived near the mouth, while the Indians themselves referred to it as Callapatscink, "where it returns," a reflection of the stream's frequent bends.

Whatever it might have been called in those first letters, and no matter from where the source of its name springs, it is generally agreed that Yellow Breeches Creek has been known by that name since Cumberland County was first settled by Europeans in the early eighteenth century.

Along with Letort, Fallings Springs, Penns Creek, Spruce Creek and Spring Creek, the Yellow Breeches is one of the best known limestone trout streams in Pennsylvania, or, for that matter, the United States. Unlike those other spring creeks, however, it does not rise full-blown from a crack in the earth's crust. Instead, it is a mixture of both freestone and limestone spring drainage, its flow dominated at times by one and then the other.

"Compare the thirty-five mile Yellow Breeches with any other stream or all the rest and the only possible conclusion one can arrive at is here is one that is different. . ." writes well known angling author and Pennsylvania angler Charles K. Fox.

Like the stream itself, the habits of Yellow Breeches trout are a bit different than those of other streams. Hatches are generally at their best early in the season, and diminish to the point where they almost disappear by the last half of the year. In line with this contrary manner, however, fishermen flock to the Yellow Breeches in some of their greatest numbers through the Dog Days of August. They come both to catch the evening fall of "White Flies" (*Ephoron leukon*), and because most other trout streams in Pennsylvania are too warm to provide good fishing so late in the season. A combination of spring feeder and old mill dams—there are some 17 on the creek—helps keep the Yellow Breeches flowing full and cold year-round.

Hatches on the Yellow Breeches can be inconsistent—strong in some sections, sparse in others—at any time during the season. Since the stream depends on runoff for part of its flow, weather is a big factor in hatching activity. Heavy rains can carry silt into the stream that effectively kills the fishing. On the other hand, if the pre-season is relatively warm and the rain light, some of the best fly fishing of all can be had around opening day in mid-April. Still, the Yellow Breeches is not a stream where a visiting angler can expect to find clear water and rising fish everyday. The fishermen who do the best on it are those who live nearby and can easily get to it when the water is right.

The "Slate Drake," imitated by the Dark Hendrickson, is the first hatch of the season on the Yellow Breeches. It does not occur everywhere along the stream, but where it does it provides some of the best fishing of the season. Caddisflies make their appearance near the same time and continue on the water through early May. Following the caddis come the "Sulphurs," a large category of mayflies that can be imitated by any sulphur-colored flies in sizes No. 10 through No. 20. The warmer weather often makes fishing the Yellow Breeches a midge and terrestrial affair, until the White Flies appear in the evening.

The Yellow Breeches Catch and Release Project is located in the town of Boiling Springs on Pennsylvania Route 174 south of Pennsylvania Turnpike Exit 16 and Interstate Route 81 Exit 14 in Carlisle. It can be reached by taking Pennsylvania Route 34 south from Carlisle to Route 174 and then following Route 174 to State Route 2003 outside of Carlisle and following it straight into town. In both instances, road signs indicate the way.

Once in Boiling Springs, parking for the project is available at the entrance to Allenberry Resort and Playhouse just east of town or further upstream near the Boiling Springs Community Park behind the lake. The Catch and Release Project runs downstream from the lake to the vicinity of Allenberry. Boiling Springs Lake is fed by one of the largest limestone springs in Pennsylvania, and the main reason for the quality of the fishing in that area. Its source is located near the clock tower in the center of town.

Anglers visiting the special regulation water for the first time should be warned that it can become quite crowded, especially in the area immediately adjacent to Allenberry. The fishermen who use it may be polite and well mannered, but crowds are what many people go fishing to escape. Good catches can be often had just above and below the Catch and Release Project, so don't be afraid of exploring those stretches, or even some further away.

Yellow Breeches stocked portion starts at the Fish Commission's Huntsdale Hatchery. It can be reached by taking the Newville, Pennsylvania Route 233 south Exit 11 of Interstate Route 81. Follow Route 233 south until it crosses the stream and meets Pine Road. Turn left onto Pine Road. The hatchery is about a mile downstream. Anglers can start fishing immediately below the hatchery, or continue on down Pine Road, which parallels the stream all of the way into Mount Holly Spring and Route 34 when Mountain Creek adds its flow. A number of side roads also afford access by running off Pine Road and across the stream.

Yellow Breeches Creek.

On the east side of Route 34, the Yellow Breeches can be reached off Route 174 and such side roads as Zion Road and Lerew Creek Road between Mount Holly Springs and Boiling Springs.

Downstream of Boiling Springs and the Catch and Release Project, the Yellow Breeches can be reached by crossing the bridge at the south end of Boiling Springs. Take the first left turn after the railroad tracks and continue on one mile toward the village of Leidighs and Criswel Drive. Turn left on Criswel Drive and back toward the stream.

Route 174, running out of Boiling Springs and past Allenbury leads to Pennsylvania Route 74, which crosses Yellow Breeches Creek at the village of Brandtsville. Immediately after Route 74 crosses the stream, a road will appear on the right that leads upstream and past an old mill dam. Anglers can find additional downstream access by turning left onto State Route 2008 just before the Route 74 bridge. Vincent Marinaro, in his classic *A Modern Dry-Fly Code,* once rated "The Stretch," or the Yellow Breeches between Brandtsville and Williams Grove as some of the best water on the entire stream.

Messiah College is located in the little town of Grantham downstream of Williams Grove. The Yellow Breeches flows along one side of this quaint little school, complete with a covered bridge, and can be reached by taking U.S. Route 15 toward Grantham and following the signs for the college. A parking lot is located near the covered bridge.

Pennsylvania Route 114 provides access to water below Grantham. Although it parallels the creek from Bowmansdale downstream to the village of Lisbon, it is at a great distance, so access must come from roads running off it. Arcona Road, which appears roughly midway between Bowmansdale and Lisbon, leads to McCormick Road, which parallels the stream. At Lisbon, Route 114 itself crosses the stream.

Mountain Creek

Small, clear and cold, heavily stocked with browns and rainbows, and with a good population of native brook trout, Mountain Creek is both a pleasure to look at and to fish. If this little freestone stream was located anywhere else but the Cumberland Valley with all its legendary limestone waters, it would undoubtedly have a much wider known reputation. As it stands, Mountain Creek is under relatively little fishing pressure and a good place for the angler to consider who finds himself being crowded off the Yellow Breeches or Falling Springs Run.

Mountain Creek runs through the heart of Michaux State Forest and Pine Grove State Park. It is stocked over a distance of 16 miles, from about the park downstream to its junction with the Yellow Breeches on the edge of Mount Holly Springs. Pine Grove State Park is accessible along Route 233. It can be picked up off Interstate Route 81 Newville Exit 11 in the north, or at Caledonia State Park along U.S. Route 30 between Chambersburg and Gettysburg in the south. The park holds roughly four miles of stream, as well as two lakes—Fuller Lake and Laurel Lake—that also are stocked with trout. Hunters Run Road (State Route 3008) joins Route 233 at the park office and follows Mountain Creek downstream toward Pennsylvania Route 34 and the town of Mt. Holly Springs. Although both Route 233 and Hunters Run Road more or less parallel the stream, a short walk is generally required to reach it.

Possible fly choices include: Adams, Hare's Ear, Royal Coachman, Hendrickson, March Brown, caddis, Renegade, Muddler Minnow, Light Cahill, Sulphurs and terrestrials.

For camping anglers, Pine Grove State Park holds 74 Class B tent and trailer sites with drinking water, pit toilets and a dump station. "However, access cannot be guaranteed in severe winter weather," according to the park's "Recreational Guide."

Besides the campground, the park also offers boating—for non-powered boats and those with a registered electric motor—on 25-acre Laurel Lake, five hiking trails, including a portion of the Appalachian Trail, picnic grounds, a camp store, a bicycle rental concession and guided tours by a park naturalist during the summer months. Two guarded swimming beaches are open from Memorial Day until Labor Day. An America Youth Hostel also is located nearby.

The park sits at the northeast end of Michaux State Forest. The forest was named in honor of Andre Michaux, a noted French botanist of the eighteenth century who explored the region. The park is named for the Pine Grove Iron Furnace, which dates back to 1764 when iron was the chief ingredient in such items as stoves, kettles, wagon wheels, cannons and even tombstones. The remains of the furnace continue to be visible near the park office, as are other remnants of the iron making age, such as old canals, raceways, a grist mill, and other buildings. Fuller Lake was once the major hole from which iron ore was dug for Pine Grove Furnace. It was abandoned when available equipment could no longer pump water out of it fast enough. The first recreational facilities were built by the railroads, and the area purchased by the state in 1913.

Details on Michaux State Forest, including a free "Public Use Map" that shows Mountain Creek and a number of other local streams, may be had by writing: District Forester, Michaux State Forest, 10099 Lincoln Way East, Fayetteville, PA 17222.

Information on Pine Grove State Park is available by writing: Pine Grove Furnace State Park, Department of Environmental Resources, R.D. 2, Gardners, PA 17324.

Old Town Run

With about five miles of stocked water, Old Town Run meets the Yellow Breeches just outside of Boiling Springs. It can be found by taking Petersburg Road off Route 174 between Mount Holly Springs and Boiling Springs. Petersburg Road is the third right east of Mount Holly Springs and Route 34.

(Also see Letort Spring Run.)

Muddy Creek
Fly Fishing Only
North Branch Muddy Creek
South Branch Muddy Creek
Toms Run, Bald Eagle Creek
York County

Muddy Creek

Ominous name not withstanding, Muddy Creek is probably the best trout stream in York County. And it certainly is the best stocked. Beginning near the Pennsylvania Dutch town of Red

Lion, it is planted with brook, brown and rainbow trout all of the way downstream beyond the village of Castle Fin just above the Susquehanna River. Along with the stocked fish, the stream also contains a good scattering of holdover browns that fall to lucky, or skillful, fishermen every year.

Besides producing some solid catches of trout, Muddy Creek also offers something else to anglers visiting its banks. Something far more difficult to find in the modern world. A splendid sense of isolation and beauty.

York and Lancaster counties' picturesque farms and their "quaint" Amish inhabitants have been a staple in Pennsylvania's tourist literature for decades. Their charms have not only attracted millions of visitors to the area, but also thousands of new residents. And along with them all the development needed to sustain a large population; growth that has turned many of the farms into congested highways, discount department stores and fast food restaurants.

Muddy Creek—even though it is located about a half hour from York and Lancaster and within an hour and a half drive of Philadelphia, Harrisburg and Baltimore—has managed to survive in a wonderfully primitive fashion probably because of the rugged, narrow gorge through which it flows. It is a terrain that limits direct access in many places, and so discourages building over much of its length.

Actually, the Muddy Creek trout fishery is made up of three different streams: North Branch, South Branch and main branch. The North Branch begins south of Red Lion and flows on a diagonal toward the southeastern corner of the York County. The South Branch starts near the Maryland line and the town of Stewartsville and continues on a northeast angle to join the North Branch at Muddy Creek Forks. The North Branch is stocked for seven miles upstream from Muddy Creek Forks and the South Branch for six miles upstream from that point, while the main stream receives fish for 16 miles downstream from the forks.

Muddy Creek's two mile long Fly Fishing Only Project runs from the State Route 2032 Bridge in the village of Bridgeton upstream to Bruce, or Bruce Station. It can be reached by taking Pennsylvania Route 74 to the village of Airville and then Pennsylvania Route 425 toward the village of Woodbine. Kennedy Road appears on the right about midway between Airville and Woodbine. Turn onto Kennedy Road and follow it for about two miles to Bruce Road then take Bruce Road, a dirt and gravel affair, for about a mile and a half to the upper portion of the project. The property at the end of Bruce Road is private, but fishing is permitted. It also is interesting in an amusing sort of way for the presence of several old railroad cars, including one around which a pleasing contemporary home has been constructed.

The lower portion of Muddy Creek's special regulation water may be found by continuing on Route 425 past Kennedy Road to Bridgeton Road (State Route 2032). Turn right on Bridgeton Road and follow it down to the stream. Piney Road, off Kennedy Road, also leads to the lower part of the project.

Downstream of the Fly Fishing Only water, Muddy Creek can be reached off Route 425 at Woodbine where a bridge crosses it. A road that appears on the other side of the Woodbine bridge parallels the creek upstream for about a mile.

Further access to the main stream's lower water is available along Route 74 at Castle Fin and Paper Mill Road (State Route 2024) just before Castle Fin. Beside trout, this lower stretch of the stream holds some large smallmouth bass and muskie. Many people also feel it is the prettiest piece of flowing water in the county. Rapids lined by giant boulders and rock ledges, deep pools, gravely riffles and a scattering of waterfalls tell the story of Muddy Creek's water. As far as Bridgeton the gorge through which the creek flows is largely undeveloped. From Bridgeton downstream below Woodbine summer homes make their appearance. After that the gorge turns primitive once again.

Fly anglers might try such standard patterns as the Adams, Quill Gordon, Hendrickson, March Brown, Gray Fox, Light Cahill, caddis, Renegade, Hare's Ear, Royal Coachman, Mickey Finn, Muddler Minnow, Black Nose Dace, midges and terrestrials.

North Branch Muddy Creek

Seven miles of North Branch Muddy Creek is stocked with trout. The planted length runs from about the village of Felton downstream to Muddy Creek Forks, where the North Branch joins the South Branch to form the main stream.

Like Muddy Creek, access to the North Branch also starts off Route 74. Felton Road meets Route 74 east of Brogue and, naturally, leads to Felton. At the bridge in Felton, a secondary road appears that follows the creek all the way downstream to the villages of Brogueville and Fenmore.

Downstream of Fenmore, the North Branch is accessible by following Laurel Road, off Felton Road a short distance below Route 74, and toward the village of Laurel. Muddy Creek Road, which runs off Route 74 at Brogue and to Muddy Creek Forks, also provides some downstream access by following the road running straight ahead when Muddy Creek Road bears to the left.

South Branch Muddy Creek

Along with providing access to Muddy Creek and the North Branch, Muddy Creek Road from Brogue on Route 74 to Muddy Creek Forks, also leads to the South Branch Muddy Creek. Anglers can reach this third tributary of Muddy Creek by continuing straight through Muddy Creek Forks. After crossing the stream, Muddy Creek Road parallels the South Branch downstream for approximately two miles.

The South Branch's upper water may be reached by taking Grove Mill Road off Pennsylvania Route 851 west of the village of New Park and the Maryland line and toward the village of Grove Mill. At its start, the road parallels the stream at a distance, but at the village pulls closer, even crossing it a short piece beyond.

Toms Run

A small tributary of Muddy Creek that might serve anglers well during high water periods, Toms Run is stocked for two miles with browns and rainbows. It may be found along Kennedy Road, between Bruce Road and Piney Road above the main stream's special regulation water. It empties into Muddy Creek downstream of Bruce Road.

Bald Eagle Creek

Another tributary of the main stream, Bald Eagle Creek, like Toms Creek, is stocked for about two miles from its mouth upstream. It can be reached along Route 425, starting near Woodbine.

Codorus Creek
Delayed Harvest Artificial Lures Only
York County

The Pennsylvania Dutch Country of York and Lancaster Counties has always been a major drawing card for the state's tourist industry. Pick up almost any magazine or other publication that focuses on Pennsylvania sights, and chances are almost 100 percent somewhere in it will be a photograph of plainly dressed folks riding in a horse and buggy. Either that or photographs of stern-looking bearded gentlemen in dark hats and coats, or women in long dresses and bonnets. For a people who dislike having their picture taken, it is unbelievable how often the privacy of the Amish has been violated and their likenesses exhibited in tourist publications.

While the idyllic settings portrayed in the tourist publications certainly do exist, visitors to York and Lancaster also should be aware that both counties have their ugly sides with factories, traffic jams and pollution. The city of York has a population of over 80,000, and the stretches of Codorus Creek it straddles are no place for the trout fisherman. Fortunately, though, it is only about a dozen miles upstream to a spot that fits the bill quite well.

Codorus Creek's headwaters form near the village of Sticks north of the Maryland state line. From there the stream flows northwest to about the village of Gnatstown where it makes an abrupt turn to the northeast and drains the center of York County. Because of the monstrous Gladfelter Papermill, which turns the stream a coffee-color at Spring Grove, only about 5.5 miles of Codorus' upper water is stocked with brown and rainbow trout. But the stretch is surrounded by a scenic array of farms, fine old houses and mills, rocky outcrops and cool woodlands of elder and birch.

Codorus Creek's 3.3-mile Delayed Harvest Artificial Lures Only Project runs from State Route 3047 upstream to State Route 116. It, as well as the stream's other stocked water, can be located by following Pennsylvania Route 116 south off U.S. Route 30 through Spring Grove. Access to the stream is available on Route 116 where that road crosses the creek above the village of Menges Mills.

Iron Ridge Road meets Route 116 on the left a short distance after Route 116 crosses Codorus Creek. It parallels the creek from the village of Porters Siding upstream. Porters Road meets Iron Ridge Road just outside of Porters Siding and also leads to the stream.

"Rapid Waters" is the translation of Codorus Creek. And, considering the number of times it switched hands between Pennsylvania and Maryland, an appropriate name in more than one sense.

The first settlers in the Codorus Creek region were intruders from Maryland who appeared in the 1720s. They built their homes on lands which the Penns had not yet purchased from the Indians. In 1729, John and James Hendricks were given a license to settle on the same land by Pennsylvania. That year, Charles Carroll also was given a warrant for 10,000 acres, including Codorus Creek, by the governor of Maryland. The following year, 1730, Thomas Cresap moved onto the lands near Wrightsville on the Susquehanna River, touching off a long fight between the settlers of the two colonies.

Six years after Cresap's arrival on the Susquehanna, the entire province of Pennsylvania—"All the lands lying on the West side of the said River to the setting of the Sun"—was purchased by the Penns from the Iroquois. But in trying to get ahead of the Calverts in Maryland, the agreement the Penns signed angered the Shawnee and the Delaware, who felt their lands had been illegally sold out from under them. From that time on the two offended tribes began drifting away from the influence of Pennsylvania and frequently were involved in fights with settlers.

Before 1736, the region west of the Susquehanna contained only about 400 people who paid taxes to Pennsylvania. After the treaty of 1736, things quickly changed and the lands surrounding Codorus Creek filled up with both Scotch-Irish and Germans. The two groups frequently fought among themselves, usually on election day, until the formation of Adams County in 1800 separated the two sides.

Monocacy Path, from Wrightsville to Frederick, Maryland, crossed over Codorus Creek at the city of York, and then followed it upstream, crossing again at Spring Grove. The trail was one of the main routes carrying settlers from Pennsylvania through Maryland, Virginia and North Carolina to the Cumberland Gap and Kentucky. Travelers even had a little ditty they sang about the path.

Me and my wife and my wife's pap,
We walked all the way to Cumberland Gap.

Hanover, just west of Codorus Creek, was the site of the first Civil War battle fought north of the Mason-Dixon Line. It occurred on June 30, 1863, when Confederate General James E.B. Stuart's cavalry rode into the town as a division of Union cavalry was leaving. The Union commanders, including one George Armstrong Custer, were at the head of their column about three miles northeast of the town when the firing started. While one unit of the division wheeled and charged back into Hanover, Custer set up artillery on a hill north of town. Eventually, the fight involved some 11,000 men who charged and counter-charged through the streets of Hanover. It ended at nightfall when Stuart withdrew. Only about 100 Confederate and 200 Union soldiers were killed or wounded in the fight, but it stopped Stuart from reaching Gettysburg in time to aid General Lee.

Anglers interested in staying near Codorus Creek can find camping accommodations at Codorus State Park. This popular 3,320 acre park has a Class A campground with 198 sites available from the second Friday in April through the third Sunday in October. The campground includes hot showers, flush toilets, water and a dump station.

For family members who do not fish, the park offers boat rentals (pontoon boats, rowboats, canoes, paddleboats and motorboats) on 1,275 acre Lake Marburg, hiking, picnicking, swimming in one of the largest pools in the nation (Memorial Day weekend to Labor Day), and environmental education programs.

Lake Marburg is a joint project of the state of Pennsylvania and the P.H. Glatfelter Paper Co. in Spring Grove. The undertaking was one of the first of its kind in the state, in that it is designed to serve both the private needs of the paper company and the public need for recreation. The $5.5 million dam on the West Branch Codorus Creek was built by the paper company and still belongs to it.

Codorus State Park can be reached by following the signs off Route 116 and Porters Siding. Further information may be had by writing: Codorus State Park, Department of Environmental Resources, R.D. 3, Box 118, Hanover, PA 17331.

Fly anglers should find some success on Codorus Creek with Adams, caddis, Hare's Ears, Hendricksons, Mickey Finns, Muddler Minnows, Matuka Streamers, Blue-Winged Olives, Soft Hackle Nymphs, March Browns, Renegades, Gray Fox, Light Cahills, Lead-Winged Coachman, midges and terrestrials.

Conewago Creek
Fly Fishing Only
Opossum Creek
Adams County

Conewago Creek

Mason and Dixon Line. Without a doubt it is the most famous political boundary in the United States. Far more than simply the

dividing line between Pennsylvania and her neighbors to the south—Maryland and West Virginia—it is the difference between the North and the South. Part history, part state of mind, part legend. The mere mention of its name is guaranteed to conjure up images of the Blue and the Gray.

Although the Mason and Dixon Line will be forever tied to the Civil War—some people even believe the southern anthem, "Dixie," was named after Jeremiah Dixon, one of the surveyors—the boundary actually was laid to settle a much earlier dispute. One that had its roots all the way back in the seventeenth century around the time of Pennsylvania's founding, and involved the lands on the west bank of the Susquehanna River and its tributary, Conewago Creek.

In 1701, the Conestoga, Shawnee and Conoy Indians entered into an agreement with William Penn in which they promised not to allow "any Strange Nations of Indians to Settle or Plant on the further side of Sasquehannah, or about the Potowmeck River. . .without the Special approbation and permission of the said Willm. Penn, his Heirs and Successors." The problem with this treaty was that New York claimed to have purchased the land on the far side of the Susquehanna down to Washinta, or the falls on Conewago Creek from the Iroquois in 1684, while Maryland

Fly Fishing Only on Conewago Creek.

said it purchased the area from the Susquehannas, or Conestogas, 30 years before that in 1652.

New York dropped out of the picture when it sold the land, property which Penn had already paid the Indians for once, to Pennsylvania. Maryland was not so quick to give up its claim, though, and as late as 1727 made a grant of 10,000 acres in the Conewago Valley to John Diggs. This warrant, known as "Diggs Choice in the Back Woods," was a constant source of trouble for claimants to the land under Pennsylvania warrants. It was finally solved in 1763 when the Privy Council in England hired Jeremiah Dixon and Charles Mason to survey a boundary between the two colonies, a boundary that was finished in 1767.

Conewago Creek, translation "at the rapids," covers nearly 70 miles, but only about 14 of those miles are stocked with trout. They extend from U.S. Route 15 south of the village of Heidlersburg, upstream beyond the village of Arendtsville. But the stretch is, without doubt, the prettiest of the entire stream. It starts as a small collection of pocket water in a hemlock-shaded gorge of big, grey boulders and ends as a medium-sized flat-water stream amidst beautiful farms, quiet forests and a receding view of Blue Ridge Mountain.

Access to Conewago Creek's upper water may be had by following Pennsylvania Route 234 (Buchannan Valley Road) east off U.S. Route 30 east of Caledonia State Park (see Conococheague Creek), and toward Bridgeport and Arendtsville. Route 234, which turns into Narrows Road, trails the stream into Bridgeport, and then crosses it east of Arendtsville. Some access also is available off Winging Road and Brysonia Road. But anglers should be careful of posted property.

Fly fishermen can find Conewago Creek's Fly Fishing Only Project by continuing east on Route 234 to Pennsylvania Route 34 in Biglerville. The project runs from Route 34 south of Biglerville, upstream for about one mile to the bridge on Russell Tavern Road (Township Road 340). It can be reached directly off Route 34, but parking is difficult and traffic heavy. The upper portion of the special regulation water can be found by taking either Goldenville Road or Zeigler Mill Road off Route 34. Goldenville Road is joined by Russell Tavern Road less than a mile off Route 34. Russell Tavern is marked by both a sign and a large stone house which was once, what else, Russell's Tavern. George Washington slept in the tavern in October of 1794.

Russell Tavern Road is not marked by a sign on Zeigler Road, but it is the first road to the left. Bridge 86 is easily visible from Zeigler Mill Road, so the stream is almost impossible to miss.

Downstream of Biglerville, Conewago Creek can be located off Rake Factory Road across from Zeigler Mill Road on Route 34, as well as Pennsylvania Route 394 which crosses over the stream. Brookside Lane appears at the Route 394 bridge and parallels the stream to Rentzel Road. A left turn on Rentzel Road leads down to the creek.

The bottom portion of Conewago's stocked water flows through State Game Lands 249. It can be found by taking Route 234 to the village of Heidlersburg. At the crossroads in the center of the village take Old Harrisburg Road (or Old Route 15) south toward Gettysburg. The road crosses the stream about a mile outside of town. Parking is available at a game lands lot.

Along with stocked browns, rainbows and brook trout, Conewago Creek reportedly holds a good population of wild browns. Fly hatches also are said to be good, particularly Blue-Winged Olives from about mid-April to early June, and Sulphurs from about mid-May to mid-June. Fly anglers also should find success with such traditional patterns as the Quill Gordon, Hendrickson, caddis, March Brown, Gray Fox, Light Cahill, midges and terrestrials. Streamers and nymphs produce good throughout the season. Possible patterns include: Muddler Minnow, Mickey

Finn, Matukas (brown, gray, black and olive), Hare's Ears and Soft Hackle Nymphs.

Opossum Creek

Beginning on Bear Mountain northwest of the village of Bendersville, Opossum Creek is the main tributary of Conewago Creek. About seven miles of the creek, from its mouth upstream, are stocked with rainbow and brown trout. The upper three miles also is said to have a good population of wild browns. But catching them is another story entirely. Clear, fast water makes Opossum Creek a tough stream to fish, especially late in the season.

Access to Opossum's upper water is available directly off Pennsylvania Route 34 east of Bendersville. The lower water can be reached off Pennsylvania Route 234 east of Biglerville. Old Carlisle Road runs off Route 234 about a half-mile before it crosses over the stream and toward the village of Center Mill. It leads to some upstream portions of the creek and, eventually, Route 34.

Center Mill Road, which also appears on Route 234, but after it crosses the stream, is another access road leading upstream. Stone Jug Road lies opposite of Center Mill Road, and leads to the mouth of Opossum Creek.

Fly fishermen can try some of the same patterns listed for Conewago Creek.

Anglers can get a good feel for the lay of Conewago Creek by sending for the "Public Use Map" of Michaux State Forest. The forest lies just west of the stream's headwaters, as does Caledonia State Park with its Class A campground (see Conococheague Creek).

Marsh Creek
Little Marsh Creek
Adams County

Marsh Creek

Undercut banks and log jams help tiny Marsh Creek maintain reproducing populations of brown and brook trout to spice up its usual quota of stocked fish. Banks lined by meadows, brush and big woods help it maintain a diverse character with a little something for just about every angler's taste, while good numbers of mayflies and caddisflies help guarantee some of the best trout fishing in all of Adams County. Fish from two to four pounds are said to be caught on a regular basis.

U.S. Route 30 is one of south central Pennsylvania's main arteries and the departure point for Marsh Creek. The stream is stocked only on the north side of Route 30 from about the village of Seven Stars upstream toward the village of Hilltown. Access is available by taking Crooked Church Road, Old Flohrs Church Road, Pine Valley Road or Fairview Fruit Road off Route 30 east of Caledonia State Park. Hilltown Road off Old Flohrs Church Road also leads to the stream.

The brushy banks that help Marsh Creek sustain a population of wild trout can also cause real headaches for fly fishermen. But anglers who do not mind losing a few flies can try Quill Gordons, Hendricksons, Blue-Winged Olives, caddis, March Browns, Gray Fox, Light Cahills, Sulphurs, midges and terrestrials. Fly fishermen also can try such impressionistic patterns as the Adams, Royal Coachman, Hare's Ear, Muddler Minnow, Mickey Finn, Matuka Streamers and Woolly Buggers.

Little Marsh Creek

The main tributary of Marsh Creek, Little Marsh Creek, is

stocked with browns and rainbows for approximately seven miles centering around the village of Orrtanna. Its upper stretches, which also hold some native brookies, is mostly rocky pocket water surrounded by mountain laurel and woods. Below Orrtanna the creek widens a bit and takes on more of a meadow character with brushy banks.

Little Marsh can be located by following the sign for Orrtanna off Route 30 near Hilltown, or Pennsylvania Route 116 near the village of Fairfield. The upper portion of the stream can be found along Jacks Road off Huhy Road in Orrtanna. Knoxlyn-Orrtanna Road across from the fruit plant in Orrtanna meets Railroad Lane (Township Road 346), which leads to the stream.

Patterns mentioned under Marsh Creek also should produce on Little Marsh Creek.

Middle Creek
Toms Creek
Adams County

Middle Creek

Brown and rainbow trout are stocked over a seven-mile stretch of Middle Creek centering around Pennsylvania Route 116 and the village of Fairfield. Aquatic insect life is said to be good and hatches heavy, considering the small size and shallow depth of the stream.

Like a number of other streams in Adams County, Middle Creek has something of a dual personality. Its upper half, starting at its source on the eastern slope of Green Ridge Mountain, has a mountain flavor of woods and fast water, while its lower portion takes on the meandering, bushy-banked characteristics of a meadow stream.

Besides the change in scenery and gradient, the lower half of Middle Creek is different from the upper because of the limestone influence it picks up in the valley around Fairfield. This added alkalinity helps to maintain the stream's flow and temperature, and sustain a good population of aquatic insects. Hatches are said to be steady and relatively heavy into the summer. The bushy banks sometimes make for tough casting, however.

South of Route 116 Middle Creek can be reached taking Bullfrog Road about a half-mile east of Fairfield off Route 116. The road follows the stream, though it is usually out of sight. Township Road 318 mets Bullfrog Road and leads to a bridge over the creek. It also marks the downstream end of the stocked water.

Middle Creek's upper water is accessible by following the signs for Mt. Hope off Route 116 east of Fairfield. This road, Mt. Hope Road, parallels the stream as it nears Mt. Hope.

Fly anglers can try such traditional patterns as the Adams, Quill Gordon, Blue Dun, Hendrickson, Hare's Ear, Muddler Minnow, March Brown, caddis, Blue-Winged Olives, Royal Coachman, Gray Fox, Light Cahill, Sulphurs, midges and terrestrials.

Toms Creek

A typical brook trout stream of fast pocket water, Toms Creek is one of the heaviest stocked streams in Adams County. It also contains some native brook and brown trout, but they are generally few and far between.

The lower portion of Toms Creek's seven miles of stocked water can be reached along Route 116 southeast of Fairfield, while its upper water can be found by taking Iron Springs Road off Route 116 near Fairfield. Fly fishermen can try some of the same patterns suggested for Middle Creek.

Gettysburg National Military Park, site of the greatest battle

ever fought on American soil, and Abraham Lincoln's immortal "Gettysburg Address," is located less than 10 miles from both Middle Creek and Toms Creek along Route 116. To describe what the town and park have to offer and the battle would take a book in itself, and has already taken hundreds. Let it suffice to say any angler who is in the area and has never visited Gettysburg is, some of the gaudier attractions aside, missing out on a truly enriching experience in American history.

No state parks are near Middle Creek or Toms Creek. However, there are countless private facilities of every type surrounding Gettysburg. Anglers also might request a "Public Use Map" of Michaux State Forest. The map gives a good overview of both Toms Creek and Middle Creek. It may be had by writing:

District Forester, Michaux State Forest, Department of Environmental Resources, 10099 Lincoln Way East, Fayetteville, PA 17222.

East Branch Antietam Creek
Fly Fishing Only
West Branch Antietam Creek
Franklin County

Sitting at the northern end of Virginia's famous Shenandoah Valley, south central Pennsylvania saw more action during the Civil War than probably any other northern state. Gettysburg, of course, was the great pivotal battle of the entire war. It was the "high water mark" of the Confederacy. Signs carrying the slogan in fact, dot the battlefield today, pointing out the furthest reach of Confederate power in the war.

But Gettysburg was not the only Pennsylvania town to suffer during the Civil War. Hanover to the east in York County was the scene of the first battle fought north of the Mason and Dixon Line. It took place on June 30, 1863, when Confederate General J.E.B. Stuart's calvary rode into town just as a division of Union calvary, including George Armstrong Custer, was leaving. The Union troops immediately wheeled about and attacked the Confederate troops. Some 11,000 troops ended up taking part in the engagement, which seesawed back and forth through the streets of the town until Stuart withdrew at nightfall.

The battle left only about 300 casualties on both sides, 100 Confederate and 200 Union, but it prevented Stuart from reaching Gettysburg until the day after the major fighting began on July 1. As a result, General Robert E. Lee was deprived of the "eyes of his army," and eventually lost the battle.

A skirmish also was fought on the southern outskirts of Harrisburg, a few days before the Battle of Gettysburg and, in 1864, Chambersburg was burned to the ground by Confederate troops, possibly in reprisal for the abolitionist John Brown having lived there before his raid on the U.S. arsenal at Harpers Ferry, Virginia.

Waynesboro, named after Revolutionary War hero General "Mad" Anthony Wayne, and sitting between the East Branch and West Branch of Antietam Creek, was another Pennsylvania town that saw Confederate troops in its streets. General Jubal A. Early entered the town on July 23, 1863. Instead of burning it or fighting in its streets, however, he only ordered the town's housewives to bake bread for his troops.

The word Antietam appears to be of Indian origin, but its meaning is now unknown, according to Dr. George Donehoo, author of *A History of the Indian Villages and Place Names in Pennsylvania*. But it will live as long as there is a United States because of the Battle of Antietam along the main stream in Maryland. As Gettysburg was the greatest battle ever fought in

North America, Antietam was the bloodiest single day in the history of the nation.

Pennsylvania holds only a tiny piece of the main branch of tietam Creek, but the entire length of both its East Branch and West Branch. Both streams are stocked with trout for about seven miles centering around Waynesboro.

East Branch

Generally considered to be the better of the two streams as far as trout fishing is concerned, the East Branch of Antietam Creek can be reached directly off Pennsylvania Route 16 on the east side of town. Weltz Road, across from Wayne Heights Mall, leads to the police station and Renfrew Museum, where parking is available for the stream's Fly Fishing Only Project. This special regulation water stretches for one mile downstream to the bridge which crosses the stream.

Renfrew Museum was given to the borough of Waynesboro by Mrs. E.A. Nicodemus, and was funded by her and Hazel Gieser. It occupies a site where legend has it the Renfrew sisters were killed by Indians in 1764. A stone farmhouse in the 107-acre park serves as the museum, holding a large collection of pre-1830 American home furnishings. It is open April through December on Thursdays, Saturdays and Sundays from 1 to 4 p.m., and by appointment at other times. The park contains a half-mile of the East Branch's Fly Fishing Only water and plenty of parking.

The East Branch's upper water can be found by following the signs for the village of Roadside along State Route 2007 off Route 16 on the east side of town. The road meets the creek about mile outside of town and parallels it into Roadside.

Fly anglers should find some success with such patterns as the Blue Dun, Adams, Quill Gordon, Hare's Ear, Muddler Minnow, Woolly Bugger, Soft Hackle Nymphs, caddis, Hendrickson, March Brown, Gray Fox, Royal Coachman, Lead-Winged Coachman, Light Cahill, midges and terrestrials.

West Branch

Like the East Branch, the West Branch Antietam Creek is accessible directly off Route 16, but, of course, on the west side of Waynesboro. It is marked by an old cast iron marker which makes it difficult to miss. Cold Spring Road (Township Road 366) appears a short distance to the west of the stream along Route 16 and provides access to some of its lower stocked water.

Upstream of Waynesboro, West Branch Antietam Creek can be found along Pennsylvania Route 316, which can be picked up off Route 16 and crosses over the stream between Waynesboro and the village of Five Forks.

Above Route 316, Pennsylvania Route 997, which again can be picked up off Route 16 in Waynesboro, parallels the West Branch from south of the village of Quincy upstream all of the way to its headwaters. Fly anglers can try some of the same patterns mentioned under the East Branch.

On its way upstream, Route 997 passes 24-acre Mount Alto State Park, Pennsylvania's first state park. Facilities are limited to picnicking, but adjacent to it is the oldest tree nursery in the state. Covering only 15 acres, it has an annual production of more than 2,000,000 trees. Also in the vicinity is the Michaux State Forest arboretum with 600 varieties of trees, both native and foreign to the state.

A "Public Use Map" of Michaux State Forest, named after the French botanist Andre Michaux and his son, Francois Andre Michaux, shows the route of both the East Branch and West Branch. It may be had by writing:

District Forester, Michaux State Forest, 10099 Lincoln Way East, Fayetteville, PA 17222.

Conococheague Creek
Franklin County

John Brown's body lies a-moulderin' in the grave.
John Brown's body lies a-moulderin' in the grave.
John Brown's body lies a-moulderin' in the grave.
His soul goes marchin' on.
Glory, Glory Halleluja. . ."

Anybody who has ever seen a movie about the Civil War probably has heard the song about the abolitionist John Brown. His raid on the federal arsenal in Harpers Ferry, Virginia (now West Virginia) is one of the most famous protest actions in the history of the United States. The picture of the bearded, anti-slavery fanatic, rifle in hand and dark eyes ablaze, is one of the most recognizable images of the entire Civil War period. His story is as well known as *Uncle Tom's Cabin,* the novel that Abraham Lincoln once said started the war. And on top of that it's true.

While even people with only the vaguest knowledge or interest in the Civil War have heard of Brown and Harpers Ferry, very few realize he planned his raid on the arsenal from Chambersburg, Pennsylvania on the banks of Conococheague Creek.

Brown, who came to be considered a martyr in the North and criminal in the South, was born in Torrington, Connecticut in 1800. He spent his boyhood years in Ohio and from a very early age became an ardent abolitionist, even operating an Underground Railroad station in Richmond, Ohio. But he was never much of a businessman. He failed in numerous business ventures, and was never able to provide his family, including some 20 children, with any type of financial security. He actually gained no prominence at all until he was well past 50 years of age.

In 1855, five of Brown's sons moved to the Kansas Territory. Their purpose was to aid the Free State cause which was then embroiled in a bitter and bloody struggle with settlers who wished to admit Kansas into the Union as a Slave State. The sons were soon followed by their father, who loaded his wagon with arms and settled in Osawatonie, Kansas. He worked as a surveyor and served as a captain in the militia, and earned the title "Old Brown of Osawatomie" after he led the successful defense of the town against pro-slavery forces.

The sack of Lawrence, Kansas by pro-slavery men drove Brown into a frenzy. Accompanied by four of his sons and two other men he attacked a small pro-slavery settlement on the Pottawatomie River in the spring of 1856. Calling himself an instrument in God's hands, he and his band killed five men in the raid.

Brown's reputation, enhanced by subsequent guerrilla attacks, spread across the country after the Pottawatomie River action. Late in 1857, he began enlisting men for his cause and in 1858 chaired a meeting in Chatham, Canada where plans were laid to establish a free mountain state in the wilderness of Maryland or Virginia. The following year, he began collecting funds from abolitionist sources to buy arms.

Calling himself a prospector, Brown moved to Chambersburg in the summer of 1859. He set up headquarters in a two and a half story limestone house at 225 King Street. And shortly afterwards started receiving large boxes labeled "tools," but that were in reality filled with carbines. These were then moved to a small farm in Maryland from which Brown, with 21 of his followers, moved to seize the Harpers Ferry arsenal on October 16, 1859.

Two days after the arsenal was seized, and after 13 of Brown's men, including two of his sons, had been killed, Brown surrendered to a mixed company of U.S. Marines and the Virginia

Militia, under the command of Colonel Robert E. Lee. Convicted on charges of treason, Brown was hanged, after riding to the gallows on his coffin, on December 2, 1859.

Chambersburg was to be touched by the violence of the Civil War period more directly five years after Brown's raid. Enraged by a Federal raid on Virginia's Shenandoah Valley, Confederate troops descended on the town on July 30, 1864. When they left most of the town was a smoking ruin. Some historians believe the ferocity of the attack may have had something to do with Brown living in the town prior to his raid on Harpers Ferry.

Concocheague Creek bends around Chambersburg on the north and west. It is a corruption of the Indian phrase Guneukitschik, meaning "indeed a long way," and lives up to its name by covering some 71 miles from its source on South Mountain at Caledonia State Park east of Chambersburg to its confluence with the Potomac River in Williamsport, Maryland. Only about 20 of those miles, however, from the park to the borough of Chambersburg, are stocked with trout. But they are very heavily planted, with over 24,000 browns and rainbows, and very popular. In fact, Conocohheague Creek is one of the most heavily fished streams in Franklin County.

Like other waterways in south central Pennsylvania's old and beautiful Cumberland Valley, Conococheague Creek is a highly civilized stream. Access is available along a network of secondary roads running off U.S. Route 30, Pennsylvania Route 997 and U.S. Route 11.

On Conococheague Creek.

Caledonia Park, along the stream's headwaters, can be easily found along Route 30 east of Chambersburg. Downstream of the park, and off Route 30, the Conococheague can be reached: off Pennsylvania Route 997 Bridge in the village of Mount Union; at Township Road Bridge in the village of Fayetteville; Mount Pleasant Road Bridge west of Fayetteville; Woodstock Road (Township Road 520) in the village of West Fayetteville; and 606 about midway between Fayetteville and the village of Stoufferstown.

The Conococheague can be located off Route 997 between Mount Union and the villages of Scotland along Coldsprings Road, Brookens Road and Mount Pleasant Road. Cook Road (Township Road 509) runs off Mount Pleasant Road and joins Woodstock Road, all of which provide access and lead to Route 30. Between Interstate Route 81 and Scotland, 606 also appears off Route 997 and leads to the stream, paralleling it down to Woodstock Road. In addition, the stream can be located off the bridge in Scotland.

Route 11 parallels and crosses Conococheague Creek between Chambersburg and Route 997. Three small dams appear on the creek from Scotland downstream to Chambersburg: a two-footer at Scotland; a seven-footer (Siloam Dam) four miles below Scotland and a seven-footer on Commerce Street in Chambersburg.

Conococheague Creek's stocked water is generally fast and rocky. A beautiful hemlock grove frames the stream in Caledonia State Park and corn fields, dairy herds and well kept farms at portions below it. Too many mobile homes, quarries and logged over hills, however, appear as the stream nears Chambersburg.

From the second Friday in April through the end of the antlerless deer season in mid-December, Caledonia State Park offers fishermen who would like to stay in the area a 191-site Class A campground with flush toilets, hot showers and a dump station.

Anglers with non-fishing family members along, will be pleased to know the park holds an abundance of diversions, possibly more than any other state park in Pennsylvania. Besides the usual picnic facilities and hiking trails (including a section of the Appalachian Trail), it has a large swimming pool open from Memorial Day weekend to Labor Day, an 18-hole public golf course and a summer stock theater, the Totem Pole Playhouse. In addition, there are environmental education programs, guided hikes, campfire programs and a historical center maintained by the Pennsylvania Historical and Museum Commission in the Thaddeus Stevens Blacksmith Shop.

Caledonia State Park takes its name from Thaddeus Stevens' Caledonia Iron Furnace, which, in turn, was named after Caledonia County, Vermont where Stevens was born. Caledonia also is the ancient Roman name for Scotland.

Thaddeus Stevens is generally touted as the father of public school education in Pennsylvania. He moved to the state from Vermont as a young man and practiced law in Gettysburg for several years, where he gained a reputation as a champion of the underprivileged, and free education for all. In 1837, he built Caledonia Furnace with an eye to providing employment for the poor. He also became an abolitionist, fighting against slavery by granting asylum, providing legal assistance to runaway slaves, and serving as the defense attorney in the first case in which blood was shed in resistance to the Fugitive Slave Law.

The incident occurred further east in Chester County. Runaway slaves belonging to Maryland farmer Edward Gorsuch were found hiding in the cabin of William Parker near Coatesville in 1851. When Gorsuch, his son and a deputy U.S. Marshall appeared at Parker's cabin with a warrant a disturbance broke out. Neighbors began to appear, threats were exchanged and, finally,

Gorsuch and his son shot. Parker and 37 others were put on trial for treason following the incident. Stevens, who was then Lancaster's delegate to the House of Representatives, was called in to defend the accused. He was so eloquent in his argument that the jury returned a "not guilty" verdict after only 15 minutes of deliberation.

Stevens' anti-slavery stand led to the destruction of Caledonia Furnace by Confederate troops in June 1863, shortly before the Battle of Gettysburg. During and after the battle the fields which now serve as the park's playgrounds were used as dressing stations for the wounded.

During the Civil War and Reconstruction Period, Stevens served as the majority leader in the U.S. House of Representatives. He was responsible in large part for much of the controversial legislation of the time

The Pennsylvania Alpine Club reconstructed the stack of the old furnace in 1927. That structure and the rebuilt blacksmith shop are all that now remain of the iron works. Caledonia Park is one of the oldest and most popular state parks in Pennsylvania. It was first operated privately and then later by local transportation companies as an amusement park, according to the "Recreational Guide." The Virginia Indian Path, from Harrisburg to Winchester, Virginia, once crossed Conococheague Creek at Scotland and followed it south to its mouth.

Fly anglers might try such patterns as the Adams, Quill Gordon, Hare's Ear, caddis, Hendrickson, Renegade, Royal Coachman, Lead-Winged Coachman, Soft Hackle Nymphs, Muddler Minnows, Woolly Buggers, Black Gnat, March Brown, Light Cahill, midges and terrestrials, as well as other traditional patterns.

Falling Spring Run
Limestone Springs Wild Trout Waters
Franklin County

If the Letort is a sort of derelict black sheep of south central Pennsylvania's limestone country, the Yellow Breeches the confused but friendly cousin and Big Spring the damaged sister, Franklin County's Falling Spring Run is the gentle, dazzling younger brother.

Ernest Schwiebert in his all-encompassing two volume work *Trout* says Falling Spring Run offers possibly the best rainbow trout fishing in the eastern United States. If not going quite that far, every other angling author who has fished Falling Spring Run has had nothing but praise for its character, fish and hatches. The list sounds like an honor roll of Eastern fishing writers: Charlie Fox, Vincent Marinaro, Charles Meck, George Harvey, Gerald Almy, Ed Koch and so on.

One look at Falling Spring Run and it is quickly apparent what has drawn all of these people. The stream along which Benjamin Chambers, for whom nearby Chambersburg is named, once lived is truly a beauty. Full of elodea and watercress, surrounded by the gentle pastures of well-tended farms and overlooked by lush cornfields, perhaps only Big Spring Creek presents a more classic limestone setting (even if year by year more houses appear along the stream).

But it is Falling Spring's wonderful hatches and colorful rainbows that most interest visiting anglers. The Fish Commission discontinued stocking the stream's special regulation water a number of years ago. The trout present there today are all stream-bred, wild and wary. They are descendants of the landlocked

Shasta River strain of rainbow, so lack a strong migratory instinct, and Falling Spring Run is one of the very few streams on this side of the Mississippi River to hold them.

To complement its lovely rainbows, Falling Spring offers some of the most marvelous, and demanding, dry fly fishing to be found anywhere in the country. Hatches of mayflies are very good, with different species emerging regularly from March through December, and even during warm, sunny days in January and February.

Baetis, or olives, are the earliest mayflies to appear on the stream. They occur in the most numbers in March and April, and then again in October. Rainy, overcast days are said to bring the most fly activity. Blue-Winged Olives, No. 18-No. 20, are recommended.

Sulphurs start as the olives are ending in the spring and continue on through June. Several species are present, and hatching generally occurs in the late afternoon and evening. Cloudy weather will make its start earlier, sunny weather later. A variety of sulphur imitations, No. 14-No. 18, are suitable.

The third major hatch to appear is the Tricorythodes. And it is this tiny, No. 26, black and white mayfly that lives only a couple of hours after hatching which really supports Falling Spring's reputation. It is tough, demanding dry fly fishing, not meant for anglers who are easily frustrated, that lures hordes of fishermen to Falling Spring's banks from July through August. The hatch, in reality a spinner fall, starts between 8:30 and 9:30 a.m. Then the "tricos" fill the air above the stream setting the fish into a dimpling, feeding rhythm that can continue well after the swarm disappears. There are few experiences in fly fishing capable of providing as much satisfaction as landing a 15 inch or larger wild trout on a No. 26 "trico" and 7X tippet.

Tricorythodes action usually ends somewhere around noon. Most fishermen then disappear until the evening when some sulphur action might occur. That is, except for a couple knowledgeable ones. For the middle of the day on Falling Spring Run often holds some fantastic terrestrial fishing. Ants, red and black, usually appear about the same time as the olives and continue to be available to the fish on through November, while beetles, small grasshoppers and crickets provide good action during the summer months. So, the fisherman who does not mind sweating in 90-degree or more heat can really get to know this gem of a limestoner while everybody else is having a beer and wondering about the evening's White Fly hatch on the Yellow Breeches.

Falling Spring Run's Limestone Springs Wild Trout Waters Project extends for 2.4 miles from the area of route Township Road 544 downstream to the wire fence crossing the Robert E. Gabler farm near Interstate Route 81. It can be reached by taking the Lincoln Way Exit 6 off Interstate 81 at Chambersburg and turning east on Route 30. Turn right onto State Route 2029 immediately east of the Interstate 81 overpass. The next three paved roads to the left lead to the stream. The first road leads to the lower end of the project, and also a swimming hole. The second road to roughly the middle of the special regulation water, and the third to the upper reaches. Parking along the second road is very limited.

The Virginia Path, from Harrisburg to Winchester, Virginia, once crossed Falling Springs near its mouth. Also known as the Potomac Road and the Great Trail, the path was well used by both the Indians and European settlers. It was the easternmost war path used by the Iroquois during raids against the Cherokee and Catawba tribes in the Carolinas.

(Also see Conococheague Creek.)

109

Letort Spring Run
Limestone Spring Wild Trout Water
Cumberland County

England has its Test and Itchen; we, on this side of the Atlantic, have "The Letort." No other single trout stream in the United States, and few in the world, has had as much written about it as Letort Spring Run. So widely known is this tiny four-mile long limestone stream in Carlisle, Cumberland County, that it borders on legend. The mere mention of its name in fly fishing circles inspires a sort of reverence, sometimes hushed, just as often profane. Travel to trout water around the country and one of the first things anglers most often want to know when they learn you are from Pennsylvania is: "Have you ever fished the Letort?" Famed angling author Ernest Schwiebert even entitled one of his articles "Legend and the Letort."

Limestone beauty.

Most of the stream's fame is owed to two men—Vincent C. Marinaro and Charles K. Fox. Together, they conducted a series of experiments in the late 1940s that changed fly fishing forever. Their work led to an understanding of the importance of both terrestrials and midges in the trout's diet, as well as their acceptance as fly fishing methods. Already a classic, Marinaro's book *A Modern Dry Fly Code* is undoubtedly due to become one of the few angling books from the twentieth century to be read a hundred years hence, while Fox's *The Wonderful World of Trout* and *Rising Trout* remain a must for any well-read angler of today.

Despite all of its notoriety, Letort Spring Run—named after early eighteenth century French trader and trapper James LeTort, who had a log cabin near the head of the stream—rarely draws much fishing pressure. Apparently, all of the tales of tiny flies and ultra-selective and skittish brown trout scare off the majority of anglers. Yet, with a little caution, and an accurate cast of maybe 40 feet, it is quite possible to catch a Letort trout or two. For along with the legendary five-pounders, there are plenty of fish in the 12-inch to 18-inch class in the stream.

In all likelihood, a first-time visitor to the Letort will probably spend most of his time looking for rise forms, a technique that will more often than not see him go home disappointed or frustrated. For even if he catches a fish, it will not be one of those that provided the inspiration for Marinaro or Fox, but almost surely a small one of under 12 inches. For the Letort does not provide the predictable surface action of neighboring limestone waters.

Fishing on the Letort is much more a subsurface affair, a search for "tailing" trout, rooting in the elodea and watercress choked banks and channels for cress bugs, scuds and freshwater shrimp. The trout shake these small aquatic insects free of the weeds and then drift downstream in the quiet current to dine. It is an energy-efficient way of feeding that helps the big fish get the most for their money. A shrimp, scud or cress bug pattern drifted to them while they are in this position is one way to achieve success, even through the winter months.

Mayfly hatches do occur on the Letort, but are not spectacular. Sulphurs, in sizes No. 16 through No. 20, occasionally offer some surface action. But the best dry fly fishing, as Marinaro and Fox long ago discovered, is with terrestrials. Ants first appear in April and sometimes in mating flights in August, and provide the best chance at some surface action. Beetles, crickets and grasshoppers also are effective. The Letort Hopper and Letort Cricket did not earn their names without reason. Grasshoppers are fished during bright midday periods, while crickets work well at dawn and dusk.

But for the first-time visitors the midday is not the time to test the stream. Dawn, after the fish have been undisturbed for several hours, seems to be the best time of the day, followed by dusk, when lines and leaders do not cast such a frightening shadow over the surface.

In the end, though, matching the mood of the Letort and its fish is more important than the hatch. Tailing trout are ready to take cress bugs, scuds or shrimp. All three occur in abundance in the stream, and the fish are not extremely picky about which one they eat first. The big secret is to get an imitation down to their depth without sending them running for cover. Even fish that have shown an interest in surface food are more apt to take something drifting straight toward them below the surface where they don't have to expose themselves. It is a simple matter of survival for a wild fish that has never known a hatchery tank.

Despite all of its fame, the Letort is not the simplest of southcentral Pennsylvania's limestone streams to find. Its 1.5-mile long Limestone Springs Wild Trout Water Project extends from about 300 yards above the Township Road 481 bridge downstream to the Reading Railroad Bridge at Letort Spring

Park in Carlisle. It can be reached by following Pennsylvania Route 34 south (Hanover Street) Exit 14 off Interstate Route 81 at Carlisle. From the exit, drive south for about one mile to Bonnybrook Road, and then left on Bonnybrook Road, which leads to the stream.

The Letort lies behind a housing plan and is bordered on the other side by railroad tracks and other trappings of industrialized America. But it is out of sight of the road and parking is scarce, except in the area of the Interstate 81 Bridge, which crosses the stream almost in the exact spot where Marinaro's and Fox's fishing hut once stood.

Both the Frankstown Path and the New Path touched on the Letort during the colonial period.

Frankstown Path, which ran from Harrisburg on the Susquehanna River to Kittanning on the Allegheny River, was the heaviest traveled path over Pennsylvania's mountains. It was used by Indians, traders and settlers. The Iroquois used it on their way to raid Cherokee and Catawba villages in the Carolinas. Colonel John Armstrong used it in his expedition against Kittanning following the massacre at Fort Granville. Kittanning was a famous gathering spot for war parties, and the place where prisoners from Fort Granville were taken to be tortured.

The New Path, from Middlesex to Shirleysburg, was a feeder trail for the Frankstown Path, and a short cut between Harrisburg and Shirleysburg. It was much used by traders and crossed the Letort near its mouth.

Carlisle, on the banks of the Letort, has a long and colorful history going all of the way back to Pennsylvania's colonial days. James Le Tort was the first European to settle in the Cumberland Valley. He established a trading post along the stream which now bears his name sometime before 1720. The town of Carlisle was laid out in 1751 and named Carlisle after the county seat of Cumberland County, England.

Land on which the town stands was originally reserved for the Indians, but sold to the Penns by chiefs of the Six Nations of the Iroquois Confederacy. Several Indian treaties were signed in the town that played a large part in shaping the province. One of the treaties, the Treaty of Amity and Friendship of 1753, was obtained from the Indians by withholding rum from them until they signed.

Throughout the colonial and Revolutionary War period, the town served as an outfitting and launching point for numerous military expeditions. Colonel Armstrong launched his attack against Kittanning in 1756. Two years later, General John Forbes mounted his successful bid to capture Fort Duquesne (Pittsburgh) from the French. In 1763, Colonel Henry Bouquet gathered his troops in Carlisle to suppress Pontiac's Rebellion. Ten days after the Battle of Bunker Hill, a regiment of riflemen was commissioned and formed in the town by none other than John Hancock. The troops arrived in Boston only hours behind another from York, Pennsylvania, and together the two units became the First Regiment of the Continental Army, and the first troops west of the Hudson River to join Washington's force.

James Wilson, Thomas Smith and George Ross, three signers of the Declaration of Independence, were Carlisle residents. Molly "Pitcher," heroine of the Battle of Monmouth, where she supplied the colonial troops with water, also lived in the town. James Buchanan, Pennsylvania's only president of the United States, graduated from Dickinson College in the town.

For several decades before the Civil War, Carlisle was an active stop on the Underground Railroad, ferrying runaway slaves to Canada. In June 1847, it was even the scene of a riot that broke out when two slaveholders from Maryland entered the town in search of three runaways.

Confederate General Fitzhugh Lee entered the town with 5,000 troops on July 1, 1863. Part of J.E.B. Stuart's army, he had hoped to find General Robert E. Lee in Carlisle. Instead, he encountered a Union force and ended up battling it in the streets of the town. When word arrived that a major battle had begun at Gettysburg, the Confederate troops burned the U.S. Army barracks on the edge of Carlisle (now the U.S. Army War College) and galloped off to join the bigger fight to the east.

Carlisle Indian School, the first non-reservation Indian school in the nation, was founded in the town in 1879. Its most famous graduate was Jim Thorpe. An old Indian graveyard still exists within the War College grounds.

Big Spring Creek
Limestone Springs Wild Trout Water
Cumberland County

A more picturesque limestone stream than Big Spring Creek near Newville, Cumberland County is impossible to imagine. From just below its source, and the Fish Commission hatchery at the village of Springfield, downstream to the mill along Pennsylvania Route 641, Big Spring Creek is a postcard photographer's dream come true. Everywhere are classic elodea and watercress beds, flat, gliding pools, pastures and farm buildings anglers have come to associate with the limestone country of south central Pennsylvania. The only thing missing is an abundance of fish.

Although still a stream worth visiting for the experience, Big Spring Creek today is a far cry from the water whose praises were once sung by none other than Theodore Gordon, the spiritual godfather of American fly fishing. "I wish that it was possible to revisit all our old haunts during the best portion of the season. . ." he wrote in a 1907 issue of *Forest and Stream*. "In June I have seen the water covered with the dimples made by rising trout as far as my view extended. This was in the evening after the sun was off the water, in Big Spring, a large spring which flows through Newville, Pennsylvania."

Former *Pennsylvania Angler* editor and well-known author Charlie Fox is another who, years later, also cherished the stream. He devoted an entire chapter of his 1967 book, *Rising Trout,* to Big Spring, dubbing it "The Commonwealth's Gem." This from the man who so loved and was so fascinated by Letort Spring Run, he purchased a stretch of it to insure its survival.

What has happened to bring about the change in the years since Gordon and Fox wrote about Big Spring seems to center around the construction of a sprawling trout hatchery at its source. Wild, stream-bred trout will not live downstream of a hatchery, and so have disappeared, killed or driven off somewhere by something in the water coming from the hatchery troughs. The Fish Commission has taken steps to correct the problem, but what is left today is a relatively short stretch of water immediately below the hatchery discharge pipe containing several hundred brook trout.

Downstream of the Thomas Dam, which marks the end of the brook trout water, Big Spring is said to hold some large browns and rainbows, 20 inches and over, but they are next to impossible to find. It takes a good pair of polarized sunglasses and a lot of patient watching. It is not a situation for a beginner or a person who craves action.

Besides the scenery, Big Spring is interesting from a historical point of view because of its connection to people like Gordon and Fox, and the fact it was the second stream, or section of stream, in Pennsylvania to be purchased and preserved for the public by the Fish Commission. The first such water was the Fisherman's

Paradise area of Spring Creek (see which) in Centre County, another trout water that has seen better days.

Big Spring's Limestone Springs Wild Trout Water Project reaches 1.1 miles from about 100 yards below its source, the area of the discharge pipe, downstream to Strohm Dam. It can be reached by taking Interstate Route 81, Newville, Route 223 Exit, and following it to Pennsylvania Route 11, then taking Route 11 south for about four miles. Turn right at the small Fish Commission sign announcing the hatchery and continue on to the project. The town of Newville and its scenic grist mill and dam may be reached by continuing on Big Spring Road, which parallels the stream and then taking Pennsylvania Route 641 toward Carlisle.

At one time, both the Virginia Path, from Harrisburg to Winchester, Virginia, and the Frankstown Path, from Harrisburg to Kittanning on the Allegheny River, crossed Big Spring.

Named for Frank Stevens, owner of a trading post near Holidaysburg, the Frankstown Path was the most important and frequently traveled Indian trail across the Pennsylvania mountains. In early colonial days, it was the preferred route of the Indian traders. Conrad Weiser, the best-known emissary between the Indians and colonial officials, traveled it to western Pennsylvania. During the French and Indian War, Colonel John Armstrong used it to attack the Indian war base at Kittanning.

The Virginia Path was the easternmost war path of the Iroquois on their raids against the Cherokee and Catawba in the Carolinas. It also was used by settlers heading south through the Cumberland Gap and on to Kentucky.

For the fisherman who elects to give this tough little stream a try, fly patterns that are said to produce the "best" include red and black ants, the Adams, the Blue Dun, olive midge pupae, shrimp, scuds and the sculpin. In addition, there is a small, bottom dwelling "redworm," imitated by some red floss or silk wrapped around the shank of a hook, that flushing of the hatchery's troughs carries into the stream. All of the patterns, except of course the sculpin, are tied small, No. 20 through No. 26 or even No. 28.

Green Spring Creek
Fly Fishing Only
Cumberland County

Back when the Indians were "Lords of the Forest," they had a marvelously simple habit of naming streams in a descriptive manner. If a river or creek flowed for a long distance, its name would reflect that fact. So we have Conococheague Creek, translation "indeed a long way." If it was full of twists and turns, then that was what its name revealed. As a result, there is the Youghiogheny River, meaning "circuitous stream" or "winding stream."

Although many of the old Indian names are still in use around Pennsylvania, numerous others have disappeared, giving way to the Europeans' habit of naming streams for historic figures, early settlers and the remembered places of their homelands. There are a few streams, though, that have managed to cross this linguistic dividing line between the two cultures. Among them tiny Green Spring Creek in western Cumberland County.

Covering just three miles from its source to its junction with giant Conodoquinet Creek, Green Spring Creek is a milk-tinted little limestone water framed by old, drooping willows, wild pastures and lush overgrown banks that literally engulf it in the color green throughout the summer months. When mixed with a scattering of dairy cows, a redheaded woodpicker at work and the occasional Amish buggy, it makes a picture worthy of any central Pennsylvania postcard. And much better looking than almost all of the area's more hallowed limestone waters. No subdivisions of overpriced sameness mar this stream's beauty. At least not yet.

But it is not all looks either. Along with its innocence, Green Spring Creek also offers some fine fishing, as good as any of its neighbor's regulars often claim (though the fish tend to be on the small side). Yet it attracts surprisingly few anglers. Throughout the latter part of summer, when fishermen from the entire eastern

Green Springs Creek.

United States are flocking to Falling Springs and the Yellow Breeches, it is unusual to encounter more than two other fishermen on Green Spring Creek. And frequently there is nobody at all in sight.

Exactly why Green Spring draws so little attention, while its sister limestoners are being overrun, probably is because it does not offer any single outstanding hatch. It has a decent sulphur hatch in late spring and some "Trico" action in the summer, along with good terrestrial fishing, but nothing to compare to the Yellow Breeches' White Flies or Falling Springs' Tricorythodes. Its fish also are not as visible or free-rising as the inhabitants of those waters. Instead of casting from one rise form to another, the angler who elects to try Green Spring will have to rely a lot more on his, or her, ingenuity and inventiveness to catch fish.

Along with its lack of a truly outstanding hatch of aquatic insects, Green Spring Creek's popularity also suffers from its seemingly isolated location. Sitting just off Pennsylvania Route 641 west of Newville, the nearest town with an abundance of amenities, such as motels, restaurants and bars, is Shippensburg, about 15 miles away. Still, for the angler seeking some solitude during his stay in the limestone country, Green Spring Creek is a viable alternative.

While it might feel remote, Green Spring Creek in reality is not very far off the beaten path. Actually, it is just down the road from famous Big Spring Creek and, like it, accessible by taking the Newville Exit 11, Pennsylvania Route 223, off Interstate Route 81. Follow Route 223 all of the way into Newville and then turn left onto Route 641 west toward Newburg. Continue on Route 641 for roughly five miles to Bulls Head Road (Township Road 398). Turn right onto Bulls Head Road, which parallels the stream. Green Spring Creek's one mile long Fly Fishing Only Project starts about a quarter of a mile down the road on the former C.F. Beckner property.

Besides tricos, sulphurs and terrestrials, fly anglers also might try streamers, Soft Hackle Nymphs, Hare's Ears, Adams, Royal Coachman, March Brown, Light Cahill and some of the other traditional Pennsylvania patterns mentioned in this book.

Fransktown Path, the most important Indian path across the Pennsylvania mountains, once crossed Green Spring Creek at the village of Green Spring. The trail ran from Harrisburg to Kittanning. It was frequently used by traders, as well as Colonel John Armstrong in his attack on Kittanning, a once famous gathering place for Indian war parties on the Allegheny River. Colonel Armstrong attacked the village to avenge the massacre of settlers at Fort Granville in the summer of 1756.

(Also see Big Spring Creek.)

Sherman Creek
Perry County

Arcing across pretty Perry County northeast of Harrisburg, Sherman Creek offers some 18 miles of trout fishing for not only stocked browns and rainbows, but also native brook trout in its upper reaches in Tuscarora State Forest. The stocked water runs from west of the village of New Germantown along Shearer Dug Trail in the forest, downstream to the village of Centre.

Pennsylvania Route 274 is the main access road to Sherman Creek's stocked portion. It parallels the stream from west of New Germantown east to the village of Loysville. Numerous roads run off Route 274 and across the stream, including: Township Road 302, State Route 3004, Mt. Pleasant Road (Township Road 391), Three Springs Road, State Route 3005, Adams Grove Road, Madison Road (Township Road 399), State Route 3009 at Cisna Run and Hidden Valley Road at Center.

At New Germantown, Sherman Creek is a mere brook. By Blaine, however, several tributaries have added their flow, enlarging the stream to a respectable size. As the stream leaves the state forest lands and enters farm country, it also picks up a limestone influence that improves its fertility and aquatic insect population. Fly fishermen should find success with such standard patterns as the Muddler Minnow, Black-Nosed Dace, Woolly Buggers, Hare's Ear, Adams, caddis, Blue-Winged Olive, Hendrickson, March Brown, Gray Fox, Light Cahill, Renegade, Royal Coachman, Lead-Winged Coachman, midges and terrestrials.

During the colonial period, the New Path, from Middlesex to Shirleysburg, followed Sherman Creek from about Shermandale to Fort Robinson near Loysville. As a short cut on the busy Frankstown path between Harrisburg and Shirleysburg, the New Path was heavily used by traders in the mid-eighteenth century.

Fowlers Hollow State Park and Big Spring State Park both lie west of New Germantown in easy reach of Sherman Creek anglers. Big Spring covers 45 acres, and is named for a nearby spring, said to be the second largest in Pennsylvania, and a source for Shermans Creek. The park area was once extensively timbered to supply local tanneries, barrel manufacturers and charcoal furnaces. Recreational opportunities include picnicking and hiking. The park is located about 5.5 miles southwest of New Germantown along Route 274.

Fowlers Hollow State Park is a 104-acre recreational area that once held a sawmill. It was served by the Perry Lumber Co. Railroad, which left the park to the state. It also is located along Route 274 near New Germantown. It has an 18-site, Class B campground open from the second Friday in April to mid-December. Facilities are limited to pit toilets, water, fireplaces, and picnic tables. Hiking and picnicking are available for guests.

Both Big Spring and Fowlers Hollow are listed in "The Thirty Best Kept Secrets of Pennsylvania's State Parks," meaning they are under utilized, translation uncrowded.

Anglers who do not mind driving a little further also can camp at Colonel Denning State Park, along Pennsylvania Route 233. Colonel Denning is a 273-acre park in Cumberland County with a 64-site Class B campground open year round. It also contains picnic areas, a nature center, children's playground, swimming at a guarded beach, from Memorial Day weekend to Labor Day, a visitor's center and hiking trails on ten miles of trails.

Colonel Denning State Park is named after Colonel William Denning, a War for Independence hero. The colonel, who lived near Newville, invented an iron cannon for which the English offered a large sum of money. Unbelievably in this day when greed knows no boundary, Colonel Denning refused the English offer and, instead, made cannons for the rebels. His earthly remains now rest in the graveyard of the Big Spring Presbyterian Church in Newville. The park became a state recreational area, under the control of the Bureau of Forestry, around 1930 and was developed by the Civilian Conservation Corps in 1936. It is situated in "Doubling Gap," so named because of the "S" turn Blue Mountain makes, doubling back on itself.

Details on all three parks may be had by writing: Colonel Denning State Park, R.D. 3, Box 2250, Newville, PA 17241.

Conodoquinet Creek
Franklin County

On a map, Conodoquinet Creek resembles a serpent; its thin tail buried deep in Franklin County, its thickening body wriggling its way northeast across Cumberland County to bite the Susquehanna River opposite Harrisburg. From the perspective of paper it is also easy to see that the Indians had once again chosen the perfect name for a stream. Conodoquinet has been translated to mean ''for a long way nothing but bends'' or, less poetically, ''long winding river'' or ''a crooked creek.''

Altogether, Conodoquinet Creek covers over 80 miles, from its source between Kittatinny and North Mountain, to its mouth on the Susquehanna. But only the headwater portion, from the village of Roxbury on Pennsylvania Route 997, upstream roughly ten miles is stocked with trout. The terrain is rugged, remote and quite pretty, with hemlock and rhododendron surrounding a clear-water little stream of sand and cobble bottom. A few hunting camps and lonely farms are the only touches of civilization in the narrow valley. State Games Lands 76 and 235 make sure there is plenty of public water. Anglers should be aware, though, that reaching it normally requires a bit of a hike.

Frankstown Path, from Harrisburg to Kittanning on the Allegheny River, followed the stream over much of its length during the colonial period. Sometimes called the Allegheny Path or Ohio Path, this Indian trail was the most important and frequently used road across Pennsylvania from the time of William Penn until after the Revolutionary War.

Conodoquinet Creek at the dam.

In early colonial days, the Frankstown Path was the preferred route for Indian traders running pack trains into the Ohio Valley. James Le Tort, whose name famous Spring Run bears; Peter Chartiers, who lent his name to a stream and town in southwestern Pennsylvania; and Andrew Montour, whose name lives on in the form of Montoursville in Lycoming County, all lived and traded along the stream. Conrad Weiser, the noted colonial ambassador to the Indians, traveled the path on his journey to a conference with the Indians at Logtown on the Allegheny in 1748. He even stopped to describe the body of a man he found who had been killed by a bear on the trail. During the French and Indian War the trail was used by Colonel John Armstron for his attack on the Indian town of Kittanning.

Besides holding a main travel route, the lands between Conodoquinet Creek and Yellow Breeches Creek (see which) to the south figured prominently in dealings with the Shawnee.

Prior to 1730, the majority of the Shawnee had departed the lower Susquehanna Valley for the Allegheny River. Because the Shawnee were always restless and ready to fight, provincial authorities did not like the idea of the tribe being so far away from the English influence. Hoping to lure them back, in 1731, they laid out a tract of land ''between Conegogwainet & Shaawna (Yellow Breeches) Creeks five or six miles Back from the River. In Order to Accommodate the Shaawna Indians or such others as may think fit to Settle there.''

Shawnee chiefs declined the offer of land, but the tract caused problems for settlers in the region when it was made a political issue in a conflict with the Quakers and Governor James Logan. The troubles occurred in 1755 when the Shawnee went on the warpath. The Quakers maintained, falsely, that the hostilities were the result of the governor allowing settlers to move into the region without purchasing it from the tribe when its chiefs demanded payment at the Treaty of Carlisle in 1753. But the Shawnee had never made such a demand. The hostilities were actually part of the series of Indian attacks that swept the frontier after General Edward Braddock's defeat in the Battle of the Monongahela that summer.

Conodoquinet's stocked water can be reached by taking Pennsylvania Turnpike Exit 15 and following Route 997 into Roxbury. Pennsylvania Route 641 west meets Route 997 in Roxbury. It parallels the creek upstream to Letterkenny Reservoir.

Horse Valley Road (Township Road 556) meets Route 641 above the dam. It follows the Conodonquinet beyond the dam, but the water is out of sight. About six miles upstream of Route 641 a road with a bridge appears on the left. Another two and a half miles beyond that road, Keefer Road appears and leads down to the creek. Otherwise, it's a hiking situation.

Fly anglers should find some success with the Adams, Quill Gordon, Blue Dun, Muskrat, Hare's Ear, Muddler Minnow, Woolly Buggers, Matuka Streamers, Mickey Finn, Hendrickson, stoneflies, Blue-Winged Olive, March Brown, Royal Coachman, Lead-Winged Coachman, Gray Fox, Renegade, caddis, Soft Hackle Nymphs, Light Cahill, midges and terrestrials.

West Branch Conococheage Creek
Franklin County

Paralleling almost the entire length of the western boundary of Franklin County, West Branch Conococheage Creek, translation ''indeed a long way,'' in many ways resembles the main Conococheage Creek, particularly in its lower reaches. Its water is often flat, shallow and rather slow moving, surrounded by the usual farms, pastures, corn fields and scrubby woods typical of south central Pennsylvania's agricultural valleys.

West Branch Conococheague Creek's stocked water runs from Fort Loudon on U.S. Route 30 upstream beyond Pennsylvania Route 641. Access is off Pennsylvania Route 75, which can be picked up either off Route 30 at Fort Loudon, or Pennsylvania Turnpike Exit 14 at Willow Hill. The stream's upper water can be reached by following Route 75 north through the village of Willow Hill. About a quarter-mile past the Fannett-Metal High School a secondary road (45-SP-E) will appear on the right and lead down to a bridge that spans the creek.

Township Road 566 appears on the other side of the bridge. Anglers can follow it under the Turnpike to a second bridge. That bridge leads to Township Road 560, which intertwines with the West Branch all of the way downstream to the village of Fannettsburg. A small dam that once turned a water wheel for a crumbling hydroelectric plant also appears at Fannettsburg.

Below Fanettsburg, access to the West Branch is available directly off Route 75. Wineman Road loops off the highway and leads to an odd, double-decker bridge across the creek. At the village of Metal another short road appears and leads to the stream.

Around the village of Richmond Furnace, West Branch Coconocheague Creek picks up some volume and gradient that adds a bit of riffle to its water. The scenery becomes wilder, too. Woods and pretty views of nearby mountains abound.

Tuscarora Path, from North Carolina to Sunbury, once followed the West Branch from Mercersburg north beyond Willow Hill. The trail was so heavily used the Valley of the West Branch even became known as "Path Valley." After their last great settlement in North Carolina was destroyed near the beginning of the eighteenth century, the Tuscarora Indians, meaning "hemp gatherers," traveled the path on their way north to seek refuge among their Iroquois kin.

Fort Loudon, at the downstream end of the stocked water, was founded in 1795. But settlement of the region actually began almost 40 years before. It started when Colonel John Armstrong erected a crude fort near the present town and named it after the Earl of Loudoun, who, for a short period, served as commander of all British forces in the colonies.

In its early years, the Valley of the West Branch formed a sort of buffer between the more densely settled sections of eastern Pennsylvania and the Indian country of the West. During periods of uprisings, the full force of Indian hostilities were regularly directed against the settlements in the valley. The remoteness of the area often required the settlers to defend themselves with little or no help from the British forces. Merchants from Philadelphia aggravated the situation with the Indians by sending pack trains loaded with everything from beads to rifles through the valley. Neglect by the British and the greed of the merchants eventually led to a revolt of sorts by settlers in the Valley of the West Branch some ten years before the Battle of Lexington.

In the summer of 1764 an Indian raid on a settlement a few miles below Fort Loudon left nine children and their schoolmaster dead. In March 1765, a pack train of 83 horses, carrying what was described as "King's goods" to the Forks of the Ohio (Pittsburgh), entered the valley. When the homesteaders found out the goods actually belonged to a Philadelphia firm bent on reopening trade with the Indians, they sent a delegation to plead with the traders to turn back. When the traders refused to change their plans one of the settlers, James Smith, decided to take matters into his own hands.

Smith had been a prisoner of the Indians for five years prior to his moving to Fort Loudon, and so had a personal reason for stopping the traders. He gathered a small band of volunteers

together. They disguised themselves as Indians and attacked the pack train at Sideling Hill west of Fort Loudon, destroying almost the entire consignment before troops from the fort could reach the scene. The British troops did manage to capture eight of Smith's "Indians," but later released them in exchange for soldiers kidnapped by Smith and his followers.

The action did little to change the attitude of either the British troops or traders in Philadelphia. After a number of other incidents involving pack trains and British troops, Smith and 300 other settlers actually laid seige to Fort Loudon, eventually forcing the entire garrison to withdrawal. The Pennsylvania Historical and Museum Commission today maintains a park on the site of the old fort just off Route 30.

Mercersburg, which lies on the West Branch Conococheague Creek south of Fort Loudon, and outside of the stream's stocked water, once was an important link in the chain of stations used to ferry runaway slaves from the South to Canada in the years prior to the Civil War. Some historians even point to it as the source for the term Underground Railroad.

The narrow passes between surrounding North Mountain, South Mountain and Cove Mountain, plus the town's close proximity to the Mason-Dixon Line, made Mercersburg an ideal location for abolitionist activities in the 1840s and 1850s. The secret, tangled trails running from the town into the mountains above it so frustrated slave hunters they complained about the ground "swallowing up" their quarry. One even declared "there must be an underground road somewhere," a phase that caught the public's fancy and evolved into the term Underground Railroad.

The area around Mercersburg, named like Mercer County in western Pennsylvania for General Hugh Mercer, a soldier and physician during the War for Independence, also saw some bloodshed over the slavery issue. It happened when a group of fugitive slaves decided to fight instead of run. They ended up killing one slave hunter and wounding two others. At least one group of blacks decided to stay in the area and not move further north. They formed a settlement called "Africa."

Cowans Gap State Park is available for anglers who would like to stay in the area. It has a 260-site Class A campground, with dump stations, flush toilets and hot showers, opened from the second Friday in April to the end of the doe season in mid-December. It also has ten family cabins available in the spring, summer and fall. The three-room cabins have a four-person overnight capacity. They contain a refrigerator, stove, fireplace, two bunk beds and a water faucet outside. Details on cabin rentals may be had from the park office.

For non-anglers, the park has a swimming beach, open from Memorial Day weekend to Labor Day, rowboat and paddleboat rentals on 42-acre Cowans Gap Lake, picnic areas and environmental education programs—including nature walks, slide shows, historical tours and campfire activities. Ten miles of hiking trails, among them a portion of the Tuscacora Path, pass through the park and surrounding Buchanan State Forest.

Cowans Gap Park can be reached by taking Richmonds Road off Route 75 at Richmond Furnace (also see Little Aughwick Creek).

Fly anglers on the West Branch Conococheague Creek should find success with the stream's browns and rainbows by using such standard patterns as the Muddler Minnow, Woolly Bugger (black, brown and olive), Matuka Streamers, Soft Hackle Nymphs, Hare's Ear, caddis, Adams, Blue Dun, Hendrickson, March Brown, Royal Coachman, Light Cahill, Lead-Winged Coachman, midges and terrestrials.

Further information on Cowans Gap State Park and Buchanan State Forst is available by writing:

Cowans Gap State Park, Department of Environmental

Resources, Star Route North, Fort Loudon, PA 17224.

Buchanan State Forest, District Forester, R.D. 2, Box 3, McConnellsburg, PA 17233.

Little Aughwick Creek
Fulton County

Land disputes between the Indians and European settlers is a story as old as America itself. By writing the rules and then changing them when they didn't fit their needs, the settlers, of course, won in the vast majority of cases. But in a few instances, the Indians did manage to obtain at least a degree of justice. Among those times was the Burnt Cabin episode on Little Aughwick Creek.

The village that now bears the name Burnt Cabins was established by a group of "squatters" who moved into the area during the first half of the eighteenth century. The Iroquois, who still owned the land, demanded time and again the settlers move. Provincial officials issued numerous proclamations ordering all whites to leave the territory, but were just as often ignored. Finally, at the Council of the Iroquois in Philadelphia in 1749, the government was forced to take firm action. Accompanied by magistrates from Cumberland County, representatives of the province went to each home along Little Aughwick Creek, as well as other locations, and ordered the inhabitants to leave, then burnt their cabins.

While no Indians were actually living around Burnt Cabins when the first settlers appeared, Aughwick, on the site of present day Shirleysburg along Aughwick Creek, was a long established Indian village. In the years following the burning of the cabins, the territory played a prominent role in the Indian affairs of the province. Several famous Indian leaders, including Queen Aliquippa, who befriended George Washington in his travels through western Pennsylvania, moved into the region and used it as their headquarters.

Prior to General Edward Braddock's 1755 campaign to drive the French from Fort Duquesne (Pittsburgh), a representative of the British made a trip to Aughwick to try to recruit Indians for the army. About 40 Indians agreed to join the campaign and traveled to Fort Cumberland in Maryland to meet Braddock's troops. Because of problems involving the British soldiers and Indian women, though, all but seven braves soon returned to Aughwick.

After Braddock's defeat on the banks of the Monongahela River, all of the Indians friendly to the British made Aughwick their refuge. In the fall of that year, Fort Shirley was erected on the site.

"This stands near the great path (Frankstown Path) used by the Indians and the Indian traders, to and from the Ohio, and consequently the easiest way of access for the Indians into the Province," Governor Robert Morris noted.

In August of 1756, Colonel John Armstrong used the fort as a staging area for his attack on Kittanning, an Indian town along the Allegheny River. At the time Kittanning was used both as a gathering place for war parties to plan attacks on settlements and as a sort of prison camp where captives were taken to be tortured or, sometimes, adopted. Colonel Armstrong's attack ended with the destruction of the town.

Little Aughwick Creek, translation "little brushy creek," is a far quieter place today. It is a typical Pennsylvania ridge and valley mountain stream running along the top of Tuscarora

Mountain to eventually join the Juniata River in northeast Huntingdon County. It is stocked with brown trout along a distance of over 18 miles, starting on its South Branch at Cowans Gap State Park and continuing upstream beyond Burnt Cabins to the Huntingdon County Line. The majority of the stocked water can be reached by taking Pennsylvania Turnpike Exit 13, Fort Littleton, then Pennsylvania Route 522 north to Burnt Cabins and following the signs for Cowans Gap State Park. Route 522 touches on Little Aughwick near the turnpike exit, and Allen Valley Road to the park parallels its South Branch, at varying distances, on the right all of the way into the park, about five miles away. Since almost the entire South Branch flows through Buchanan State Forest there is no problem with posted property.

South Branch Aughwick Creek also may be reached off U.S. Route 30 between McConnellsburg and Chambersburg. A sign for the park appears at the summit of Sideling Hill. Aughwick Road, which appears at the summit, parallels the stream on the left from just outside of the park.

Cowans Gap State Park has a 260-site, Class A campground with dump station, flush toilets and hot showers open from the second Friday in April until the day after the antlerless deer season in mid-December. It also has ten family cabins with refrigerator, stove, fireplace and two sets of bunk beds to accommodate four people. There is no indoor plumbing, but a water faucet is located outside. The cabins are available in the spring, summer and fall. Rental information may be had from the park office.

For those visitors who don't fish, or the off-hours, the park has a swimming beach, open from Memorial Day weekend to Labor Day, boat rentals on 42-acre Cowan Lake, picnicking, ten miles of hiking trails, environmental education programs and a food concession.

The park takes its name from Major Samuel Cowan, a British soldier who fell in love with the daughter of a Boston merchant during the Revolutionary War. Because her father supported the colonist, Major Cowan was forbidden to see his love and returned to his home in England alone. But he could not forget his American sweetheart. After the war he returned to Boston and the couple eloped to Chambersburg.

The Cowans remained in Chambersburg for a few years until the urge to move West overcame them. Like two more famous Pennsylvanians—Daniel Boone and John Jacob Audubon—they decided to move to Kentucky. The Cowans' journey ended far short of the Bluegrass State, though. The family made it only as far as the next county when their wagon broke down and they sold it to the Indians in exchange for the land which became Cowans Gap State Park in 1937, when the Civilian Conservation Corps built the first recreational facilities.

Long before the park, the land on which the Cowans settled was an important part of the Raystown Path, the major southern Indian trail between Harrisburg and Pittsburgh.

Possible flies to try include: Adams, Hare's Ear, caddis, Hendrickson, stoneflies, Lead-Winged Coachman, Renegade, Light Cahill and terrestrials.

Further information on Cowans Gap State Park may be had by writing: Cowans Gap State Park, Department of Environmental Resources, Star Route North, Fort Loudon, PA 17224.

Cove Creek
Roaring Run, Spring Run
Fulton County

Cove Creek

Easy access off U.S. Route 522 and Pennsylvania Route 928 helps to make Cove Creek (sometimes also called Big Cove Creek) the most popular trout stream in Fulton County. Stocked from south of McConnellsburg through the villages of Webster Mills and Big Cove Tannery, Cove Creek offers a combination of meadow and woods fishing in its upper portion that changes to mostly forest by the time it empties into Licking Creek. Along with Route 522 and Route 928, most of the secondary roads running off those two highways lead to this medium-sized stream. These side roads are mostly unmarked, but generally include all those running to the west.

McConnellsburg was laid out along the banks of Cove Creek in 1786 by Daniel and William McConnell. "Squatters," however, began moving into the area in the 1730s and 1740s. The presence of these early Europeans did not sit well with the Indians, who never sold the land to the colony until 1758, and they were frequently attacked by war parties. In 1755, emboldened by the defeat of General Edward Braddock in the Battle of the Monongahela outside Pittsburgh, an Indian raiding party killed or captured more than half the 93 families living around McConnellsburg. Two years later, a force of colonial militia also was annihilated by local tribes.

Fly choices for Cove Creek and its tributaries might include: Adams, Hendrickson, caddis, March Brown, Soft Hackle Nymphs, Muddler Minnows, Woolly Buggers, Hare's Ear, Light Cahill, Sulphurs and terrestrials.

Roaring Run

Roaring Run feeds Meadow Grounds Lake, Fulton County's only warmwater fishing spot. It is stocked with trout both above and below the lake for 4.5 miles through State Game Lands 53. Access may be had by following State Route 1003 off either U.S. Route 30 west of McConnellsburg, or Route 522 south of the town. Follow the signs for the lake and the game lands. A dirt road leads to the stream both above and below the lake. Bear Trail, which appears on the west side of the stream at the dam, follows Roaring Run downstream.

Access to the lower stocked water of this Cove Creek tributary is available by taking Township Road 372 off Route 522 midway between Webster Mills and Big Cove Tannery. Traveling south from McConnellsburg, T-372 runs to the right.

Spring Run

Cove Creek's other planted tributary, Spring Run can be found by again taking Route 522 south through McConnellsburg. Route 522 parallels the stream for a short distance just north of Webster Mills. Above the village, Spring Run and its 2.5 miles of trout water is reachable along Township Road 381 toward the village of Cito.

On the other side of Tuscarora Mountain from Cito in Franklin County is Buchanan's Birthplace Historical State Park. The 18-acre park and its pine grove mark the birthplace of James Buchanan, fifteenth president of the United States, and the only one from Pennsylvania. The site of the cabin where Buchanan was born is today covered by a 25-foot high stone pyramid, called Stony Butler. Buchanan was born in 1791 and, along with serving as president from 1857 to 1861, also spent time in the U.S. House of Representatives, the Senate and as ambassador to England and Russia. He is not highly regarded as a president, some historians even pointing to his policies as part of the reason for the Civil War.

The park is located off Pennsylvania Route 16 between Mc-Connellsburg and Mercersburg. Facilities are limited to some picnic areas and comfort stations. Details may be had by writing: Park Superintendent, c/o Cowans Gap State Park, Fort Loudon, PA 17224.

While never touching on Cove Creek or its tributaries, Buchanan State Forest still surrounds the stream. Anglers can obtain a free "Public Use Map" that will help them find not only Cove Creek and its tributaries, but also several other trout streams, by writing: District Forester, Buchanan State Forest, R.D. 2, Box 3, McConnellsburg, PA 17233.

(Also see West Branch Conococheague Creek, Conodoquinet Creek and Little Aughwick Creek.)

Blacklog Creek
Huntingdon and Juniata Counties

Sandwiched between Blacklog Mountain on one side and Shade Mountain on the other, Blacklog Creek cuts a straight path down skinny, pastoral Blacklog Valley to join Aughwick Creek near the village of Orbisona. It is stocked with brown trout over a distance of 17 miles, from Orbisona upstream through southern Huntingdon County into Juniata County. Some natural reporduction also may occur in its upper stretches, but most of the fish are hatchery bred.

Located off the beaten path, away from any main highways, Blacklog Creek is reportedly one of the most underfished trout streams in Huntingdon County. Access is available by taking U.S. Route 522 and turning onto State Route 2017 near Orbisona. The creek can be reached at many points near the road, but those spots also are the most heavily fished areas. As might be expected, the pools that require some walking generaly hold the better fishing.

Fly fishermen might try such traditionally productive Pennsylvania patterns as the Quill Gordon, Blue Quill, stoneflies, Hendrickson, March Brown, Gray Fox, Sulphurs, Light Cahill, caddis, Blue-Winged Olive, Lead-Winged Coachman, and terrestrials.

Tucked away in its rugged, backwater valley, Blacklog Creek has never played an important role in Pennsylvania history. But Frankstown Path, from Harrisburg to Kittanning on the Allegheny River, did pass over it. A spot near Orbisona even served as a "sleeping place," or campground, along the trail.

Somewhat longer than the equally famous Raystown Path, Frankstown Path for a time was "by far" the more important and frequently traveled Indian path across Pennsylvania's mountains. It was named after Frank Stevens who operated a trading post at Frankstown in Blair County. Colonel John Armstrong used the path during his expedition against the Delaware Indian's war gathering place at Kittanning in 1756. Conrad Weiser, noted early explorer of Pennsylvania, also traveled the path and, as recorded in *Indian Paths of Pennsylvania* by Paul A.W. Wallace, had at least one unusual encounter along it in 1748.

"Found a Dead Man on the Road who had killed himself by Drinking too much Whiskey; the place being very stony we cou'd not dig a Grave—He smelling very strong we covered him with Stones & Wood." But the grave did not last long. On his return he found "the bears had pulled him out and left nothing of him but a few naked bones and some old rags."

Honey Creek
Kishacoquillas Creek
Mifflin County

Honey Creek

Paralleling the southern edge of Bald Eagle State Forest through the agricultural New Lancaster Valley, Honey Creek may be better known as a geological attention-getter than a trout stream. What makes it so unusual is its leaky limestone base, which at low water periods actually takes the stream on an underground detour through Alexander Caverns near the village of Shrader northeast of Reedsville. The opening is through a debris clogged channel near an old lime plant.

Its oddities aside, Honey Creek is a trout stream of some merit, holding both stocked and wild brook and brown trout from its junction with Kishacoquillas Creek at Reedsville upstream toward the Snyder County line. Caddis and sulphurs provide good fly fishing action during May and June. Other flies an angler might try on this little stream include such traditional patterns as the Adams, March Brown, Hendrickson, Light Cahill, Hare's Ear, midges and terrestrials.

Reeds Gap State Park lies astride Honey Creek about six miles northeast of Reedsville and U.S. Route 322. Only 220 acres in size, the park has 16 Class B, tent-only, campsites with flush toilets. Sites are available on a first come, first served basis from the second Friday in April to the third Sunday in October.

For the non-fishing visitor and the off-hours, Reeds Gap offers a 4,000 square foot swimming pool. It is open from Memorial

Day weekend to Labor Day, but usually closed on weekdays until the middle of June. There also are four picnic areas, about four miles of hiking trails and an environmental education program.

Indians from the village of Ohesson (Lewistown) used the New Lancaster Valley as a hunting grounds long before the white man appeared on the scene. In the late eighteenth century the Reeds Gap area was used as a "bush meeting ground," where local settlers gathered to hear circuit preachers and socialize. The practice continued well into the 1920s, according to the park's "Recreational Guide."

Around the middle of the nineteenth century, Edward Reed built a sawmill along Honey Creek near the western boundary of the park. Part of the old dam which powered the mill is still visible along the Honey Creek Trail. About 1900 a steam-powered sawmill, which was located in the maintenance building, took over the lumbering operation. The state purchased the land on which the park sets in 1904, after all of the timber had been depleted. Civilian Conservation Corps members from a camp further up the valley worked building pavilions, fireplaces, tables, toilets and playgrounds in the park through the 1930s. The swimming pool was added in 1965.

Reeds Gap State Park, the only state park in Mifflin County, can be reached by following the signs for seven miles off Route 322 from Milroy. New Lancaster Valley Road parallels Honey Creek from Locke Mills through the park and on up towards its headwaters.

Information on the park may be had by writing: Reeds Gap State Park, Department of Environmental Resources, R.D. 1, Box 276-A, Milroy, PA 17063-9735.

Details on neighboring Bald Eagle Forest, including a valuable map, are available by writing: District Forester, Bald Eagle State Forest, P.O. Box 111, Mifflinburg, PA 17844.

Residents.

Kishacoquillas Creek

In 1755, in the wake of General Edward Braddock's defeat on the Monongahela River outside of Pittsburgh, Governor Robert Morris ordered the construction of a number of frontier forts, including one along Kishacoquillas Creek. Word of the completion of Fort Granville about one mile north of Lewistown was received on January 29, 1756. It lasted only six months. On July 30, 1756 it was destroyed by Indians under the command of a French officer. Twenty-two men, three women and several children were taken as prisoners to Kittanning, a gathering place for war parties and holding area for prisoners on the Allegheny River in Armstrong County. The destruction of Fort Granville and capture of these prisoners filled the entire frontier with fear and sent settlers scurrying for the security of more settled areas.

Lined by the well-kept farms of the gentle Amish, Kishacoquillas Valley is a far safer place today. And still quite beautiful. After passing near a factory and some big farms around the town of Belleville, the stream enters a gorge bordered by the slopes of Jacks Mountain on one side and wide, expansive pastures leading up to Stone Mountain on the other.

Access to Kishocaquillas Creek may be had by taking Pennsylvania Route 655 south off U.S. Route 322 at Reedsville. Even though Route 655 parallels the stream over its entire stocked length, from Reedsville upstream almost to Allensville, Kishocaquillas Valley's size often puts it out of sight of the road. Side roads do run off Route 655 to the creek at various points, however. These include: Taylor Mill Road, Spring Run Road, Kishocaquillas Avenue and Walnut Street.

According to Dr. George Donehoo in his *A History of Indian Villages and Place Names in Pennsylvania,* the name Kishocaquillas, as translated by early explorer John Heckewedler, may be a corruption of Gisch-achgook-wailieu which means "the snakes are in their dens." It also could have been named for "Kissikah-quelas," a Shawnee chief friendly to the English who once lived at the village of Ohesson on the Juniata River into which Kischocaquillas Creek flows.

Besides the traditional patterns mentioned for Honey Creek, Sulphurs from late May to the middle of June are good, and Slate Drake patterns such as the Lead Winged Coachman through the summer.

Standing Stone Creek
East Branch Standing Stone Creek
Laurel Run
Huntingdon County

Few streams anywhere can offer such a good variety of trout fishing experiences as Standing Stone Creek. Through its upper portions in Logan State Forest on the Huntingdon/Centre County line it holds a mixture of stocked and native brook trout in a mountain setting of rhododendron, pine and hemlock. Below McAlveys Fort, its character is altered by the addition of some limestone springs to its flow, and its setting changes from mountains and forests to meadows and flat farmlands. Browns and rainbows also take over as the predominant species.

Access to the greatest part of Standing Stone Creek's 31½ miles of stocked water may be had along Pennsylvania Route 26 north off U.S. Route 22 in the town of Huntingdon. Route 26 both crosses and parallels the stream, at varying distances, all of the way from Huntingdon to McAlveys Fort. Generally speaking, any side roads running off to the right lead to the stream.

At McAlveys Fort, State Route 1023 meets Route 26 on the right and follows Standing Stone Creek upstream into Rothrock State Forest. Anglers who choose to fish the stream's upper water, and enjoy the feel of big woods, should make certain they continue into the Alan Seeger Natural Area of the forest. There they will find a tiny, laurel shrouded Standing Stone Creek braiding its way through a magnificent stand of virgin hemlocks.

The name Standing Stone was derived from a large "standing stone" erected by the Iroquois Indians at the mouth of the stream in what is now the town of Huntingdon. According to various historical accounts, the standing stone was a pillar 14 feet high and six inches square where Iroquois war partires returning from the south met to celebrate their victories. The stone also marked the intersection of the Warriors Path and Frankstown Path, which provided important links to numerous other Indian paths leading to the Ohio River, the North Branch and West Branch Susquehanna River, and the Potomac River. It was a central point for all the great Indian trails. From it every part of the entire trail system could be reached. Some historians believe the stone even provided the name for the Juniata River, which is a corruption of "Tyu-na-yate," the Seneca name for the place.

The original standing stone was removed by the Indians after the Purchase of 1754 which ceded the area to the whites. A memorial stone was erected in the town of Huntingdon in 1896 bearing the inscription: "Onojutta, Juniata, Achsinnink. Erected September 8, 1896, as a memorial of the ancient standing stone, removed by the Indians in 1754."

During the War for Independence the Standing Stone area was a gathering place for central Pennsylvania Tories. The loyalists mounted at least two attacks on local settlers who pledged allegiance to the rebel cause from the area.

Standing Stone fly fishermen can try Quill Gordons, Adams, Hendricksons, Matuka Streamers, Hare's Ears, Muskrats, Soft Hackle Nymphs, Royal Coachman, caddis, March Browns, Blue-Quills, Light Cahills, Sulphurs, Renegades, midges and terrestrials.

East Branch Standing Stone Creek

The main tributary of Standing Stone, East Branch Standing Stone, is stocked for some 8.5 miles from east of the village of Jackson Corner upstream to Greenwood Furnace State Park. It can be reached by taking East Branch Road (State Route 1019) off Route 26 at Jackson Corner. It follows the creek upstream to Pennsylvania Route 305, which then picks up the stream and parallels it into the park.

Although only 340 acres in size, Greenwood Furnace Park has 50 Class A campsites with showers, flush toilets, a laundromat, and a dump station. It is open from the second Friday in April to mid-December.

Family members who do not fish will find picnic grounds, a children's playground, swimming at a guarded beach on six-acre Greenwood Lake (open from Memorial Day weekend to Labor Day and also stocked with trout), a historical center highlighting the area's ironmaking past and hiking.

Further information on the park may be had by writing: Greenwood Furnace State Park, Department of Environmental Resources, R.D. 2, Box 118, Huntingdon, PA 16652.

Laurel Run

Joining Standing Stone Creek between the villages of Ennisville and McAlveys Fort, Laurel Run is stocked for eight miles from its mouth upstream into Whipple Dam State Park. It can be reached off Route 26 north of McAlveys Fort. It is the second stream

Route 26 passes over, the first stream, at the junction with Route 305, is Standing Stone Creek.

Route 26 parallels Laurel Run at a distance between McAlveys Fort and the turn-off for Whipple Dam Park. Roads running off the north side of the highway generally run toward the stream. In Whipple Dam Park, Laurel Run Road trails the stream above Whipple Lake, a 22-acre impoundment that also is stocked.

Camping is not available at Whipple Dam State Park, but visitors will find opportunities to picnic, swim at a guarded beach (Memorial Day weekend to Labor Day) and boat (no rentals). Details on the park are available by writing: Greenwood Furnace State Park.

ROTHROCK STATE FOREST

The "Public Use Map" of Rothrock State Forest provides a good overview of all of the above streams, as well as several others in the general area. It may be obtained, free of charge, at the forest office, or by writing: District Forester, Rothrock State Forest, P.O. Box 403, Huntingdon, PA 16652.

Raystown Lake Tailrace
Raystown Branch Juniata River
Huntingdon County
(No Closed Season)

Raystown Dam on the Raystown Branch Juniata River was built by the U.S. Army Corps of Engineers between 1968 and 1978 to control flooding along the Juniata and lower Susquehanna Rivers. From the start, the 8,300-acre impoundment the dam formed has been a popular recreation spot for boaters, water skiers, campers, hunters, hikers and especially fishermen. Almost every year the lake, the largest entirely within Pennsylvania, produces a new state record striper bass. The current record is in excess of 35 pounds.

While Raystown's record-breaking stripers naturally garner the most publicity, the lake also is said to hold some of the largest trout outside of Lake Erie, trophy fish in the eight-pound plus range. And some of these beauties naturally end up in the tailrace of the dam. It happens mainly during the high-water periods of late winter and early spring when baitfish congregate in the warmer water near the dam gates. As the trophies move closer to the discharge area to feed on the minnows, some are flushed into the tailrace when the gates are open. These refugees—which also include some stripers—tend to gather in the fast water just below the dam. Because the phenomenon is not predictable, anglers who do not live in the immediate area, or know people who live there, and can keep an eye on the situation, will find hitting it right mostly a matter of luck.

The water below the dam may be the best bet for a big trout, but the Raystown Branch flows for approximately five miles from the dam downstream to the Juniata River near the town of Huntingdon, and the entire length is open to trout fishing on a year-round basis. It can be reached by following the signs for "Raystown Dam" and "Point Access" off U.S. Route 22 east of Huntingdon. The dirt and gravel road which runs down to, and then past, the Fish Commission's Point Access to the Juniata River parallels the stream all the way up to the dam. The area is fairly isolated and without services. However, Corbin Island Access below the dam has a comfort station, drinking water, picnic tables and a boat launch for anglers who might like to bring their canoe along and float the stretch down to the Point Access.

Minnows, spoons and spinners pick up most fish during high-water times. Fly anglers might try streamers and bucktails in brown, black, yellow and white, or large nymph and wet patterns such as Woolly Buggers, stoneflies, Montanas and so forth.

Numerous campgrounds, motels, restuarants and other facilities have sprung up in the area to accommodate the crowds that use the lake. Seven Points is the major outdoor recreational complex on the lake. It contains five separate campgrounds, swimming, boating and picnicking facilities, as well as a marina. The campground is operated on a first-come, first-served basis. Lake Raystown Resort offers even a greater variety of recreational opportunities, including a campground, water slides, boat rentals and a restaurant. It accepts reservations by calling: (814) 658-3500.

Information on the Raystown project may be had by writing: Manager, Raystown Lake, Corps of Engineers, R.D. 1, Hesston, PA 16647.

Little Juniata River
Blair and Huntingdon Counties
(No Closed Season)

Until the end of the 1960s, the Little Juniata River was nothing more than a stinking, open sewer for a papermill and several towns along its banks. Then better environmental protection laws, coupled with a decline in production at the Westvaco plant in Tyrone, turned its black waters clear. Nourished by a dozen limestone springs, aquatic insect life multiplied and the Fish Commission began stocking fingerling brown trout, as many as 100,00 a year. And the Little Juniata quickly evolved into a top-shelve trout river. But it was still just a sampling of things to come.

The single biggest turning point in the Little Juniata's return was Hurricane Agnes. Within a matter of hours, that historic storm of June 1972 dumped more than ten inches of rain on central Pennsylvania. Fed by the downpour and runoff from its numerous tributaries, the Little Juniata became a racing flood of mud and debris. Disaster was probably the word on most people's minds. Only after the waters abated did the truth surface. The storm had been a blessing in disguise. Its range had flushed the river and scoured its bottom of the accumulated wastes of a hundred years.

Hurricane Agnes left one other entirely unexpected gift: Monster brown trout. The storm had conducted its own stocking program when it swept dozens of big browns out of a hatchery along Spruce Creek and into the Little Juniata. Word-of-mouth began to spread about the great fishing below the village of Spruce Creek.

Throughout the 1970s and early 1980s, the reputation of the Little Juniata as a quality trout river, one of the best in Pennsylvania, continued to grow. Increased pressure might have made the fishing tougher, but the trout were still there, and with the right mixture of skill and luck an angler could take any number of wild browns of 15 inches and over. At least they could in the river downsteam of Tyrone and before 1984 when a real tragedy of a different sort struck.

Whether it was by accident or intention—many locals feel it was the latter—it makes no difference, but a highly toxic pesticide entered the Little Juniata. And wiped out an estimated 95 percent of the trout in a six-mile stretch of the middle river. Hundreds upon hundreds of giant browns washed up dead on the banks. Fishermen and landowners were enraged. Rewards were offered and an investigation conducted by the Department of Environmental Resources and the Fish Commission, but the perpetrator remains free. The one saving grace in the factor was that the kill did not destroy the river's best fishery in the area below the village of Spruce Creek.

In the years since the fish kill, the Little Juniata has once again rebounded in dramatic fashion. Aided by Fish Commission stockings and a plea from the local chapter of Trout Unlimited urging anglers to release their catch, the portion of river contaminated by the pesticide is once again producing some nice trout.

The Little Juniata flows northeast from Altoona to Tyrone and Bald Eagle Creek, where it takes a sharp turn to the southeast. Its trout water runs from the mouth of Bald Eagle Creek in Tyrone downstream to its confluence with the Frankstown Branch Juniata River, a distance of over 15 miles. Some fishing also is available above Tyrone, but the quality is only marginal when compared to the lower river.

Access to this big stream is good along most of its length. Pennsylvania Route 453 can be picked up off U.S. Route 220 and Pennsylvania Route 550 near Tyrone. It parallels the river from Tyrone through the villages of Ironville and Birmingham. The river can be reached directly off Route 453 or along several bridges leading to side roads. Anglers who are train buffs should keep their eyes open when either fishing or traveling along the Little Juniata. Nearly 20 railroad bridges, many of them of handcut stone arches, span the river between Tyrone and its mouth.

Immediately before Route 453 crosses the river a secondary road appears and leads further downstream. This road then crosses the stream to join with State Route 40061, which provides access to the Little Juniata all of the way to the village of Spruce Creek.

Between Spruce Creek and the village of Barree, access is walk-in only. But it is a place no trout fisherman should miss. The gorge the river has cut through Tussey Mountain is the most scenic part of the experience.

Barree and the lower river can be reached by taking Route 453 to the village of Water Street and U.S. Route 22. From Water Street continue east on Route 22. Just before the road begins to cross the Frankstown Branch Juniata River, State Route 4014 will appear on the left leading to the village of Alexandria. Follow S.R. 4014 to its junction with State Route 4014 about a half-mile outside of Alexandria. S.R. 4004 is marked by a sign leading to Barree, where it crosses the Little Juniata and then parallels it downstream to Pennsylvania Route 305.

At least four different Indian paths touched on the Little Juniata River at one time. Bald Eagle Path, from Lock Haven to Frankstown, closely followed the river from Altoona to Tyrone. It was part of a warrior's path stretching all of the way south into Virginia and the Carolinas, and an important link in a complex system of north/south trails.

Penns Creek Path, from Sunbury to Frankstown, was the continuation of the Great Warriors Path from the Iroquois country of New York to Sunbury. It crossed the Little Juniata at Spruce Creek, and was the trail used by the Indians at the outset of the Penn's Creek Massacre, the fight which followed General Edward Braddock's defeat by the French and Indians in the Battle of the Monongahela in July, 1755 (also see Penns Creek). The path also was used by the Indians returning from the raid with their captives.

Raystown-Chinklacamoose Path, from Bedford to Clearfield, was a part of the Warriors Mark Path and another trail that crossed the Little Juniata River near Spruce Creek.

As befits a Pennsylvania limestone stream, the Little Juniata River has a world of good fly hatches. The best Mayfly hatch by far is the Sulphur, which occurs from about the middle of May to the end of June. The regular hatch schedule includes: mid-April to mid-June, Blue Quill, Green Caddis and Sulphurs; mid-June to mid-July, Sulphurs, Light Cahill, Blue-Winged Olive, Slate Drake; mid-July to September, Sulphurs, Cream Cahill, Yellow Drake, Tricorythodes and White Flies.

Caddis are an extremely abundant insect on the river, so fly anglers should never overlook any caddis imitations in their fly box. They also should not forget about terrestrials.

(Also see Bald East Creek West and Spruce Creek.)

Spruce Creek
Catch and Release
Huntingdon County

Let a president of the United States become interested in something and, thanks to the miracle of modern communications and journalistic overkill, the object of his affection immediately obtains an importance all out of proportion to its merits in the real world. Which is exactly what happened when former President Jimmy Carter began fishing Spruce Creek in Huntingdon County. Not that the stream is overrated when it comes to trout fishing and fly hatches. It is generally agreed to be one of the finest little limestone streams in central Pennsylvania. The problem, instead, lies in the fact so very little of it is accessible to the general public.

Except for its one-half mile long Catch and Release Project on Penn State's Experimental Fisheries property and small stretches just above the village of Spruce Creek and near Baileyville on the Centre County line, Spruce Creek is private property. Among the holders of some of the very best water is the exclusive Spruce Creek Rod & Gun Club, one of former President Carter's hosts, and home water of well-known fly tyer, angling writer and former Penn State University fly fishing instructor George Harvey.

Even though public water on Spruce Creek is at a premium, that does not mean what is open is worthless. Its Catch and Release Project holds plenty of difficult wild brown trout guaranteed to provide all the hair-pulling challenge any angler might desire. Hatches of Blue Quills and "Tricos" are reported in late July and August, and terrestrial fishing is often good.

The Catch and Release Project also is interesting because its fish were the subjects of Dr. Robert Bachman's doctoral thesis, "Foraging Behavior of Free-Ranging Wild Brown Trout in a Stream," at Penn State University.

The gregarious Dr. Bachman spent nearly everyday, from April through November, for four years in the late 1970s and early 1980s sitting in a camouflaged observation tower studying the behavior of Spruce Creek's fish. What he learned has sparked controversy in some trout fishing circles, as well as changed the way many fishermen now view the behavior of wild trout.

"One thing that sitting out in that tower day after day taught me is the fact that fish don't feed on a bright day and that they're hiding is just a bunch of garbage," he points out.

The brown trout Bachman observed often occupied feeding sites throughout the center of the stream in water only inches deep and frequently awash in bright sunlight. Actually, the only time he found his fish hidden away undercover was when they were disturbed. Then their natural wariness would make them dash out of sight so quickly visitors sometimes claimed the pool they were watching was empty. When undisturbed, he never saw them take cover to rest as many anglers believe.

"Why would a fish rest?" he asks. "What else are they going to do besides feed? They don't have any PTA meetings to go to. They don't have any jobs or parties to go to. They're always feeding out in Spruce Creek. I don't find any time when they're not feeding. In Spruce Creek, where there is probably more drift (food) than any stream you find anywhere, the fish never stop feeding."

According to data Bachman collected with the aid of his "Trout Tracker" computer, Spruce Creek's fish spent the lion's share of their time, over 85 percent, simply sitting and waiting for food to arrive at their feeding station. These sites were extremely precise spots in the water to which the fish returned year after year. They were usually on the downward sloping sides of rocks and comprised of certain hydraulic properties that required the expenditure of a minimum amount of energy to maintain.

Even when Bachman's trout did move, they did not cruise around a pool searching for food, but went almost directly from one feeding station to another. Their world was incredibly small, no bigger than the size of the average living room floor. The few, odd times his fish did cruise a pool and feed was when there was a great amount of food on the water at one time, such as during a spinner fall.

"And they had to be getting a lot of energy to make up for it," he explains.

While the feeding rates of the trout he observed did differ from hour-to-hour and day-to-day, over the long run there was little difference between the different hours of the day and different days. Even when "Beethoven," one of the nearly 100 trout he was able to positively identify by the spot pattern on its back, devoured two huge crayfish within 20 minutes of each other his appetite was little affected. Throughout the remainder of the day he continued to feed regularly on drifting flies.

Along with discovering that his fish never stopped feeding during daylight hours, Bachman also found that less than 12 percent of the food they consumed came from the bottom of the stream; from under rocks, between the gravel and in the mud. He says the reason such a small percentage of food was taken from the bottom is visibility and availability. Although nearly every rock in the study pool sheltered nymphs, for the most part they were unavailable to the trout, hidden far under the rocks and deep in the spaces between them. In addition, Bachman points out, trout can see only a small portion of the bottom at any one time and the nymphs are extremely adept at blending into it. On the other hand, food passing in the drift is silhouetted against the sky and highly visible.

As Spruce Creek's trout grew older, they also fed less frequently. The average feeding rate of a four-year-old fish was only half that of a yearling. Larger trout would pass up food smaller fish took because they would have to expend more energy getting it than it was worth.

"There is no point in expending energy on a piece of food that will only return part of it," he says.

Another thing Bachman discovered, was that trout grow well only until they are about 11 inches long. Beyond 11 inches, a drift-feeding fish just about balances the food he receives with the energy he expends getting it. Even in food-rich Spruce Creek, the 16-inch and bigger fish is rare. And it was the best feeding stations, holds where a trout could pick off a crayfish or minnow from time to time for instance, which produced the largest fish, and not the other way around. He says a trout has no way of knowing what are or are not the best feeding stations in a stream, so a larger fish will not steal a site from a smaller one simply because it is better than the one he already owns. In any case, fish of 16 inches and larger were rare.

An experiment with stocked trout also proved to Bachman that

wild fish and stocked fish do not mix well. Stocked fish did not know how to conserve their energy to, so to speak, get the most for their money, and only made the wild fish expend energy chasing them when they violated their territory.

Although it would not be very scientific, or fair, to apply Bachman's findings about Spruce Creek's wild brown trout to all trout in streams everywhere, from an angler's viewpoint his study still has turned up a number of things worth considering. First of all, since his fish fed on a regular basis, it shows the old adage, "the best time to fish is whenever you can" to be truer than probably anybody thought. The reason more fish are caught in the morning and in the evening is because those are the times when the most fishermen are out, and also when it is the most difficult for a fish to spot an angler.

The study also reveals just how precious is a trophy trout. If fertile Spruce Creek produces only a handful of wild trout in the 16-inch and larger range, imagine what the situation is like in less food-rich streams. And don't forget, it takes years to produce a trophy fish. So the angler who wants to catch more big fish should release more of the big fish he does catch.

Something else the study shows is that it may not pay to mix hatchery fish with wild fish. Stocked fish don't make it through the winter; only two of the 170 that were stocked during Bachman's study survived to the following spring. The hatchery fish also forced the wild fish to needlessly expend energy chasing them off, thus decreasing their survival chances.

Feeding sites that produced large fish in the past may be expected to produce large fish in the future, according to data collected during the study. So anglers looking for a trophy should remember where they caught big fish in the past. Provided, of course, no drastic changes have taken place, such as a tree falling in the water or a flood.

Finally, the study reveals that simply placing a rock in the middle of a stream can improve it. If a trout finds the rock makes a suitable feeding station, the carrying capacity of a pool or run has instantly been increased.

Spruce Creek parallels Pennsylvania Route 45 from the village of Spruce Creek upstream beyond the village of Rockspring. All of its public water can be reached off Route 45. The Catch and Release Project lies about 0.6 of a mile above the village of Spruce Creek and is marked by a small Penn State University sign.

A more detailed presentation of Dr. Bachman's study is available in the Spring 1983 issue of Trout Unlimited's *Trout* magazine and in the February 1982 issue of *Sports Afield,* as well as in the Penn State University Library at State College, Pennsylvania.

Hatches on Spruce Creek include: April through mid-May, Blue-Winged Olives, Blue Quills, caddis, Yellow Cranefly and Sulphurs; mid-May to mid-June, Sulphurs, March Browns, Green Drakes, Light Cahills, Lead-Winged Coachman and Slate-Winged Olives; mid-June through the summer, Yellow Drakes, Blue-Winged Olives, Tricorythodes and terrestrials.

(Also see Little Juniata River.)

Author's Note: *Central Pennsylvania's Bald Eagle Valley contains two Bald Eagle Creeks. They both begin in the same marshy area southwest of Port Matilda. One, however, the far longer eastern stream, flows northeast to form the Foster Joseph Sayers Lake in Bald Eagle State Park, Centre County, and eventually drains into the West Branch Susquehanna River near Lock Haven. The other, much shorter eastern stream flows southwest into the Little Juniata River near Tyrone, Blair County.*

Bald Eagle Creek
(West)
Blair County

Five miles of Bald Eagle Creek (West) is stocked with a healthy dose of trout from Tyrone upstream beyond Pennsylvania Route 350. Although not quite as wide as its longer cousin, it is still a fair-size trout water, and, like the other stream, is readily accessible off a good road.

The upper portions of this Bald Eagle Creek are the more scenic. Being hemmed in by highways, however, it is still far from a picturesque trout fishing experience. U.S. Route 220 toward Port Matilda follows the creek upstream from the traffic lights at the junction of Route 350 in the village of Bald Eagle.

Old Route 220, which leads to Tyrone, also provides access to some of the nicer water. The road is not marked by a sign, but can be picked up at the traffic lights in Bald Eagle. For the angler coming from the south on Route 220 it will be a left turn where the expressway ends at the traffic lights. While old Route 220 parallels and eventually crosses Bald Eagle Creek, the stream is much closer to the Route 220 bypass and so generally out of sight. Since the state police frown on parking along the bypass, a short hike is required to reach it.

Tyrone, near the mouth of the stream, was settled in 1850 by immigrants from Ireland, specifically the Scotch-Irish of what is now Northern Ireland. It has long been an industrial center starting with the iron industry.

"This is a model iron establishment," wrote Eli Bowen in his 1852 *Pictorial Sketch Book of Pennsylvania*. "There are upward of 200 hands regularly employed, averaging ten dollars per week each, and a more cheerful set of men we never saw. . .It is so unusual a circumstance to hear overseers complimented by their workers, that for the novelty of the thing we must beg to be excused for mentioning it."

The lower stretches of Bald Eagle Creek clearly reflect Tyrone's industrial past. Anglers who try it will find themselves surrounded by railroad tracks, garages, old frame workers' homes and a variety of industrial facilities. Whereas the upper waters are full of rocky riffles, runs and pools, the lower stream is somewhat calmer and rimmed with high mud banks.

Flies for spring fishing, mid-April to late May, include: Blue Quills, Quill Gordons, Black Quill, Hendricksons, Sulphurs and Gray Fox; late May and June, Sulphurs, Light Cahills, Lead-Wingd Coachmen, Yellow Drake and caddis; summer flies, Lead-Winged Coachmen, Yellow Drakes, caddis and midges.

The Bald Eagle Indian Path, from Lock Haven to Frankstown, followed both Bald Eagle Creeks. It was an important link between two trail complexes in the north and south. The creek, path and village are all named for Chief Bald Eagle, a Munsee Indian who once lived on the site of Milesburg.

(Also see Bald Eagle Creek East, Centre County.)

Pennsylvania brown trout.

Frankstown Branch Juniata River
South Poplar Run, Poplar Run
Blair County
Beaverdam Creek
Bedford County

Frankstown Branch Juniata River

Conveniently situated along U.S. Route 220 south of Holidaysburg, Frankstown Branch Juniata River would seem a likely candidate to attract droves of anglers. But indications are it has few real devotees. A lot of anglers dislike either its coffee color, proximity to the highway, the many homes surrounding it, or other touches of civilization, like the garbage around Claysburg.

While the Frankstown Branch's eight miles of stocked water may not be among the prettiest, or quietest, in Pennsylvania, neither are they the worst. And its little riffles and runs are said to hold a solid population of nice holdover fish.

The Frankstown Branch's planted brown and rainbow water extends from approximately the village of Sproul near the Bedford County line upstream to about the village of McKee. Access is available to the river directly off Route 220 in many places. In other locations, easily spotted side roads lead to the water. Route 220 itself crosses the river between Sproul and Claysburg. Above Claysburg, the Frankstown Branch flows on the east side of the highway.

Like the Frankstown Path and the village of Frankstown, Frankstown Branch Juniata River takes its name from Frank Stevens, who established a trading post in the region in the mid-1750s. (Though some historians believe the name comes from the Frank brothers, prominent Philadelphia traders.) Touched by the Frankstown Path, the most frequently traveled Indian Path over Pennsylvania's mountains, but also the Frankstown-Burnt Cabin Path, the Frankstown-Conemaugh Path, the Warriors Path and the Kittanning Path, Frankstown became an important trading center for central Pennsylvania during the period around the Revolutionary War. The decision to place the eastern terminus of the Huntingdon-Cambria-Indiana turnpike at John Blair's homestead further west, however, changed everything. As Holidaysburg grew—becoming also the western terminus of the Juniata Branch of the Pennsylvania Canal and then the eastern terminus of the Portage Railraod—so did Frankstown decline. Today it is but a tiny hamlet on U.S. Route 22 east of Holidaysburg.

Encouraged by the completion of the Erie Canal in 1825, the Pennsylvania legislature, in 1826, authorized the construction of a water/rail transportation system linking Philadelphia and Pittsburgh. Operating from 1834 to 1857, the Portage Railroad was a fascinating system of incline planes and levels over the mountains between Holidaysburg and Johnstown. It ran for 37 miles, carrying cargo and canal boats, which could be broken down into segments, 1,400 feet up the mountains from Holidaysburg and 1,200 feet down to Johnstown. A hemp rope was used to connect and counterbalance boats going up and down the mountains. Horses and mules, and then later locomotives were used to move the loads across the level stretches.

Among the most famous people to travel the Portage Railroad was Charles Dickens. The creator of Scrooge, Tiny Tim, David Copperfield, Nicholas Nickleby and all the rest, crossed Pennsylvania's Allegheny Mountains in 1842 on his way to Pittsburgh. And he wrote about the experience: "Occasionally the rails were upon the extreme verge of a giddy precipice; and looking from the carriage window, the traveler gazes sheer down, without a stone or scrap of fence between, into the mountain depths below. . .It

was very pretty traveling thus at a rapid pace along the heights of the mountains in keen wind, to look down into the valley full of light and softness; catching glimpses, through the treetops, of scattered cabins; . . .men in their shirtsleeves, looking on at their unfinished houses, planning out tomorrow's work; and we riding onward, high above them, like a whirlwind. . ."

Allegheny Portage Railroad is now a National Historic Site located off U.S. Route 22 near the village of Cresson. Anglers can visit the site, and museum which tells the story of the venture, by following the signs of Route 22 west of Holidaysburg.

Along with being transportation and trading centers for central Pennsylvania, both Frankstown and Holidaysburg were the scene of several Indian attacks during the colonial period, and a hotbed for Tory activity during the Revolution. Fort Fetters was erected just outside of Holidaysburg to protect settlers from Indian raids and Fort Holiday inside of the town. Tories from the "Frankstown District" attempted to get the British and Indians from Kittanning to launch an attack on local patriots. They gave up the idea when one of the chiefs in Kittanning suspected the Tory leader of actually being a patriot and scalped him in front of the others.

Fly fishermen along the Frankstown Branch and its tributaries might try: Quill Gordon, Adams, stoneflies, Hare's Ear, Muskrat, Muddler Minnow, Woolly Bugger, Soft Hackle Nymphs, Hendrickson, caddis, March Brown, Light Cahill and terrestrials.

Beaverdam Run

The first of the Frankstown Branch's three stocked tributaries, Beaverdam Run, flows across northern Bedford County to join the main stream in Sproul. It is stocked from its mouth upstream to about the village of Queen. Access may be had by taking the road west for the village of Queen Station off Route 220 in Sproul. Further access to its upper reaches may be had by taking the road from Queens Station toward Queens.

South Poplar Run

South Poplar Run is stocked from its mouth on the southern edge of Claysburg to about the village of Ski Gap. Anglers can reach the stream by taking State Route 3002 toward the village of Friesville, which runs off Route 220 to the west near Claysburg.

Poplar Run

Poplar Run joins the Frankstown Branch above that stream's stocked portion east of the village of Newry south of Holidaysburg. The upper portion of its 7.5 miles of planted water can be found by following State Route 3003 toward the village of Puzzletown off Route 220 west of Newry. In Puzzletown, the road running to the right, State Route 3010, follows Poplar Run. (Also see Bobs Creek and Canoe Creek.)

Canoe Creek
Blair County

Wedged tight between Brush Mountain and Canoe Mountain, Canoe Creek has almost no tributary streams feeding it and none whatsoever of any length. This limited runoff makes it a possible choice for early spring, when most other Pennsylvania freestone streams are running high or coffee-colored. The presence of

Canoe Creek State Park makes it a fine pick for a family outing anytime.

Canoe Creek is stocked from the backwaters of Canoe Lake (stocked) in the park, upstream for about 7.5 miles. It can be found by taking Beaver Dam Road (State Route 1011) off U.S. Route 22 just east of the entrance to the park at the village of Canoe Creek. The village and road are located about 11 miles east of Holidaysburg in Blair County. Beaver Dam Road parallels the stream over its entire stocked length.

No camping is available at Canoe Creek State Park, but the angler with non-fishing family members along will be glad to know there are plenty of other things to do. Swimming is available at a guarded beach on 905-acre Canoe Lake from Memorial Day weekend to Labor Day, boat rentals, picnicking, hiking trails, bridal paths, a snack bar, and comfort stations.

Canoe Creek also is within easy reach of the Allegheny Portage Railroad National Historic Site on Route 22 west near the village of Cresson. Operating from 1834 to 1857, the Portage Railroad was a fascinating system of levels and inclined planes over the mountains between Holidaysburg and Johnstown. It was designed to help connect Philadelphia to Pittsburgh. Cars moving up and down the mountain were used to counterbalance each other, while first mules and horses, then locomotives moved the cars across the level summit. The site holds a museum that tells the entire story of the enterprise (also see Frankstown Branch Juniata River).

In the years of the War for Independence, both Canoe Valley and neighboring Sinking Spring Valley were hotbeds for Toryism in central Pennsylvania, even launching conspiracy in 1778.

". . .a further & very dangerous correspondence," General Daniel Roberdeau wrote Pennsylvania officials about the plan, "between the Commandant at Detroit & disaffected persons among us, some of whom he says have suddenly disappeared, & expected to be joined by others, to associate with Indians & others sent by the Enemy to scalp the Inhabitants & break up the Settlements."

The plan called for local Tories to unite with other British sympathizers and the Indian allies in Kittanning and attack patriots in the "Frankstown District." An Indian chief at Kittanning brought an abrupt end to the conspiracy when, suspecting the Tory leader of actually being a patriot, scalped him in front of the others. The remaining members of the Frankstown party quickly fled Kittanning after the scalping, so saving the area from a probably very bloody attack.

Fly fishermen on Canoe Creek should find some success with the Adams, stoneflies, Hendrickson, March Brown, caddis, Hare's Ear, Muskrat, Soft Hackle Nymphs, Renegade, Muddler Minnow, Matuka Streamers, Woolly Buggers, Light Cahill and terrestrials.

Details on Canoe Creek Park may be had by writing: Canoe Creek State Park, Department of Environmental Resources, R.D. 2, Box 560, Holidaysburg, PA 16648.

Piney Creek
Blair County

Another little spring-fed Blair County stream, Piney Creek flows tight against Lock Mountain through a wide, rolling, out-of-the-way farm valley. It is stocked with brown and rainbow trout for 12 miles, from the village of Clappertown downstream to its mouth on the Frankstown Branch Juniata River near Williamsburg.

Pennsylvania Route 866 follows Piney Creek's upper planted water at varying distances between the villages of Clappertown and Royer, where it pulls away from the stream and toward Williamsburg. Side roads run off Route 866 at both Clappertown and Royer. At Royer, Township Road 378, marked by a sign pointing to Frankstown, also leads to another secondary road which follows the creek downstream.

Piney Creek's mouth can be reached off Route 866 north of Williamsburg on the edge of State Game Lands 147 near where the road crosses over the Frankstown Branch.

Like its neighbor Clover Creek to the east, Piney Creek also once laid along the Frankstown-Burnt Cabin Path, from Frankstown on the Frankstown Branch Juniata River to Burnt Cabins on Little Augwick Creek. While not itself a very important Indian trail, the Frankstown-Burnt Cabin Path was a link between the Warriors Path (Frankstown Path) and the Raystown Path, two major highways through the wilds of early Pennsylvania.

For fly fishermen, the Sulphur hatch is the main event of the trout season on Piney Creek. The normal time for the hatch on Pennsylvania streams is late May to mid-June. Other possible patterns for the fly angler are: Adams, Hendricksons, Hare's Ears, Muddler Minnows, Mickey Finns, Matuka Streamers, Soft Hackle Nymphs, Royal Coachmen, March Browns, Gray Fox, Blue-Winged Olives, caddis, Black Gnat, Lead-Winged Coachmen, Light Cahill, Renegade, midges and terrestrials.

(Also see Clover Creek.)

Clover Creek
Blair County

Anybody who has ever driven through Pennsylvania's pleasant farm valleys has seen plenty of pastures with tiny mud-banked streams. Generally, these little feeder streams hold nothing but minnows, and often not even those forage fish. But there are always exceptions to the rule, and Blair County's Clover Creek is a good one.

Looking exactly like every other small pasture stream in many places, spring-fed Clover Creek in reality is the longest trout stream in Blair County. From its headwaters south of the town of Fredricksburg upstream to the villages of Shellytown and Larke, it is stocked water, full of browns and rainbows. From Shellytown and Larke downstream to its mouth on the Frankstown Branch Juniata River near the village of Cove Forge, it is designated as Wild Trout Water, pure enough to sustain a population of streambred fish. Altogether, it offers more than 17 miles of places, spring-fed Clover Creek, in reality, is the longest trout

Because of its small size and surroundings, Clover Creek is extremely susceptible to changes in the weather. Anglers interested in trying it should keep in mind that a heavy downpour can knock it out of commission for days, and leave it cloudy for weeks.

Reaching Clover Creek is relatively easy over most of its length. Pennsylvania Route 164, which can be picked up off U.S. Route 220 south of Altoona in the west and Pennsylvania Route 26 alongside Raytown Lake on the east, crosses the creek at Fredricksburg, providing access at that point.

Upstream of Fredricksburg, Clover Creek can be found by taking Martinsburg Road (Township Road 320), which runs off Route 164 next to the bridge.

Anglers can fish the stream's wider lower water by turning off Route 164 at the sign marked Williamsburg 12 miles. State Route 2011 parallels and crosses the creek for over 11 miles before turning away from it toward Williamsburg. Less than a mile outside of Fredericksburg, Mill Race Road (Township Road 341) runs off S.R. 2011 and to the stream.

Other secondary roads providing access to Clover Creek off S.R. 2011 and to the stream include: Township Road 369 at the village of Drab, Township Road 377 and Township Road 454.

Anglers traveling to Clover Creek's pretty, rolling agricultural valley from Route 26 may notice the Captain Phillips Ranger Memorial across the Blair County line in Bedford County.

Captain William Phillips was the commander of a troop of men recruited to defend the frontier. On July 16, 1780, he and 11 of his men were attacked and killed by Indians near the village of Saxton. The next day Colonel Piper learned of the massacre and set off after the Indians with only ten men.

Reaching the site of the fight, Colonel Piper found the house where Captain Phillips had been station burned to the ground "with sundry Indian tomahawks that had been lost in the action. . ." About a half-mile away they found Captain Phillips and his men "with their hands tied and murdered in the most cruel manner."

The memorial on Fisher Summit was erected and dedicated on July 16, 1926 by the Saxton American Legion Post. Seven years later, while post members were working on the memorial, the remains of seven more victims of the massacre were found at the base of an old tree stump. The Frankstown-Burnt Cabin Path from, naturally, Frankstown to Burnt Cabin crossed Clover Creek at Shellytown.

The Sulphur hatch in May is said to be the highlight of the angling year on Clover Creek. Other patterns that should produce fish include: Adams, Renegade, Hare's Ear, Blue-Winged Olives, Muddler Minnows, Matuka Streamers, caddis, Royal Coachman, Black Gnat, March Brown, Gray Fox, Light Cahill, midges and terrestrials.

(Also see Piney Creek.)

Yellow Creek
Delayed Harvest Fly Fishing Only
Potter Creek, Three Springs Run
Beaver Creek
Bedford County

Yellow Creek

Another limestone stream outside of the renowned Carlisle-State College-Chambersburg triangle, Yellow Creek springs to life in the pasture lands along Pennsylvania Route 36 north of the village of Woodbury, Bedford County. It offers angling for both stocked and native brook, brown and rainbow trout over a distance of about 11 miles, from the dam at the village of Waterside downstream to its junction with the Raystown Branch Juniata River at Hopewell.

While Yellow Creek is certainly a limestone stream, it resembles more a freestone than a classic spring creek. Full of fast-flowing riffles, deep pools and slow-moving flats, the first-time visitor might even argue it could not possibly have a limestone source. But one ride up Route 36 past Waterside should end those doubts. There sections of Yellow Creek could double for famous Falling Springs Run.

Almost all of Yellow Creek can be fished either off Route 36 from Waterside downstream, or Pennsylvania Route 26 from Hopewell upstream. Its one mile long Delayed Harvest Fly Fishing Only Project can be found just downstream of the Route 36 bridge between the villages of Loysburg and Yellow Creek. The project runs from the mouth of Maple Run (Jacks Run) upstream to Red Bank Hill. No signs appear at the Route 36 Bridge, but the special regulation water starts just downstream from it and is well marked by Fish Commission posters.

State Route 1024 parallels the Fly Fishing Only Project, at a distance, downstream from the bridge, and also leads to another bridge that crosses the stream below the project water, then meets Best Avenue, which provides access even further downstream.

Yellow Creek is a good size stream flowing through a variety of scenic settings from pasture to forest and mountain. A short distance upstream of the Route 36 bridge anglers will spot a steep bank of giant boulders running down the mountain to the stream. At the end of the last glacial episode, nearly all of the mountains in Pennsylvania were covered with such a blanket of broken stone. The boulders were formed by natural freezing and thawing action splitting apart the mountain surface rock, and gravity pulling the stones downward.

Boulder field on Yellow Creek.

Besides its link with the natural history of Pennsylvania through its boulder field, Yellow Creek also has witnessed man's passage across the region along the Warriors Path through Bloody Run (Everett). Warriors Path was a fairly important route for both Indians and early settlers. It ran from Standing Stone (Huntingdon) south, over Yellow Creek, to Opessah's Town (Oldtown) on the Potomac River in Maryland. Christopher Gist, famous earlier western Pennsylvania settler and guide for George Washington, was among the many people who traveled the path, making his passage on October 31, 1750 north from Oldtown.

Fly life is said to be abundant on Yellow Creek. Fly fishermen might try such traditional Pennsylvania patterns as the Quill Gordon, Hendrickson, March Brown, Gray Fox, Light Cahill, Sulphurs, Green Drake, Yellow Drake, Blue Quill, Blue-Winged Olive, caddis and terrestrials.

Potter Creek

Feeding Yellow Creek at Waterside, Potter Creek holds 3.5 miles of stocked water easily accessible off Pennsylvania Route 868 toward the village of Maria. Fly anglers might try some of the same patterns mentioned under yellow Creek on any of its tributaries.

Three Springs Run

Another little feeder brook with good access and three miles of stocked trout water is Three Springs Run. It can be found lying alongside Pennsylvania Route 869, running off Route 36 between Loysburg and Waterside and toward the village of new Enterprise.

Beaver Creek

No major road follows Beaver Creek's four miles of planted water, but access is still good off a secondary road. Anglers can find it by turning onto State Route 1005 where Route 36 makes its sharp bend in Loysburg and heads toward Waterside. State Route 1026 runs off S.R. 1005 and parallels the creek upstream.

Bobs Creek
Bedford County

Rushing down off the Allegheny Front out of State Game Lands 26 and Blue Knob State Park, Bobs Creek offers a good mixture of forest and meadow fishing. It is well stocked from the park downstream to its junction with Dunning Creek near Reynoldsdale, a distance of about 13.5 miles. Some native, or streambred, fish also can be found in the upper, forested portions of this freestone stream.

Besides offering a combination of angling scenes, the varied topography surrounding Bobs Creek also holds a rich assortment of flora and fauna. The different elevations and soil types, especially in the territory around the park, sustain a full range of plants and animals found scattered throughout Pennsylvania's wilderness regions. Bird life is particularly abundant, making the area a sort of mecca for bird watchers.

History, with a taste for legend, touches the stream in the form of the "Lost Children of the Alleghenies" along Ciana Run, a small tributary of Bobs Creek on Game Lands 26. A monument marks the site where George, 7, and Joseph, 5, sons of Samuel and Susanna Cox, were discovered after being lost in the wilderness near the village of Lovely in April 1856. Upwards of 2,000 people searched the area for the children after they were reported lost. They were not found, until Jacob Dibert, a nearby settler, told of a recurring dream he had envisioning the spot where the boys could be located. Dibert's brother-in-law, Harrison Whysong, recognized the spot in Jacob's dream and together the two men went there and found the boys' bodies near the stream on May 9. They had died of starvation and exposure. The monument marking the location was erected in 1906. The boys are buried in the Mt. Union Church Cemetery in Lovely.

Lost Turkey Trail now leads to the spot where the youngsters were discovered. The Conemaugh Indian Path from Bedford to Johnstown also crossed the stream near its mouth.

Access to the majority of Bobs Creek may be had directly off Pennsylvania Route 869, which can be picked up off U.S. Route 220 at St. Clairsville north of Bedford, or U.S. Route 219 north of Johnstown near St. Michael. The stream's upper waters in Blue Knob Park and Game Lands 26 may be reached by turning off Route 869 onto a dirt road across from a ball field just west of the park entrance and the village of Pavia.

Fly choices are similar to those on many other Pennsylvania freestone waters: Quill Gordon, Adams, Hendrickson, March Brown, caddis, Light Cahill, Sulphurs, Hare's Ear, stoneflies, Soft Hackles and terrestrials.

Blue Knob State was developed by the federal government's National Park Service and Works Progress Administration in the mid-1930s and turned over to the state in 1945. It is named after Blue Knob, the second highest peak in Pennsylvania at 3,146 feet, just 67 feet shorter than Mt. Davis, the state's tallest peak. Because Blue Knob sets on the Allegheny Front overlooking several ridges and valleys, its view is actually more dramatic than Mt. Davis, which stands in the middle of a plateau.

Anglers who decide they like Bobs Creek and might want to explore it for more than a day, will find a 75-site campground in the park. The sites are all Class B with water, a dump station and pit toilets. No hookups are available. It operates from the second Friday in April through the third Sunday in October. Visitors who do not fish will find a swimming pool, open Memorial Day through Labor Day, picnic grounds and, of course, hiking trails to help them occupy their time.

Backpacking anglers can pick up the 22-mile long Lost Turkey Trail in Blue Knob Park. According to the park's "Recreation Guide," this back country trail was built in 1977 by the Youth Conservation Corps. It has been mapped and distance markers installed at one kilometer intervals to aid hikers in determining their location. Guidebooks are available at the park office, or from the Gallitzin State Forest, Department of Environmental Resources, 13 Hillcrest Drive, Ebensburg, PA 15931. The trail leads to Clear Shade Creek (see which), another excellent trout stream in Somerset County.

Further information on the park may be had by writing: Blue Knob State Park, Department of Environmental Resources, R.D. 1, Box 230A, Imler, PA 16655.

Raystown Branch Juniata River
Bedford County

From its headwaters in the Allegheny Mountains of Somerset County through Raystown Lake to its confluence with the Juniata River, Raystown Branch covers about 120 miles. It is both the longest and largest tributary of the Juniata, draining nearly 1000 square miles. Only about 21 miles of the river is a stocked trout fishery, however, from the village of New Baltimore on the

Somerset/Bedford County line to just east of the town of Bedford. It holds all three major species of trout: browns, rainbows and brookies.

As could be expected of a stream as long as Raystown Branch, its character varies quite a bit. Anglers who choose to try some of the upper water from New Baltimore to roughly the first Pennsylvania Route 31 Bridge at the village of Kegg will find an often swift moving little stream tumbling over cobble-sized stones and sharp ledges while splitting apart into a twisted array of channels. The narrow and cultivated valley surrounding the stream in this area provides some of the most pleasant scenery along the entire river.

Below the first Route 31 Bridge the gradient lessens and the stream's flow turns moderate, becoming even placid by the time it reaches Pennsylvania Route 96 between Shawnee State Park and the village of Manns Choice. The scenery also becomes a lot tamer, being comprised mostly of a mixture of houses, trailers and a couple of busy, noisy highways.

New Baltimore and the start of Raystown Branch's stocked water may be reached by taking State Route 1017 off U.S. Route 30 east of the village of Reels Corners in Somerset County. The Pennsylvania Turnpike appears upstream of New Baltimore and follows the river through the town of Bedford. Route 31, however, provides the greatest access to the stocked water. From about two miles upstream of Kegg to Route 30 and Wolfsburg it closely parallels the river, crossing it twice.

Camping is available at Shawnee State Park off Route 96 north. It has 300 Class A sites with flush toilets, showers, a dump station, water and picnic tables, as well as some with electrical hookups. It is open from the second Friday in April to mid-December.

For those off hourrs, or family members who do not fish, the park has a swimming beach, picnic grounds, children's playfield, snack bar, boat rentals on 451-acre Shawnee Lake and 12 miles of hiking trails.

Shawnee State Park occupies the site of a prominent stopping place for Shawnee Indians on their way from the Potomac River on the Warriors Path, and west to the Ohio Valley on the Raystown Path. A point on Shawnee Run, the tributary of Raystown Branch which is the main feeder stream of Shawnee Lake, was said to have been a manufacturing point for arrowheads.

Shawnee has been translated as "south," "southerners," "southward or south place," and even "south wind." The Shawnee were a branch of the Algonquin, and one of the most mysterious of Indian tribes. Driven out of South Carolina by the British in the late seventeenth century, their wandering habits after that linked their history with the entire United States east of the Mississippi River. In Pennsylvania they lived, among other places, along the Delaware, Susquehanna, Monongahela, Allegheny, Ohio and Youghiogheny Rivers. Following General Edward Braddock's defeat in 1755, they joined the French and remained hostile to the English through the War for Independence, and then after the war the Americans. In 1869 they became incorporated with the Cherokee of Oklahoma. Their great chiefs included Tecumseh.

Cutting a rather flat path through the mountains, Raystown Branch has been a heavily traveled route long before the construction of the Turnpike, Route 30 and Route 31, major roads that all follow the river at various times. The Raystown Path, from Harrisburg to Pittsburgh, was an important Indian trail that followed the river from about Breezewood to the present area of Shawnee State Park. General John Forbes chose to use the path on his march west to capture Fort Duquesne (Pittsburgh) from the French in 1758. Portions of the path became incorporated in the

Forbes Road, which after the British occupation of the Ohio Valley became the nation's main highway east and west for nearly a century.

Fly anglers might try the Adams, Quill Gordon, Hendrickson, March Brown, Light Cahill, Royal Coachman, Lead Winged Coachman, Hare's Ear, Soft Hackle Nymphs, caddis, terrestrials and midges.

Information on Shawnee Park can be had by writing: Shawnee State Park, Department of Environmental Resources, P.O. Box 67, Schellsburg, PA 15559.

Cove Creek
Bedford County

Almost 18 miles of stocked water makes Cove Creek one of Bedford County's longest trout streams. Its planted portion runs from the edge of Buchanan State Forest west of Rainsburg north through a wide, lovely farm valley almost to its mouth on the Raystown Branch Juniata River.

Despite its length, Cove Creek has few tributary streams of any consequence, and so is not a very large stream. Look at it from Pennsylvania Route 326 in late summer, and its shrunken size makes it difficult to imagine the Fish Commission even bothering to stock it. Of course, the situation is somewhat different in the spring when rains and melting snow swell the creek to a more respectable size.

Access to Cove Creek, like much of the rest of Bedford County, begins off the Pennsylvania Turnpike and U.S. Route 30. Bedford Exit 11 of the Turnpike will lead to Route 30, and Route 30 east leads to Route 326, which takes a path south through the valley between Evitts Mountain and Tussey Mountain. The upper reaches of the stream can be found by continuing south on Route 326. The road passes over Cove Creek just north of Rainsburg, where Valley Road (State Route 3013) appears and runs toward the village of Patience and Centerville. Harriet Lane splits off Valley Road just outside of Rainsburg and also crosses the stream. Wertz Road, a dirt trail leading back into the state forest, parallels the stream along its headwaters.

Although very tiny in size, Rainsburg is actually a borough. It is named after pioneer hunter John Rains. During the middle of the nineteenth century, it was known as the home of Rainsburg Academy, which housed the Allegheny Male and Female Seminary. Samuel Williams chartered the school in 1853. It remained in operation, offering an education equivalent to a high school and junior college, until almost 1870, when the Odd Fellows took over the building and, in turn, started a normal school. After the normal school closed its doors in 1912, the building was used as an elementary school until 1952. In 1969, it was purchased for a private home.

Cove Creek's lower waters north of Rainsburg can be located by following Route 326 off Route 30. Egolf Road (State Route 2014) appears at the top of a hill where Route 326 bends to the right. It leads toward the village of Ott Town, where access to the creek may be had off Ott Town Road. Yellow Lane runs off both Egolf Road and Ott Town Road, and near the stream.

A short distance after Egolf Road meets Deihl Road (State Route 2017) two dirt roads appear on the left leading back to State Game Lands 97, another place where Cove Creek can be found. Knootzsville Road, which can be found running off Deihl

Road upstream of the Game Lands, also leads to the creek. Deihl Road eventually joins Route 326 between Rainsburg and Charlesville.

Buchanan State Forest at the headwaters of Cove Creek was named in honor of James Buchanan, the fifteenth president of the United States and the only Pennsylvanian to hold that post. Buchanan was born further to the east, near the village of Cove Gap, at a spot known by early traders as "Stony Batter."

During his term in office, Buchanan frequently visited the Bedford Springs Hotel on the other side of Evitts Mountain from Cove Creek, earning it the name "Summer White House." A popular resort, particularly with wealthy Southerners, the hotels also was used during the summer months by the U.S. Supreme Court. Some historians maintain the court reached the Dred Scott Decision, making slaves property and not people, while staying at the hotel.

Bedford Springs Hotel was established around 1800 by Dr. John Anderson on the site of a magnesia mineral spring long praised by the Indians and early settlers of the region for its medicinal qualities. On August 17, 1858, Buchanan received the first transatlantic cable from Queen Victoria while staying at the hotel.

"Come let us talk together," the Queen signaled. "American genius and English enterprise have this day joined together the Old and the New World. Let us hope that they may be closely allied in bonds of peace, harmony and kindred spirit."

Buchanan replied with, "New England accepts with gladness the hand of fellowship proffered by Old England."

In 1859, after a poor first term plagued by corruption and nepotism, Buchanan announced from the hotel that he would not seek a second term in office. The start of World War II found the hotel being used as a holding place for Japanese embassies and then a training facility for the navy. It is located along Business Route 22 off Route 30.

Cove Creek fly fishermen might try Adams, caddis, Soft Hackle Nymphs, Muddler Minnows, Matuka Streamers, Hare's Ears, Blue-Winged Olives, March Browns, Gray Fox, Renegades, Light Cahills, Royal Coachmen, Lead-Winged Coachmen, and terrestrials.

Town Creek
Bedford County

At the top of the ridge they stopped. The escape route ran ahead to the north. Far behind them now were the slave hunters. So far they could not even hear the dogs anymore. It was beginning to look as if they might make it. But they were not free yet. Even though they had crossed the Mason-Dixon Line into Pennsylvania, they were still in the United States. And, legally, somebody's property. With any luck at all, though, by morning they would be safely hidden in Bedford, and within a few days Canada. Where they would be truly free.

Then they caught their first glimpse of the torches. Arrayed across the valley floor in front of them, they formed a line solid enough to make it plain their escape route to the north was gone. Probably, they felt then they still had a chance. They were a special group, individually chosen for the quiet strength they had always exhibited in the face of the overseer and even the "massa." Besides they had come too far from the plantation fields, from the stink of the slave quarters, from having every

waking hour owned by someone else to really believe their journey could end so close to freedom.

Maybe the change first started when one of them looked back to the south and the creek and the mill they had just left and saw another line of silent torches approaching. If not at that moment then almost for certain when they turned toward the east and saw the beginnings of a third line. Only the west remained. And then as quick as they could turn in that direction, it, too, was gone. The trap was closed.

For a time, after the panic had given way to resignation, they stood completely motionless. Then one by one the realization sank in. The running was over. Images of the beatings, the humiliation, the shame they had always known and would now know again flooded their minds. Then maybe one began to sing. Music had always been a refuge. Now, it also was an inspiration. 'And before I'll be a slave I'll be buried in my grave, and go home to my God, and be free. . .'

For several choruses the voices grew stronger, ringing through the trees and down the mountain into the valley. Then, in the same manner, they grew weaker. The voices dying one after the other until there was only silence.

Nobody, of course, will ever know exactly what happened on Smiths Mountain in the decade before the Civil War. But David Bradley, a Temple University history instructor and native of Bedford County, has provided a stunning premise in his award winning novel *The Chaneysville Incident*. It is a book that has been compared to Ralph Ellison's classic *The Invisible Man* for its depiction of the Black experience in America. And flowing close to the center of it is Town Creek.

Formed by the meeting of Wilson Run and Elk Lick Run below the village of Chaneysville, Town Creek follows a narrow valley between Warriors Ridge on the west and Polish Mountain on the east to empty into the Potomac River near Oldtown, Maryland. Of medium size, it is stocked with browns and rainbows for about ten miles from Chaneysville to the Maryland line. It is accessible off Pennsylvania Route 326 south from U.S. Route 30 near the town of Bedford, and Township Road 306 at the village of Hewitt.

Fly anglers might try the Adams, Hendrickson, March Brown, Soft Hackle Nymphs, Light Cahill, Sulphurs, Gray Fox, Hare's Ear, Renegade, caddis, midges and terrestrials.

Although the Warriors Path through Bloody Run (Everett), from Huntingdon to Oldtown, Maryland, passed along Town Creek, Southampton Township through which it flows has always been a backwater sort of place. Rimmed by several mountain peaks of over 2,000 feet that cut it off from the rest of Bedford County and Pennsylvania, it has closer ties to Maryland and the South. Captain Thomas Powell of Virginia became the first white man to visit the region in 1625. He was so little impressed by it, his lackluster account of the territory discouraged any further exploration for years. It was not until nearly 100 years later, in 1728, that settlers led by Thomas's grandson, Joseph, moved permanently into the area. They were all Virginians, and during the Civil War some were said to have borne arms for the Confederacy.

Chaneysville today is a rundown mountain village nearly surrounded by Buchanan State Forest.

A "Public Use Map" of Buchanan State Forest that shows Town Creek and other nearby streams may be had free of charge by stopping in at the office in Chaneysville or writing: District Forester, Buchanan State Forest, R.D. 2, Box 3, McConnellsburg, PA 17233.

(Also see Raystown Branch Juniata River and Cove Creek in Bedford County.)

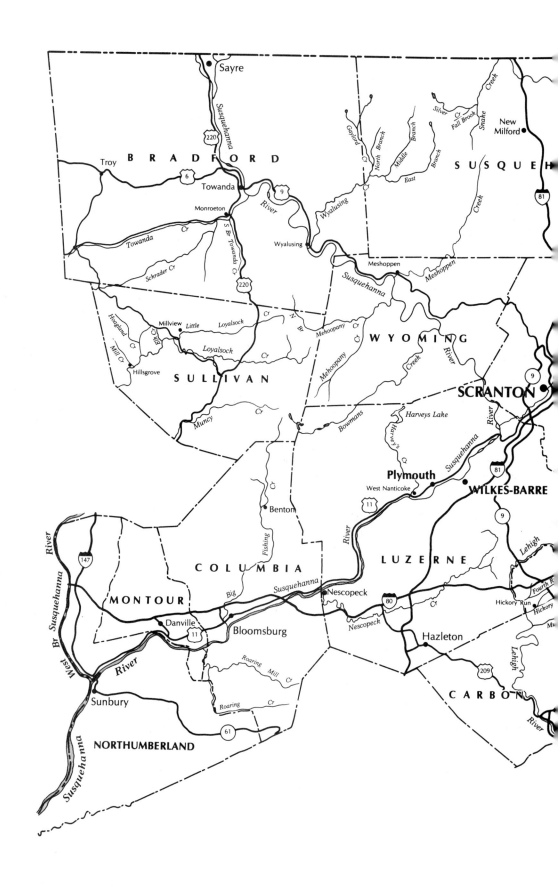

NORTHEAST

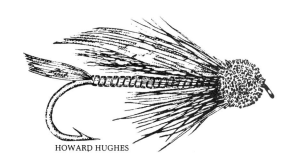

HOWARD HUGHES

Bradford County
Gaylord Cr
Schrader Cr
Susquehanna River
Towanda Cr
Towanda Cr S. Br
Wyalusing Cr

Carbon County
Aquashicola Cr
Fourth Run
Hickory Run
Hunters Cr
Lehigh River
Mud Run

Columbia County
Big Fishing Cr
Roaring Cr
Roaring Mill Cr
Susquehanna River

Lackawanna County
Lackawanna River

Luzerne County
Bowmans Cr
Harveys Cr
Harveys Lake
Lehigh River
Necopeck Cr

Monroe County
Aquashicola Cr
Brodhead Cr
Buckwha Cr
Bushkill Cr
Delaware River
Tobyhanna Cr

Montour County

Northumberland Co
Susquehanna River

Pike County
Bushkill Cr
Delaware River
Lackawaxen River
Little Bushkill Cr
Sawkill Cr
Shohola Cr

Sullivan County
Elk Cr
Hoagland Cr
Little Loyalsock Cr
Loyalsock Cr
Mehoopany Cr
Mill Cr
Muncy Cr

Susquehanna County
Gaylord Cr
Lackawanna River
Meshoppen Cr
Silver Cr
Snake Cr
Starrucca Cr
Wyalusing Cr
Wyalusing Cr E. Br
Wyalusing Cr Mid. Br
Wyalusing Cr N. Br

Wayne County
Delaware River
Dyberry Cr E. Br
Dyberry Cr Mid. Br
Dyberry Cr W. Br
Equinunk Cr
Lackawanna River
Lake Wallenpaupack
Sherman Cr

Wyoming County
Bowmans Cr
Mehoopany Cr
Mehoopany Cr N. Br
Meshoppen Cr
Susquehanna River

Northeast Region

Aquashicola Creek, Buckwha Creek Hunters Creek
Monroe and Carbon Counties

Aquashicola Creek

Long stretches of sand and gravel in the streambed are said to make Aquashicola Creek an ideal breeding ground for a wide variety of aquatic insects. Mayflies, stonefies, caddisflies, midges and mosquitoes all occur in relative abundance. As do black-nosed dace minnows, sculpins and other forage fish. And feeding off this cornucopia are good numbers of large trout, many of them carryovers or wild, stream-bred fish.

With such a variety of things working in its favor, an angler, upon first hearing of Aquashicola Creek, might think it is some sort of overlooked fly fishing paradise. While the fishing can be good, a pleasure it is not. The Indians named this little tributary of the Lehigh River in the shadow of famous Blue Mountain Aquashicola, "where we fish with a bush-net," for good reason. So thick is the brush along the stream's banks that frustration is the only constant when it comes to casting. Simply putting a fly in the right spot amid the overwhelming tangle of alders, assorted downed trees, fences and low bridges can leave the angler with a fulfilling sense of accomplishment, especially after the new growth of late spring begins to appear.

The valley through which Aquashicola flows was evidently occupied by Indians long before recorded history. Archaeologists exploring the region have discovered numerous relics that were never used by the Delaware Indians who inhabited the valley when the white settlers arrived. The Wechquetank Path, from Bethlehem to Wilkes-Barre, passed over the stream at Smith Gap near Kunkletown. It was used by the Moravian missionaries in 1765 when they moved with their Indian converts to Wyalusing (see Wyalusing Creek). The Moravians had been driven out of the region in 1763 when the Paxton Boys, a vigilante group from the Harrisburg area, threatened them during Pontiac's Rebellion. The Indian town of Meniologameka, meaning "a rich spot of land surrounded by barren lands," also once stood along the stream near Kunkletown, but was abandoned in 1754 when Richard Peters, who owned the land on which the town stood, ordered the Indians to move.

Barely a hint of the beautiful valley which must have drawn the Indians to Aquashicola Creek a thousand years ago has made it into the twentieth century. Some of the stream's upper water, above its junction with Buckwha Creek, remains fairly attractive. Below the village of Little Gap, though, things change rapidly until the creek passes through what may be the most abused piece of earth in the entire commonwealth.

The town of Palmerton was laid out in 1898 by the New Jersey Zinc Co. and named for its President, Stephen J. Palmer. In the years following the company built two plants, the East Plant and the West Plant, each of them a mile in length. For decades before air pollution control laws became the norm, the huge stacks in these two facilities belched an acrid yellow smoke. It coated the town's houses and stores, filled the lungs of its residents and killed practically every bit of vegetation on the portion of Blue Mountain above it. With the trees and undergrowth gone the soil washed away, leaving mainly rocks and trunks bleached as white as skeletons.

While Aquashicola Creek's 15 miles of stocked water begins roughly midway between Palmerton and Little Gap, the best fishing reportedly lies above its confluence with Buckwha Creek. That point also marks the start of some of the better scenery. So if an angler can overlook the slag piles and general moonscape around Palmerton, he (or she) still can find a somewhat pleasant setting in which to fish.

No major roads follow Aquashicola Creek, but reaching it is not terribly difficult. Finding it hidden away between the brush is another story, though. Exit 34 of the Northeast Extension of the Pennsylvania Turnpike leads to U.S. Route 209. Near the town of Leighton Route 209 joins with Pennsylvania Route 248. Take Route 248 east to the Palmerton Exit then continue straight through the center of town to the village of Aquashicola. State Route 2002 runs through Aquashicola where a sign will appear pointing the way to Little Gap, four miles away. S.R. 2002 parallels the stream, but the water is generally out of sight.

In Little Gap turn right at the crossroads in the center of the village and continue over a smaller stream and then a covered bridge, under which Buckwha Creek flows. A short distance beyond the covered bridge a junction appears and State Route 2006, which leads to the village of Danielsville and a bridge across Aquashicola Creek. Lower Smith Gap Road (State Route 3002) appears on the left just before the bridge and follows the creek at varying distances upstream into

Monroe County. It also offers access by crossing the stream at different points along the way.

Aquashicola Creek's abundance of aquatic insects and its overhung banks from where terrestrials can find their way to the streams should keep any fly angler who can contend with the brush happy. Starting at the beginning of the season and continuing through the summer, fly fishermen can try Blue Quills, Quill Gordons, Hendricksons, stoneflies, Black-Nosed Daces, Muddler Minnows, Mickey Finns, Black Quills, Black Gnats, caddis, Sulphurs, Blue-Winged Olives, Gray Fox, Light Cahill, Lead-Winged Coachman, Yellow Drake, midges and terrestrials.

Buckwha Creek

Many people confuse Aquashicola Creek with Buckwha Creek. According to the "Stream Map of Pennsylvania" put together by Penn State University, Buckwha Creek is a tributary of Aquashicola Creek, the two joining together about a mile below Little Gap.

Like Aquashicola, Buckwha Creek originates near Pennsylvania Route 33 in Monroe County and contains a fairly good supply of mayflies, stoneflies and caddisflies. Along with stocked fish, it also holds some wild or carryover trout. Unlike its neighboring stream, however, it is quite a bit more open and forgiving to poor casters. Fly anglers can try some of the same flies mentioned for Aquashicola Creek. Buckwha's stocked water runs from its confluence with Aquashicola Creek upstream for approximately 9.5 miles.

As with Aquashicola Creek, Buckwha Creek can be reached by taking the Palmerton Exit off Route 248 and continuing through town to Little Gap on Kunckletown Road (State Route 2002). At Little Gap continue straight on S.R. 2002 toward Kunkletown. The bridge in Kunkletown provides access and joins Chestnut Ridge Road (State Route 3001) which leads to Aquashicola Creek.

Chestnut Ridge Road also traces the route of the Wechequetank Path, from Wilkes-Barre to Bethlehem, over both Aquashicola and Buckwha Creeks. The trail was the "new path" to Wyoming, and sometimes called David's Path. It was used by Moravian missionaries and their Indian converts in 1765 on their return to Wyalusing from Philadelphia. They had fled Wyalusing two years earlier when threatened by the vigilante Paxton Boys during Pontiac's Rebellion.

Hunters Creek

A small tributary of Buckwha Creek, Hunters Creek is stocked for about three miles from its mouth in Little Gap upstream. Anglers traveling from Palmerton to Little Gap can find the stream by turning left on State Route 2004 at the crossroads in the center of Little Gap.

Brodhead Creek
Monroe County

Tradition has made New York's Catskill Mountains the spiritual cradle of fly fishing in America. And it is not an inaccurate assessment. For its streams—the Beaverkill, Neversink, Esopus, Schoharie and Willowemoc—are among the most famous trout waters in the United States. And certainly no other region has inspired as many great anglers as the Catskills. There Theodore Gordon, the godfather of fly fishing in America, adapted British dry-fly theories to waters on this side of the Atlantic, Roy Steenrod first tied the Hendrickson and Harry Darbee the Coffin Fly. George LaBranch wrote *The Dry Fly* and *Fast Water* while living in the region, Preston Jennings' *A Book of Trout Flies;* Art Flick, *A Streamside Guide to Naturals and Their Imitations;* Edward Ringwood Hewitt, *A Trout and Salmon Fisherman for Seventy-Five Years;* Sparse Grey Hackle, *Fishless Days and Angling Nights,*

and Ray Ovington, *How to Take Trout on Wet Flies and Nymphs.* The impressive list continues on and on, through such contemporary masters as A. J. McClane and Ernest Schwiebert.

Despite all of its acclaim, however, one honor has managed to escape the Catskills. It is not the birthplace of sport fishing in America. That accolade belongs to the Pocono Mountains of eastern Pennsylvania and Brodhead Creek.

Although the Brodhead tradition revolves around the private waters of Henryville House, the stream was already famous for trout when it was known as Analomink Creek (meaning unknown) and the Indians camped along its banks. Indentured servant contracts frequently carried stipulations limiting the number of brook trout dinners a master on the frontier around the stream could feed his servants each week.

Captain Daniel Brodhead negotiated with the sons of William Penn to purchase some 1,500 acres of land in the colony in 1734. Three years later he moved into the Pocono region and, with his sons, built a log cabin and sowed his first crop along Analomink Creek, which almost immediately became known as Brodhead Creek.

The arrival of the Brodheads to the Analomink Valley came close on the heels of the "Walking Purchase" (see Hickory Run) that defrauded the Delaware and Minisink tribes of more than 1,200 square miles of their ancestral lands, including Brodhead Creek. It was a scheme the Indians never forgave, and during the uprising that followed General Edward Braddock's defeat in the Battle of the Monongahela in western Pennsylvania in 1755, the stone manor house Captain Brodhead built to replace the family's original cabin served double duty as a fort. The Brodheads came from a long military line and were among the few people who refused to flee their frontier home. Barricading themselves in the house, they successfully repelled a number of attacks by Indian war parties. Later the captain's five sons would serve as officers in the Continental Army during the War for Independence.

While there were fly fishermen in Pennsylvania even when the Brodheads lived along the creek, fishing was mainly a source of food. According to Ernest Schwiebert in his book *Remembrance of Rivers Past,* sport fishing on the Brodhead did not start until the mid-1830s when Arthur Henry built a small inn, Halfway House, along the stream. It was that little inn, host to rough teamsters and the occasional hunter or fisherman, which grew to become Henryville House, the first trout fishing hotel in America.

The first well-known person to fish the Brodhead was John Jefferson, a famous actor of the mid-nineteenth century and later fishing companion of President Grover Cleveland. Thaddeus Norris, probably the best known of the United States early angling writers, appeared soon after Jefferson, and featured the stream in his *The American Angler's Book* in 1864. Joining Norris on the stream, Schwiebert notes, were Samuel Phillips, a gunsmith and violin maker from Easton, Pennsylvania, who developed the first modern cane rod, and Chancellor Levison, a founder of the Anglers' Club of New York and the Brooklyn Flyfishers' Club.

In the years between the Civil War and the Great Depression, Henryville House became a favorite stomping ground for the rich and famous across the eastern United States. General Philip Sheridan is said to have recuperated from his campaigns at the hotel, even supplying the name Paradise Valley for the valley through which the Henryville Branch of the Brodhead flows. Buffalo Bill and Annie Oakley both fished and demonstrated their marksmanship along the stream. Grover Cleveland and Benjamin Harrison stayed at the hotel while running against each other. And Gifford Pinchot, the nation's first professional forester and a two-term governor of Pennsylvania, brought Theodore Roosevelt to the Brodhead from his home in nearby Milford.

The list of famous fly fishing innovators and writers who tested their skills and worked to form their theories on the Brodhead include every major member of the Catskill fraternity, among them Gordon, LaBranche and Hewitt. Other angling figures with links to the stream are: Preston Jennings; the fly tyer Charles Wetzel; James Leisenring of the "Leisenring Lift" nymphing technique; Charlie Fox, who along with Vincent Marinaro revolutionized fly fishing theory on the Letort in the years after World War II; *Field & Stream's* Ed Zern; and Ray Bergman, whose *Trout* was the standard guide for generations of trout fishermen. Like the Catskills list, the Brodhead list goes on and on.

The Brodhead today is said to still contain some truly outstanding trout water. Unfortunately, all of it is privately owned and lined with the typical Pocono signs, "KEEP OUT," "POSTED," "NO TRESPASSING," "PRIVATE," "NO FISHING." Only about eight miles of the lower Brodhead, from near Stroudsburg upstream, is open to the public. But fishing in this relatively swift water is fairly good early in the season, as well as during the fall and winter.

Access to the Brodhead's public water may be had by taking Interstate Route 80 Exit 50, Park Avenue, and following Pennsylvania Route 191's circuitous path through the town of Stroudburg. Route 191 parallels the Brodhead upstream and across the creek to Pennsylvania Route 447 which follows it the rest of the way. Stokes Avenue and Stokes Mill Road both run off Route 191 and down to the stream, but the area is residential and parking at a premium.

Hurricanes Connie and Diane dumped over 14 inches of rain on Brodhead Creek in 1955, and almost completely destroyed the stream's aquatic life for years. The stream now has sporadic hatches of mayflies, caddisflies and stoneflies. Anglers might tempt the stream's browns and rainbows with Adams, Quill Gordons, Hare's Ear, Hendricksons, stoneflies, Muddler Minnows, Sculpins, Mickey Finns, Soft Hackle Nymphs, March Browns, Renegades, Royal Coachman, caddis, Light Cahills and terrestrials.

Fishermen can obtain a view of the Brodhead's upper water, and several other trout streams in the area, through the Delaware Forest's free "Public Use Map." One can be had at forest offices, most nearby state parks, or by writing: District Forester, Delaware State Forest, 474 Clearview Lane, Stroudsburg, PA 18360.

Big Bushkill Creek
Fly Fishing Only
Monroe County

Renowned as one of the most aesthetically pleasing streams in eastern Pennsylvania, Big Bushkill Creek also may be one of the most heavily posted. People who own land along this picturesque jewel like to save it for themselves. "No Trespassing" and "Private Property" signs abound. So, of its entire length, from its source in Pecks Pond, Pike County, to its mouth at the village of Bushkill on the Delaware River, a distance of roughly 30 miles, only 12 miles are stocked by the Fish Commission.

But what does remain available to the public of the stream, which in Dutch means "forest water," nonetheless, is quite beautiful, especially the upper portion on the Boy Scouts of America reservation around Rescia Falls. Anglers who visit there will find a relatively large stream loaded with numerous good pools and swift, cobble runs surrounded by forests of hemlock and pine, and watched over by natural ledges and a stunning set of falls.

Big Bushkill Creek's six-mile long Fly Fishing Only Project lies in the upper half of the stocked water on the Boy Scout property. It can be found by taking Interstate Route 84 Exit 8 and following Pennsylvania Route 402 south to the village of Resica Falls, or by picking up Route 402 off U.S. Route 209 at the village of Marshalls Creek and driving north to Resica Falls. Route 402 passes over the stream on the Boy Scout property, and parking is available nearby. The special regulation water is clearly marked with signs. No fishing is permitted within 200 yards upstream and downstream of the falls.

The lower portion of the Bushkill's stocked water can be reached by taking Route 209 to the village of Bushkill. Route 209 parallels the stream between the villages of Shoemakers and Bushkill. Access also is available by taking Township Road 301 across the mouth of Little Bushkill Creek in Bushkill and following it up to Winona Falls Road where a bridge crosses the stream.

Strictly a seasonal stream, the tea-colored waters of Big Bushkill Creek are at their best in the spring and fall. Summer will see its trout either entering cooler tributaries or moving downstream to the deeper Delaware River.

Popular flies include: Blue Quills, Quill Gordon, March Brown, Hendrickson, Hare's Ear, stoneflies, caddis, Soft Hackle Nymphs, Renegade, Muddler Minnows and Mickey Finns.

Anglers looking for a map with a good view of Big Bushkill Creek, as well as several other trout streams in this book, should obtain a free "Public Use Map" of Delaware State Forest. It may be had at forest offices, most local state parks or by writing: District Forester, Delaware State Forest, 474 Clearview Lane, Stroudsburg, PA 18360.

Nescopeck Creek
Luzerne County

Interstate Route 80 and Interstate Route 81 may cross each other just over the hill, but thanks to undeveloped Nescopeck State Park and State Game Lands 187, the angler who chooses to visit Nescopeck Creek can easily feel he is a million miles away from everywhere. This is especially true after the traditional early-season crowds have thinned out.

From Pennsylvania Route 437 downstream to approximately the Interstate Route 80 bridge, the Nescopeck flows mostly smooth and clear through an utterly beautiful wilderness valley of hardwood and white birch forests, glades and alder swamps typical of southeastern Luzerne County. The only blemish in the whole scene is the presence of a private club on the first mile below the Route 437 bridge. Otherwise, the entire stretch, roughly six miles, is open to the public. Or at least that segment of the population not opposed to a hike. For no road touches the water and all the fishing is of the walk-in variety, mainly over State Game Lands 187.

Centuries before the nation's interstate highway system was even imagined, Nescopeck Path, which crosses the stream near the town of Conyngham, was a major route between Bethlehem and the town of Nescopeck on the Susquehanna River across from Berwick. It was used by traders and missionaries, Indian war parties during the French and Indian War, and by settlers fleeing the Wyoming Valley after the Wyoming (Wilkes-Barre) Massacre of 1778. In that fight, Indians hired by the British went out of control and murdered some 300 men, women and children after they had surrendered.

In the wake of British General Edward Braddock's defeat in the Battle of the Monongahela during his march on Fort Duquesne (Pittsburgh) in 1755, the village of Nescopeck became a rallying point for Indians hostile to the English. In 1756, Silver Heels, an

Rescia Falls on Big Bushkill Creek.

Iroquois, was sent by the English to investigate the Indian situation along the Susquehanna River. He found some 140 warriors at Nescopeck making preparations to raid a frontier settlement. That same year word was sent out to all hostile Indians in the region to meet at Nescopeck. The village and surrounding territory remained a center for Indians hostile to European settlers into the Revolutionary War.

Nescopeck Creek between Route 437 and Interstate Route 80 is well-stocked with brown trout. For the first mile and a half, which includes the private club water, the stream is a small brook measuring only about ten feet in width. It is full of rocks, fast chutes and broken channels. The addition of Creasy Run's flow and a decrease in gradient begin to change things, but the angler can expect about another mile of broken channels before the Nescopeck really begins to live up to its name "deep and still water."

The presence of swamp lands around the stream makes a good insect repellant a must, but it also makes mosquito imitations deadly for the fly fisherman. Other effective flies include the Adams, caddis and midges. The usual Pocono region hatches include: April, Blue Quill, Quill Gordon, Hendrickson and Black Quill; May, Sulphurs, March Brown, Blue-Winged Olive, Gray Fox and Green Drake; June, Light Cahill, Isonychia and Yellow Drake.

Nescopeck Creek can be reached by taking Interstate Route 80 Exit 39, Pennsylvania Route 309 south toward Sand Springs and Hazelton, or Exit 40, Route 437 north through White Haven toward Mountain Top and Wilkes-Barre.

The lower part of the state park/game lands stretch starts less than a mile off Exit 39, Route 309 south. Honeyhole Road runs parallel to the stream all of the way to Route 437. As of publication, the sign for Honeyhole Road is missing. Anglers can find it by following the signs for Beech Mountain Lakes, a private resort, and turning left next to a heavy equipment company.

Honeyhole Road on the upper reaches of the stretch, also unmarked, can be reached by turning left immediately after crossing the stream on the Route 437 bridge. In both cases, numerous signs will make the angler aware of when he is on game lands propery. Parking is available at many locations.

Both the Lehigh Path, from Bethlehem to Wilkes-Barre, and the Nescopeck Path, from Bethlehem to Nescopeck, once crossed Nescopeck Creek.

The Nescopeck Path was used by traders and missionaries, Delaware war parties during the French and Indian War, and settlers fleeing the Wyoming Valley after the Wyoming Massacre. The path was sometimes also called the Fort Allen Path. Benjamin Franklin ordered the construction of Fort Allen at Weissport in 1756 to deny the use of the path to Indian war parties.

The Lehigh Path was a short, but difficult, route to Wyoming, frequently used by the Indians. It was so hard, travelers could not help expressing their feelings. Christian Post wrote after climbing a mountain along the trail ". . .all my Limbs trembled as if I had a fit of the Ague, & in descending the same it made both Man & Beast tremble. . .My horse being formerly a Gentleman's & not used to such hardships & to climb such craggy hills & steep mountains, laid him twice flat on the ground with me. . ."

Lehigh River
Wayne, Monroe, Lackawanna, Carbon and Luzerne Counties
(Float Trip)

Transportation and the Lehigh River have been closely linked since long before the first European landed in Pennsylvania. The Lehigh Path, from Easton/Bethlehem to Wilkes-Barre, was a heavily-used Indian trail that followed the river well over half its distance. During the early years of the nineteenth century the Lehigh Navigation & Coal Co. and the Lehigh Valley Railroad utilized the waterway to carry anthracite coal from the fields of northeastern Pennsylvania to Philadelphia and New York. So, somehow it seems proper that the river is now within easy reach of four interstate highways, as well as the Northeast Extension of the Pennsylvania Turnpike.

Such convenient access has made the Lehigh River—whose name is an English corruption of a German shortening of the Indian name Lechauweeki, or "at the forks,"—one of Pennsylvania's most popular whitewater streams. Every year rafters and canoeists from all over the East Coast descend upon the river by the thousands. Fortunately for trout anglers, however, most of their attention is focused on the 26-mile long stretch between the towns of White Haven and Jim Thorpe. Consequently, many other portions of the Lehigh are uncrowded, even underfished. This despite the fact it has an abundance of insect life, and good populations of wild, stocked and carryover brown, brook and rainbow trout.

The Lehigh River starts at Westend Pond in the village of Gouldsboro on the northern edge of what the Indians called the "Great Swamp." It is stocked from its source downstream for about 13.6 miles to the Luzerne County line. Along these headwaters the small, tannic acid-stained river forms the boundary between first Wayne and Lackawanna Counties, and then Lackawanna and Monroe Counties. Possibly because of its close proximity to Gouldsboro and Tobyanna State Parks, and the unposted property of State Game Lands 127, it also attracts quite a bit of angling pressure. In spite of the pressure, though, it is still said to hold a number of streambred and carryover browns and rainbows, along with a good yearly quota of hatchery fish.

Interstate Route 380 is the first major highway to touch on the Lehigh River. Anglers can gain access to the river's headwaters by taking Exit 6 and following Pennsylvania Route 507 toward Gouldsboro and Gouldsboro State Park. Route 507 parallels the stream at a distance through the village and up to Westend Pond. Fishermen should beware of trespassing on private property. Pennsylvania Route 435, which appears at Exit 6, also crosses the stream.

Both Gouldsboro and Gouldsboro State Park are named after nineteenth century industrialist Jay Gould. One of the original "Robber Barons," Gould at one point owned approximately one out of every nine miles of railroad track in the United States. During the Grant Administration he also was responsible for a gold trading scheme that helped bring about a stock market crash in the early 1870s. His ties to the upper Lehigh Valley center around a tannery he built along the river in 1857 near the start of his career.

No overnight facilities are available at Gouldsboro State Park along Route 507. However, it does have a one mile long hiking trail, picnic areas, boating and swimming, from Memorial Day Weekend to Labor Day, on 250-acre Gouldsboro Lake.

For anglers who would like to spend a few days in the area, camping facilities can be found at Tobyhanna State Park, which abuts Gouldsboro Park on the east. Tobyhanna has a campground with 140 Class B sites open on a year round basis. There are no flush toilets or showers, but a dump station is open from May 1 to October 1. And there are ten miles of hiking trails, picnic area and Tobyhanna Lake for boating and swimming, from Memorial Day weekend to Labor Day. (Also see Tobyhanna Creek.)

Downstream of Gouldsboro the Lehigh River can be reached by following State Route 2013 toward the village of Clifton, which meets Route 435 near a crossroads sign a short distance north of where it crosses the river. A better choice, however, might be the road leading into Game Lands 127. It runs off Route 507 south at Exit 6 (Gouldsboro) of Interstate 380. Traveling north, it would be a left turn immediately at the bottom of the exit ramp. The road parallels and crosses the river, essentially a medium-sized stream, all of the way out to Clifton. Beginning as a paved secondary road, it turns to dirt and gravel in the Game Lands. Plenty of parking is available at various locations.

The Lehigh River in Game Lands 127 is a clear, but dark, stream hurrying over gravel beds and small boulders and under the fallen trees typical of mountain waters. At Clifton State Route 2013 appears and follows the river downstream through the village of Thornhurst, where Jay Gould once had his tannery.

From Clifton downstream through Thornhurst the Lehigh again becomes a "civilized" river. Houses frequently appear along its banks, and its flow shows the smooth and flat waters usually associated with plateau streams. Below Thornhurst S.R. 2013 turns into State Route 2015 and the upper portion of the river's stocked water ends. The road also begins to pull away from the river, allowing it to quietly slip back into a forest setting. .

S.R. 2013, which appears outside of Thornhurst, ends on Pennsylvania Route 115. A left turn on Route 115 leads to Stoddartsville, where access to the Lehigh is available from a parking area next to the bridge. Less than a hundred yards below the Route 115 bridge the Lehigh slips over a picturesque set of falls. Anybody who decides to stop at the Stoddardsville bridge should be sure to keep an eye open for private property. About two miles below the bridge, Tobyhanna Creek also joins the Lehigh, nearly doubling its volume.

After Thornhurst, stocking of the Lehigh River does not resume until the Francis E. Walter Dam. The river below the dam can be reached by following Route 115 through Stoddarsville to the village of Blakeslee and then taking Pennsylvania Route 940 west toward White Haven. A short distance east of Pennsylvania Turnpike Exit 35 a road, marked by a large sign, leads to the dam. After crossing over the dam a dirt road leads from a picnic area at the top to a smaller picnic area roughly a half mile downstream of the dam.

Francis E. Walter Dam marks the start of the Lehigh's most floatable water. The river from there through White Haven down to Jim Thorpe is canoeable or raftable from the opening of the trout season in mid-April through the end of May. In wet years the river sometimes can be floated into June, as well as in November and early December. During the summer months the Corps of Engineers also regularly schedules "Release Weekends," when it releases water from the dam to raise the river for rafting purposes.

White Haven is the center of rafting activity on the Lehigh River. And just a quick look at its location shows why. Situated at the junction of Pennsylvania Routes 940 and 437, it is easily accessible off Exit 35 of the Pennsylvania Turnpike, as well as Exit 40 of Interstate 80. It is less than ten miles from the campgrounds and other facilities of Hickory Run State Park, and near the head of 6,000-acre Lehigh Gorge State Park, an undeveloped piece of public real estate that protects some 30 miles of the river, including the 1,000-foot high cliffs of Lehigh Gorge, from Francis E. Walter Dam downstream to Jim Thorpe.

Numerous legends have arisen over the centuries in connection with the discovery of anthracite coal in Pennsylvania. One of the earliest has a party of Indians building a signal fire on an outcropping and suddenly finding that the black rock would burn. In 1762 Connecticut pioneers supposedly were aware of "stone coal" in the Wyoming Valley. Blacksmith Obadiah Gore reportedly used it in his forge near what is now Wilkes-Barre as early as 1769, and just six years later a shipment of anthracite was floated down the Susquehanna River to market. But since it was much more difficult to burn than the soft, bituminous coal of western Pennsylvania, it found no purchasers. The next year, some anthracite was used as a fuel to fire ironmaking furnaces that supplied the Continental Army with arms. It was another quarter of a century, though, before the hard coal started to find domestic and commercial use. Frederick Grass of Philadelphia burned it in a large stove in 1802; the following year another Philadelphian, Oliver Evans, used it in a grate; and in 1808 Judge Jesse Fell of Wilkes-Barre used it in an open grate under a natural draft.

Following the discovery of anthracite coal near Mauch Chunk (Jim Thorpe) in 1791 a group of Philadelphia businessmen organized the Lehigh Coal Mine Co. The purpose of the company was to supply the Philadelphia area with anthracite. The investors hoped it would catch on as a fuel source, and in the process make them wealthy. Because few people knew how to use it, or had the proper equipment, the venture met with a great deal of public skepticism. The company was forced to give away large quantities of the coal to try and build a market. Still, only about 385 tons of the coal was being mined a year up until 1820.

"My father procured a lump of Lehigh Coal about as large as his two fists, and tried it on his wood fire in an open Franklin stove," Abijah Hall wrote in his travel diary as late as 1824. "After two days he concluded that 'if the world should take fire, the Lehigh Coal Mine would be the safest retreat, the last place to burn.' "

The seed of change already had been germinating for a dozen years, however, when Hall wrote those lines. It was planted in 1812 when an employee of Josiah White and Erskine Hazard's Fairmont Nail & Wire Works on the Schuylkill River near Philadelphia returned to the factory to pick up something he had forgotten. When he arrived at the plant he found an experimental anthracite fire flowing with intense heat. That fire rekindled White's interest in anthracite coal. Convinced it could be of commercial value, White and Hazard took out a 20-year lease on the coal fields around Mauch Chunk. Then, in the winter of 1817-1818, White left Philadelphia to explore the possibilities of using the Lehigh River to transport anthracite coal to Philadelphia. His trip led to the merging of the Lehigh Coal Co., established 1818, and the Lehigh Navigation Co. in the Lehigh Coal & Navigation Co. in 1820. Nine years later the merger resulted in the opening of the Lehigh Canal, built to carry anthracite coal from Mauch Chunk to Bethlehem-Easton and then down the Delaware River to Philadelphia and New York City.

White Haven, about 25 miles up the Lehigh River from Mauch Chunk, was first settled in 1824 by John Lines and his family. Lines operated a sawmill and tavern along the river, and for a time the village was known as Linesville. Then in 1839 the Lehigh Canal reached the town and in 1841 the Susquehanna & Lehigh Railroad Co. built a line from Wilkes-Barre to White Haven, turning it into an important intersection between the anthracite fields and pine forests of the Wyoming Valley and the cities of the East Coast.

A flood in 1862 destroyed all of the dams along the northern portion of the canal. A few years later the Susquehanna & Lehigh Railroad Co. joined with Asa Packer's Lehigh Valley Railroad Co. to build a rail line from White Haven to Mauch Chunk and further cement the town's link in the transportation chain of northeastern Pennsylvania.

Asa Packer was a classic American success story of the Golden Age of Capitalism. A native of Mauch Chunk, Packer was an unemployed carpenter when he took a job as a boatman on the Lehigh Canal. As coal production in the region increased in the 1830s and the canal began to expand, he noticed a need for more boats. He decided to put his carpentry skills to work by establishing a boat yard. That venture turned out so well he soon opened a second yard on the Schuylkill Canal in Pottsville.

Packer's boats were well-built and seaworthy enough to enable his company to become the first to ship anthracite coal along the Atlantic Seabord to New York City. In the 1840s he began buying up coal rights along Nesquehoning Creek west of Mauch Chunk. When his coal company went into operation he was able to control large amounts of anthracite all of the way from his mines to New York and Philadelphia on his own boats.

By 1850 Packer was one of the wealthiest men in Carbon County. Sixteen years later he used a portion of his fortune to establish Lehigh University in the city of Bethlehem, being generous enough that no tuition was required of students for over 20 years, from 1871 to 1892, when the enrollment grew so large a small fee was required. Through the same period Packer's political clout also grew to the point where in 1876 he was Pennsylvania's candidate for president of the United States at the Democratic convention.

The decline of northeastern Pennsylvania's lumber and coal empires as the twentieth century neared brought change to White Haven and the Lehigh River. From a transportation/industrial hub the town became a center for tourists interested in visiting the Lehigh Gorge, and a retreat for victims of tuberculosis or, as it was known then, consumption. Its clean air eventually attracted several rest homes, among them the Free Hospital for Poor Consumptives, which later became the White Haven Sanatorium and today operates as the White Haven State School.

White Haven can be reached by taking either Interstate Route 80 Exit 40, or Pennsylvania Turnpike Northeast Extension Exit 35 and following signs along Route 940 into the town. In the center of town, on the west side of the Lehigh River, an Historical Marker appears commemorating Josiah White. Across from the marker is a small shopping center with a supermarket. Turn into the shopping center and drive straight through the parking lot. At the end of the pavement a black cinder road appears that leads under the Interstate 80 bridge back to the river and Lehigh State Park, marked by a large wooden sign and a gate barring further access to the road. Anglers can follow the river downstream by walking along the road, which is really an abandoned railroad bed, or the active railroad bed, but floating gives the easiest access.

The Lehigh around White Haven has been stocked with fingerling trout. The river's stocked waters officially end on the Carbon County line at the mouth of Hickory Run. Unofficially, trout fishing along the Lehigh ends about two miles above Jim Thorpe where Nesquehoning Creek adds its acid mine-tainted waters.

Roughly two miles below White Haven the Lehigh River can be reached by getting back on Interstate 80 and taking Exit 41, Pennsylvania Route 534 into the village of Lehigh Tannery. Access may be had by turning right at the ''T'' in the village.

Route 534 also leads to Hickory Run State Park. Fishermen interested in staying in the area will find a 381-site Class A campground with showers, flush toilets, dump station and camp store in the park. It is open from the second Friday in April to the end of the antlerless deer season in mid-December. The park, which covers some 15,500 acres, also offers swimming at Sand Spring Lake from Memorial Day weekend to Labor Day, picnicking, an environmental education program on weekends during the sum-

At rest above the Lehigh River.

mer, hiking along 30 miles of trails and fishing in Hickory Run, Mud Run (see which), Sand Spring Lake and Hickory Run Lake. Since the park borders on the river, anglers also can fish the Lehigh by following Hickory Run Trail.

The next road access point to the Lehigh after White Haven is about 9.5 miles downstream at the village of Rockport. It can be found by following Route 940 west out of White Haven. A short distance beyond Interstate 80 Exit 40 the White Haven-Weatherly Road (State Route 2044) appears on the left. Six miles down the road an obscure left turn, marked by a well farmed area, appears. The river can be reached by following this road downhill and making the first right and then the next left.

After Rockport, and State Route 4014, the next road access to the Lehigh is behind the old railroad station in Jim Thorpe. Although all the best trout fishing is far above Jim Thorpe, anglers floating the river should consider continuing all of the way into the town for a number of reasons. First of all it is a very pretty place with gingerbread trim and ornate cast iron railings. Secondly, it has the facilities—especially bars and restaurants—that tired anglers crave. Float fishermen who do not go the full distance from White Haven to Jim Thorpe also miss a chance to see Glen Onoko. The waterfalls tumbling down this short hemlock-dressed side canyon just a few miles above Jim Thorpe have charmed visitors to the Lehigh Gorge since the nineteenth century when special excursion trains chugged their way in from cities downstream. Some people feel Glen Onoko may be the most beautiful spot in the whole gorge, and travelers who want, can again visit the area by a steam-powered tourist train that runs out of Jim Thorpe.

Until 1953 Jim Thorpe was actually two separate municipalities—Mauch Chunk ("bear mountain" in the Indian language) and East Mauch Chunk—on opposite banks of the Lehigh River. Through most of the nineteenth century and early years of the twentieth it was one of the most prosperous railroad, canal and coal centers of northeastern Pennsylvania. Mansions along Broadway were said to equal any of the time in much larger cities and the town's new millionaires decorated them with the finest money could buy.

With the decline of the coal industry and the railroads during the Great Depression both Mauch Chunk and East Mauch Chunk fell on hard times. Unemployment increased, businesses closed and young people began leaving the towns for greener pastures.

Around the same time Mauch Chunk and East Mauch Chunk began experiencing troubles, so did Jim Thorpe. At the 1912 Olympics in Stockholm, Sweden, Thorpe was at the peak of his abilities and fame. He had just become the first person in history to win both the decathlon and pentathlon, and had been proclaimed "the greatest athlete in the world" by King Gustaf V of Sweden.

Soon after the Olympics, however, Thorpe's famous problems began. They started when a reporter discovered he had been paid $60 a month to play baseball in North Carolina while he was a student at the Old Carlisle Indian School in south central Pennsylvania. Despite Thorpe's protests that he had not known he was forfeiting his amateur status by taking the money the International Olympic Committee stripped him of his medals.

In the years following the Olympic scandal, Thorpe made his living by playing both professional baseball and football, including a stint with the old New York Giants of the National League. In 1950 the nation's sportswriters paid him overdue honor by voting him the greatest male athlete of the half century. The title was clearly a case of too-little, too-late, though. Within a year, Thorpe was a charity case in a Philadelphia hospital.

"We're broke," his wife reported at the time. "Jim has nothing but his name and his memories. He has spent his money on his own people and has given it away. He had often been exploited."

When Thorpe died in 1953, his widow learned his native state of Oklahoma was not interested in establishing a memorial in his honor. About the same time, she also heard of Mauch Chunk and East Mauch Chunk, and of their citizens' efforts to spur the town's economies by donating a nickel a week to a special development fund. She decided to approach local officials. The idea of honoring Jim Thorpe by accepting his remains and changing the names of the two towns was approved by local voters in two referendums. He now lies buried in a quiet, grassy site under the Olympic flag on Route 903 north of the town.

Hatches on the Lehigh River include: mid-April to late May, Blue Quills, Quill Gordons, stoneflies, Hendricksons, Black Quills, Sulphurs, March Browns, Blue-Winged Olives, caddis, Gray Fox, Green Drakes and Brown Drakes; June and later, Blue-Winged Olives, Sulphurs, caddis, Green Drakes, Light Cahills, Isonychias, Yellow Drakes and terrestrials.

Information on Gouldsboro and Tobyhanna State Parks may be had by writing: Gouldsboro and Tobyhanna State Parks, Department of Environmental Resources, P.O. Box 387, Tobyhanna, PA 18466.

Details on Hickory Run are available by writing: Hickory Run State Park, Department of Environmental Resources, R.D. 1, Box 81, White Haven, PA 18661.

The "Public Use Map" of Delaware State Forest also provides a good overview of the upper Lehigh. It can be had free of charge at forest offices, most local state parks, or by writing: District Forester, Delaware State Forest, 471 Clearview Lane, Stroudsburg, PA 18360.

(Also see Tobyhanna Creek and Hickory Run.)

Hickory Run
Catch and Release
Mud Run
Fly Fishing Only
Fourth Run
Carbon County

Hickory Run

Over the past one million years at least three glaciers have descended the polar regions to encompass northern Pennsylvania. Chief among these was the Wisconsin Glacier, which came to a halt less than a mile northeast of Hickory Run State Park. It came making the climate similar to Greenland's ice cap, and pushing before it much of the earth and stone known today as the Pocono Mountains. When it retreated, some 20,000 years ago, it also left behind one very strange remnant: a boulder field.

Blanketing an area of approximately 400 feet by 1,800 feet, this odd scar is comprised of thousands upon thousands of rocks—red conglomerate, sandstone and siltstone. They measure mostly four feet in diameter and lay startlingly naked, devoid of vegetation in the midst of a lush forest.

How the boulders reached their present location has fascinated visitors to the area since they were first discovered. Looking at them it is easy to imagine primitive travelers and early settlers shying away from the spot in fear of the nether world. While such horrific visions might make for good ticket sales at the box office, they do nothing at all to explain the true origins of the boulder field.

According to the park's "Trail of Geology" guide, the boulder field was formed by water running off the glacier face and entering cracks in the ridge ahead of it. Repeated freezing and thawing action during the Ice Age seasons then broke the ridges apart, piling the debris at their bases. This debris was eventually spread out into its present form by the same freeze and thaw periods pushing it across the surface of the frozen land. A roundness was added to the boulders as they rubbed together on their journey.

Hickory Run State Park's boulder field is so unique a phenomenon it is listed as a National Natural Landmark. But from the trout angler's perspective, it is much more interesting as the source of Hickory Run with its population of both stocked and wild brook and brown trout.

Running from the boulder field area through the heart of the park until it joins the Leigh River roughly three miles below Leigh Tannery, Hickory Run is a completely protected stream, open to

Mud Run in Hickory Run State Park.

the public along practically its entire length.

Despite its privileged location, however, swift little Hickory Run is not totally untouched by the hand of man. Only a few yards below the park office, and just above the stream's Catch and Release Project, sits a sewage treatment facility. While there is no denying such an operation is preferable to having raw sewage destroy the stream, its presence does little to enhance the aesthetic beauty of Hickory Run's surroundings. And it also probably contributes to the stream reaching the highest water temperature (72 degrees) of all the creeks in the park.

Still, the plant's existence apparently has not caused any great harm to Hickory Run's aquatic insects or trout. Fish up to 20 inches have been reported, and there are hatches of both caddisflies and mayflies. Imitations to try in April include: Blue Quills, Baetis, Quill Gordons, Hendricksons and Black Quills; May, Sulphurs, March Browns, Blue Winged Olives, Gray Fox, Green Drakes and Brown Drakes; June, Light Cahill, Isonychia and Yellow Drakes. Caddis occur in abundance throughout the spring and summer. Most of them can be imitated by impressionistic patterns such as the Elk Hair Caddis, Humpy, Adams, Soft Hackle Nymphs and Henryville Special.

Hickory Run's 1.5-mile Catch and Release water runs from its junction with Sand Spring, near the park office, downstream to the mouth. Hickory Run Trail runs off Route 534 in the park and down to the stream.

Mud Run

Like Hickory Run, Mud Run is a tributary of the Leigh River, joining that famous waterway about five miles downstream of Leigh Tannery. Unlike Hickory, though, only 2.6 miles of Mud Run are protected by Hickory Run State Park. The remainder flows across private property, starting east of the village of Albrightsville.

While it might not enjoy such a privileged status as Hickory Run, Mud Run is by far the prettier of the park's two special regulation waters. Loaded with canyons, rapids and waterfalls, it may be one of the most scenic trout streams in the Pocono region. The one item marring the picture is the presence of a Pennsylvania Turnpike bridge. It appears high overhead about midway into Mud Run's passage through the park, and just downstream from lovely Hawk Falls.

The existence of the bridge aside, thanks to the fact Mud Run is not directly accessible from any road, it still offers as near a wilderness fishing experience for brook and brown trout as can be found in Carbon County. But anglers looking to fish here will have to do a little hiking. The stream can be reached by either Orchard Trail or Hawk Falls Trail. Both trails run off Route 534 in the southeast corner of the park. They are clearly marked by wooden signs and parking areas are provided.

Fly hatches on Mud Run are similar to Hickory Run. Since the stream is well-shaded its temperature seldom rises above 65 degrees, so it is generally a better bet than Hickory Run in warm weather. At least a few fish also can be found rising along it most of the time. Midge patterns and emerging caddis imitations are said to be particularly effective. Anglers also might try some of the other patterns mentioned under Hickory Run.

Fourth Run

A third stocked trout stream in Hickory Run State Park is Fourth Run, a little tributary of Hayes Creek and the Lehigh River. Running through both the park and State Game Lands 40, it is stocked for over 3.5 miles from its confluence with Hayes

Run upstream. It can be reached by following Fourth Run Trail in the park.

HICKORY RUN STATE PARK

Land on which the park sits was acquired through the infamous "Walking Purchase of 1737" that forcibly removed the Delaware Indians from their ancestral lands in eastern Pennsylvania. The pact, purporting to be the confirmation of an old deed made in 1683 with William Penn, provided for a boundary line starting at Wrightstown, Bucks County, and running parallel to the Delaware River "as far as a man could walk in a day and a half."

Extraordinary measures, some of them grossly unfair, were taken by the colonists to make certain as much land as possible would be obtained in the deed. Among them were the surveying of the route in advance and the use of the fastest walkers in the province to follow it.

Repeated complaints by the Indians that they could not keep up with the walkers led them to quit in disgust at the end of the first day. The colonists completed the walk the next day on their own, finally covering between 60 and 65 miles, or about twice what the Indians had expected when they signed the deed. The line, which was to be drawn from the point where the walk stopped east to the Delaware River, also was drawn on a slant to encompass still a larger area. By the time the affair was concluded, the territory claimed embraced all of the hereditary lands of the Minisink Tribe of the Delawares.

The entire transaction provoked bitter resentment among the Delawares, and marked the beginning of Indian troubles in Pennsylvania.

To help spur development of the territory obtained in the Walking Purchase, the state, from 1790 to 1835, sold warrants of 400 acres to anyone who would pay for registration and survey work. Among those who took up the offer were Robert Morris and Stephen Decatur. Morris, who is known as the "Financier of the American Revolution," was a signer of both the Declaration of Independence and the Constitution. Decatur was a naval hero during the Tripolitan War against the Barbary pirates of the north African coast and the War of 1812.

Prior to the Civil War, according to the park "Recreational Guide," the area was known as "Shades of Death" because of the dense growths of white pine, hemlock, oak and maples which covered it. After 1865, numerous lumber camps and villages sprang up, both in the present-day park and surrounding mountains, including the village of Hickory Run, at the junction of Sand Spring Run and Hickory Run. Isaac Gould, a relative of railroad magnate Jay Gould, one of the best known "Robber Barons" of the late nineteenth century, for a time owned a lumbering operation in Hickory Run.

Saylorsville was another lumber town within the park boundaries, and one of the stops on the main Bethlehem to Wilkes-Barre stage route. Its most famous structure was an inn that could house up to 150 guests.

By 1880, just 15 years after it all began, however, the mountains were fairly stripped of trees and everything came to an end. The lumber companies pulled up stacks and moved west to the still virgin forests of central Pennsylvania, where they started the process all over again as the towns they left behind gradually withered and died. The present park office and chapel are all that remain of the village of Hickory Run, while Saylorsville's existence is attested to only by the presence of Saylorsville Dam on the upper reaches of Hickory Run. The stream itself bears witness to the past with the ruins of several mills.

The establishment of the park can be attributed to Allentown businessman Harry Trexler. He purchased several tracts of land within the park boundary in the early years of the twentieth century. Following his death, trustees of his estate made 12,908 acres available to the National Park Service. The Hickory Run Recreation Demonstration area was built with the help of the Works Progress Administration during the 1930s. At the end of World War II, the project was turned over to Pennsylvania and became Hickory Run State Park.

For the angler thinking about staying in the area, the park contains a family campground with 381 sites for large tents and trailers. Facilities include hot water, showers, a dump station and camp store selling firewood, ice, general camping supplies and packaged foods. The campground is open from the second Friday in April through the end of the antlerless deer season in late December.

Non-fishing members of the family can swim at a guarded, sand beach (open from Memorial Day weekend to Labor Day), hike along some 30 miles of trails, picnic and sightsee.

Hickory Run State Park may be reached by taking Exit 41, the Hickory Park Exit, of Interstate Route 80, and then traveling south for approximately six miles on Route 534. From the Northeast Extension of the Pennsylvania Turnpike, take Exit 35 and drive west on Pennsylvania Route 940 for three miles then south on Route 534 for six miles. According to the park's "Recreational Guide," which provides a map with a good overview of all the streams, the park is within three hours drive of Harrisburg, Philadelphia and New York City, and one hour from Allentown, Scranton and Wilkes-Barre.

Further details, including a free "Recreational Guide," write: Hickory Run State Park, Department of Environmental Resources, R.D. 1, Box 81, White Haven, PA 18661.

(Also see Lehigh River.)

Tobyhanna Creek
Delayed Harvest Artificial Lures Only
Monroe County

Depending upon the source, Tobyhanna Creek has been translated from the Indian to mean either "dark waters" or "alder stream." Which one is correct it is difficult to say for certain. The "dark waters" translation seems suitable because of the stream's reddish-brown "tea" color, the result of a high tannic acid content. By the same token, though, "alder stream" also appears to be a proper choice since the stream originates in Bender Swamp and passes through other wetlands in which the species grows.

Exactly what the Indians might have meant by its name aside, Tobyhanna Creek is without a doubt one of the prettiest little trout streams in Monroe County. Even if only about seven miles of it are without orange "Posted" signs and available to the public, they are all scenic miles protected first by Tobyhanna State Park and then State Game Lands 127.

While fishing is available in the park, the stretch of stream winding through it is too accessible to dilettantes. The serious trout angler's Tobyhanna is in Game Lands 127, beginning below the village of Tobyhanna, off Pennsylvania Route 423, Exit 7, of Interstate Route 380. After the last few houses of Tobyhanna, and a couple more where Route 423 south crosses the stream at Wernertown, the stream is a splendidly isolated wilderness experience all of the way down to Pocono Lake. The angler who ventures into this area will find hardwood forests of beech, birch

and maple mixed with patches of hemlock and rhododendron along the banks.

The Tobyhanna in the game lands is full of long riffles and easy rapids during the spring months, which turn into quiet flats and pools as the season wears on. In keeping with its presence within what the Indians called the "Great Swamp," marshy areas also abound along the stream, helping it to live up to its name.

A short distance downstream from Wernertown the angler will find a large, reedy glade marked by an old dam at the outflow. This was once the bottom of an ice pond. Today, it sits only as a reminder of the region's once prosperous ice industry.

From the turn of the century to the mid-1930s, the Tobyhanna-Gouldsboro-Klondike area shipped boxcar loads of ice, sometimes as many as 150 a day, to cities on the East Coast and even Florida. The ice was cut from lakes around the three villages in the winter, stored in barn-like structures and then sent out to customers as the need arose, most often at the height of summer.

Long before the ice industry, Tobyhanna Creek was well-known to the Indians and settlers of the region because of the Wechquetank Path, one of the oldest Indian trails in Pennsylvania and a main link between Bethlehem and Wyoming (Wilkes-Barre), which followed it. Sometimes called "David's Path," the trail was used by the Moravians traveling from Philadelphia to Wyalusing, Bradford County with their Indian converts in 1765. The path derives its name, which refers to a species of willow, from the fact it passed through Wechequetank (Gilbert, Monroe County), an Indian mission town founded in 1760 by the Moravians.

Only three years after the town was established by the missionaries, it had to be abandoned during Pontiac's Rebellion when it was threatened by the "Paxton Boys"—a collection of frontiersmen from Dauphin County who, following a series of Indian attacks in their area, formed a vigilante troop and began killing Indians all through eastern Pennsylvania. Among their victims, were the last of the Conestoga Indians in the state. Feelings against all Indians were so strong among the settlers that the Christian Indians of Wyalusing were constantly in fear for their lives and a decision was made to move them to Philadelphia.

Many history books claim the "Paxton Boys" were so hungry for revenge they followed the Indians to Philadelphia and actually began preparations to storm the city in order to kill them. Dr. George Donehoo in his book *A History of Indian Villages and Place Names in Pennsylvania,* however, points out that while the "Paxton Boys" did approach the city, no demands were ever made for the Indians, but rather for representation in the General Assembly.

During the Revolutionary War, Wechquetank Path was used by General John Sullivan in his expedition against the Iroquois in the summer of 1779. Sullivan, for whom Sullivan County is named, was sent on the expedition by George Washington, who conceived it as a means to punish hostile Indians in northern Pennsylvania and New York, whom the British had armed and hired to harass frontier settlements. One of the Indian attacks led to the Wyoming Massacre in which an estimated 300 men, women and children were slaughtered.

Setting out from Easton with a force of 5,000 soldiers, Sullivan passed through the "Shades of Death," as the forest around present day Hickory Run State Park was known. They camped at Hungry Hill (The Chowder Camp) in Tobyhanna Twp. and passed through the Great Swamp which surrounds the stream before stopping at Wilkes-Barre to pick up supplies and additional equipment. His army then proceeded up the North Branch of the Susquehanna River to Tioga Point (Athens, Bradford County).

By the time General Sullivan was done, he had laid waste to the homelands of the Senecas, Cayugas and Onondagas in New York.

Altogether, he destroyed some 40 towns and more than 150,000 bushels of corn and vast quantities of other crops. Hardly a single vestige of life or food supplies was left untouched in the region. In his report to Congress that fall, the general noted he had done it all without losing more than 40 men "in action or otherwise since taking command."

Hatches in Tobyhanna Creek are similar to other streams in the Pocono region. April provides action with Blue Quills, Quill Gordons and Hendricksons; May, Sulphurs, March Browns, Blue-Winged Olives, Gray Fox, Green Drakes and Brown Drakes; June, Light Cahills, Isonychias and Yellow Drakes. Various caddis patterns also will take fish, as will the Adams and mosquito. The stream's Delayed Harvest Fly Fishing Only Project covers the last mile of water in the game lands, from the Confluence of Still Swamp Run downstream to the PP&L service bridge.

Tobyhanna State Park, at the head of the stream, holds a 140-site Class B campground—no showers or flush toilets—for fishermen interested in staying near the stream. It is open year-round, but the dump station operates only from May 1 to October 1. Along with camping, the park offers picnicking, playgrounds, hiking trails and 170-acre Lake Tobyhanna (stocked) with swimming, from Memorial Day weekend to Labor Day, and boat rentals. Because the park is 2,000 feet above sea level, visitors should be ready for cool weather, even in the middle of summer.

Additional information on Tobyhanna Park may be had by writing: Tobyhanna State Park, Department of Environmental Resources, P.O. Box 387, Tobyhanna, PA 18466.

To help put the lay of Tobyhanna Creek in better perspective, anglers might want to obtain a free "Public Use Map" of Delaware State Forest. Along with Tobyhanna Creek, the map also shows several other northeastern Pennsylvania trout streams in this book. One can be had by stopping at a forest service office, most local state park offices, or by writing: District Forester, Delaware State Forest, 474 Clearview Lane, Stroudsburg, PA 18360.

(Also see Lehigh River.)

Sawkill Creek
Pike County

When the name Gifford Pinchot is mentioned today, it is most often in reference to environmental conservation efforts at the turn of the century and the founding of the U.S. Forest Service. Or, somewhat less frequently, in connection with his friend Teddy Roosevelt and the Progressive Party, the great liberal social movement of those years.

Within Pennsylvania, Pinchot's name also occasionally crops up as a former governor. Born August 11, 1865, he served two terms in that office, from 1923 to 1927, and again from 1931 to 1935. His most noted efforts as governor included his fight for stronger state regulation of public utilities; his remodeling of state government operations; and his secondary road paving program, or "getting the farmers out of the mud," the benefits of which are still evident throughout rural Pennsylvania.

While those public events are the main reason Pinchot's name has not disappeared into the obscurity that almost immediately descends upon a governor when he leaves office, they by no means reflect the extent of his accomplishments or interests. For Pinchot led an extremely rich and varied life, one that carried him not only into politics and the infant conservation movement, but also gained him recognition as an author, teacher, world traveler, and fisherman.

Of all the interests Pinchot cultivated during this long life, none was dearer to his heart than the "brotherhood of the angle," as Isaak Walton might have said. From childhood through old age, fishing remained one of his consuming passions. And, like many a man before and since who has been hopelessly bitten by the "fishing bug," he pursued his muse far and wide: chasing blue fish in the waters around Massachusetts Nantucket Island, tuna in the Gulf Stream, barracuda and bonefish in the flats of the Florida keys and billfish in the South Seas.

Pinchot's many fishing excursions gave him subjects for a ream of magazine articles and a couple of books, *Let's Go Fishing* (1930) and *Just Fishing Talk* (1936). A third angling volume was among the projects he was planning when he died in New York City on October 5, 1946.

In line with the oldest traditions in sporting literature, Pinchot's fishing tales all offer a generous dose of philosophy and adventure along with his opinions on tackle and technique. And, as befits the man who fought the secretary of the interior to keep Alaska's coal reserves in the public domain, the governor also was an early promotor of catch and release in his stories.

"Then we chose white and brown spiders, with long hackles and little hooks, out of my horn snuff box, with Napoleon's tomb carved on the cover; made sure that the barbs had been broken off with a pair of sharpnosed pliers (we never fish for trout with barbed hooks any more); tied leaders to spiders with the Turle Knot; and oiled the hackles of our spiders with three parts of abolene and one of kerosene. Then the war was on.

"It was a good war, and a swift. Before you could say Jack Robinson, Giff (his son) had a nine-inch native. Untouched by human hands, back into the stream he went, thanks to the debarbed hook, with nothing but a little healthful exercise to remember his adventure by. I always get satisfaction out of that."

The money Pinchot inherited from his grandfather, a New York real estate speculator, allowed him to fish many far-off places, but he never forgot the streams and rivers of northeastern Pennsylvania and his beloved home in Milford, especially Sawkill Creek.

"Men may come and men may go," he wrote in *Just Fishing Talk,* "but the Sawkill brook flows on—feeding its trout, protecting its insects, molluscan, and crustacean life—a home and hiding place for myriads of living creatures—a thing of beauty and a joy forever."

The story, "Time Like an Ever Rolling Stream," goes on to imagine the flow of the Sawkill from a time when its only company was the giant pines and hemlocks along its banks through the arrival of the Indians and the first European settlers, "when axe began to modify the face of the earth, and the days of the wilderness were numbered." It then moved forward to the arrival of the first Pinchot and finally the governor's own experiences with his son, an at first reluctant angler.

"What a shock was there, my country men! Rubia and I were struck with horror. I couldn't be consoled even by the fact that I had just taken several trout on a leader made by me out of a knotted succession of single strands of Rubia's hair. Was it possible that the son of such parents could fail to love to fish? We couldn't believe it, and, what was more, we didn't intend to stand it."

Fortunately for young Giff, he did come around to his parents' point of view, and by age ten was casting a "workmanlike fly" on the Sawkill that filled his father with pride.

Pinchot's positions as head of the U.S. Forest Service and governor of Pennsylvania may have brought him in contact with many nationally prominent people of his time, but when it came to fishing, his usual companions were simply anglers who lived near his home. He even fished with Dan Cahill, a railroad brakeman who lived across the Delaware River in Port Jervis,

New York, and invented the Light Cahill pattern. In another of his stories, "When the Dry Fly Was New," the governor actually maintains he proved to Cahill the advantages of the dry fly over the wet in certain situations.

"On our way to the brook he (Cahill) had condemned the dry fly without mercy. Now he had seen a trout taken which the wet fly could not have possibly reached. To make the story short, throughout the afternoon the wet fly took no fish, while the dry fly made a score of eight, four of which, being natives, were returned to the stream."

Gifford Pinchot is one of a now seemingly lost breed of public servants. He entered politics not for fame or power, but rather to repay the debt he felt he owed the nation for providing his grandfather with the wealth the governor inherited. He was a politician who was much more than image and a blow dryer, a man who saw beyond the narrow range of his own life. He would not be a bad role model in many ways today, among them angling.

"But with all the endless charm of fishing, there is one essential condition of its true enjoyment. Be not too anxious to fill your basket or your boat. The first and ostensible object of fishing is indeed to catch fish, but it is only the first. There is far more. Unless you are willing to take thankfully what the Red Gods send, whether it be little or much, you cannot really love fishing, you will not continue to love it until the end of your days."

Only a relatively small section of Sawkill Creek is stocked by the Fish Commission and open to the public. The stretch runs for 1.5 miles along the south side of Milford and can be reached by taking U.S. Route 209 to Milford. At the red light in the center of town, anglers coming from the south should turn left off Route 209. The Sawkill is located at the end of the block. A tiny side street parallels the creek upstream from that point. The stocked portion ends at the American Legion Post.

Grey Towers, Pinchot home on rainy Sawkill creek.

Fly anglers on the Sawkill should try various caddis patterns, including: Elk Hair, Henryville Special, Soft Hackle Nymphs, Adams, Breadcrust, Grannom, Hare's Ear and Honey Bug.

Grey Towers, the Pinchot home in Milford, is administered by the U.S. Forest Service. Tours are generally scheduled throughout the year, except in January, February and March, when appointments are necessary. Details may be had by writing: Grey Towers National Historic Landmark, U.S. Forest Service, P.O. Box 188, Milford, PA 18337.

Shohola Creek
Pike County

Streams flowing across plateaus are generally known to have placid natures. At least until they reach the edge of their table tops and come plummeting and crashing down toward their end, they are usually smooth, winding, quiet affairs. And Shohola Creek is no exception. Actually, this central Pike County stream fits the image so well its name in the Indian language means "meek" or "weak."

Shohola Creek covers more than 30 miles from its source in the swamp country south of Blooming Grove until it finally gushes into the Delaware River at the village of Shohola. But it has only about a four-mile stretch which is of real interest to the trout angler. It starts on Pennsylvania Route 739 and ends at the tailwaters of Shohola Dam. In between, it offers some excellent fishing for stocked and holdover trout from spring all the way into fall.

Because the stretch is almost entirely surrounded by State Game Lands 180, anglers visiting it have a chance to fish in a wild, unspoiled environment without even a trace of the "No Trespassing" or "Private Property" signs so prevalent all over the Pocono region.

And not only is the section open to anybody with a willingness to do some walking, but it also is quite beautiful. Through it Shohola Creek's clear, brownish waters cut a writhing path between sandy banks framed by meadows and hardwood forets dotted by the occasional appearance of dark pines. Except for a touch of rapids right at the Route 739 bridge, the rest of the stream lives up to its "faint" title by providing plenty of smooth flowing water that should make any angler who loves meadow streams ecstatic.

Shohola Creek is open to all types of fishing. Anglers who prefer spinners and bait are usually successful in the early spring. Fly fishermen can do well throughout the season. Fly patterns to try in April include Blue Quills, Quill Gordon, Hendrickson and, of course, the Adams. Possible flies for May are Sulphurs, March Browns, Blue-Wing Olives, Gray Fox and, again, the Adams. June fly choices include the Light Cahill, Isonychia and Yellow Drake.

Caddisflies also occur in good numbers. Among the species are the Grannon, brown sedge, black sedge, spotted sedge, cream sedge and green sedge. They can usually be imitated by impressionistic patterns such as the Elk Hair Caddis, Henryville Special and Adams. Soft hackle patterns are a good choice when the fish are not feeding on the surface.

Access to Shohola Creek is simply a matter of taking the Lords Valley, Route 739, Exit 9 off Interstate Route 84. The Route 739 bridge lies to the north in sight of Interstate 84. Anglers can begin fishing at the bridge, though there is not much room to park. Fishermen who do not mind hiking should continue on to the village of Lords Valley and make a right onto State Route 1001. The road parallels the stream at distances varying from just under a mile near Lords Valley to probably over three miles as it nears the dam. Parking is available at various locations along the road.

Since Shohola Creek is never far off Interstate 84, an easier way to gain access is off the highway. But remember, it is illegal to park along an interstate except in an emergency.

Heavily used Minisink Indian Path, which ran from Wilkes-Barre to Minisink Island in the Delaware River below Milford and then on into New Jersey, once crossed Shohola Creek in the Lords Valley area.

Visiting anglers who would like to do a little sightseeing should consider a visit to Shohola Falls on U.S. Route 6. The falls, listed in *Outstanding Geological Features of Pennsylvania,* end in a normal enough manner, but then shoot through a fearsome, sheer-walled chasm sure to send a chill up the spine, especially when considering a rumor that some whitewater lovers have run the shoot.

The village of Greeley, named for newspaper publisher Horace Greeley, also lies a little further north on Pennsylvania Route 434. Back in 1842 the idealistic young Greeley, in line with his "Fourierism" philosophy, attempted to establish a commune known as Sylvania on the site.

Formulated by the French philosopher Charles Fourier, the philosophy held that the ideal system of social organization was the "phalanstery" consisting of 1700 to 1800 people whose different psychological traits, when allowed free-play, would complement one another to produce total happiness for everyone. All work in the phalanstery would be attractive because nobody would undertake a job that was not associated with a "passionate stimulus." Instead of spending long hours at the same job, workers would frequently vary their occupations. Work groups would be moved by love within the group and a friendly competition with neighboring groups. The competitiveness between the groups would not lead to any enduring hostile relationships, Fourier asserted. The experiment was a failure.

A good perspective on the lay of Shohola Creek, and several other Pocono trout streams in this book, can be obtained with a copy of the "Public Use Map" of Delaware State Forest. The map is available free of charge at forest offices, most state parks in the area, or by writing: District Forester, Delaware State Forest, 474 Clearview Lane, Stroudsburg, PA 18360.

Butternut Creek
Fly Fishing Only
Wayne County

Riffles and pools dominate Butternut Creek in its dash from the swamplands on the Wayne/Lackawanna County line to its end at the backwaters of famous Lake Wallenpaupack. It is stocked with trout over a distance of three miles, from its mouth upstream, and is said to hold a fairly good population of stream-bred fish. Its Fly Fishing Only Project runs for 2.5 miles from its mouth upstream.

Locals report access to Butternut Creek's special regulation water has been limited by a change in land ownership. The stream may still be easily reached, however, by taking Interstate Route 84 Exit 5 and following Pennsylvania Route 91 south toward New Foundland. Route 191 crosses the creek less than a mile off the in-

Shohola Creek.

Pennsylvania Route 196 also provides some access when it crosses Butternut Creek south of the village of Sterling. State Route 3002, which runs off both Route 196 and Route 191, is another road that provides some access.

Among the flies an angler might try on the stream's amber waters are: Blue-Winged Olives, Quill Gordons, March Browns, Hare's Ears, Adams, Hendricksons, caddis, Soft Hackle Nymphs, Black Gnats, Light Cahills, Sulphurs and streamers such as the Black Marabou.

Butternut Creek is not directly connected to a state park, or any other public lands for that matter, but it is between two good ones where an angler can camp, hike, swim and even boat.

Tobyhanna State Park can be reached by continuing south on both Route 191 and Route 196. It has 140 Class B campsites open year-round, as well as a picnic area, a playground, swimming beach, boat rentals on a 170-acre lake, ten miles of hiking trails and a dump station. (See Tobyhanna Creek.)

Promised Land State Park lies to the east of Butternut Creek off Interstate Route 84 Exit 7 on Pennsylvania Route 390 south. Facilities include 535 Class A and B campsites, picnic areas, a playground, swimming beach, boat rental on a 595-acre lake, 29 miles of hiking trails and a dump station. In addition, there are 12 family cabins that can be rented on a weekly, and sometimes half-week, basis. Reservations are needed.

Details on the parks may be had by writing:

Tobyhanna State Park, Department of Environmental Resources, P.O. Box 387, Tobyhanna, PA 18466.

Promised Land State Park, Department of Environmental Resources, R.D. 1, Box 96, Greentown, PA 18426.

An overview of Butternut Creek also may be had by obtaining a "Public Use Map" of the Delaware State Forest. It is available free of charge at forest offices, most state parks in the area, or by writing: District Forester, Delaware State Forest, 474 Clearview Lane, Stroudsburg, PA 18360.

Lackawaxen River
Wayne County

Through books such as *The Last of the Plainsmen* and the classic *Riders of the Purple Sage,* the name of Zane Grey will be forever linked to the "Wild West." Some sportsmen also might recognize him as a renowned fisherman. One who pursued his sport to the far corners of the earth. The flats of the Florida keys, deep blue of the Gulf Stream, white water of Oregon and the crystalline streams of New Zealand were all home to him. A few literary types might even known him as a rival of sorts to Hemingway, at least in that younger writer's mind.

Zane Grey certainly was all of those things and a great many more, including a movie maker and Pennsylvania angler, who for years called the confluence of the Delaware and Lackawaxen Rivers home.

Born January 31, 1872, in a town named for an uncle, Zanesville, Ohio, Pearl Zane Gray was the fourth of five children. As with most writers who earn at least part of their fame in the outdoor field, his early years were spent roaming in the woods around his home. When he was not fishing or hunting, he was playing baseball. An accurate pitching arm and hot bat gained him a baseball scholarship to the University of Pennsylvania, while a desire by his father to have him follow in his footsteps pushed him into the field of dentistry.

After graduation from the University of Pennsylvania, the future master of the Western moved to New York City, about as faraway from the world of the cowboy and Indian as a person could get. He then changed the spelling of his hame from "Gray" to "Grey," and set up a dental practice under the name P. Zane Grey.

While his dentistry practice paid the bills, it left him unsatisfied, at times even unhappy. With his younger brother, Romer, he began playing baseball for the New Jersey Athletic Club and making frequent trips to the country, particularly the Delaware River. In the summers, when they were making good money playing baseball, the brothers often stayed at the Delaware House, a resort hotel on the New Jersey side of the Delaware directly across from the village of Lackawaxen, Pennsylvania. It was while Zane and Romer were staying at the resort that the author first spotted Lina Elise Roth, a 17-year-old student at New York Normal School (Hunter College), who five years later would become Mrs. Zane Grey, or "Dolly," as her husband always called her.

His dislike of the routine that is dentistry spurred Grey to begin writing. Many of his earliest stories focused on fishing and hunting, often in northeast Pennsylvania. "Fighting Qualities of Black Bass" appeared in the May 1912 issue of *Field & Stream* and relates some of the things Grey learned about bass on the Delaware River. "Mast Hope Brook In June" focuses on a small stream the author and his brothers fished while staying at

Zane Grey home on Lackawaxen River.

Lackawaxen and was published in his 1928 book *Tales of Freshwater Fishing*. But perhaps his best story about Pennsylvania angling is "The Lord of the Lackawaxen," which saw print in the May 1909 issue of *Outing* magazine.

In *The Lord of the Lackawaxen,* Grey writes of his experiences over the course of a year with a six-pound smallmouth who chose to call a swimming hole on the Lackawaxen home. Having already lost one battle with the monster, Grey decides to trick his unsuspecting brothers into fishing the pool. The first one, Reddy, Grey gets to visit the spot with a tiny rod the fish splinters as soon as it is hooked, and leaves Reddy uttering words no publisher would have dared print in 1909. Cedar, the other brother, who Grey describes as "a white-duck-pants-on-a-dry-rock sort of fisherman," ends his try for the fish with a muddy, shin-bruising dunking in the creek. Grey finally hooks the fish solidly on one of his trips to the pool, but it wedges itself between two rocks on the bottom. After a fight that includes the author diving into the pool and trying to force the bass loose with his hands, he finally realizes that such a fish deserves to live and breaks off his leader.

In 1902, hidden away in his dingy New York flat, Grey completed his first novel, *Betty Zane,* for which he also did the illustrations. But, as countless other aspiring writers have found out since, nobody was interested in publishing the work of an unknown author. The work saw the light of day only after Grey borrowed money from Dolly and published it himself. A second edition was picked up by Charles Frances Press, but it did not sell well. The book remained one of Grey's least successful efforts throughout his life. For some unknown reason, however, the book began to sell in 1979, rapidly going through four printings.

New writers will take encouragement anywhere they can find it, however, so after the appearance of *Betty Zane,* Grey quickly followed it up with *Spirit of the Boder* and *The Last Trail.* Both books found a publisher, but neither sold well.

Grey and Dolly married in 1905, and, even though the reception his first three books received was less than thrilling, together they decided Zane should quit his dental practice and devote himself full time to his writing. With money from Romer, who had recently married a wealthy woman, the couple purchased a two-story house on five acres near the mouth of the Lackawaxen River. It was there Grey seriously set about winning his fame and fortune as a novelist.

Except for a number of fishing stories in outdoor magazines, success continued to elude Grey on the banks of the Lackawaxen. Reward for all of his hard work did not begin to raise its heads until a friend invited him to attend a lecture by J.C. "Buffalo" Jones, a buffalo hunter during the great slaughter of the herds in the 1870s, who later saw the ruin of his ways and became a game warden in Yellowstone National Park. Jones was speaking on his plan to breed buffalo with cattle, and obtain what has since become known as the beefalo. In those days, though, Jones was too far ahead of his time and often hooted and hollered off stage by a laughing crowd. But Grey saw something different. He approached Jones after his talk, showing him a copy of *Betty Zane* and convincing him he wanted to go West with him. Jones eventually agreed to take the author along on a project to capture mountain lions for zoos. That was the real beginning of Grey's exposure to the West, and led directly to the publication of his first two best-selling novels.

Zane Grey actively used his house on the Lackawaxen from 1905 to 1918, and made periodic visits to it until 1929. His days on the river are today preserved in the Zane Grey Museum next to the Fish Commission's Lackawaxen Access to the Delaware River in the village of Lackawaxen.

Born at the junction of West Branch Lackawaxen River and Van Auken Creek, the Lackawaxen has been translated to mean "swift water" or "where the way forks," and is the first major tributary of the Delaware River. It drains some 600 square miles of Pike and Wayne Counties, and offers some 25 miles of trout and, as Zane Grey found out, smallmouth bass fishing. Its stocked—rainbows and browns—water is broken into three separate sections. The first runs from the village of Pompton downstream about halfway to Honesdale. This stretch holds a good deal of commercial and residential development, as well as the accompanying beer bottles and old tires. Access is available off U.S. Route 6.

The second stocked portion reaches from Honesdale and Dyberry Creek (see which) downstream to the village of White Mills. It is a relatively quiet, but swift, section where the river gains quite a bit of size. Except for one huge junkyard, the stream flows mostly out of sight of the road, winding its way past woods, grassy banks, low hills and the ruins of an old canal.

Despite the river's steep gradient, early nineteenth century engineers laid out and built the Delaware & Hudson Canal to link the anthracite coal fields of northeast Pennsylvania with New York City. Completed in 1829, the canal ran for 108 miles from Honesdale to Eddyville on the Hudson River. It took 34 locks just to carry the barges between the Delaware River and Honesdale. The canal operated for about 75 years. This second stretch of planted water also is accessible off Route 6.

The Lackawaxen's third, and longest, stocked section runs from about Hawley downstream to the Delaware River and Zane Grey's home. Here the Lackawaxen begins to cut a path through a narrow valley and become a true river. It is wide, rocky and swift, even the pools move fast. And it also is dangerous. The Pennsylvania Power & Light Co. dam at Lake Wallenpaupack is a hydroelectric facility that during release periods quickly raises the river's level. Signs shouting "CAUTION: RIVER LEVEL CHANGES RAPIDLY" appear all along the banks and it pays to listen to them. They mean what they say. The cobble-sized rocks of the Lackawaxen are extremely slippery. An angler can easily lose his footing and be swept away to his death. In a less fatal vein, he can get caught on the wrong side of the river from his car. So when the river starts to rise get off it. The one saving grace in the whole situation is that releases from Lake Wallenpaupack are ordinarily scheduled only for weekdays. Saturday and Sunday normally belong to the fishermen.

Route 6 leaves the river at Hawley, but access remains good along practically its entire length. Follow Pennsylvania Route 590 out of town to State Route 4006, which leads toward the village of Kimble and closely follows the river all of the way to the village of Rowland. Route 590 once again picks up the steam at Rowland and shadows it all of the way to the village of Lackawaxen.

Over 125 years before Zane Grey moved to Lackawaxen and added his fame to it, the village gained a more notorious fame as the site of the Battle of Minisink. It occurred on July 22, 1779. Chief Joseph Brant of the Mohawks led 300 Tories and Indians against Minisink (Port Jervis) and burned the settlement. Laden with booty, the force was headed for home when a group of about 175 settlers under the command of a Major Wood attacked. In the ensuing fight nearly all of the settlers were killed. Wood and about two dozen of his men managed to escape only because of his unintentional use of the Masonic distress signal. After seeing the signal, Chief Brant, for some reason, allowed the group to escape into the surrounding forest.

The Lackawaxen Path once ran from the village of Lackawaxen to the village of Indian Orchard. It was an incredibly straight Indian trail, taking only 13 miles to join the two villages. Route 6 and Route 590 now take 20 miles to do the same thing.

For the fly fisherman, the Lackawaxen offers miles of often

superb water. Anglers should find success with the Adams, Quill Gordon, Blue-Winged Olive, Muddler Minnow, Woolly Buggers (black, brown and gray), Matuka Streamers, Black-Nosed Dace, Mickey Finn, Hare's Ear, stoneflies, Hendrickson, March Brown, Royal Coachman, caddis, Light and Dark Cahills, Gray Fox, Lead-Winged Coachman, Renegades and terrestrials.

A good idea of the lay of the Lackawaxen's lower waters may be had by obtaining a free "Pubic Use Map" of Delaware State Forest. The map, which also includes several other trout streams in this book, is available at forest offices, most local state parks, or by writing: District Forester, Delaware State Forest, 474 Clearview Lane, Stroudsburg, PA 18360.

Dyberry Creek
Delayed Harvest Fly Fishing Only
East Branch Dyberry Creek
West Branch Dyberry Creek
Middle Branch Dyberry Creek
Wayne County

All four branches of Dyberry Creek hold trout. Between them they also offer as wide a variety of fishing opportunities as an angler can expect to find in an individual watershed. There are smooth runs over gravel bottoms, succinct riffles, rocky rapids and flat pools. There are wild, bushy stretches accessible only on foot where native trout or hook-jawed holdovers might be found, and wide open places flowing tight against the road where an angler can catch stocked brookies and browns without wrapping every backcast around a branch.

With so many things working in its favor, Dyberry Creek, particularly the main stream below the junction of the East Branch and West Branch, is understandably among Wayne County's most popular trout streams. Which also means it gets crowded, especially early in the season before much of its freestone water warms and becomes marginal habitat for trout.

Dyberry Creek proper, as well as the East Branch, West Branch and Middle Branch, may be reached by taking U.S. Route 6 to the county seat of Honesdale and then following Pennsylvania Route 191 north. The big Dyberry can be fished right off Route 191 upstream from Honesdale. The water downstream from the General Edgar Jadwin Dam, however, is not among the stream's best. Chubs might be more likely to take a fly or lure here than a trout.

Not quite a mile and a half north of the dam, Route 191 is joined on the left by State Route 4009, which then becomes State Route 4007. These two roads—follow the sign for the "Gun Range"—trail the main stream and the lower East Branch into State Game Lands 159. The upper East Branch is accessible from State Route 4023. The stream's Delayed Harvest Fly Fishing Only Project runs from the Widmer property about a mile below Tanner's Falls—once a collection of house and a tannery, but now just a name—downstream to the Mary Wilcox Bridge. It is clearly marked, and there are plenty of parking spaces along both the main stream and the East Branch, which both flow close to the road.

The West Branch and Middle Branch are a bit further off the beaten path than the East Branch and main stream. But they may be found by turning right onto State Route 4017 and the fourth bridge near a game lands parking lot. This dirt and gravel road

follows the West Branch, crossing it at a pretty waterfall. It also leads to another parking lot from which anglers can walk upstream a bit to fish the Middle Branch.

Generally speaking, the Dyberry Creek's Main Branch and East Branch are medium-sized streams that receive the heaviest pressure since they flow so close to paved roads. The West Branch and Middle Branch are under considerably lighter pressure because they are tougher to reach. Their upper reaches are typical brook trout water with pine shaded pools punctuated by some boggy meadows. The East Branch is famous for its gnats, so go prepared.

The big Dyberry is stocked for seven miles, the East Branch for six, the West Branch for five, and the Middle Branch for one mile. Fly choices include: Blue-Winged Olives, March Browns, Hendricksons, Black Gnats, Gray Fox, Sulphurs, Brown Drakes, Cream Dun, Yellow Dun, caddis, Tricorythodes and terrestrials.

Honesdale, at the junction of Dyberry Creek and the Lackawaxen River, is now the quiet county seat of Wayne County. But during the early years of the nineteenth century it was a main coal storage and shipping point for the anthracite fields of northeastern Pennsylvania.

In 1826, Philip Hone, mayor of New York City and later president of the Delaware & Hudson Canal Co., came to the town to push for the construction of a canal along which coal could be transported to his city. In 1829, Hone's canal company imported the first two locomotives into the United States from England. One of these engines, the "Stourbridge Lion," became the first locomotive to run on an American railroad. Horatio Allen, a construction engineer for the canal company, had the "Lion" brought to this country to replace the mules used to pull coal from the mines to the canal.

"The impression was very general that the iron monster would break down the road, or that it would leave the track at the curve and plunge into the creek," Allen would later write. "My reply to such apprehension was that it was too late to consider the possibility of such occurrences; that there was no other course but to have a trial made of the strange animal which had been brought there at great expense, but that it was not necessary that more than one should be involved in its fate; that I would take the first ride alone, and the time would come when I should look back to the incident with great interest.

"As I placed my hand on the handle I was undecided whether I should move slowly or with a fair degree of speed, but holding that the road would prove safe, and proposing, if we had to go down, to go handsomely, and without evidence of timidity, I started with considerable velocity, passed the curve over the creek (Lackawaxen River) safely, and was soon out of hearing of the vast assemblage present. At the end of two or three miles I reversed the valve and returned without accident to the place of starting, having made the first locomotive trip on the western hemisphere."

Although the first trip went off without a hitch, a second test proved the locomotive too heavy for the rails. Since it was cheaper to return to mules and wagons than replace the rails, the canal company removed the "Lion's" boiler for use in the shop and put the remainder of the engine in storage. In 1889, what was left of the locomotive was sent to the Smithsonian Institute.

(Also see Lackawaxen River.)

Equinunk Creek
Wayne County

Upper Wayne County's rolling hills carry a gentle, remote feeling. Sparsely settled by farms and villages without a single major highway, they might make a good subject for the landscape artist's brush. Which is why it is difficult to believe they are barely 100 miles from the skyscrapers of Manhattan.

Equinunk Creek is an often swift, cobble-strewn bit of stream whose clear waters do justice to the region. It is stocked for nearly 12 miles upstream through a narrow valley from its mouth on the Delaware River at the village of Equinunk. It is said to hold some nice trout. Fishing is reportedly good all of the way from the opening of the season in April through September when some of the Delaware River's big trout enter the stream to spawn.

Anglers who favor fly fishing might try Blue-Winged Olives, Adams, Hendricksons, Hare's Ears, March Browns, Soft Hackle Nymphs, Renegades, Light Cahills, Gray Fox, Sulphurs, caddis and terrestrials.

From the name Equinunk, translation "where articles of clothing are distributed," seems to indicate the area might have served the Indians as a trading site. Early settlers frequently found arrowheads, stone tools and other artifacts at Indian campsites.

Josiah Parks was one of the earliest white men to live along the stream. He moved there before the Revolutionary War, and during that conflict served as a scout. He was driven away by local Tories and their Indian allies. Fleeing to the Wyoming Valley, he was able to warn settlers in the region of an impending series of attacks that eventually ended in the Wyoming Massacre in which an estimated 300 men, women and children were slain.

Equinunk Creek can be found by following Pennsylvania Route 191 to the village of Equinunk. Legislative Route 63050 joins Route 191 in the center of the village. Intertwined with the stream, it provides access at numerous spots.

(Also see Delaware River.)

Lackawanna River
Susquehanna, Wayne and Lackawanna Counties

Delaware Indians were the first people to live along the Lackawanna River. They occupied the land surrounding the stream and fished its waters long before William Penn was even a glint in his father's eye. The Lackawanna Path, which followed a portion of the river's lower waters, was the gateway to the "great meadows" of Wyoming and the Iroquois country of New York.

Within historic times, two villages existed near the mouth of the Lackawanna upstream of the Susquehanna River. Attempts by settlers to take control of this area was one of the chief causes of trouble with the Indians, and, eventually, led to the Wyoming Massacre at Forty Fort (see Wyalusing Creek) in 1778. The massacre spread panic throughout the upper Susquehanna region. Whites fled the area in droves, leaving the Lackawanna Valley virtually uninhabited for ten years until Philip Abbott built a cabin and girst mill on Roaring Brook near the present city of Scranton.

Ten more years passed before Ebenezer and Benjamin Slocum arrived on the scene to build a forge and distillery. They named their settlement Unionville and then in 1816 changed it to Slocum Hollow. The name stuck to the middle of the nineteenth century when two other brothers, George and Selden Scranton, moved to the Lackawanna River from New Jersey.

The Scranton brothers and their firm, Scranton, Grant and Co., were the first people to succeed in manufacturing iron with the region's abundant anthracite coal. In 1845, in honor of President William Henry Harrison, the Scrantons also changed the name of the settlement from Slocum Hollow to Harrison.

With a view to expanding their operations, the Scranton brothers obtained a loan of $10,000 from their cousin John Scranton in Georgia. Then in 1847 John bought out Sanford Grant's interest in the company and came north to manage the Lackawanna Iron Works.

Three years after John Scranton's arrival on the scene a post office was established at Scrantonia. Less than a year after that name was shortened to Scranton.

Throughout the last half of the nineteenth century and first quarter of the twentieth Scranton sat as the capital of Pennsylvania's anthracite and coal empire. Development of the coal mines attracted thousands of immigrants to the city on the Lackawanna. By 1860 the village Philip Abbott had started reached a population of 9,000. And by 1886 was home to some 50,000 individuals.

Such frenzied growth naturally took an awesome toll on the Lackawanna River and neighboring mountains. For years the waters of the river ran dark and lifeless, while the mountains became overshadowed by ugly black piles of slag. Even today the environs of the Lackawanna River certainly are not a tourist attraction. Mother Nature may have healed some of the worst scars, or at least hid them under a skirt of greenery, but plenty of others still remain. Yet the river itself, or at least 9.5 miles of it, survives as a trout fishery. It may be far from the best trout stream in the state, but it is not the worst either. And it is convenient to thousands of people, most of whom probably do not take advantage of it.

The Lackawanna River starts north of Stillwater Dam in Susquehanna County. Averaging between 75 and 100 feet across in many places, it is stocked with brook, brown and rainbow trout for two miles in Susquehanna County, two miles on its bend through Wayne County and for 5.5 miles in Lackawanna County. Access to the river is mainly along Pennsylvania Route 171 which can be picked up off U.S. Route 6 at Carbondale on the downstream end of the stocked water. Route 171 crosses the river at Simpson and then veers away from it until north of Forest City. About two miles above Forest City Route 171 crosses the stream again. From that point it parallels the river past Stillwater Dam and the village of Union Dale to the junction with Pennsylvania Route 311 which marks the upper end of the stocked water.

Even though Route 171 turns away from the Lackawanna at Simpson, the river still can be reached by turning right onto Jefferson Street immediately after crossing the bridge. A series of back streets and an old railroad bed trail the river, though at a short distance, all the way into Forest City. About 0.6 of a mile above the Route 171 bridge north of Forest City, an old, dead-end road also appears and leads back to the river.

The scenery around Stillwater Dam holds rhododendron and birch, and is the most beautiful of the entire river. Gradually, it deteriorates to the scrubby growth of old slag piles and coke ovens. Because very few houses appear along the river, however, it still manages to produce a pleasant feeling of remoteness all of the way to Simpson. The presence of Stillwater Dam also helps to keep the river fishable beyond the time other streams in the area have become too low and warm.

After Simpson, the Lackawanna's banks are wall to wall industry or houses.

Fly anglers might try the usual Pennsylvania patterns, including: Adams, Blue Dun, Quill Gordon, caddis, Hendrickson, Soft Hackle Nymphs, March Brown, Royal Coachman, Lead-Winged Coachman, Light Cahill, Hare's Ear, Sulphurs, Muddler Minnows, Mickey Finn, Woolly Bugger in black or olive, midges and terrestrials.

Delaware River
West Branch Delaware River
Wayne County
(Float Trip)

Delaware River

No historical painting, at least not in the United States, is better known than that of George Washington crossing the Delaware River. Standing chin out, protected against the elements only by a plain cloak, defiant of both the enemy and the cold around him, the general cuts perhaps the ultimate heroic image. He is the true rebel leader, the individual battling the might of an empire, surrounded by the simple folk "yearning to breathe free." It is a stirring picture, even to the most cynical American.

In the eyes of those unfortunate millions who do not fish, or enjoy the outdoors, that painting of Washington on Christmas night 1776 on his way to surprise Britain's Hessian mercenaries and capturing Trenton, New Jersey, is the only knowledge they have of the Delaware River. Those higher beings who do angle, however, know the river in a much different light. To them it is one of the finest pieces of fishing water in the entire eastern United States, a place where they can find American shad, herring, striped bass, largemouth and smallmouth bass, pickerel, walleye, muskellunge, and trophy brown and rainbow trout.

Defining Pennsylvania's eastern border, and surrounded by the largest concentration of population in the country, the Delaware is an anomaly. Beginning by draining New York's magnificent Catskills and Pennsylvania's famous Poconos, it flows for some 197 miles from the junction of its East Branch and West Branch near Hanock, New York downstream to the site of Washington's victory at Trenton. From there it ebbs and flows with the tides another 85 miles past the cities of Philadelphia and Wilmington, Delaware where it starts spreading out to form Delaware Bay. It is the last major river in the East to be unshackled by a dam. No major highway or railroad line follows it very far. There are only a scattering of big factories along its banks, and above its tidewater but one city.

Despite this lack of development the Delaware is not entirely without problems, or safe from future abuse. New York City draws part of its water supply from two dams located on the East Branch and West Branch. In dry years, the city has been more than a little reluctant to release water from those impoundments. This reluctance has hampered the flow of the main river at times. New York and Philadelphia even ended up in a fight before the U.S. Supreme Court over the issue during a period of record drought back in the mid-1960s. And plans developed after the drought for a dam on the river above the Water Gap remain available, awaiting the next drought and some political push.

Besides being an occasional point of contention between New York and Philadelphia, the Delaware also is a refuge for millions of rat-race-weary residents of those two great metropolitan areas. The hills above much of the river are filled with second homes, plush resorts, private hunting and fishing preserves, great estates and simple camps. Between Hanock and Trenton there are probably two dozen large canoe liveries with close to 5,000 craft available for rent. Add to that total all the smaller rental operations and private rafters, canoeists, kayakers, boaters and tubers, and it is easy to see why the river is not a place to do some contemplative trout fishing on a hot summer weekend, or in the spring when the shad are running. Fortunately, however, the river's banks themselves are partially protected from the crush of civilization by parks and other public lands. The Upper Delaware Scenic and Recreation Area shelters the river from Hanock to Port Jervis, New York; the Delaware Water Gap National Recreation Area envelopes it from Port Jervis to the Water Gap; and Roosevelt State Park from Easton to Morrisville, New Jersey.

Although a few big trout are caught each year along the entire length of the river, usually by fishermen tossing shad darts, the Delaware's best trout water runs from its start near Hanock downstream to about Callicoon, New York. The further up the river, the better seems to be the rule. Many people feel the stretch between Hanock and Lordsville, New York is actually the cream of the river for trophy browns and rainbows.

Its large size notwithstanding, bank fishing along the river's trout water is generally good. And access is a rather simple affair. On the Pennsylvania side of the border, Pennsylvania Route 191, which can be picked up off Interstate Route 84 Exit 5, closely parallels the river from the village of Equinunk (also see Equinunk Creek) upstream all of the way to Hanock. Almost any place along the side of the road where it is wide enough to park is an access point.

In Pennsylvania, the river also can be reached off State Route 1016 across from Callicoon and road 966, which runs off Route 191 near the village of Lookout to the village of Stalker on the river.

A reciprocal agreement with the state of New York permits anglers with a valid Pennsylvania fishing license to fish from the Delaware's banks in New York and vice-versa. Access to the river's trout water on the New York side may be had along Route 97, which roughly follows the river from Callicoon to Hanock.

Direct road access to the Delaware's trout water is unavailable only between Lordsville and Long Eddy, a distance of approximately six miles. Another gap in road access appears at Callicoon and runs upstream a couple of miles.

The number of weekend canoeists and rafters aside, float fishermen could not ask for a better trip than the upper Delaware River. Relatively gentle and smooth, with only a few, widely spaced Class 1 rapids and riffles, it is a first-class tour of a mountainous region of high, rounded and forested hills, rugged cliffs over which delicate waterfalls plummet in the spring, and low, grassy banks and islands. A trip over the Delaware's trout water from Hanock to Callicoon runs 27.5 miles, but it can be broken up into several smaller trips. Free launching sites are available on both the Pennsylvania and New York sides of the river. In Hanock, floaters can reach the river at the south end of town in the Fireman's Park and float 5.7 miles to take out at the Pennsylvania Fish Commission's Buckingham Access Site just north of Equinunk. Another Fish Commission access site is located at Equinunk, 2.2 miles further downstream.

Floaters also can take out or put in at the bridges in Lordsville, and Stalker about nine miles downriver. The stretch between Lordsville and Stalker is probably the most isolated on the Delaware, especially between Lordsville and Long Eddy, where no roads or homes touch the river. From the bridge at Stalker to the Fish Commission access below Callicoon is a distance of 9.4 miles. A New York state access point is available below Callicoon.

Anglers who want to make their trip along the Delaware a two, or even three day long affair can add 3.6 additional miles to their float by putting in at the Fish Commission's Ball's Eddy Access Site on the West Branch Delaware River. It can be found by following State Route 4014 upstream toward the village of Winterdale. S.R. 4014 meets Route 191 just before the bridge crossing over into Hanock. The river is always canoeable, except when frozen or flooding, but can very very, very shallow in places.

By all accounts, fly fishing on the upper Delaware is exceptional. It holds good populations of all three major aquatic insects. Hatches include: mid-April to mid-May, Blue-Winged

Olives, Hendricksons, caddis, Sulphurs, March Browns; mid-May to mid-June, caddis, Sulphurs, March Browns, Green Drake, Brown Drake, Isonychia, Slate-Winged Olives; summer, Isonychia, Slate-Winged Olives, caddis, Blue-Winged Olives, Tricorythodes and terrestrials. Fly anglers also might try such impressionistic or attractor patterns such as the Adams, Hare's Ear, Muddler Minnows, Crayfish, Woolly Buggers, Matuka Streamers, Royal Coachmen, Renegades and Zug Bugs.

The name Delaware is derived from that of the governor of the English colony at Jamestown, Virginia, Lord De la Warre, who succeeded Sir Thomas Gates as head of America's first English colony in 1610. The Indians had a number of different names for the stream. The Delaware Indians, whose original name was Lenape, called the river "Lenapewihittuck," or "river of the Lenape." It also was called Kithanne or "great stream," Kikhittuk or "large river," and Makeriskhickon or "Great River of the Mohawk." Early Swedish settlers, for their part, called the Delaware the South River.

About 150 years before Washington took his famous boat trip across the Delaware, the lower river already was making history. Delaware Bay was discovered by Henry Hudson, an Englishman working for the Dutch, on August 28, 1609. Lord Delaware entered the bay the following year on his way to Jamestown. The first attempt to settle along the river was made by the Dutch in 1623, when they established a trading post and fort at Gloucester, New Jersey.

In 1638, a group of Swedes led by Peter Minuit of the Swedish West Indian Co. settled on the present site of Wilmington, Delaware. Three years later the English established colonies at Salem Creek, New Jersey and near the mouth of the Schuylkill River, or Philadelphia. The erection of those settlements brought the first clash between the colonial powers, when the Dutch and Swedes joined forces to drive the English out of the area. Charles II of England, in March 1664, gave the Duke of York and Albany a land grant which included what was then known as New Netherlands. The duke reacted by seizing New Amsterdam from the Dutch and naming it New York in September 1664. Nine years later the Dutch returned the favor by recapturing New York. A year after that the Treaty of Westminister ceded the land back to the English, and, after several other deals involving various noblemen, the Delaware River and much of the rest of Pennsylvania was granted to Admiral Sir William Penn by Charles II in payment for 16,000 pounds owed the admiral. The date was March 4, 1681.

While the lower Delaware Valley has had a rich and varied history, the upper river has remained comparatively untouched. The Delaware River Path, from Philadelphia to Fort Hunter, New York, closely followed the upper river along the New York side from Port Jervis to its start near Hanock.

West Branch Delaware River

Originally known as the Mohawk Branch, the West Branch runs along the Pennsylvania-New York line from Hanock almost to Hale Eddy, New York. Like the river it helps to form, the West Branch is said to hold some real trophy browns and rainbows. It is a wide stream of moderate flow, with a scattering of riffles and deep pools, and long stretches of rocky flats. Except during periods of high water in the spring, the river is wadable from bank to bank.

One difference between the Main Branch and the West Branch is that the West Branch is usually less crowded. Many reports have it as underfished. This despite a good supply of aquatic insect life. Fly anglers can try some of the same patterns recommended for the main river.

Access to about half of Pennsylvania's portion of the West Bank may be had by following S.R. 4014, which appears at the Route 191 bridge leading into Hanock. The rest of the river can be reached off Route 17 in New York. However, anglers who do not own a New York fishing license should be careful to stay within the portion of river bordered by Pennsylvania and not wander too far upstream out of the water covered by the reciprocal agreement between the states.

The Delaware Path, for a period a major war path of the Mohawk tribe, followed the West Branch from Hanock upstream through Deposit and then on to Fort Hunter on the Mohawk River.

Starrucca Creek
Susquehanna County

Overshadowed by the presence of the tall, stately arches of the old Erie & Lackawanna Railroad Viaduct, Starrucca Creek quietly slips into the Susquehanna River near the start of the "Great Bend," where the river makes a sharp turn to the west. By then it has already offered some 13 miles of very enjoyable trout angling through a narrow and thinly populated farm valley.

Although the name Starrucca is almost assuredly of Indian origin, it has been so corrupted in the years since European settlers first moved into the region in 1787 that few historians will even venture a guess at its meaning. Since it is tucked far out of the way in the northeastern corner of Susquehanna County, though, it seems unlikely it may have been tied to any important events. But there is evidence a Tuscarrora Indian town once stood at the present location of Lanesboro near the mouth of the stream. The tribe, whose name means "hemp gathers," was the sixth member of the Six Nations of the Iroquois Confederacy.

Native to North Carolina, the Tuscaroras began moving north in the early eighteenth century after a number of clashes with settlers in their homeland. General John Sullivan's expedition of 1779 against British-paid Indians of the area who had been harassing settlers resulted in the destruction of at least one Tuscarora village in the region. Ingaren at the site of the present town of Great Bend on the Susquehanna River was wiped out on August 17, 1779.

Its fine fishing and picturesque setting notwithstanding, Starrucca Creek's main claim to fame today is the old railroad viaduct at Lanesboro. Built in 1847-1848, it is the oldest stone railroad bridge in the state in use today. Listed as a National Historic Civil Engineering Landmark, it is 1,040 feet long, 100 feet high and 25 feet wide at the top. The quality of its stone work and grace of its arches are a truly impressive sight, too, to people who are not particularly interested in such things.

While Starrucca Creek still remains somewhat off the beaten path, reaching it is a relatively simple matter thanks to Interstate Route 81. At the town of Great Bend take the Pennsylvania Route 171 Exit off Interstate 81 and drive south toward the villages of Hickory Grove and Oakland. In Oakland turn right across the Susquehanna River to the town of Susquehanna. From there continue east on Route 171 to Lanesboro. The location of the stream is clearly marked by the viaduct.

Immediately before the bridge crosses Starrucca Creek at Lanesboro there is a road running off to the right under one of the viaduct arches. That is Viaduct Street (Township Road 296). It follows the stream for more than ten miles all of the way to the village of Starrucca. Access to the creek is available at numerous locations.

Starrucca Creek is a rocky, cobble-strewn stream full of ledges reminiscent in some ways of Potter County's much better known Kettle Creek. Fly fishermen might try impressionistic caddis patterns, as well as old reliables such as the Quill Gordon, Adams, Hendrickson, March Brown, Soft Hackle Nymphs, Light Cahill, caddis, Renegade, Sulphurs and Terrestrials.

Lackawanna Path, from Pittston to Windsor, New York, crossed Starrucca Creek near its mouth at Lanesboro. It was used by a group of young Tuscaroras coming north late in 1766. While the sick and old traveled in canoes by way of Wyalusing, Tioga and Owego to the Great Bend, the younger people took the shorter, but more d. ficult, Lackawanna Path. When the last Indian left Scranton around 1771, they also traveled the path, as did the Iroquois after the battle of Wyoming.

Starruca Creek.

Snake Creek
Silver Creek, Fall Brook
Susquehanna County

Snake Creek

Flowing out of Lake Montrose in central Susquehanna County, Snake Creek cuts a crooked path north to join the North Branch of the Susquehanna River at Corbettsville, New York. It is well stocked for about ten miles, from south of Franklin Forks to about Brookdale, and generally considered to be one of the better trout streams in the county.

Along with being fine trout water and heavily stocked, Snake Creek also is easily accessible off Pennsylvania Route 29, which it hugs for practically its entire length. Fishing the stream involves nothing more than pulling off Route 29 and avoiding posted property. Besides direct access off Route 29, Snake Creek also may be reached by bridges on Shadow Brook Drive, Liberty Park Road, State Route 4002 at Lawsville Center and Forks Hill Road at Franklin Forks.

With most of the population between the county seat of Montrose and the New York State line clinging to Route 29, anglers might expect to find Snake Creek overrun by people and surrounded by noise. While it is under considerable early-season pressure, as are almost all Pennsylvania trout streams, its length allows for an occasional quiet spot. Because the stream is separated from the road by flat bottomlands of cornfields, pastures and woods, it also is much more serene than many people might think.

Fly fishing usually does not get good on Snake Creek until the water warms a bit. Once it does heat up, however, such traditional patterns as the Royal Coachman, Adams, Hare's Ear, caddis, Hendrickson, March Brown, Renegade, Light Cahill, Sulphurs and terrestrials will often produce fish.

Although Snake Creek itself is not rich in history, the hills just to the east of it are dear to the hearts of millions of Mormons all over the world. For it was while living amongst those gentle peaks that the church's founder, Joseph Smith, is said to have begun translating the golden tablets on which the church's gospel is based.

Smith reportedly came to Pennsylvania in about 1825 from Palmyra, New York, in search of a Spanish silver mine legend claimed was somewhere along the Great Bend of the Susquehanna. This was after he had aroused a great deal of ridicule in his home town by proclaiming he had been in contact with God, who had promised to reveal a new gospel to him carved by an angel on gold plates.

The prophet may not have found any Spanish silver while living along the Great Bend, but he did meet a girl. She was Emma Hale, the daughter of Isaac Hale, a farmer from Harmony near present day Hallstead. Because he was considered strange and did not have any solid prospects when it came to making a living, Smith's request to marry Emma was denied by her father.

Immediately after he was denied Emma's hand, Smith returned to Palmyra and announced he had unearthed the gold plates God had told him about. He then acquired the services of a young school teacher, Oliver Cowdery, to help him translate the tablets. Together the two men returned to the Great Bend and a small miner's cabin where Smith dictated to Cowdery what was on the plates.

Having gained a reputation as an eccentric during his earlier stay, once it was learned Smith had returned to the Harmony area attempts were made to drive him out. But they proved unsuc-

cessful, and, one day in February 1826, he appeared at the Hale farm to sweep Emma away in a sleigh.

Following their marriage in New York State, and another trip to Palmyra, where he found a publisher, Smith and Emma moved back to Harmony where he finished translating the plates. They were published as the Book of Mormom in March 1830 in an edition of 5,000 and at a price of $2.50.

Smith and Emma remained in Pennsylvania until the fall of 1830 when they moved to western New York, where his followers had organized a church, and then on into history.

Silver Creek

The only stocked tributary of Snake Creek, Silver Creek holds brown and rainbow trout from its mouth at Franklin Forks upstream five miles. It can be reached following State Route 4008 off Route 29 at Franklin Forks and toward Salt Spring State Park. S.R. 4008 parallels the stream from its mouth, past the entrance to the park and onto Pennsylvania Route 167, which then provides access.

Fall Brook

Fall Brook joins Silver Creek near the picnic area in Salt Spring State Park. It is stocked for about 3.5 miles upstream from its mouth. It can be fished by walking upstream from the picnic area or by following Salt Spring Road (Township Road 601) through the park to Buckleys Road (Township Road 677), which crosses the stream. Salt Spring Road also parallels the stream in its upper reaches.

Covering just 400 acres, Salt Spring Park does not hold any camping facilities. However, there is a hiking trail, restrooms and a picnic area. The park takes its name from the two unique salt springs within its boundary. The salt it produces was very important to the Indians of the area and a secret that they closely guarded from European settlers for years.

According to a Susquehanna County Historical Society flyer, a mill was open on the site in 1811 and made rough cloth for local residents. The area also was a popular rest spot because of the curative powers the springs were believed to possess. Nathan Wehaton, a brick layer from Connecticut, purchased the property in 1848.

The springs are listed as one of the "Outstanding Scenic Geological Features of Pennsylvania." Fall Creek itself contains three waterfalls tumbling through a deep, rock gorge and is touched by a glen of virgin hemlock estimated to be between 600 and 700 years of age. The springs and land for the park were purchased in the early 1970s by the Nature Conservancy from the Wheaton family and then resold to the state.

Fly fishermen can try some of the same patterns mentioned under Snake Creek on both Silver Creek and Fall Brook.

Further information on the springs, the park and surrounding area may be had by writing: Salt Springs State Park, Department of Environmental Resources, R.D. 1, Dalton, PA 18414.

Susquehanna County Historical Society, Monument Square, Montrose, PA 18801.

Wyalusing Creek
East Branch Wyalusing Creek
Middle Branch Wyalusing Creek
North Branch Wyalusing Creek
Gaylord Creek
Susquehanna County

"The place of the old man," or "the dwelling place of the hoary veteran," Wyalusing Creek carves a gentle path through the rugged plateau of Susquehanna and Bradford Counties to the village of Wyalusing, where it empties into the Susquehanna River. But only a very small portion of the main stream is stocked by the Fish Commission. Most of the watershed's trout water is on the East, Middle and North Branches.

Winding through a valley of steep slopes and narrow flats that don't lend themselves to many crops, Wyalusing Creek and its branches are primarily dairy country streams, but with a nice touch of New England added. The area was originally settled by migrants from Connecticut and the villages and towns along the stream still bear their neat, whitewashed influence.

If the Yankee touch seems picturesque and friendly today, it was anything but that during the years surrounding the Revolutionary War. For the presence of Connecticut settlers in northeastern Pennsylvania was far from a welcome one. In fact, it led the two colonies to fight a series of battles for control of the territory known as the "Pennite Wars."

Connecticut based her claim to northeastern Pennsylvania on her charter of 1662, which set her western boundary at the Pacific Ocean, excepting "any territory then possessed by a Christian prince or state." This charter overlapped the Penn's claim to all of what is now northern Pennsylvania.

In 1750, a few Connecticut pioneers made their way to the Wyoming Valley, a then nearly trackless wilderness. They reported their discovery to officials back in their home colony, describing the area as beautiful, fertile and quite desirable for settlement. As a consequence, three years later, the Susquehanna Company was formed with the purpose of developing the region.

No colonization of the area was attempted by the New Englanders until about 1762, when some 200 settlers moved into it with their families. The first Wyoming Massacre ended that first stab at development only a year later. Connecticut was not ready to give up, though, and quickly formed the Delaware Company which began purchasing from the Indians all the land lying between the Wyoming Valley and the Delaware River.

The Penns, having bought the same land from the Indians earlier, had no intention of letting the Connecticut challenge go unopposed. They quickly secured a letter from the King of England ordering colonial officials in Connecticut to stop their people from moving into the Wyoming Valley. In addition, through the Treaty of Fort Stanwix in 1768, the Penns got the Indians to renounce all of their land sales to Connecticut.

Ignoring all the Penns' actions, the Susquehanna Company went ahead and surveyed five townships along the Susquehanna and, in 1769, sent in 40 settlers who built a block house near what is now Wilkes-Barre.

Because the Penns had already leased some of the best land in the region to Pennsylvanians, the two colonies quickly found themselves in a highly explosive situation. The result was the first Pennite War during which the New Englanders were driven out of the region, only to return in greater numbers and start a stalemate that continued to 1771 when the Pennsylvanians apparently gave up.

Since the Susquehanna Company was formed as a private business, the government of Connecticut disavowed any connection with the problem until 1774 when it formally made the area, all of the way into Northumberland County, part of Litchfield County.

As more Yankee settlers moved into the region, they spread both south and west along the West Branch of the Susquehanna all of the way to Pine Creek in Lycoming County. In 1775 an expedition of Pennsylvanians attacked the Connecticut settlers along the West Branch and the second Pennite War was ignited.

The hostilities lasted for several months, with neither side able to gain the upper hand, until the Pennsylvanians again retreated downstream.

The arrival of the Revolutionary War brought a truce of sorts. Then, once independence was won, Pennsylvania approached Congress to settle the issue. In 1782 a Court of Commissions met in New Jersey and ruled, in the Decree of Trenton, unanimously in favor of the Keystone State. That decision may have ended the political fights, but not the question of property rights, and another series of clashes occurred between settlers from the two colonies which became known as the third Pennite War.

It was five years later, 1787, before the dispute was finally ended by the Confirming Act which gave the land to the original Connecticut settlers and paid Pennsylvania claimants with land elsewhere in the state.

Besides being part of the land involved in the Pennite Wars, the village of Wyalusing at the mouth of Wyalusing Creek also was once a famous Indian mission. Called Friedenshutten, "Tents of Peace," it was even considered a model wilderness town. Unfortunately, however, the settlement did not see much peace. Its inhabitants had to flee the town during Pontiac's War of the 1760s, again during Colonel Thomas Hartley's march through the area to avenge Indian attacks in 1778, and was finally destroyed by General John Sullivan's troops in his famous scorched-earth march against British-paid Indians in the upper Susquehanna River basin in 1779.

Wyalusing Creek also has been touched by a more gentler, and perhaps longer lasting, type of fame, too. The village of Camptown upstream from Wyalusing provided the inspiration for Stephen Foster's immortal song "Camptown Races."

Wyalusing Creek (East Branch)

All of East Branch Wyalusing Creek's stocked water—Fairdale to Rushville (including a small portion of the main stream—is accessible off Pennsylvania Route 706. Other access is available at bridges running off Route 706, including, State Route 3023, State Route 3033, Township Road 348 and 14 SP E. Route 706 can be picked up off U.S. Route 6 at the village of Wyalusing or Interstate Route 81 Exit 67 and U.S. Route 11 at New Milford.

Middle Branch

Stocked water on the Middle Branch covers about seven miles from just above Lawton upstream beyond the village of Birchardville. Like the East Branch and main stream, all of it is easily accessible off a main road, in this case Pennsylvania Route 267, which runs off Route 706 near Lawton, and parallels and crosses the Middle Branch over its entire seven-mile stocked length.

North Branch

Seven more miles of stocked trout water can be found in the North Branch Wyalusing Creek. And like both the main stream, East Branch and Middle Branch, it is all readily accessible off a main highway. Pennsylvania Route 858, running off Route 706 between Rushville and Lawton, follows the stream over its entire stocked length beyond the village of Middletown Center.

Gaylord Creek

Gaylord Creek is a tributary of the North Branch holding some 7.5 miles of stocked trout water. It has good access off Route 858 along Township Road 498, or the third road running to the left after Route 858's junction with Route 706.

As the early season pressure ends and the water begins to warm a bit, fly anglers in the Wyalusing watershed often score with Hare's Ears, Blue Duns, Quill Gordons, Adams, Hendricksons, March Browns, Soft Hackle Nymphs, Ginger Quills, Gray Fox, Green Drakes, caddis, Light Cahills, midges and terrestrials.

Meshoppen Creek
Susquehanna and Wyoming Counties

East of the crossroads in the Susquehanna County village of Springville, down at the foot of a long hill, a narrow bridge passes over a quiet bit of clear, green water hemmed in by overgrown mud banks and known as Meshoppen Creek. The weedy banks soon give way to a thick forest of ghostly, dead trees, but the smooth water remains typical of the "place of beads" along the upper portion of its stocked water. It is a pleasing, if sometimes eerie, scene interrupted only rarely by a few houses and pastures until the stream enters Wyoming County,and passes under Pennsylvania Route 29. Then its gradient steepens and the placid water turns into an almost unbroken series of riffles and ledges, punctuated by a 20-foot high waterfall, about two miles upstream of the village of Meshoppen.

Altogether 15.5 miles of Meshoppen Creek is stocked with brook, brown and rainbow trout. Nine miles of that length, from its mouth upstream to the Wyoming/Susquehanna County line, are in Wyoming County, and six and a half miles, centering around Springville, are in Susquehanna County.

No single road parallels Meshoppen Creek, but several cross it or follow it at various points throughout its stocked length. State Route 3004 toward the village of Hop Bottom appears at the crossroad on Route 29 in Springville. Quarry Road meets S.R. 3004 on the right just before the bridge and trails the stream at a distance for about four miles downstream where it meets State Route 3017, which leads down to another bridge over the creek and the approximate end of Susquehanna County's stocked water.

In Wyoming County, Route 29 provides easy access when it crosses over the Meshoppen a short distance north of the village of Lemon. About another mile north of the Route 29 bridge State Route 3015 appears to the east and runs down to the stream.

Approximately a quarter of a mile north of Lemon, State Route 4008 meets Route 29 on the west. This road parallels Meshoppen Creek at varying distances downstream to the village of Kaiserville. Bridges appear on Stang Road, roughly a half-mile off Route 29, and at Kaiserville. S.R. 4008 continues on the left across the bridge in Kaiserville and follows the creek downstream to U.S. Route 6 and the village of Meshoppen.

Settled in 1742, Meshoppen was a stagecoach stop until about 1870 when the railroads arrived. General John Sullivan, during his campaign against the Tories and their Indian allies in 1779, forded Meshoppen Creek at its mouth and camped a few miles beyond at Vanderlip's Plantation, near the present village of Black Walnut on Route 6.

Fly fishermen can try such standards as the Blue Dun, Quill Gordon, Adams, Hendrickson, stoneflies, Blue-Winged Olive, Hare's Ear, Muddler Minnow, Mickey Finn, Matukas, Woolly Buggers, Royal Coachman, caddis, Soft Hackle Nymphs, March Brown, Light Cahill, Sulphurs, midges and terrestrials.

Mehoopany Creek
Wyoming County
North Branch Mehoopany Creek
Wyoming and Sullivan Counties

Mehoopany Creek
Countless bogs, swamps and ponds make the North Mountain Plateau .on the Wyoming/Sullivan County line the birthplace of numerous streams. Among the trout waters which form on the plateau, or have tributaries that run off it, are Bowmans Creek, Loyalsock Creek, Fishing Creek and Mehoopany Creek.

Translated as "place of wild potatoes," Mehoopany Creek is stocked with brown trout for a distance of about nine miles from between the villages of Mehoopany and North Mehoopany on the Susquehanna River upstream. Through its headwaters on State Game Lands 57 northeast of Ricketts Glen State Park, the stream is designated as "Wild Trout Water" and holds a population of native brook trout. The stocked portion of this little stream is easily reachable off Pennsylvania Route 87 to the village of Forkston. State Route 3001 appears on the right after Route 87 crosses the stream at Forkston and leads further upstream, turning to dirt and gravel, through the village of Kasson Brook and into Game Lands 57. Fishing along the creek's upper water is a walk-in affair once S.R. 3001 begins pulling away from the stream.

Typical of plateau streams, Mehoopany Creek's upper waters above Stony Brook are fast and rocky. As it nears Forkston the gradient begins to decrease and the valley widen turning the Mehoopany into a meandering stream of braided channels and hillside farms. Two high, cascading waterfalls a short distance upstream of Mehoopany add a nice scenic touch for visiting anglers to admire.

Fly anglers should find some success with traditional patterns such as the Blue Dun, Adams, Hare's Ears, Soft Hackle Nymphs, stoneflies, Muddler Minnows, Mickey Finns, Matukas, Woolly Buggers, caddis, Quill Gordons, Hendricksons, March Browns, Light Cahills, Gray Fox and terrestrials.

North Branch Mehoopany Creek
Although a tributary of Mehoopany Creek and smaller in size, North Branch Mehoopany Creek actually offers the trout angler one more mile of stocked water to fish. It is planted with brooks, browns and rainbows for ten miles from its mouth on Mehoopany Creek at Forkston, upstream to about the village of Colley in Sullivan County. Access to the stream's entire length is available off Route 87 starting in Forkston.

Wyalusing Path, a very difficult Indian trail from Wyalusing to Muncy, once crossed the North Branch near Lovelton and the "Sign of the Goose," a cabin that was probably established by the Moravian missionaries and became a frequent stopping place for travelers. Bishop John Ettwein used the trail to help lead some 200 Indian converts from Friedenshutten, a Morvaian settlement near Wyalusing, to the Beaver River after the Iroquois sold the land to the Penns and trouble erupted between the Connecticut settlers and the Pennamites (see Wyalusing Creek).

"After we crossed the Susquehanna at the ford our way led straight to the mountains," the bishop wrote, "and after proceeding two miles, we entered the Great Swamp, where the undergrowth was so dense that ofttimes it was impossible to see one another at the distance of six feet. The path was frequently a blind one and yet along it sixty head of cattle and fifty horses and colts had to be driven, and it needed careful watch to keep them together. We lost but one young cow from the entire herd. Every morning, however, it was necessary to send drivers back, as far as ten miles, to whip in such as would during the night stray off. At our first night's encampment two of our Indians lost themselves while in search of straying cattle, and several hours elapsed before we could reach them with signal guns. It was a daily matter of astonishment to me, that any man should presume to traverse this swamp, and follow what is called a path. . ."

Samuel Harris, a surveyor who passed along the path two years later, also found the going so tough he chose to write about it:

"May 10. Left Woyalusing 6 minutes after Six in the morning, Dyned at the Sign of the Goose. Left it 1/4 after one Oclock and got over to the Elk Lick on Muncy Creek 1/4 before Six. Incampt got our Suppers feed our Horses have made our Beeds and not quite dark. I think we had a Hard days Ride OVER THE WORST ROAD IN THE WORLD . . ."

Fly anglers can try some of the same patterns mentioned under Mehoopany Creek.

Bowman Creek
Fly Fishing Only
Wyoming County

Dropping off wild North Mountain Plateau and fascinating Ricketts Glen State Park, Bowmans Creek begins life full of nearly unlimited scenic potential. A busy highway, abundance of houses and ugly, if necessary, rip-rapped banks soon quash much of that promise. What remains, however, is still good enough to make the stream a Mecca of sorts for trout anglers from throughout the Wyoming Valley, as well as much of the rest of northeastern Pennsylvania.

Relatively large in size, Bowmans Creek is stocked with brook, brown and rainbow trout for about 15 miles from its mouth on the Susquehanna River near the village of Eatonville upstream through southeastern Wyoming County to the Luzerne County line. It has a one-mile long Fly Fishing Only Project extending from the vicinity of Pennsylvania Route 292 downstream to near its confluence with Marsh Creek. Pennsylvania Route 29/309 intertwines with the stream to provide plenty of easy access from Eatonville to the village of Noxen. State Route 3002 appears at the bridge on the right in Noxen and follows the creek further upstream.

Bowman Creek's Fly Fishing Only water can be found by taking the Route 292 bridge over the stream. Jenks Road appears to the left a short distance on the other side of the bridge and leads to a parking area, marked by the usual Fish Commission posters.

As is common on most Pennsylvania freestone streams, nymphs and streamers usually produce the best for fly fishermen on Bowmans Creek during the early part of the season. Possible early season patterns include: Hare's Ear, Lead-Winged Coachman, Woolly Bugger (brown or yellow), stoneflies, Muddler Minnow, Mickey Finn, Matukas, Soft Hackle flies and caddis pupa. Dry fly anglers can try such standards as the Adams, Quill Gordon, Hendrickson, Blue-Winged Olives, Royal Coachman, March Brown, Light and Dark Cahill, caddis, Gray Fox, Sulphurs and terrestrials.

The headwaters of Bowmans Creek form in Ricketts Glen State Park on the Luzerne/Sullivan County line. The stream is not stocked in that area, but the park has a 101-site family campground open on a year-round basis where anglers can stay (also see Fishing Creek, Columbia County). From mid-April to mid-

November the campground is operated as a Class A facility with hot showers and flush toilets. Winter sites are Class B with pit toilets.

Ricketts Glen also offers ten modern rental cabins on a year-round basis. The cabins are furnished and have a living area, toilet and shower, and two or three bedrooms. Advance reservations are required. Application forms may be had by writing the park office.

For the non-fishing visitor Ricketts Glen's 13,050 acres hold a wealth of sightseeing and other recreational opportunities. Boat rentals are available on Lake Jean during the summer, swimming may be done at a guarded beach from Memorial Day weekend to Labor Day. There also are 20 miles of hiking trails, an environmental education program, five miles of bridle trails and a world of picnic sites. The most fascinating offering of the park, however, is the Glens Natural Area.

A Registered National Natural Landmark, the Glens Natural Area, holds some 22 named waterfalls. They range in height from 11 feet to 94 feet, and occur on the two branches of Kitchen Creek as they cut their way through the deep gorges of Ganoga Glen and Glen Leigh. The area also marks the meeting of the northern and southern hardwood types, and so contains an extensive variety of tree species.

Ricketts Glen itself is named after Colonel Robert Bruce Ricketts. As leader of Battery F during the Battle of Gettysburg, Colonel Ricketts helped repel "Picketts Charge." The colonel at one time owned, or controlled, over 80,000 acres in and around the park. His heirs, through the Central Penn Lumber Co., sold about 48,000 acres to the Pennsylvania Game Commission between 1920 and 1924. The area actually was approved as a site for a national park in the 1930s, but World War II put an end to those plans. In 1942 the Ricketts family sold the falls and land bordering it to the state. The first recreational facilities were opened two years later.

For the angler fishing Bowmans Creek, Ricketts Glen can be reached by following Route 29 south through Noxen to its junction with Pennsylvania Route 118 near the village of Pikes Creek. Follow Route 118 west to the village of Red Rock where state Route 487 appears and leads into the park.

Further information of Ricketts Glen is available by writing: Ricketts Glen State Park, Department of Environmental Resources, R.D. 1, Box 251, Benton, PA 17814.

Harveys Creek
Luzerne County

Natural lakes are relatively rare in Pennsylvania, particularly outside of the northeast region. The state's rugged mountains and narrow valleys lend themselves far more to the creation of streams and rivers than lakes. Still, there are a few scattered here and there, and one of the largest among them is 658-acre Harveys Lake, the source of Luzerne County's most popular trout stream, Harveys Creek.

Stocked all of the way from Harveys Lake downstream to its mouth on the Susquehanna River at the village of West Naticoke, Harveys Creek holds some 13 miles of heavily planted, and fished, water. Access is good, but because most of the land surrounding the creek is owned by the Pennsylvania Gas & Water Co. or the state (in the form of a prison and Lackwanna State Forest), free of development. Practically the entire creek lies within a pretty gorge of forests and cliffs, besmirched only by the sound of nearby roads, which is very surprising, considering the fact that Nanticoke, across the Susquehanna River from the mouth of the stream, was once a great anthracite mining center. During the first half of this century up to 10,000 miners worked shafts in the immediate vicinity of the town. Avondale Mine just east on U.S. Route 11 from Harveys Creek was the site of a mining disaster in 1869 that took the lives of 108 men, when fire and smoke blocked the only entrance to the facility.

Before the miners, the Nanticoke Indians built a village on the site of Nanticoke. The Great Warriors Path, from Athens to Sunbury, crossed Harveys Creek near its mouth. Its name aside, the trail also was used during times of peace, being the designated route for Iroquois ambassadors traveling south for talks with colonial officials in Philadelphia, Maryland and Virginia.

Access to Harveys Creek's lower water through Lackawana State Forest is available by taking Pennsylvania Route 29 north off Route 11 at West Nanticoke. Route 29 follows the creek upstream beyond the village of Ceases Mills and the state prison,

giving further access off Mizdale Road (Township Road 499) and Township Road 497.

Near the prison, Route 29 bears to the west and Pine Creek Reservoir. Anglers can gain access to Harveys Creek's upper water by turning right onto a secondary road and following the stream toward Harveys Lake. The road parallels the creek to Pennsylvania Route 118, which then picks it up and follows it into the village of Meeker. In Meeker, turn right onto Mercer Road, leading to Harveys Lake. Mercer Road parallels the stream to the lake, which also is stocked with trout.

Harveys Creek fly fishermen can try Quill Gordons, Adams, stoneflies, Hendricksons, March Browns, Royal Coachman, Muddler Minnows, Matuka streamers, Woolly Buggers, Hare's Ears, Muskrats, Soft Hackle Nymphs, Renegades, Gray Fox, Light Cahills, Sulphurs, midges and terrestrials.

A free "Public Use Map" of Lackawanna State Forest, with an overview of lower Harveys Creek, may be had by writing: District Forester, Lackawanna State Forest, 401 Scranton State Office Building, 100 Lackawanna Avenue, Scranton, PA 18503.

Mountain brookie.

Muncy Creek
Sullivan and Lycoming County

Renegade, Black Gnat, Gray Fox, Royal Coachman, Light Cahill, Sulphurs, midges and terrestrials.
(Also see Loyalsock Creek.)

"No respect." That's what Muncy Creek seems to get. At least in comparison to her neighbor to the west Loyalsock Creek. Yet it certainly is not a bad place to wet a line. Its surroundings are mainly scenic forested slopes, floodplain woods and pretty farms. Hunting camps and second homes are at a minimum. While its waters hold a good mixture of stocked brown trout and native brookies, fish that are usually under less pressure than those in the famous Loyalsock.

Muncy Creek is of good size, too. Anglers can find plenty of room to cast in most places. And it is long. Its stocked water covers some 28 miles, all the way from its mouth on the West Branch Susquehanna River near Muncy in Lycoming County, upstream toward the village of Nordmont in Sullivan County. Most of the fishing pressure is focused on the Lycoming waters below the village of Beech Glen.

Access to Muncy Creek also is good. Pennsylvania Route 405 follows the stream from its mouth upstream through Muncy to Hughesville. A Fish Commission access area allows anglers who want to try its mouth to reach it with no problem. Route 405 itself crosses the stream just above Pennsylvania Route 147. Pennsylvania Route 118, which runs east off Route 405 in Hughesville, gives further access to the lower stream.

Upstream of Hughesville, U.S. Route 220 takes over, closely paralleling and crossing the creek through the villages of Picture Rocks (named for the Indian painting that once graced the cliffs overlooking the settlement), Tivoli, Glen Mawr, Beech Glen, Muncy Valley and Sonestown. Several bridges and side roads run off Route 220 between Hughesville and Sonestown, giving additional access to the stream.

At Sonestown, Muncy Creek bends away from Route 220, but access still remains good off State Route 2002 running toward Nordmont. S.R. 2002 meets Route 220 on the right a short distance after Muncy Creek turns away from the highway.

Wyalusing Path, from Wyalusing to Muncy, once followed Muncy Creek from its mouth upstream through Nordmont. It was known for both its ruggedness and beauty.

"On the highlands where the Loyalsock and Muncy creeks head, it is very rocky and almost impassible," Moravian Bishop John Ettwein wrote of his trip along Wyalusing Path in 1772. "There were indications of abundance of ores here. The timber is principally Sugar-maple, Lindens, Ash, Oak and White-pine. What told me the most was that several days it rained incessantly, and I was wet all day. The path led thirty six times across Muncy creek. At intervals here there were exceedingly rich bottoms, and the noblest timber I have seen in America, excepting the cypress in South Carolina and Georgia."

Fort Brady once stood along the creek near the town of Muncy. Captain John Brady built the stockard in the fall of 1777 after being ordered to the West Branch Susquehanna by Washington. Captain Brady was a noted Indian fighter and pioneer who had already seen action in the French and Indian War, Pontiac's Rebellion and the Revolutionary War. He had been seriously wounded in the Battle of Germantown just before Washington sent him north. He was killed in an Indian ambush at nearby Wolf Run in 1779. After his death the British and their Indian allies overran the region.

Fly anglers along Muncy Creek should find some success with caddis, Adams, Muskrat, Soft Hackle Nymphs, Hare's Ear, Hendrickson, Muddler Minnow, Woolly Buggers, March Brown,

Loyalsock Creek
Fly Fishing Only (Float Trip)
Sullivan and Lycoming Counties
Little Loyalsock Creek
Elk Creek, Hoagland Branch Elk Creek
Mill Creek
Sullivan County
Little Bear Creek, Wallis Run
Lycoming County
(Northcentral Map)

Loyalsock Creek
Primeval pine forests and a gorge as steep as they come in Pennsylvania kept the Indains from living along most of the Loyalsock Creek, or their paths from following it over any great distance, for a thousand years. When the first road finally pierced the valley, it ran high along the slopes of the gorge and was so precipitous it left many travelers believing they were at the "end of the world."

For another hundred years after the first Europeans reached what is now Sullivan and Lycoming Counties, the lands around the Loyalsock remained wild and sparsely settled. Then the Industrial Revolution struck. Lumber became an important ingredient in the rush of progress. The expanding railroads needed it for ties, the mines for supports and the manufacturers for factories. And then all the new workers had to be housed and stores built for new merchants. By the turn of the century, the slopes above Loyalsock Creek were bare and the stream itself a silt-filled slug.

If anybody requires evidence of Mother Nature's ability to withstand man's greed and rejuvenate herself, then the valley of the Loyalsock is the place to look. From the wasteland of the lumber barons, the stream today is one of the most picturesque in all of Pennsylvania. Resplendent solitude, at least after the first few weeks of the trout season, once again engulfs its gorge and more than 40 miles of deep pools and swift rapids. Given a second chance, Mother Nature has proven even more generous than in the heydays of the lumber industry. The lands of Wyoming State Forest, Tiadaghton State Forest and State Game Lands 134, which all border Loyalsock Creek, not only provide a magnificent setting to escape the stresses of too many people, but now hold some of the most valuable hardwood forests in the world. Let's hope we use them better this time.

Despite the often primitive feel of its environs, the "Sock," as locals refer to it, is easily accessible to any angler who wishes to explore its waters. Pennsylvania Route 87 and Pennsylvania Route 154 parallel the stream along its entire stocked length. Route 87 and the lower Loyalsock can be picked up off Interstate Route 180 at Montoursville east of Williamsport in Lycoming County, near where the stream empties into the West Branch Susquehanna River. Route 154 and the upper portion of the stream can be found off U.S. Route 220 near the Sullivan County seat of Laporte (with a population of just 200, the smallest county seat in Pennsylvania).

Loyalsock Creek, whose name means "middle creek," in reference to its position midway between Lycoming Creek and Muncy Creek, is stocked with brown and rainbow trout from the village of Loyalsockville upstream to where it turns away from Route 154 outside of Laporte, or a total of 22 miles in Lycoming County and 20 miles in Sullivan County. Its three mile long Fly Fishing Only Project runs from the Lycoming County line downstream to Sandy Bottom and is well marked with signs.

Camping accommodations for fishermen visiting Loyalsock Creek are available at Worlds End State Park along Route 154. Named after the feeling early travelers to the region had when transversing the first road along the top of the valley, the park has a 70-site Class B campground. It is open year-round, but access is not guaranteed in winter. Facilities are limited to water, toilets and a dump station.

Along with the campground, World End also has 19 family cabins for rent by the half-week or week during the spring and fall, and by the week in the summer. Due to large demand, however, a lottery system is used to distribute the cabins. Further information and application forms may be had from the park office. The cabins are equipped with a refrigerator, range, fireplace, table, chairs and beds.

Besides fishing in Loyalsock Creek, Worlds End Park offers guests swimming in a small, guarded dam area from Memorial Day weekend to Labor Day, picnicking, and hiking along the 57-mile long Loyalsock Trail, as well as several shorter routes. Excellent sightseeing opportunities also exist, particularly in June, when the Mountain Laurel, Pennsylvania's State Flower, is blooming, and in the fall, when the leaves are changing. Canyon Vista holds an outstanding view of the Loyalsock Gorge and surrounding mountains.

Whitewater boating may be done on Loyalsock Creek in the park during the high-water months of the spring, and the park is the site of annual whitewater races. With rapids that can run to Class 4, the Department of Environmental Resources discourages floating the stream through the park in open canoes. From the village of Forksville downstream of Worlds End State Park, however, the stream becomes a lot more receptive to anglers who might want to try floating it. Edward Gertler, in his book, *Keystone Canoeing,* rates the Loyalsock's whitewater from Forksville to its mouth as no higher than Class 1+, or just enough to make the trip a little lively. The stretch is said to be floatable in the spring during snowmelt and within one week of a hard rain.

The gorge towering above the Loyalsock kept major Indian paths from following it over any great distance. However, the Towanda Path from Muncy to Towanda did cross the stream near the village of Hillsgrove on Route 87. Also known as Genesee Road, the path actually was one of the main routes for emigrants from southern Pennsylvania, Maryland and Virginia to the fertile Genesee Valley of New York.

Caddisflies are now the predominant aquatic insects on Loyalsock Creek, and fly anglers should do well with just about any imitation of that species. The heavy mayfly hatches are gone, but fishermen can still find some action with the traditional hatches: mid-April to mid-May, Quill Gordons, Hendricksons and March Browns; mid-May to mid-June, March Browns, Gray Fox, Light Cahills. Other fly patterns anglers might try include: Adams, Hare's Ear, Muddler Minnow, Matuka Streamers, Royal Coachman, Renegade, Black Gnat, Lead-Winged Coachman and terrestrials.

Details on Worlds End Park may be had by writing: Worlds End State Park, Department of Environmental Resources, P.O. Box 62, Forksville, PA 18616-0062.

A map and other information on Wyoming State Forest, and the eastern section of Tiadaghton State Forest, is available by writing: Wyoming State Forst, District Forester, Old Berwick Road, Bloomsburg, PA 17815.

Anglers/hikers interested in finding out more about the Loyalsock Trail can contact: Alpine Hiking Club, P.O. Box 501, Williamsport, PA 17701.

TRIBUTARIES

Being a large stream, Loyalsock Creek can sometimes become too high and discolored for good fishing early in the season. Instead of letting the weather ruin a trip, fishermen might consider trying one of the stream's small tributaries, which are much less susceptible to the weather. Fly fishermen can use some of the same patterns listed under Loyalsock Creek.

Little Loyalsock Creek

Flowing through a lovely, narrow farm valley, Little Loyalsock Creek is the main tributary of Loyalsock Creek, joining the bigger stream at Forksville. Its 10 miles of stocked water extend from its mouth on Loyalsock Creek upstream almost to the village of Dushore. Access to its entire stocked length is available off Route 87 between Route 220 and Forksville.

Countless immigrants to the United States have had their family names butchered by officials and neighbors of different nationalities. Dushore, near the head of Little Loyalsock's trout water, is the Americanization of Aristide Aubert Dupetit Thouras name, a refugee of the French Revolution and early settler of the area.

Elk Creek

Splashing down a slender valley of hemlocks, spruce and sycamores along the edge of Wyoming State Forest, Elk Creek is stocked for six miles from its mouth upstream. Access may be had off Elk Creek Road (State Route 4001), which can be found on Route 154 in the village of Lincoln Falls and Route 87 about a mile upstream of Hillsgrove.

On really bad days, or during off hours, anglers might consider a little sightseeing at Lincoln Falls. This beautiful cascading piece of water—listed in *Outstanding Geological Features of Pennsylvania* (Commonwealth of Pennsylvania Department of Environmental Resources Bureau of Topographic and Geologic Survey) is located on a tributary of Elk Creek about a quarter-mile east of the village of Lincoln Falls. It can be pinpointed on the "Public Use Map" of Wyoming State Forest.

Hoagland Branch Elk Creek

Six more miles of stocked trout water can be found on this tiny stream, accessible along the dirt and gravel Hoagland Branch Road off Elk Creek Road at the village of Wissingers, really a collection of hunting and fishing camps. The stream is completely surrounded by state forest lands.

Mill Creek

Gushing out of Wyoming State Forest to join the Loyalsock at Hillgrove, Mill Creek holds still another six miles of stocked water, running from its mouth upstream. Dirt-surfaced Mill Creek Road (State Route 4010) meets Route 87 in Hillsgrove and parallels the stream over its entire stocked length.

Little Bear Creek   (Northcentral Map)

Lycoming County holds two stocked tributaries of Loyalsock Creek. Little Bear Creek and its four miles of trout water, stretching from its mouth upstream, can be found flowing next to the

Forest Headquarters off Route 87 between the villages of Barbours and Butternut Grove. A dirt and gravel road parallels the stream past the headquarters building.

Wallis Run   (Northcentral Map)

Located roughly seven miles above Montoursville, Wallis Run has eight miles of stocked water, running from its mouth upstream.

Unlike the Loyalsock's other tributaries, Wallis Run is not accessible off Route 87. Anglers who wish to try it must turn off Route 87 and onto Pennsylvania Route 973 at Loyalsockville. Immediately after crossing the Loyalsock, Wallis Run Road (State Road 1003) appears. This secondary road parallels the Loyalsock upstream along its north bank. It picks up Wallis Run when it turns away from the Loyalsock just before the village of Butternut Grove.

Towanda Creek
South Branch Towanda Creek
Schrader Creek
Bradford County

Towanda Creek

General John Sullivan's march up the Susquehanna River to revenge attacks by British-paid Indians on settlers who supported the War for Independence is a very famous piece of Pennsylvania history. His successful action against the Indians of the upper Susquehanna and Gennessee basins of New York State brought him a great deal of recognition in the Continental Army, and eventually lead to Pennsylvania naming a county after him. Some historians also point out that while General William T. Sherman is generally credited with developing the "scorched earth" philosophy of warfare on his flaming "March to the Sea" during the Civil War, General Sullivan actually provided the example nearly 100 years earlier when he destroyed some 40 Indian villages and laid waste to thousands of acres of cropland.

Involving an army of some 5,000 men, Sullivan's expedition may have been the first large scale example of total war, but even he had a model to follow. His name was Colonel Thomas Hartley. Riding at the head of a troop of 200 men, Colonel Hartley, in 1778, about a year before Sullivan marched out of Easton, attacked and destroyed the Indian settlements of Queen Esther's Town (Milan), Tioga and Sheshequin (Ulster). In an era when wars were fought by professional soldiers away from civilian populations, Hartley's actions were, to say the least, unusual.

Besides revealing the possibilities of all out war, Colonel Hartley's march also demonstrated the practicality of moving troops through the forests and mountains of the region on Indian paths. He did it by traveling up the Sheshequin Path (translation "at the place of the gourd rattle") between Williamsport and Ulster, and along Towanda Creek from about East Canton to Powell.

Before General Sullivan, the Sheshequin Path was an easy, short route between the Indian villages around Athens and those at Lock Haven and Sunbury. Conrad Weiser, colonial Pennsylvania's ambassador to the Indians, and his companion Shickellamy used the path in March 1737, when two to three feet of snow and flooding creeks made their passage less than a pleasure.

St. Joseph Path, from Powell to Ulster, was one of several,

smaller crossing paths over Towanda Creek. It forded the stream in the vicinity of Powell. It may have been named by Moravian Bishop Gottlieb Spangenberg, who traveled it with Weiser in 1745.

Most tributaries of the northern Susquehanna River are relatively short. The main exceptions to this in Pennsylvania are the Lackwanna River, Tunkhannock Creek, Fishing Creek and Towanda Creek. Draining approximately 278 square miles, Towanda Creek, meaning either "the place where we bury our dead" or "swift water," rises near the town of Canton in the southwestern corner of Bradford County and enters the Susquehanna through the broad, swampy wetlands below the town of Towanda. Between the grand Victorian homes of those two towns, it flows through a scenic agricultural valley of rolling dairy farms and scattered corn fields.

The 13.5-mile stretch of Towanda Creek from Canton to West Franklin is annually stocked by the Fish Commission with plenty of brown, rainbow and brook trout. Access to just about the entire length of stocked water is available off Pennsylvania Route 414 from U.S. Route 220 at Monroeton. Parking is available at various locations along Route 414, as well as at six bridges which cross the stream between West Franklin and Canton. These include: 08003 SP E, Curtwright Road, Crofut Road at Woodruff Corners, Mill Street at Leroy, West Leroy Cross Road, Van Fleet Road and East Canton Road.

Anglers should be aware that rain can quickly turn the gentle waters of Towanda Creek off-color. Flies such as the Adams, Blue Dun, Hare's Ear, Soft Hackle Nymphs, Hendrickson, caddis, Gray Fox, March Brown, Renegade, Light Cahill, Sulphurs and terrestrials.

South Branch Towanda Creek

As a high-banked, steeply dropping mountain brook, South Branch Towanda Creek is almost the exact opposite of its pastoral parent stream. Starting as a trickle south of Laddsburg, it flows almost directly north through a narrow valley of summer homes, trailers and hunting camps to join Towanda Creek proper near Monroeton. It is stocked with browns and rainbows roughly from the village of New Albany to the village of South Branch.

Since South Branch Towanda Creek is paralleled and crossed by U.S. Route 220, access is simply a matter of pulling off the highway and avoiding any posted land. Fly fishermen might start their fishing with patterns similar to those used on Towanda Creek.

Schrader Creek

Cutting through the heart of a wild, wooded sandstone plateau, Schrader Creek is an outstanding scenic addition to the Towanda Creek watershed. And one which should never fall victim to "progress," since more than 15 of its 22 miles are under the protective custody of State Game Lands 12 and 36.

But unlike certain people, Schrader Creek is much more than the sum of its looks. By all accounts it is an excellent spring and fall trout fishery, loaded with stocked fish, a good number of holdovers and even some streamborne individuals. The best section runs from Cold Springs near the Bradford/Sullivan County line to the old lumbering village of Laquin.

Schrader Creek can be reached by taking U.S. Route 220 to Monroeton and then following Route 414 toward Franklindale. About a mile outside of Monroeton turn left across the Towanda Creek bridge and continue on State Route 3006 to the village of Powell, which sits at the forks of Schrader Creek and Towanda Creek. Immediately before crossing the bridge into Powell there will be a dirt and gravel road off to the left. The stream paralleling

Towanda Creek.

that road is Schrader Creek. The road shadows the stream for about 12.5 miles to a game lands service road. The service road is marked by a locked gate and closed to motor vehicles. From that point on the best fishing water is strictly a walk-in proposition.

Fly fishermen who frequent this cobble and boulder studded beauty report good success with the Royal Coachman, Adams and Blue Dun and other patterns mentioned under Towanda Creek.

FRENCH AZILUM

Much history has touched the upper Susquehanna River basin. Anglers who enjoy a little sightseeing when taking a break from Towanda Creek, South Branch Towanda Creek and Schrader Creek might consider a trip to French Azilum.

Located on the Susquehanna between Towanda and Wyalusing, Azilum (Asylum) in 1793 became the home for 200 aristocratic refugees from the French Revolution. Traveling up the river on Durham boats, the colonists built several log cabins, including a two and a half story log mansion for the deposed queen and her son, the dauphin, who were never able to escape France.

Refined and backed by substantial wealth, members of the colony also added a genteel touch to the frontier, mixing buckskin with lace, serving venison on fine china, and building log cabins with wine cellars. The colony lasted only nine years, until 1802, when the new Emperor Napoleon granted the refugees amnesty and they responded by returning to their homeland.

The Pennsylvania Historical Society now controls the site of French Azilum and administers it as a state historic property. It lies between Durrell on Pennsylvania Route 187 and Rummerfield on the other side of the river on U.S. Route 6.

Big Fishing Creek
Catch and Release
Columbia County

Big Fishing Creek

Draft resistance has had a long and colorful history in the United States. From its beginnings in the Civil War, when crowds nearly burned down New York City at Abraham Lincoln's proposal to conscript soldiers for battle in the cottonfields of the South, to the Age of Aquarius when rioting crowds nearly burned down the nation's institutions of higher learning rather than journey to the rice paddies of Viet Nam, Americans have often resisted efforts to forcibly put them in uniform.

"Draft resistance is as American as applie pie," is the way one slogan of the late 1960s put it.

While thousands of resistance plots have been hatched by both individuals and groups in every war, very few have lived beyond their immediate generation. Among those exceptions is the "Fishing Creek Confederacy."

The "Confederacy" came into being late in the Civil War when a group of residents of northeastern Pennsylvania decided they did not want to become a part of Mr. Lincoln's Army, or pay the $300 needed to hire a replacement, and went into hiding in the wilderness of Columbia County's Big Fishing Creek Valley.

Travel through the mountains being what it was at the time, the evaders probably would have been completely overlooked had not

rumors of fortifications and Fifth Columns reached Washington. Unable to ignore such a threat, the federal government hurriedly displatched a thousand troops to crush the rebellion in its rear. What resulted was worthy of a M*A*S*H episode. A member of the expedition later wrote:

"Well do we remember the heroic charge on the supposed battlements after a fortnight's preparation and quite vivid is the picture of the disgusted countenance as they reached the summit of the mount where we were taught to believe the Fishing Creek Army was massed and found not a man, nor evidence that a man had been there . . . In a word, such a thing as a confederacy to resist the U.S. Government never existed in Columbia County."

The "Fishing Creek Confederacy" may have been a mirage, but Big Fishing Creek (also sometimes simply called Fishing Creek) itself is real enough. And among the finest freestone trout streams in the state.

Although its source reaches far back to an East Branch and a West Branch in the big woods between the slopes of North Mountain and Huckleberry Mountain on State Game Lands 13 in Sullivan County, Big Fishing Creek proper really does not come into being until south of Pennsylvania Route 118. The main stream then flows southwest, draining some 385 square miles, to enter the North Branch of the Susquehanna River near Bloomsburg—the only municipality in Pennsylvania incorporated as a "town." Along the way, it flows over abandoned mill dams and under covered bridges that recall an era when villages like Cole Creek, Stillwater and Benton were prosperous centers of milling and lumber industries.

Farmers hauling grain to the mills and lumberjacks looking for a little fun on a Saturday night are today long gone from the Big Fishing Creek scene. But along with them also all of the siltation and erosion of those "rape and run" days. What remains in their place is some classic, big stream Eastern-style angling for brown trout with a dash of rainbows thrown in for good measure.

Roughly 23 miles of Big Fishing Creek is currently listed as stocked by the Fish Commission. The stocked water runs an intermittent course from north of Interstate Route 80 in the Lightstreet area, all the way upstream to the main creek's beginnings below Route 118. Portions that are not stocked can generally be identified by the presence of "No Trespassing" signs of one sort or another.

The upper stretches of Big Fishing Creek flow through a narrow valley bordered by generally low hills covered in a patchwork of woods and pastures. Except in really high water, it is often surprisingly clear, even early in the season. The presence of the stream's Catch and Release Project in this upper water, though, also means it draws a good deal more pressure than many other sections of the stream; including the water from the covered bridge at Zaner's Station downstream, an area that many of the creek's largest fish reportedly favor.

As far as the village of Benton, about seven miles downstream from Route 118, development along Big Fishing Creek is scarce. Below Benton, clusters of summer homes and cabins begin to appear, but they never really take over the stream, and except for a pass at Interstate Route 80 south of Lightstreet, Big Fishing Creek continues in a mostly rustic vein all of the way around Bloomsburg.

Unlike most other freestone streams in Pennsylvania, and the eastern U.S. as a whole, Big Fishing Creek is one waterway where the word hatch still means a healthy appearance of mayflies. Highlights of the season are Hendricksons in April, and Sulphurs, March Browns and Gray Fox in May. In between there also are excellent emergences of caddis and some great terrestrial fishing through the summer. Imitations and presentations must be good, however, since Big Fishing Creek trout are wary and selective, definitely not given to suicide.

Almost the entire length of Big Fishing Creek can be reached by taking Interstate Route 80, Exit 35 east of Bloomsburg to Pennsylvania Route 487 north. Bridges provide further access by crossing the stream in several locations all of the way up to Route 118. Parking also is available in numerous locations along Route 487. The Catch and Release water extends for one mile from the confluence of the East Branch and the West Branch at Grassmere Park downstream to the Gary Cook property line. It is clearly posted and can be reached by making a left turn off Route 487 north onto Road No. 16 (marked by a small, white legislative route-type sign), which is located a short distance above the village of Coles Creek. Road No. 16 crosses the stream and continues along the special regulation water through Grassmere Park to Route 118.

No state parks touch on Big Fishing Creek, but 13,050-acre Ricketts Glen State Park is located only about five miles northeast on Route 487/118 in Luzerne and Sullivan Counties. The park offers 110 tent and trailer campsites open year-round. From mid-April to mid-November a Class A campground with hot showers and flush toilets also is operated. Winter sites are Class B with pit toilets. The campground also includes a sanitary dump station, shaded sites and gravel spurs.

Besides the tent and trailer sites, Ricketts Glen offers 10 modern rental cabins on a year-round basis. Cabins are furnished with a living area, kitching/dining area, toilet/shower and two or three bedrooms. Advance reservations are required.

Anglers with family members along who do not fish will be glad to know the park also has a swimming beach, open from Memorial Day weekend to Labor Day, and boat rentals on 245-acre Lake Jean. Twenty miles of hiking trails and an environmental education program are other activities available in the park.

But the main attraction is the Glens Natural Area. Two branches of Kitchen Creek cut through the deep gorges of Ganoga Glen and Glen Leigh to join at "Waters Meet." In the process they tumble down no less than 22 named waterfalls ranging in size from 11 to 94 feet, and surrounded by a wide variety of hardwood trees, many over 500 years old. The area is so beautiful and unusual that in 1969 it was placed on the federal Register of National Natural Landmarks.

Ricketts Glen honors Colonel Robert Rickett, who enlisted in the U.S. Army as a private in 1861. He eventually rose to command Battery F, which helped repulse "Pickett's Charge" during the Battle of Gettysburg. Colonel Rickett at one time owned or controlled over 80,000 acres in the park area. His heirs, through the Central Penn Lumber Co., sold 48,000 acres to the Game Commission between 1920 and 1924. After World War II brought an end to plans to develop a national park in the region, the state purchased more land from Colonel Rickett's son, William, in 1943 and 1949, and opened the first recreational facilities in 1944.

Before the "Confederacy" and lumber companies, the Great Warriors Path, from Athens to Sunbury, crossed Big Fishing Creek near Bloomsburg. The path was used not only for war, but also was the designated route for Iroquois ambassadors traveling to Philadelphia, Virginia and Maryland.

Additional information on Ricketts Glen Park, including its family cabins, may be had by writing: Ricketts Glen State Park, Department of Environmental Resources, R.D. 1, Box 251, Benton, PA 17814.

Roaring Creek
Columbia County

Here is another little trout stream involved in the "Pennsylvania Name Game." The Fish Commission's "Summary of Fishing Regulations and Laws" distributed with each fishing license lists the stream only as Roaring Creek. As does Howard Higbee's "Stream Map of Pennsylvania" published by Pennsylvania State University. However, half the other publications, including the Fish Commissions's "Trout Fishing in Pennsylvania," booklet, also refers to the stream, or at least the upper part above the village of Slabtown, as Roaring Mill Creek. So take your pick. Apparently, half the stream is Roaring Creek, the other half Roaring Mill Creek.

By whatever name it is called, in this case we'll drop the "Mill," Roaring Creek still holds 13.5 miles of stocked brown and rainbow water, running from about Slabtown downstream to the Susquehanna River. As far as its confluence with the South Branch, Roaring Creek flows through a fairly narrow, remote farm valley surrounded by hardwood forests. Unfortunately, several spots are marred by old slag piles and trailer parks. Below the South Branch, the stream gains in size and enters a secluded hemlock grove decorated by rock cliffs. Both Roaring Creek and South Branch Roaring Creek are good places for the angler who enjoys covered bridges. No less than five of the old bridges cross the two streams.

Roaring Creek can be reached by taking Pennsylvania Route 487 south from Bloomsburg, the only Pennsylvania municipality incorporated as a "town," every other municipality in the state is either a borough or city. Route 487 and Pennsylvania Route 42 join at Catawissa and continue as the same road for a few miles. When they again split apart, Route 42 leads to the stream's upper water, crossing and paralleling Roaring Creek to Slabtown. No sign appears at Slabtown, but anglers can be sure they have found it when they see the sign for Our Lady of Mercy Catholic Church.

At the bridge where Route 42 crosses Roaring Creek, Queen City Road (Township Road 377) appears and trails the creek downstream, offering access at four different bridges before it meets Route 487. That road then parallels the stream to its junction with the South Branch.

About half of the four miles of Roaring Creek lying between its confluence with the South Branch and its mouth on the Susquehanna River is not touched directly by a road. Anglers can reach the lower part of the stream, though, by backtracking on Route 487 to its junction with Route 42. State Route 3012 joints the two roads on the west at almost the same point. It leads back to the mouth of Roaring Creek, and, a short distance upstream, a waterfall.

Fly fishermen on Roaring Creek should find some success with Quill Gordons, Hare's Ear, streamers, Adams, Hendricksons, caddis, March Browns, Gray Fox, Light Cahills, Renegades, Lead-Winged Coachmen, midges and terrestrials.

SOUTHEAST

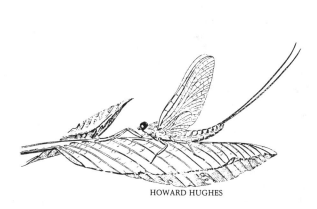

HOWARD HUGHES

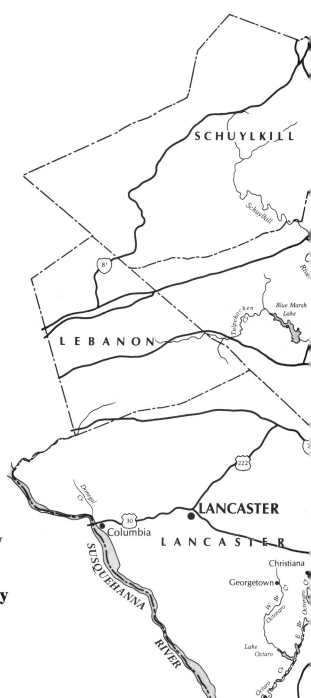

Berks County

Mantawney Cr
Schuylkill River
Tulpehocken Cr

Bucks County

Delaware River
Tohichan Cr

Chester County

Beaver Run
Brandywine Cr
Brandywine Cr E. Br
Brandywine Cr W. Br
French Cr
Valley Cr
White Clay Cr
White Clay Cr E. Br
White Clay Cr Mid. Br
White Clay Cr W. Br

Delaware County

Ridley Cr

Lancaster County

Donegal Cr
Octararo Cr
Octararo Cr E. Br
Octararo Cr W. Br
Susquehanna River

Lebanon County

Lehigh County

Cedar Cr
Jordan Cr
Lehigh River
Little Lehigh Cr

Montgomery County

Skippack Cr

Northampton County

Delaware River
Bushkill Cr
Lehigh River
Monocacy Cr

Philadelphia County

Schuylkill County

Schuylkill River
Tulpehocken Cr.

NORTHAMPTON

Bushkill

Bath

Lehigh

Northampton

9

Cr

22

Easton

LEHIGH

Whitehall

Cr

Monocacy

River

DELAWARE

Jordan

Cedar

Cr

ALLENTOWN

Little Lehigh

Cr

Lake
Nockamixon

ERKS

Tohickon

Cr

ING

Mantawney

Cr

9

RIVER

BUCKS

422

MONTGOMERY

Beaver
Run

French

Cr

Skippack

Cr

276

Brandywine

Phoenixville

95

RIVER

30

Cr

PHILADELPHIA

30

Valley

3

Coatesville

Cr

Ridley

Brandywine

Cr

95

DELAWARE

CHESTE

Cr

DELAWARE

Mid

Br

1

East Br

White Clay

White Clay Cr

Southeast Region

Ridley Creek

Delayed Harvest Fly Fishing Only
Delaware County

Southeastern Pennsylvania is people country. It was where William Penn landed, and the first part of the state to be settled. Philadelphia was a metropolis before the United States was a nation. For a trout stream with water clean enough to merit a Delayed Harvest Fly Fishing Only Project to exist amidst all the suburbs, fast food joints and industry is a true credit to the Department of Environmental Resources, the Fish Commission and everybody else involved. Some people might even view it as a miracle.

But the real reason Ridley Creek can sustain a special regulations section within the shadow of Independence Hall, so to speak, is the presence of Ridley Creek State Park, a 2,606-acre sanctury of open space for man and beast in north central Delaware County.

Property for Ridley Park was purchased back in the 1960s and developed under the "Lands & Water Conservation Fund." It was open to the public in August 1972. And although it does not contain any camping facilities, there is still plenty for an angler's family to do while he is on the stream. There are 14 picnic areas in the park, several of which are attached to large fields suitable for athletic activities, four playgrounds for children, 12 miles of hiking trails, a riding stable where horses can be rented, and regularly scheduled historical and environmental programs.

Besides all of the usual outdoor activities, Ridley Creek also holds the Colonial Pennsylvania Plantation. Staffed and operated by the Bishop's Mill Historical Institute, the plantation is designed to give visitors an accurate picture of life on a Quaker farm in 1776. Visitors can observe the making of farm tools, clothing, furniture, wool spinning, butter churning, meat smoking and food preparation. There is a small fee.

The park, near the start of Ridley Creek's Fly Fishing Only water, also holds a small eighteenth century village known as Sycamore Mills. The miller's house, office and library, and several smaller workers' homes still exist. The area has been designated the Ridley Creek Historic District by the National Register of Historic Places. A self-guided brochure is available at the park office, a beautiful stone structure that was once the "Hunting Hill" mansion of the wealthy Jeffords family.

Ridley Creek is stocked over a distance of eight miles from above the park downstream to the town of Media. The park's main entrance is located on Pennsylvania Route 3, about 2.5 miles west of Newton Square. It also may be reached from the east by taking Pennsylvania Route 351 to Gradyville and then following Gradyville Road to the park, or from the west off Pennsylvania Route 252 and Providence Road. The routes are generally marked by park signs.

The Delayed Harvest Fly Fishing Only Project of Ridley Creek runs for one mile from the falls downstream to the mouth of Dismal Run. It can be reached by taking either Bishop Hollow Road or Chappel Hill Road off Providence Road. White Trail in the park also leads to the project, as well as some nice water upstream of it. Because of heavy traffic around the park that might make spotting some of the roads leading to the project difficult, anglers should consider stopping at the park office to obtain a "Recreational Guide" with a map. Ridley Creek Road, which appears at the bridge at the junction of Chappel Hill Road and Bishop Hollow Road, leads to the lower reaches of the special regulation water and downstream to Media.

While Ridley Creek may be clean enough to support trout, fishermen who go there for the first time should not expect to find a lot of privacy. Ridley Creek State Park is a well-used respite from the rat race of one of the largest cities in the United States. Paths along the stream are worn bare from the tread of so many anglers' feet, and joggers, bicyclists, and strollers abound.

Okehocking Path, from Valley Forge to Gradyville, forded Ridley Creek when William Penn first arrived on the scene. It was a southern extension of the Perkiomen-Lehigh Path, which ran from the Schuylkill River to Pawling Ford near Valley Forge.

Dark-colored flies are said to generally produce the best on this tributary of the Delaware River. Possible fly patterns include: the

Adams, Dark Hendrickson, March Brown, black and brown Woolly Worms, Muddler Minnow, bivisibles, Hare's Ear, caddis, Soft Hackles and terrestrials.

Further information on Ridley Creek Park may be had by writing: Ridley Creek State Park, Department of Environmental Resources, Sycamore Mills Road, Media, PA 19603.

Skippack Creek
Montgomery County

A gravel and sand bottom should make Skippack Creek a joy for anglers who like to fish flat water interspaced by gentle riffles.

Ridley Creek State Park.

No rocky pockets and gushing whitewater here, just a nice, civilized flow heavily stocked with browns and rainbows, and within easy reach of millions of nature-hungry suburbanites. Fortunately, Evansburg State Park's 3,349 acres protect most of the stream's trout water from a crush of second homes and other "development."

Stocked water on Skippack Creek, or "Skippy" as it is known locally, covers ten miles, from its mouth on Perkomen Creek upstream beyond Pennsylvania Route 73 and the village of Skippack. The upper portion of the stream is generally surrounded by second, or even third, growth brush, while the lower sections are touched by evermore remote forest. Access is available off both Route 73 and U.S. Route 422 east of Collegeville.

A number of side roads also lead to the stream, often crossing it on picturesque stone arch bridges. Grange Avenue parallels the stream on its east side, giving access to the lower water off Ridge Pike Road and Visitation Road, and the upper water off Mill Road and Water Street.

Above Water Street, Grange Avenue becomes Green Hill Road and pulls closer to the stream. Anglers can continue further upstream on the east side by taking Stump Hall Road off Green Hill Road. Stump Hall Road follows the stream to Route 73. Turn left on Route 73 and follow it over the stream. Old Forty Fort Road appears near the bridge and leads to the upper end of the stocked water.

From the west, Skippack Creek can be reached by taking Route 422 into the village of Evansburg. In the village, Level Road leads downstream toward the village of Arcola at the confluence of Skippack Creek and Perkiomen Creek. Ridge Pike Road and Cedar Lane both run off Level Road and to the stream.

Upstream on the west side, the Skippack can be reached off Skippack Creek Road (part of which may be closed) and Evansburg Road out of the village. Wayland Road and Mill Road both run off Evansburg Road and to Skippack Road on the stream. Mayhall Road, which joins Skippack Road at Mill Road, leads to the office of Evansburg Park and provides further access.

Because so many roads touch on the Skippack even in the park, anglers are well-advised to obtain a "Recreational Guide" from the park. The guide contains a good map of the park and nearby lands that should help the fishermen reach the stream. Six miles of the Skippy's trout water flows through the park.

Along with fishing, Evansburg State Park also holds picnic grounds, ballfields, hiking trails, bridal paths, a golf course and, during the summer, environmental education programs. The Fried Visitor Center is a Revolutionary War era home which was owned for 190 years by the same family of German Mennonites. Inside displays tell the story of the Mennonite lifestyle and highlight the natural history of the area. Outside is a root cellar, well, herb and flower gardens used by the family. Further details may be had by writing: Evansburg State Park, Department of Environmental Resources, P.O. Box 258, Collegeville, PA 19426.

A Youth Hostel also is located in the park to accommodate members of the American Youth Hostel Association. Information on it may be had by writing: Evansburg State Park Youth Hostel, 837 May Hall Road, Collegeville, PA 19426.

Possible fly choices for the Skippack include: Muddler Minnows, Woolly Buggers, Soft Hackle Nymphs, Hare's Ears, Muskrats, Adams, Hendricksons, Royal Coachman, March Browns, Gray Fox, Lead-Winged Coachman, Light Cahill and terrestrials.

Valley Creek
No Kill
Chester County

"Valley Forge." No two words in American history are as capable of evoking the horrors and deprivation of men at war as the name of that once simple ironmaking village in Chester County. Every schoolchild learns the story of how Washington and his ragged troops suffered through the winter of 1777-1778 living in huts, short of food, blankets, shoes, uniforms, food and even wood. As Cyrus Townsend Brady once wrote, "No spot on earth, not the plains of Marathon, nor the passes of Sempach, nor the Place of the Bastille, nor the dykes of Holland, nor the moors of England, is so sacred in the history of the struggle for human liberty as Valley Forge."

Washington was forced to take his army into winter quarters at Valley Forge after the British beat him at the Battle of Brandywine and Battle of Germantown. Victory at the Battle of Brandywine allowed the British to capture Philadelphia, victory of Germantown allowed them to stay in the city, well-fed, clothed, quartered and entertained.

The Continental Army's encampment site today is a National Historical Park administered by the National Park Service. It contains reconstructed huts in which Washington's men lived during that brutal winter, officers' quarters, a chapel, hospital, and enough memorials, markers, statues and monuments to keep a history buff busy for days. Interpreters in period customs act as guides to the many exhibits, while a museum and films tell the story of the encampment and the National Memorial Arch preserves Washington's feelings on February 16, 1778.

"Naked and starving as they are, we cannot enough admire the incomparable patience and fidelity of the soldiery."

Along with being a sacred historical site, Valley Forge today is a popular outing place with hiking and biking trails, horseback riding, picnicking, boating on the Schylkill River and, under the gaze of Washington's headquarters, fishing in pretty Valley Creek, a no-kill trout fishery.

Certainly, there are no shortage of signs for Valley Forge, and anglers can find Valley Creek by following the signs. Pennsylvania Turpike Exit 24 will lead to U.S. Route 422, and Route 422 west to Pennsylvania Route 23, which crosses the lower stream near the Schuylkill River. A secondary road runs off Route 23 near the bridge and along the stream to a covered bridge.

Before the Continental Army's trial, the Okehocking Path, a southern extension of the Perkiomen-Lehigh Path, ran from Valley Forge to Gradyville.

Fly fishermen on Valley Creek might try the Adams, caddis, Blue Dun, Hare's Ear, Muskrat, Quill Gordon, Muddler Minnow, Woolly Bugger, March Brown, Light Cahill, midges and terrestrials, as well as any other favorite patterns in their fly box.

French Creek
Fly Fishing Only
Beaver Run
Chester County

French Creek
Ironmaking in America began only a year after the establishment of the first permanent English settlement at Jamestown,

Iron Master's Home, French Creek.

Virginia in 1620. By the middle of the next century, however, Pennsylvania's abundance of iron ore and limestone, its numerous rushing streams and extensive hardwood forests had made it the leading iron-producing colony in British America. By 1771 well over 50 iron furnaces and forges were operating within the colony. Among these was Hopewell Furnace near the headwaters of French Creek on the Berks/Chester County line.

Mark Bird was a second generation ironmaker who learned the trade at his father's forge near the Schuylkill River—and Daniel Boone's birthplace—at what is now Birdboro. He started buying land after his father's death in 1761. By 1770, he was one of the largest landowners in Berks and Chester Counties, controlling roughly 10,000 acres of woodlands, iron ore mines and water rights. In 1771, he started Hopewell Furnace on a site along French Creek, between his father's forge and Hopewell Mine.

The Iron Act of 1750 limited the importation of American iron into England to raw, pig iron that could be reworked into finished products by British forges. The restriction turned many ironmasters on this side of the Atlantic against the mother country. Among them was Mark Bird. Even before hostilities broke out at Lexington and Concord in 1775, Bird joined radical groups in Pennsylvania. After the Declaration of Independence was signed he became one of the leading patriots of eastern Pennsylvania. He served as an officer in the local militia and a judge, and even won election to the Pennsylvania General Assembly. In the wake of George Washington's defeat at Brandywine in 1777, Bird

marched his men to the relief of the Continental Army and stopped the British from advancing up the Schuylkill Valley.

While Bird's action following the Battle of Brandywine was valuable to the War for Independence, it was not his major contribution. As Quarter Master General of Pennsylvania he shipped thousands of barrels of flour down the Schuylkill River to Washington's troops at Valley Forge. His ironworks, including Hopewell Furnace, also supplied cannon and shot to both the Continental Army and Navy throughout the war.

Congress was quick to recognize Bird's contributions to the war effort, but not so fast when it came to paying its bills. Like most creditors of the new government, he had trouble getting paid. The money Bird received for his work came infrequently and was always insufficient. In 1776 Congress advanced him $2,000 and in 1780 authorized payment to him of $125,000, but there is no record he ever received the cash.

At the end of the war Bird asked Congress for the great chain strung across the Hudson River at West Point to obstruct British Warships as partial payment for the money owed him. Congress denied the request, saying he was only one of many creditors. The economic recession of the 1780s also hit him hard. By 1786 he was desperate for cash and put Hopewell Furnace and some 4,000 acres up for sale. He could find no buyers. And in 1788, after Hopewell was auctioned off, he fled Pennsylvania for North Carolina.

Ensuing years saw Hopewell Furnace change hands several

times, until 1800 when it was bought by Daniel Buckley, Matthew Brooke and Thomas Brooke. It remained in their families for the next 83 years until it ended operations for good in 1883.

Mark Bird was to return to Pennsylvania one more time in 1807. He wrote two letters during that stay. One was to Dr. Benjamin Rush, a Philadelphia physician, the other to Matthew Brooke. In his letter to Brooke, Bird said: "I shall not think well of the Iron masters, when they come to know my Situation, if they do not fall on some mode . . . to relieve me, either by lone, or other wise they know I was Ruined by the warr, it was not Drunkeness, Idleness or want of Industry."

Bird's letter to Dr. Rush carried a similar tone. "I was Bankrupt by the Vile unatural war, and never Able to get anything of Acct. in my hands since . . . There is no doubt my principle ruin, was by the Warr and Depretiation." His request for help was rejected because, as Rush wrote, "all his friends of 1776 were dead or reduced."

Like its builder, Hopewell Furnace gradually fell into ruin. By the turn of the twentieth century the village that had sprung up around it was deserted and the massive stone furnace crumbling. At the beginning of the 1930s members of the Franklin Institute in Philadelphia and then the federal government became interested in the furnace and village as a historic site. Civilian Conservation Corps members undertook restoration work and in 1938 the federal government designated the area Hopewell Village National Historic Site within the National Parks System.

Hopewell today depicts a typical industrial community of the early nineteenth century, although in a somewhat more romantic than realistic vein. Along with the restored iron furnace, the village contains charcoal hearths, a charcoal house and cooling shed, anthracite furnace, a store of the period, cast house, ore roaster, blacksmith shop, tenant house, school, ironmaster's mansion. Special programs are conducted throughout the summer. Visitors to the village not only can see how iron was made back in the eighteenth and early nineteenth centuries, but also watch people knowledgeable in the arts of blacksmithing, weaving, candlemaking and other crafts of the period conduct demonstrations.

Nearby French Creek, which once supplied the water for Hopewell Furnace, now is the most popular trout stream in the area. It is stocked for 14 miles, from the village of Knauertown downstream toward the town of Phoenixville and its mouth on the Schuylkill River. Its 1.2-mile Fly Fishing Only Project runs from the dam at Camp Sleepy Hollow about one mile east of Pennsylvania Route 100 and the village of Pughtown, downstream to Sheeder Road, and is clearly marked. Since French Creek is the best stream in a very densely populated county, anglers should be aware it is often crowded.

Before and during the colonial period, French Creek Indian Path followed the stream. It ran from Conestoga Indian Town (near Washington on the Susquehanna River) to Phoenixville, which once held a considerable Indian population, and now a hulking steel mill. The course of French Creek Path also was one of the earliest roads marked off by the colonial courts after Lancaster County was cut out of western Chester County.

These days Route 100 is the main artery leading to French Creek. In the south, it can be picked up off Pennsylvania Turnpike Exit 23. From the north, it can be reached off U.S. Route 422 at Pottstown. Pughtown Road runs off Route 100 in Pughtown south of Pennsylvania Route 23, and provides access to French Creek's lower waters, including the Fly Fishing Only stretch. It is unmarked, but meets Route 100 near a small general store just north of the Route 100 bridge over the stream.

Bertolet School Road, Township Road 499, Sheeder Mill Road and Hollow Road, which appears next to an abandoned slaughter house and holds a covered bridge, all run off Pughtown Road and down to French Creek. Pughtown Road itself crosses the stream about a mile below Hollow Road where it joins French Creek Road which provides more access, both upstream toward Hollow Road and downstream to Lucas Road and Seven Stars Road, two other access routes.

A portion of French Creek's upper water can be found by taking Route 23 west from the village of Bucktown to the village of Coventryville and toward French Creek State Park. The stream can be reached off the Township Road 517 bridge in Coventryville.

French Creek is a shallow and rocky stream of about medium size. Riffles and easy rapids appear frequently and turn into a succession of pleasant flats and pools as the water level drops. It follows a fairly attractive path through woods and farmlands interrupted only by an occasional dam. Like most other streams in populous southeastern Pennsylvania, however, it is never far from a home or a road. But many of the houses which line it are of the old variety with quaint gingerbread and other adornments, so not all that horrible to view.

Anglers interested in camping near Hopewell should enjoy beautiful and spacious French Creek State Park. It can be found by taking Route 23 west past Coventryville to the junction of Pennsylvania Route 345 and then following the signs along Route 345 into the park. Three family camping areas with 200 Class A sites and 110 Class B sites are available on a first-come, first-served basis. The sites are suitable for tents, trailers or recreational vehicles. They are furnished with a picnic table and campfire ring. The Class A campground also includes showers and flush toilets. Campers should contact the park office to determine local conditions.

With 7,339 acres, French Creek State Park has a lot to offer both the angler and any family members who do not fish. Swimming is permitted at a guarded pool, from Memorial Day weekend through Labor Day. More than 500 picnic tables are scattered throughout the park. There are two lakes—Hopewell Lake and Scotts Run Lake (stocked with trout)—where boating is permitted. Rental boats are available on Hopewell Lake. Hiking is possible along some 32 miles of trails, and there are environmental education programs offered from Memorial Day to Labor Day.

Hopewell Village National Historic Site is adjacent to the park on Route 345. It is open year-round from 9:00 a.m. to 5:00 p.m. The weavers, blacksmiths, cooks, candlemakers and so forth ply their crafts during the months of July and August.

Traditional Pennsylvania fly patterns that should work on French Creek include: Hare's Ear, Blue Dun, Quill Gordon, Woolly Worm, Muddler Minnow, Mickey Finn, Hendrickson, Royal Coachman, Lead-Winged Coachman, Adams, March Brown, caddis, Light Cahill, midges and terrestrials.

Further information on Hopewell Village is available by writing: Hopewell Village National Historical Site, R.D. 1, Box 345, Elverson, PA 19520.

Details on French Creek Park may be had by writing: French Creek State Park, Department of Environmental Resources, R.R. 1, Box 448, Elverson, PA 19520.

Beaver Run

When fishing a freestone stream in Pennsylvania, particularly early in the season, it always pays to have a small, feeder stream in mind for when the larger streams are running high and discolored. For anglers on French Creek, Beaver Run is the ticket.

Stocked for approximately three miles from its mouth on French Creek at Pughtown upstream, Beaver Run's lower water can be reached directly off Route 100 south of Pughtown. Its upper reaches are accessible by taking Fairview Road off Route 100 and toward Nantmeal Village. Fly anglers can try some of the same patterns mentioned for French Creek.

East Branch Brandywine Creek
West Branch Brandywine Creek
Chester County

And once they peaceful tide
Was filled with life-blood from bold hearts and brave;
And heroes on they verdant margin died,
The land they loved, to save.

These vales, so calm and still,
Once saw the foeman's charge, — the bayonet's gleam;
And heard the thunders roll from hill to hill
From mourn till sunset's beam.

—Bayard Taylor

On June 14, 1777, the Continental Congress adopted a resolution decreeing that the "flag of the United States be thirteen stripes, alternate red and white, that the union be thirteen stars, white in a blue field, representing a new constellation." Nobody knows for certain when "Old Glory" was first flown in battle, but some historians believe it might have been during the Battle of Brandywine on the banks of Brandywine Creek and Chadds Ford.

Less than a month after the decree adopting the stars and stripes as the official flag of the new nation, the British fleet entered Delaware Bay. They departed without causing too many problems, but by early September had invaded Pennsylvania and were marching toward Philadelphia with plans to capture the Continental Capital and put an end to all the foolishness.

Washington knew he had to do something or his cause was lost. On September 11, 1777, he hurled 12,000 troops of the Continental Army against some 18,000 British regulars and Hessian mercenaries. After fighting back and forth in a heavy fog for hours, the British finally managed to cross Brandywine Creek, a much larger stream than now, and outflank the Americans, forcing them to retreat. The British captured Philadelphia after their victory in the Battle of Brandywine, but congress, and the Liberty Bell, was able to escape.

Bayard Taylor, who wrote the poem quoted here, was born in Kennett Square near the headwaters of the West Branch Brandwine Creek in 1825. He was a noted novelist, poet, journalist and diplomat of the mid-nineteenth century. His *Views Afoot, or Europe Seen with Knapsack and Staff,* was a best seller in 1846. He also was the first person to translate Goethe's *Faust* into English. He died in Berlin while serving as American minister to Germany in 1878.

Trout fishing is not available in the main branch of Brandywine Creek, but two of its tributaries, the East Branch and the West Branch, are popular Chester County trout waters.

East Branch Brandywine Creek
Flowing through the center of beautiful, and expensive, Chester County is East Branch Brandywine Creek. It is stocked with trout for about eight miles, from just upstream of the village of Glenmore to just downstream of Lyndell. Access to the stream's entire stocked length may be had off Pennsylvania Route 282 between those two villages. Several bridges running off Route 282 also provide access and run into Marsh Creek State Park on the east side of this boulder-strewn little stream. Route 282 can be picked up off U.S. Route 30 north of Dowingtown.

Marsh Creek State Park preserves 1,705 acres of central Chester County from the hands of developers. It does not have a campground, but there is a pool, open from Memorial Day weekend to Labor Day, a playground for children, a snack bar, picnic areas, boats available for rent on 535-acre Marsh Creek Lake, six miles of hiking trails and six miles of bridal paths. Further information may be had by writing: Marsh Creek State Park, Department of Environmental Resources, R.D. 2, Park Road, Dowingtown, PA 19335.

West Branch Brandywine Creek
The headwaters of the West Branch Brandywine Creek lie right beside those of the East Branch. But that is where the connection between the two branches ends. For the West Branch is a much faster stream of pocket water and rock bottoms than the quiet little East Branch.

Access to the West Branch's roughly five miles of stocked water is not nearly as good as that of the East Branch. Interested anglers can find it, though, by taking Pennsylvania Route 82 north off Route 30 near Coatsville. About midway between Route 30 and U.S. Route 322 turn left on S.R. 4005 toward the village of Cedar Knoll. Hibernia Road follows the creek both up- and downstream from Cedar Knoll, giving access off numerous bridges. The stream is stocked for four miles in the area of Hibernia Park, a beautiful place to fish or take a break. The park can be reached by following Cedar Knoll Road across the stream. There is a Fish Commission parking area at the village of Brandamore.

Fly fishermen on both the West Branch and the East Branch might start with Adams, Hare's Ear, Soft Hackle Nymphs, caddis, Hendrickson, Muddler Minnow, Royal Coachman, Renegade, March Brown, Gray Fox, Bivisible, Woolly Bugger, Light Cahill, Sulphurs, midges and terrestrials.

Middle Branch White Clay Creek
Delayed Harvest Artificial Lures Only
East Branch White Clay Creek
Chester County

Middle Branch White Clay Creek
Tucked along the Pennsylvania/Delaware line at the southwest corner of its great arc around Wilmington, Delaware, White Clay Creek Preserve State Park is one of the newest additions to Pennsylvania's state park system. It covers 1,234 acres, but its facilities are currently limited to some hiking, picnicking out of baskets and fishing in pretty White Clay Creek, a medium-sized trout stream and one of the main reasons for the park.

The White Clay Creek watershed has been a popular cold water fishery for many anglers from Philadelphia's suburbs for years. The Fish Commission, in 1987, acknowledged both the stream's popularity and quality when it established a Delayed Harvest Artificial Lures Only Project along its Middle Branch. Now anglers willing to limit their tackle to flies or artificial lures, and release their catch between March 1 and June 15, can enjoy their sport

171

year-round on a portion of this Chester County tributary of the Delaware River.

The Middle Branch is stocked for about seven miles from its confluence with the East Branch upstream to about Pennsylvania Route 841. Its special regulation water runs from State Route 3009 (Good Hope Road) downstream to its junction with the East Branch. Several combinations of secondary roads will take the angler to the project from all four directions of the compass. But probably the easiest way for fishermen coming from the west to reach the stream is to take Route 896 south past the Ginns Airport and toward the village of Stickersville. Turn right onto Good Hope Road and follow it back to the stream and the park.

Anglers coming from the east can reach the Middle Branch's special regulation water by taking Penn Green Road south off Pennsylvania Route 41 and toward the village of Landenberg. Penn Green Road joins Route 41 south of Avondale near the village of New Garden and meets Good Hope Road southeast of Landenberg. Turn left on Good Hope Road and follow it back to the project.

Inside White Clay Park, South Creek Road parallels the Middle Branch downstream of London Tract Road. By turning right and crossing the creek, the fisherman can gain further downstream access by taking the first road to the left and continuing on it to a "T" intersection. Turn left at the "T" and the stream lies just ahead.

Above the Delayed Harvest Project, the Middle Branch's upper water can be reached along North Creek Road running off Good Hope Road.

Possible fly choices for the Middle Branch include: Quill Gordon, Adams, Royal Coachman, Hendrickson, Hare's Ear, Soft Hackle Nymphs, caddis, Muskrat, Muddler Minnow, Woolly Bugger, March Brown, Renegade, Light Cahill, Black Gnat and terrestrials.

East Branch White Clay Creek

Almost 10 miles of East Branch White Clay Creek is stocked with trout. Its planted water extends from its confluence with the Middle Branch in White Clay Creek Park upstream beyond U.S. Route 1. Like the Middle Branch, it can be reached via numerous back roads.

The East Branch's upper water can be found by taking London Grove Road off Route 41 near the village of Chatham and following it east toward the village of London Grove. Spencer Road and McCue Road both run off London Grove after it makes a sharp bend to the right and lead to the stream.

Two major highways also offer access to the stream's upper water. Route 1 crosses the East Branch east of Route 41 near Glen Willow Road. Route 41 crosses over the stream at Avondale, a quaint old market town.

Spring Creek morning.

172

Below Avondale, Elliot Road parallels the stream, giving further access off Garden Station Road, running to the right near Elliot Road's end on Starr Road. A left turn onto Starr Road will lead to Penn Green Road, which follows the stream through Landenberg. Another left turn at the end of Penn Green Road will take the fisherman to London Tract Road and further along the stream. Sharpless Road, which meets London Tract Road on the left in the park leads to the end of the East Branch's stocked water. Fly fishermen can try some of the same patterns mentioned under the Middle Branch, as well as any other favorites they might have hidden away in their boxes.

Conestoga-Newport Path, a minor Indian trail connecting Washington Boro on the Susquehanna River to Newport, Delaware, once crossed the East Branch at Avondale.

Although no information is presently available on White Clay Park, a ''Recreational Guide'' and other items will no doubt be printed in the future as more of the park is developed. The park address is White Clay Creek Preserve State Park, Department of Environmental Resources, P.O. Box 172, Landenberg, PA 19350.

West Branch Octararo Creek
Delayed Harvest Fly Fishing Only
Lancaster County
East Branch Octoraro Creek
Lancaster and Chester Counties

Passed in 1972, Pennsylvania's Scenic Rivers Act ''authorizes the establishment of a state scenic rivers system and specifies procedures for designating certain waterways and waterway segments which have outstanding aesthetic and recreational values. The purpose is to provide for the protection of these segments for the benefit of present and future generations through cooperative and voluntary resources management.''

The Pennsylvania Scenic Rivers Program is a wonderful idea. But so far a variety of political, landowner, business and other problems have kept the project from being implemented in all but a few cases. To freely paraphrase a famous saying: ''Many have been called, but only a very few have been able to weave their way through the tangled web of private versus public rights.'' One of the half dozen or so streams to so far gain final approval—more than 200 have been nominated—is Octoraro Creek in southern Lancaster County. It carries the program's ''Scenic and Pastoral'' classification, and anybody who has ever seen this little beauty would understand why. Translated to mean ''rushing waters,'' its trout water actually is a rather mellow collection of long pools and gravely riffles, framed by rolling woods and farms.

West Branch Octoraro Creek
Generally considered to be the best of the two streams, the West Branch holds about seven miles of stocked brown and rainbow water. Its Delayed Harvest Fly Fishing Only Project runs for 1.9 miles from about 220 yards below Pennsylvania Route 472, downstream to near the second unnamed tributary below Legislative Route 37052. It can be reached by following Route 472 to Puseyville Road (State Route 2010) and then following that to the parking lot on State Game Lands 136, where a sign announces the stream's ''Scenic Rivers'' designation. In the village of Puseyville, Wesley Road appears and paralles the creek downstream.

East Branch Octoraro Creek
Forming the boundary between Lancaster and Chester County, the East Branch holds just over nine miles of stocked water planted with browns and rainbows. Its lower trout water is accessible off Pennsylvania Route 896 at the village of Octoraro.

Above the village of Octoraro, the stream can be reached by following Route 896 to the village of Homeville. In the village take Homeville Road (State Route 3085) north toward Cochranville. Bryson Road appears outside of Homeville on the left and leads down to the stream. Ross Fording Road runs off Bryson Road and on across the stream.

The East Branch's upper water also may be found by taking Route 372 to the village of Ninepoints, and turning onto Noble Road, which runs toward the village of Atglen and the creek.

Fly fishermen might try the following patterns on both the West Branch and East Branch: Quill Gordons, Adams, caddis, Hare's Ears, Hendricksons, Muddler Minnows, Matuka streamers, Royal Coachmen, Soft Hackle Nymphs, Renegades, March Browns, Gray Fox, Light Cahills, Lead-Winged Coachmen, midges and terrestrials.

Octoraro Creek Region
Like Codorus Creek to the west (see which), Octoraro Creek figured prominently in the border dispute between the Penns of Pennsylvania and the Calverts of Maryland. In the documents relating to the dispute, a number of references are said to have been made concerning the exact location of the ''Susquehannock Fort'' on the mouth of Octoraro Creek. The fort was important because it marked the southern boundary of Pennsylvania.

James Hendricks, one of the earliest settlers in the region, in his statement said: ''That the Affirmant was then told, by some of the Indians there residing (at the mouth of the creek), that they called the same Place Meanock, which they said, in English, signified a Fortification or Fortified Town. Has also seen the Ruins of another such Fortified Town on the East side of Susquehannah River aforesaid, opposite to a Place where one Thomas Cersap lately dwelt.''

Cersap's Fort was located on the west side of the Susquehanna River across from the present town of Washington Boro. A Susquehanna Indian fort was located on the site in 1670. The name Meanock that Hendrickson mentions in his statement was indeed the name of the town at the mouth of Octoraro Creek, but of other fortified Indian settlements, too. A line drawn west from the old section of Philadelphia crosses the Susquehanna at few miles south of Cresap's Fort, and was the line recognized by the Calverts. The problem was finally solved by a Royal order in 1739 setting the boundary above the mouth of Octoraro Creek.

When the dispute was going on, however, it was often bitter, even producing threats of kidnapping, or hostage taking. In 1684, it was reported to William Penn that, ''Jonas Askins heard Coll. Talbot say, that if Govr. Penn should come into Maryland, he would Seize him and his retairee in their Journey to Susquehanna fort.''

Peach Bottom Path, from Hayesville to Peach Bottom, once crossed Octoraro Creek at Pine Grove near the present site of Chester-Octoraro Reservoir. It was an offshoot of the Nanticoke Path, a major north-south Indian trail linking Calvert, Maryland to Reading and Nanticoke.

Donegal Springs Creek
Delayed Harvest Fly Fishing Only
Lancaster County

Almost everyone who is acquainted with Irish history knows of the potato famine of 1847 and the way it practically halved the country's population. An estimated one million people died of starvation, while four million others, mostly Roman Catholics, left their homeland forever to settle in the United States.

Far fewer people, though, probably are aware of another mass migration from the Emerald Isle more than 100 years before the potato famine. This first exodus involved mainly the Scotch-Irish who had moved to Northern Ireland from Scotland in the mid-seventeenth century at the urging of England's King James I. It also revolved around a number of natural disasters: a drought in 1717, a famine in 1728, and the "black frost" and famine of 1740, during which more than 400,000 died. But even more than frosts and famines, it was the result of Ireland's English rulers denying these "Ulstermen" even a small degree of economic and religious freedom.

All told, some 300,000 Scotch-Irish left Northern Ireland for Colonial America. They settled in Virginia, the Carolinas, Kentucky, Tennessee and especially Pennsylvania. So many of them descended upon Penn's Woods, in fact, that for a time many people feared they would completely take over the state.

"If the Scotch-Irish continue to come they will make themselves masters of the Province," wrote William Penn's scretary and Proprietary Council President James Logan.

"They are in a fair way to taking possession of the state," Benjamin Franklin would add later.

Believing land was theirs for the taking in the wilderness west of Philadelphia, thousands of these new settlers found their way to Lancaster County and York County. There, without making arrangements to purchase the property from the province, they built their farms and settlements, naming them after places they remembered from their homeland. Bainbridge. Colebrooke. Donegal. Maytown.

As might be expected, the idea of the Scotch-Irish obtaining land free of charge displeased a great many people who had paid for their property. To check the tide until the misunderstanding could be resolved, legislation actually was enacted that forbade the sale of land in Lancaster and York to immigrants from Ulster.

Among those who settled in Lancaster County was Andrew Galbraith. Arriving in America in 1718, he built a farm in the northwest corner of the county on the banks of Spring Creek. Calling the area Donegal Township, he and his fellow countrymen established a church on his property in 1719 or 1720. They named the church Donegal Presbyterin Church and changed the name of the stream to Donegal Springs Creek.

Over the years, Donegal Church was the scene of a number of events of local historical significance. The most famous of which occurred on a Sunday morning in June 1777.

With a history of persecution by the English behind them, Pennsylvania's Scotch-Irish were fiercely anti-English during the Revolutionary War. Five of them signed the Declaration of Independence, a sixth was secretary of the Congress that adopted it and a seventh printed it. So when the pastor of Donegal Church, in accordance with the prescribed order of service, persisted in praying for the king the congregation did not take it lightly. Leading the pastor from the altar to the yard, the parishioners formed a circle around him while he stood against an oak tree, and forced him to cheer for the cause of the colonies. The rest of the congreation then renewed their pledge to continue the fight. After that the oak became known as "The Witness Tree."

Donegal Church still stands at the source of Donegal Springs Creek. It is a picturesque limestone country church surrounded by a low wall, cemetery and stately old trees. With its smooth, steady flow, cress beds and scattering of domestic ducks, the stream in the vicinity of the church is a fine accompanying scene. Anglers

passing through the area, however, should not expect to fish near the church, since much of the land surrounding the stream is private and posted against trespassing. Donegal Springs Creek's two-mile long Delayed Harvest Fly Fishing Only Project is located further downstream after a lot more runoff water has had a chance to enter the stream and dairy cattle an opportunity to stir up the bottom a bit.

According to the Fish Commission's "Summary of Fishing Regulations and Laws," the stream's special regulation water runs from the "upper boundary of the John Heir Farm below Rt. 141 downstream to a bridge on Rt. T-334 near the mouth." The only problem nobody seems to have informed either the Pennsylvania Dept. of Transportation or Donegal Twp. officials. For it is next to impossible for a visting angler to find the stream by following those instructions. The situation is a perfect example of the problem the state as a whole has when it comes to directional signs.

Donegal Springs Creek can be reached by taking the Columbia, Pennsylvania Route 441 Exit off U.S. Route 30, on the east side of the Susquehanna River, and following it north toward Marietta where it joins Pennsylvania Route 23 and the real fun begins. For the Route 141 listed in the summary book is actually posted by PennDOT as Pennsylvania Route 772, or Mount Joy Pike. Residents of the area can give directions to Route 141, which will turn out to be Route 772, but no traveler will ever find a sign with that road number on it. Sound like "Catch 22?"

Be that as it may, Donegal Springs Creek can be found by taking the Route 441 Exit off Route 30 and then turning right onto Route 772 (Mt. Joy Pike) at Marietta. The road dips down to cross the stream a couple of miles later just before the turn-off to Donegal Mills Plantation, marked by a sign. Anglers can park along Route 772, but be careful, and walk downstream about a hundred yards to the upper boundary of the project.

Route 772, and the stream, also can be reached by taking Exit 20 off the Pennsylvania Turnpike and following P.R. 72 to Manheim, then turning right onto Route 772 toward Mount Joy. The lower end of the project is accessible by taking Route 772 past the plantation sign and turning right onto Long Lane and continuing on it to Donegal Creek Road and the Marietta Pike, or Route 23 west.

Fly fishermen venturing to the stream might try such traditional patterns as Royal Coachman, Bivisible, Renegade, Adams, Henryville Special, Hare's Ear, Soft Hackle Nymphs, Muskrat, March Brown, Gray Fox, Light Cahill, Sulphurs, Mickey Finn, and especially terrestrials.

Tulpehocken Creek
Delayed Harvest Artificial Lures Only
Lebanon and Berks Counties

Wooded bluffs and tangled, overhanging bottoms make lower Tulpehocken Creek seem as if it's a lot further away from the city of Reading than just a couple of miles. Yet that is it. Venture down the streets leading to its mouth on the Schuylkill River, and suddenly you are in the land of shopping centers and rush hour traffic.

But then traffic is nothing new to Tulpehocken Creek or Reading, for that matter. Both have been busy with travelers since before the earliest colonial days. The Tulehocken Path, from Sunbury To Womelsdorf, and the Allegheny Path, from

Philadelphia to Pittsburgh and Kittanning, both followed the stream for a portion of their lengths. Reading served as a junction for the Maxatawny Path, from Easton to Reading; the Nanticoke Path, from Nanticoke to Calvert, Maryland; the Oley Path, from Bethlehem to Reading; the Perkiomen Path, from Philadelphia to Reading; and, through the Tulpehocken Path, the Red Hole Path, from upper Swatara Creek to the West Branch Schuylkill. In later years, Reading also would become a canal and railroad center, famous enough to be included on the "Monopoly" game board.

Of all the various Indian paths which once converged on the "Tully," as it is sometimes called, and Reading, the longest and the most important was the Allegheny Path. John T. Faris in his *Old Trails and Roads in Penn's Land* calls it "the oldest road in Pennsylvania which passed between the Delaware and the Susquehanna." William Penn himself is said to have supervised the laying of a road along the path in Philadelphia. The Tulpehocken Path, also sometimes called the Shamokin Path, crossed the stream at Womelsdorf. It was used by embassies of the Iroquois traveling from the Syracuse area of New York to Philadelphia.

Along with being a vital link in the Indian's trail system, Tulpehocken Valley was a major trouble spot in relations between the early settlers and the Indians. In 1723, a group of Germans from the Schohary Valley crossed the headwaters of the Susquehanna River, followed it to Swatara Creek and then up that stream to the Tulpehocken. Conrad Weiser, an early explorer of Pennsylvania and chief intermediary between the Indians and colonial officials, moved to the area in 1729. This occupation of the Tulpehocken Valley resulted in quite a bit of trouble with the Indians because it had not been purchased by the settlers. After the Delaware King Allummappees complained about the matter at a council in Philadelphia, colonial officials asked if the Germans could remain in the valley until a solution was found.

The officials did nothing about the settlers, however, until 1732, when the valley was bought from the Indians. The purchase opened the Iroquois eyes to the value of land in the province. They quickly laid claim, by conquest, to land owned by the Delaware. That action also turned the Delaware against Weiser, who they believed influenced the Iroquois to sell their lands along the Susquehanna River. Raids which followed this change in the Delaware's attitude led to the construction, supervised by Weiser, of a series of forts to protect the frontier.

Relatively wide and shallow, with a good sprinkling of rocky riffles, Tulpehocken Creek, meaning "stream of turtles," is accessible by several different routes. Among the easiest way to reach it, is by taking the Papermill Road Exit off U.S. Route 422. Follow the exit around to the Reading Motor Inn and then turn right directly in front of the inn. The stream also can be located by taking Palisades Road off P.R. 183 and following it past the Dry Brooks Access to Blue Marsh Lake. The Tully's 4.1-mile long Delayed Harvest Artificial Lures Only Project runs from the first deflector below Blue Marsh Dam downstream to 225 yards above the junction of Township Roads 702 and 602.

About four miles below the dam a long covered bridge provides a pleasant addition to the lower Tulpehocken. At the same time, on a hill overlooking the stream, an imposing black and yellow painted wooden building will appear. The structure is the Gruber Wagon Works. Anglers of a mechanical mind and love of gadgets should make certain to visit the building during a break in their fishing. Originally, built in 1882 on a site now covered by Blue Marsh Lake, the factory produced wagons, sleighs, wheelbarrows and, after the turn of the century, wooden truck bodies. It operated all of the way up until 1972 and was moved to its present location in 1976. It can be found along Route 183.

Tulpehocken Creek's upper stocked water runs from west of the Route 422 bridge west of Myerstown in Lebanon County downstream beyond Womelsdorf in Berks County. It occupies a pleasant, pastoral setting of old farms, a few summer cottages, and plenty of woods and open fields. There is even a scenic old mill at Route 422 near Womelsdorf.

Besides providing a romantic touch with its mill, Route 422 also is the main access artery to the upper Tully. It parallels the stream from Womelsdorf upstream beyond Meyerstown. Other roads running off Route 422 that touch on the creek include: State Route 3039, Pennsylvania Route 419, Sheridan Road, State Route 3061, State Route 1015, Pennsylvania Route 501 at the Myerstown Recreation Area and Township Road 560.

History buffs among the angling fraternity chasing the Tulpehocken's browns and rainbows might consider visiting the Conrad Weiser homestead off Route 422 near Womelsdorf. Operated by the Pennsylvania Historical and Museum Commission, the homestead contains the graves of Weiser (1696-1760) and his wife, Anna, their small limestone house and various memorabilia of the early colonial period.

Possible fly patterns for Tulepehocken Creek are: Blue Quills, Adams, Quill Gordons, Hare's Ears, Soft Hackle Nymphs, Muddler Minnows and other streamers, caddis, Hendricksons, March Browns, Light Cahills, Blue-Winged Olives, Sulphurs, midges and terrestrials.

Manatawny Creek
Berks County

Covered bridges and old mills, quiet woods and rock cliffs make Manatawny Creek calendar perfect in many places. Add to those special spots a roomy farm valley with pastures full of fat dairy cows and stone houses next to well-kept barns and it is hard, even on first glimpse, not to be enchanted by this tributary of the historic Schuylkill River. The surroundings are built up only around the village of Earleville, near the center of the stream's 15 miles of stocked water, and at Pottstown on its mouth. In between those two towns the angler is more likely to find ducks and geese than people.

The region around Manatawny Creek, translation "where we drank liquor," was settled by Germans prior to 1704. The stream once laid on the main road from Paxtang (Harrisburg) through Reading to Philadelphia. The road followed the Perkiomen Path, passing over the stream at the Indian town of Manatawny (Pottstown). Governor John Evans used the route in 1707 to travel to and from councils with the Indians in Lancaster County. In 1712 Lieutenant Governor Charles Gookin met with four Indian kings along the stream. Various tribes lived in the area until about 1730 when troubles with settlers forced them to move.

John Penn's description of the land surrounding the road and stream during his passage through the region in 1788 still serves well along the upper reaches of the Manatawny. "Beautiful," he writes, "a little heightened in some places by the sublime. It is, indeed, perfect . . ."

Beauty and brushes with politicians and Indians aside, Manatawny Creek's main claim to fame lies in a different direction. The first known iron forge in Pennsylvania was erected by Thomas Rutter, a one time bailiff in Germantown, along the stream just outside of Pottstown in 1716. It was named "Pool." The forge and another one, Pine Forge, which Rutter built along the stream in 1725, helped to supply the Continental Army with cannon, shot and other ordinance during the Revolutionary War.

Up Pennsylvania Route 100 from Pottstown in the region of the Manatawny also is a place that was once known as "Free Love Valley." The name derives from a religious sect known as the "Battle Axes"—'Thou art my battle axe and weapon of war,' Jeremiah 51:6—that was founded in the middle of the nineteenth century by Theophilus Gates.

Born in Connecticut in 1787, Gates is said to have experienced hallucinations from early childhood. At different times he was a law student, itinerant school teacher and writer of religious prophecy. In 1837 he published the *Battle Axe* which contained an article entitled "The Order of God," declaring "among the present fashion and usages of this world that will fade away is that of man and wife so called, living in strife and disagreement."

While hawking his papers in Philadelphia, Gates met Hannah Williams, "earner of a public and unconventional livelihood," and the two moved to the village of Shenkel. Attracted by Gates' teachings, local residents began to visit his home and within a short time a series of meetings were conducted—in the nude—at different members' homes. Eventually, any Battle Axe member was free to visit another member's house and, after explaining they were being led by a divine voice, walk out with that member's wife or, in true equal rights fashion, husband.

Believing that Heaven was near, one night Gates attached wings made of shingles to his arms and attempted to fly off a roof. Shortly afterwards his following began to decrease.

Manatawny Creek's stocked portion, the heaviest stocked water in Berks County, can be reached by taking Route 100 to the intersection of Pennsylvania Route 73 between Boyertown and Gilbertsville. Take Route 73 west through Boyertown to Pleasantville at the upstream start of the stocked water. Covered Bridge Road appears at the red light in the center of Pleasantville. It crosses the stream and then parallels it downstream toward Pennsylvania Route 662 and the village of Yellow House. Church Road, Spangsville Road and Fisher Mill Road all run off Covered Bridge Road and across the stream to Manatawny Road, which follows the creek on the other side down toward Earleville and Pennsylvania Route 562.

Between Route 662 and Route 562 Old Airport Road and Blacksmith Road lead to the stream, and, eventually, the other highway. Pine Forge Road off Route 662 south of Amityville and Worman Road off Route 562 east of Earleville also lead down to Manatawny Creek.

Anglers who like to fish with flies might try the Blue Dun, Adams, Quill Gordon, Hare's Ear, Hendrickson, Renegade, caddis, March Brown, Soft Hackle Nymphs, Light Cahill, Sulphurs, Woolly Buggers, Muddler Minnows, Mickey Finn, midges and terrestrials.

Manatawny Creek.

Little Lehigh Creek
Fly Fishing Only, No Harvest Fly Fishing Only
Berks and Lehigh Counties
Jordan Creek, Cedar Creek
Lehigh County

Little Lehigh Creek

For anglers after more than dead fish, streams with special regulation projects are heaven sent. Not only do they allow fishermen to practice their sport year-round, but over a high density of trout (which is what you get when you don't kill your catch). They are wonderful places to hone skills, cure cabin fever before the season opens and escape the worst of the crowds once it starts. Pennsylvania has approximately 60 such waters in eight different categories but only one stream with two separate projects—Little Lehigh Creek.

Originating in eastern Berks County, the Little Lehigh runs the entire gauntlet of civilization in the twentieth century. Its waters flow past woods and rolling dairy farms, housing plans of increasingly beautiful and expensive homes, the fairways of a country club, the wide open, tidy green spaces of a city park, well-preserved native stone buildings, and, finally, the remains of industrial America. The stream itself winds relatively unnoticed and undisturbed until it slips under the Pennsylvania Route 100 bridge south of Trexlertown. There Schaefer Spring Creek adds its rich, cool limestone flow, swelling the Little Lehigh to its normal width of between 15 and 20 feet, and depth of two to three feet.

Little Lehigh's dozen miles of stocked trout water are nearly as interesting as its surroundings. Its planted portion is broken into roughly two equal sections. The first part extends from north of Mertztown in Berks County downstream to the Laudenslager's Mill dam at the downstream end of the stream's Fly Fishing Only Project. The second stretch reaches from upstream of the creek's No Harvest Fly Fishing Only Project at the Lehigh Valley Country Club to its confluence with Jordan Creek and then the Lehigh River in Allentown.

Unlike most Pennsylvania trout streams, Little Lehigh Creek's upper stretches are fairly warm and unproductive. The stream's good water does not begin until the appearance of Schaefer Spring Creek, and its best water is said to lie within the city limits of Allentown, after numerous small springs have contributed their share. The lower stream is even reported to have some natural reproduction of its browns and rainbows.

As with other streams in heavily populated southeastern Pennsylvania, access to the Little Lehigh is available along numerous roads. Its marginal waters can be reached by following Spring Creek Road (State Route 3004) upstream from the Route 100 bridge. Spring Creek Road also parallels the creek downstream for about 2.5 miles, meeting Mill Creek Road, which crosses the stream.

Shortly after crossing the Little Lehigh on Mill Creek Road, Sauerkraut Road (Township Road 475) will appear on the left. Sauerkraut Road trails the creek downstream at a distance, but running off it are several roads that cross the stream, including: Willow Lane, Brookside Road, Wild Cherry Lane (which leads to the Fly Fishing Only Project), MaCungie Road and Millrace Road.

All of the roads running across the stream also can be reached by taking the Cedar Crest Boulevard Exit south off Pennsylvania Route 309 and following it for about two miles. Before crossing the stream, turn right up the hill on Lower MaCungie Road. Continue on that road for about a mile and then turn left on Wild Cherry Lane. The Fly Fishing Only water runs from Wild Cherry Lane downstream one mile to an old mill dam.

Little Lehigh's No Harvest Fly Fishing Only Project, and its lower stocked water, can be found by again taking the Cedar Crest Boulevard Exit off Route 309 south and then turning left on Hatchery Road, which crosses the stream at the bottom of the hill. From that point, Hatchery Road parallels the creek downstream, while Keystone Road trails it upstream to the Lehigh Valley Country Club.

Hatchery Road ends on Oxford Drive. Anglers can continue to follow the creek downstream by turning left and crossing it on Oxford Drive and then taking Park Drive to where it is joined by Lehigh Parkway and Jefferson Street. Both of those roads lead to Lawrence Street, which trails the Little Lehigh to its confluence with Jordan Creek.

Immigrants from Germany began settling on the banks of Little Lehigh Creek around 1723. William Allen, who would later become chief justice of the Pennsylvania Supreme Court, acquired a large tract of land on the site of Allentown in 1735. He erected a hunting and fishing lodge on the property in the 1750s, but the city which bears his name was not actually laid out until 1762.

Originally called Northampton or Northamptontown, Allentown grew slowly until the outbreak of the Revolutionary War when the valley's arms industry brought in more people. The war also provided the city with perhaps its most interesting historical footnote. It took place in September 1777 when the British army captured Philadelphia. In hopes of keeping the Liberty Bell out of British hands, and stopping the disastrous effects its capture would have on morale, colonial troops, in the dead of night, removed the bell from Independence Hall and spirited it through the battle lines to Allentown. There it was hidden in the basement of the Zion Reformed Church, which also served as a hospital during the war, for more than a year. The town changed its name from Northampton to Allentown in 1838. The Liberty Bell Shrine in downtown Allentown today commemorates the episode with the Liberty Bell.

Fly hatches on Little Lehigh Creek include: April to mid-May, Blue-Winged Olives and caddis; mid-May to late June, Sulphurs, caddis, Blue-Winged Olives and terrestrials; July and later, caddis, Blue-Winged Olives, Tricorythodes, terrestrials and midges. Anglers also should not overlook such impressionistic patterns as the Adams, Renegade, Muddler Minnow, Matuka Streamers, Hare's Ear and Soft Hackle Nymphs.

Jordan Creek

Like the Little Lehigh, which it joins in Allentown, Jordan Creek is planted with trout in two separate sections, a meandering, rural upper portion from approximately Route 100 to Kernville, and a heavily developed lower stretch from Route 309 downstream to its mouth. It is both the longest stream in Lehigh County and the most heavily planted. But not the widest. It packs most of its size into great, fitful loops through the rolling countryside.

Although the Allentown, or lower, stretch of Jordan Creek is said to contain some good fishing, the traffic and crowds take quite a bit away from the setting. Anglers looking to fish in more pleasant surroundings should think about visiting the stream's upper water in State Game Lands 206. It can be reached by taking Route 100 to the village of Lowhill where it crosses the creek. Long Lane (Township Road 369) meets Route 100 on the south side of the stream and State Route 4031 on the north bank right after Route 100 crosses Jordan Creek. Both roads parallel the creek at varying distances and eventually cross it, S.R. 4031 after joining Township Road 653 and then State Route 4025.

Lower Jordan Creek can be found by following Main Boulevard downstream off Route 309 at the village of Guthsville. Herman Lane, Wehr Mill Road and Cedar Crest Boulevard all run off Main Boulevard and down to the stream. Iron Bridge Road parallels the water between Wehr Mill Road and Cedar Crest Boulevard. Albright Road off Cedar Crest Boulevard and then Pirma Avenue provides further downstream access at Jordan Park.

Although Jordan Creek is now essentially a put and take fishery, it was once a premier trout stream, teeming with wild fish. James Allen, son of the founder of Allentown, named his hunting and fishing lodge Trout Hall in recognition of the abundance of trout in Jordan Creek and the Lehigh River. During the Revolutionary War, the lodge became the home in exile of James Hamilton, a cousin of Benjamin Franklin, after the Continental Congress decreed "that the Old Royalist Governor be not permitted too near the British garrison in Philadelphia."

Fly anglers on Jordan Creek can try some of the same patterns recommended for Little Lehigh Creek.

Cedar Creek

A small tributary of the Little Lehigh, Cedar Creek has a split personality. Its lower water, downstream of Lake Muhlenberg, is said to be strictly put and take, while its upper reaches are Class A wild trout water loaded with wild brown trout. Some people claim its upper section is the best in all of Lehigh County.

Nearly all of Cedar Creek is surrounded by public lands in the form of parks. That helps to make the fishing pleasant, despite the stream being in the middle of a busy city, but also lures a lot of the non-fishing public, which can be distracting to the angler and frightening to the fish, keeping them tucked out of sight under the stream's numerous undercut banks. Locals say the best time to fish Cedar Creek is early in the morning or in the evening when fewer people are around. Hatch activity is similar to what is found on the Little Lehigh.

Access to Cedar Creek's best water—between Dorney Park and Lake Muhlenberg—may be had by taking the Hamilton Boulevard Exit east off Route 309 and following it to the Dorneyville crossroads. Turn left at the crossroad light onto Cedar Crest Boulevard. About a mile from the crossroads the boulevard passes over the stream. Turn right at a traffic light and continue on for roughly a mile to Ott Street. The stream appears on the right.

Monocacy Creek
Northampton County

Religious freedom has been a tenet of Pennsylvania since the arrival of William Penn and the Quakers in 1682. The quiet garbed plain speaking founders of the province welcomed anybody willing to live in peace and face the hardships and dangers of the wilderness. This almost unknown liberalism and spirit of tolerance attracted members of every major Christian religion, as well as many colorful smaller sects. The Mennonite descendants of the Anabaptists came first, followed by the Dunkards, a German Baptist sect, the Schwenkfelders, a tiny group caught between the Lutherans and Catholics, the French Hugenots and the Moravians of Bohemia and Moravia.

Founded in the middle of the fifteenth century by John Hus, the Moravians were a highly persecuted sect in their homeland for over two centuries. Then in 1722 Count Nicholas Ludwig von Zinzendorf opened his Saxony estate to them. A few years later von Zinzendorf, himself, became a convert and in 1735 financed the immigration of two groups to the New World. One group went to the Savannah, Georgia area, the other to Philadelphia.

In the spring of 1740 several members of the Georgia group moved north to Pennsylvania after Evangelist George Whitfield offered them work building a school for former slaves in what is now Upper Nazareth Township. A year later Bishop David Nitschmann obtained a 500-acre tract at the confluence of Monocacy Creek and the Lehigh River. The community the Moravians built on the site became the center of the sect's activities in America. From it they undertook their missionary work among the Indians, work that produced David Zeisberger, a noted explorer of colonial Pennsylvania.

On Christmas Eve in 1741 the sect also welcomed their benefactor, Count von Zinzendorf, to America at the site. Ceremonies were held in a new common house, part of which contained some of the community's cattle. "Because of the day, and in memory of the Birth of our dear Savior," one Moravian wrote, "we went into the stable in the tenth hour and sang with feeling, so that our hearts melted:

Not Jerusalem
Rather Bethlehem
Gave us that which
Maketh life rich."

And so the community on the banks of Monocacy Creek and the Lehigh River came to be known as Bethlehem.

As befitting a city named as the result of a song, Bethlehem from its earliest years gained a reputation as a music center. The founders had a "Singstude" in 1742 and operated a school of music from 1744 to 1820. It also is reputed to be the first place in America where the complete rendition of *Bach's Mass in B Minor* and Hayden's *The Creation* were played. The Moravians actually published some Bach scores in Bethlehem before they were available in Europe.

"We listened to very fine music in the Church, close by," Benjamin Franklin wrote to his wife in 1756. "Flutes, oboes, French horns and trumpets do accompany the organ for our Bethlehem brethren."

Because of the friendship between the Moravians and the Indians, Bethelehem was a refuge for settlers during the French and Indian War. In 1776 a hospital was established in the town to treat colonial troops wounded in Morristown, New Jersey. American casualties from the Battle of Brandywine also were treated at the hospital, and British prisoners quartered nearby.

The opening of the Lehigh Canal and construction of the Lehigh Valley Railroad in the middle of the nineteenth century changed Bethlehem into an industrial center. While still having a fine cultural side with Lehigh University and other institutes of learning, Bethlehem and its surroundings today hold the usual malls, discount department stores, four-lane highways, franchise restaurants and bumper to bumper traffic of a modern city. Amid it all, though, Monocacy Creek has somehow managed to survive as a trout stream, and not simply as a put and take fishery. This little limestone tributary to the Lehigh River (see which) is said to hold a good mixture of stocked and wild brook and brown trout even inside the city limits of Bethlehem, while about a two-mile stretch of the stream north of the city has water pure enough to be classified as "Wild Trout Water," capable of sustaining its own population of trout. Traffic, street tangles and the general pulse of life, however, probably makes this lower stretch of the

Monocacy of interest mainly to local anglers. Visitors might be better served by heading for the stream's upper water around the town of Bath.

Named after Bath, England, Northampton County's Bath is a town of under 5,000 residents, full of white-painted frame homes, some of them well-kept, some of them rundown, that sit close to the street and still impart a touch of nineteenth century eastern Pennsylvania. Monocacy Creek means "a stream with several large bends" and its upper stocked water begins on one of those bends downstream from where Penn. Route 512 passes over the creek about two miles south of Bath. Although Route 512, which can be picked up off U.S. Route 22 at Bethlehem, parallels the Monocacy's stocked water, the tiny stream is usually out of sight. It is separated from the road by cement works, trucking firms, contractors and so forth. Streets running to the left generally provide access to the creek. The angler might be able to park at some of the business establishments. Jacksonville Road off Route 512 leads to both the creek and School Road, which follows it for a short distance through some nicer farm country. Fishermen also can find some of the stream's more pleasant portions by walking along the railroad bed that follows it.

Monocacy Creek's stocked water runs into the center of Bath, North of the town the stream is designated "Wild Trout Water." Access is available off first Penn. Route 987 and then again Route 512.

Fly patterns the anglers might consider include: caddis, Soft Hackle Nymphs, Hare's Ears, Adams, Blue Quills, Hendricksons, sulphurs, March Browns, Blue-Winged Olives, Gray Fox, Light Cahills, Tricorythodes, midges, terrestrials, Muddler Minnows, Mickey Finns and Matuka Streamers in olive, black and brown.

Bushkill Creek
Northampton County

"Limestone" and "Pennsylvania," when spoken to a collection of trout anglers, almost guarantees an image of the fertile farm country in the south central part of the state. The picture will include streams with names such as Letort, Falling Springs, Big Springs, the Yellow Breeches and, perhaps, Spring Creek. Unless one of the anglers lives in the Delaware Valley, chances are excellent the name Bushkill won't enter a single thought. Which is unfortunate. For here is a stream that can provide some good, often uncrowded fishing for a lot of people in densely populated southeastern Pennsylvania. That is, at least, after the hatchery trucks—and their followers—have stopped making their rounds.

Even though Bushkill Creek qualifies as a limestone stream, like the more famous Yellow Breeches it does not begin life in such a lofty manner. Instead, it starts as a humble freestone trickle near the Northampton/Monroe County line on the slopes of Blue Mountain, the long ridge which stretches all of the way across Pennsylvania to Vriginia's Appalachian Mountains.

For over half of its length, Bushkill Creek also is a rather undistinguished, though at times pretty, stream of only marginal interest as a trout water. The big change occurs near the town of Stockertown. It takes place quietly, almost without notice. The only point of reference is a small limestone building. It is there that a spring quietly adds it cold, alkaline water to the stream, and

in the process changes everything. From that point on to its end in the city of Easton, a distance of roughly eight miles, the Bushkill turns into an excellent trout fishery. Its water is so clean the Fish Commission has chosen to designate a portion of the stream as "Wild Trout Water," meaning it is capable of sustaining its own population of stream-born fish.

The quality of its water aside, anglers who choose to sample the Bushkill should not go expecting a quiet wilderness experience. Investors, speculators, entrepreneurs and industrialists of every stripe have been wreaking havoc on the creek since the late eighteenth century. Beginning at Jacobsburg with the Henry and Boulton gun works, and Henry Forge, where the first bar of iron was poured in Northampton County in 1809, and continuing through a succession of mills to Easton, the Bushkill has seen all the worst industrialized society has to offer. It has been dammed, dredged, channeled and filled with more waste than some sewers. Yet throughout it all the stream whose name in Dutch means "forest creek" has managed to survive, even prosper. It is a remarkable example of nature's rejuventating powers. And, even with noisy roads, houses and sometimes trash nearby, once a couple of good fish are spotted rising regularly, it still retains the ability to carry an angler far away to a better place.

Bushkill Creek is essentially a caddis stream when it comes to aquatic insects. Caddis pupae patterns, streamers and Muddler Minnows fished slow and deep are among the early-season favorites of local anglers. Dry fly action starts in early May with patterns like the Green Caddis imitations, followed by Sulphur hatches through the middle of June, and decent Tricorythodes and midge activity during the summer months. Terrestrials also offer very good fishing from June into September, and even later. But don't look for the dry fly fishing to be easy.

As a suburban stream that has been industrialized for roughly 200 years, the Bushkill is readily accessible throughout its length. However, the best way for a visiting fisherman to reach it without getting lost in the side streets of Easton is to take the Pennsylvania Route 191 Stockertown Exit off Pennsylvania Route 33 north of Easton. Pick up Stockertown Road in Stockertown and follow it south toward Easton. About a mile and a half outside of Stockertown turn right onto State Route 1002. Bushkill Road is off to the left just before the S.R. 1002 bridge. It parallels the creek all of the way to Easton.

Stockertown Road follows a route similar to an old Indian path. It became known as Sullivan's Road after General John Sullivan used it on his march north from Easton in 1779 to retaliate against Indians the British had paid to harass settlers in northeastern Pennsylvania.

Although Jacobsburg State Park contains a couple of miles of Bushkill Creek's freestone water, it does not offer any camping facilities for fishermen looking to stay in the area. But history buffs may be interested in visiting it because of the historic sites it holds, including the village of Jacobsburg, Henry Gun Factory, Boulton Gun Factory, Henry Forge and the Henry Homestead. The homestead, which the Henry family, owners of the gun works, lived in during the years it was in operation, has been completely restored and is open to the public on special occasions.

When the stocking trucks are rolling in the spring, the park's waters also offer a picturesque setting for trout fishing. It is accessible by taking Route 33 to the Belfast, Jacobsburg State Park Exit and following the signs.

Further details are available by contacting: Jacobsburg State Park, Department of Environmental Resources, 435 Belfast Road, Nazareth, PA 18064.

Salmon & Steelhead Waters

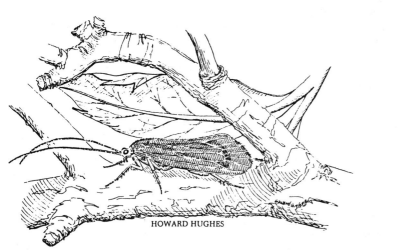

HOWARD HUGHES

Lake Erie Tributary Streams

Presque Isle Bay

Eastern Streams
Conneaut Cr
Eightmile Cr
Fourmile Cr
Sevenmile Cr
Sixmile Cr
Sixteenmile Cr
Twelvemile Cr
Twentymile Cr

Western Streams
Crooked Cr
Elk Cr
Godfrey Run
Raccoon Cr
Trout Run
Walnut Cr

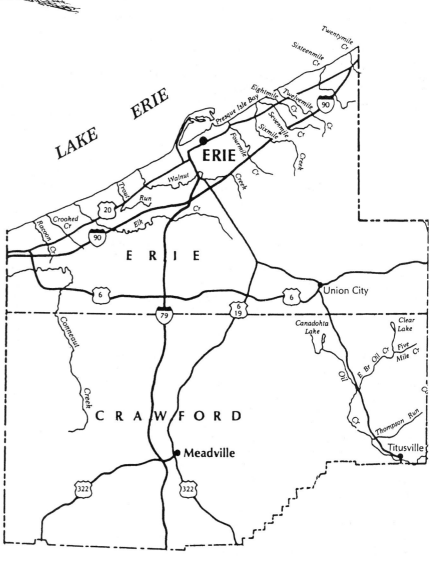

Salmon & Steelhead Waters

Erie and Crawford Counties

Lake Erie Tributary Streams
Erie County

Compared to a state such as Michigan, or even neighboring New York, Pennsylvania does not possess a very extensive salmon and steelhead fishery. But this is understandable when it is considered the state touches Lake Erie over a straight stretch of less than 50 miles, and holds only about a half dozen tributary streams of any size, while those other states contain hundreds of miles of shoreline with dozens of tributary streams.

Despite Pennsylvania's geographic limitations, however, salmon and steelhead fishing remains a very popular sport. Lake Erie fish are the only ones in all the Great Lakes that have not been contaminated by mercury, PCB, PBB, DDT, dieldrin, chlordane, toxaphene or dioxin or some other toxic chemical. There are no health warning limits on the consumption of salmon and steelhead from it, which is one reason the fishery attracts not only anglers from Pennsylvania, but also a scattering from Ohio, Maryland, West Virginia, and even New York. The lines of cars, trucks and campers heading toward Erie County in the fall at times can rival those at the opening of the whitetail deer season. And no state turns out more deer hunters than Pennsylvania, which annually sells over one million hunting licenses.

Salmon runs in Lake Erie tributary streams generally occur between the middle of September and the end of October. Fish can be found in the streams both before and after that period, but their totals are usually small.

Steelhead follow the chinooks and cohos into the stream to feed on any loose or unguarded eggs, and many hang on through the winter months, providing some action all of the way into April. Anglers who decided to go after these fish, however, should be aware that winter can be extremely harsh along the Erie lake shore. Since only the most dedicated fishermen venture out during this period, the streams are frequently empty, offering rare opportunities to angle for these big fish in near solitude.

In hopes of expanding Pennsylvania's steelhead fishery, the Fish Commission has been working with a spring-run strain of the big fish that could carry the action into the warmer months. Anglers will have to watch the newspapers and listen to the grapevine to find out the results of this experiment.

During the fall runs of both salmon and steelhead the most popular baits and lures include: salmon eggs or skein, egg sacks, nightcrawlers, No. 4 Rooster Tails, particularly in black, yellow and fluorescent colors, smaller K-O Wobblers or Little Cleos with touches of blue, green and orange, Blakemores, Flatfish and jigs, especially in white and black. Popular fly patterns are: the Skunk, Orange Comet, Fall Favorite, Double Egg Fly, Silver Minnow, Brad's Brat, Woolly Bugger and Polar Bear. Streamers tied with black, green, brown, orange and yellow bucktail also will produce fish on occasion.

When it comes to finding Lake Erie's tributary streams, the key is Pennsylvania Route 5. Running close to the lake shore over nearly the entire length of the county from New York to Ohio, Route 5 crosses all of the state's best salmon and steelhead streams, and in many cases provides the main access.

Presque Isle Bay

Obviously, the sheltered waters of Presque Isle Bay do not qualify as a Lake Erie tributary stream. But they do hold salmon and steelhead during the fall run, as well as through the winter into the spring. And it is the only safe place for anglers in small boats to fish when Lake Erie is in the midst of one of her famous tantrums that can change her character from a gentle farm pond to a raging ocean within minutes.

The center for public use of Presque Isle Bay is Presque Isle Bay State Park, a 3,202-acre spit of land that juts seven miles out into Lake Erie directly across from the city of Erie. It offers miles upon miles of fishable shore line and six boat launching ramps in four different areas, along with a seasonal marina of nearly 500 slips and a boat rental concession. It can be reached by taking Interstate Route 90 Exit 5, and following Pennsylvania Route 832 directly into the park.

Boats also may be launched, and Presque Isle Bay fished, from the 538-foot long public dock at the foot of State Street in the city of Erie. State Street can be located by following Alternate Route 5 (also known as West Lake Road and East Lake Road) into the center of the city.

Anglers who decide to visit the public dock will find themselves surrounded by both local and national history. Near the entrance to the dock is the U.S.S. Niagara and the bow of the U.S.S. Wolverine, while just up the street is the old Custom House and former home of newspaper legend Horace Greeley.

Built in 1813, the Niagara was Commodore Oliver Hazard Perry's second flagship in the Battle of Lake Erie during the War of 1812. It became the flagship for the September 10, 1813 battle after Perry's original ship, the U.S.S. Lawrence, was severely damaged, and the commodore boarded the Niagara along with his famous flag bearing the motto: "Don't Give Up The Ship."

Perry's report on the battle to General William Henry Harrison also is famous in naval lore: "We have met the enemy and they are ours: two ships, two brigs, one schooner and one sloop." The Niagara was sunk upon government orders in Misery Bay on Presque Isle near the entrance to Preseque Isle Bay. It was raised in 1913 and rebuilt to celebrate the centennial of the battle, which was found near Sandusky Point, Ohio. Since 1939, the ship has been administered by the Pennsylvania Historical and Museum Commission. It is opened to the public. A monument commemorating Commodore Perry and his victory in the Battle of Lake Erie stands across the bay in Presque Isle Park.

The bow of the U.S.S. Wolverine next to the Niagara is all that remains of the first iron-hulled warship in the United States Navy. It was designed for lake patrol and built in 1842-1843 at the foot of Peach Street, the same place where part of Perry's fleet was built. The ship was the only U.S. warship on active duty on the Great Lakes for more than 80 years. An agreement with Canada limited its armory to only one gun during its entire life. In 1949, most of the ship was sold as scrap.

The old Custom House, 407 State Street, was designed in the Greek Revival style by William Kelly of Philadelphia and built between 1837 and 1839. Besides serving as a custom house, it also has been a bank, post office and headquarters for the Grand Army of the Republic from the 1890s into the 1930s. Now a museum, it is operated by the Pennsylvania Historical and Museum Commission.

A few doors away from the old Custom House, at 414 State Street, is the Joseph M. Sterrett house where Horace Greeley lived while working as a printer for Sterrett in 1830-1831, long before his famous entreaty to "Go West young man." The house is now a piece of commercial property.

Further information on Presque Isle State Park and bay may be had by writing: Presque Isle State Park, Department of Environmental Resources, P.O. Box 8006, Erie, PA 16505.

Western-Eastern Streams

Lake Erie tributary streams are divided into two major categories: Eastern and Western. The category denotes nothing more than a particular stream's geographic relationship to the city of Erie. The Western streams are: Walnut Creek, Trout Run, Godfrey Run, Elk Creek, Crooked Creek and Raccoon Creek. Eastern streams, which are named for their approximate distance from the city, include: Four Mile Creek, Six Mile Creek, Seven Mile Creek, Eight Mile Creek, Twelve Mile Creek, Sixteen Mile Creek and Twenty Mile Creek. Of the streams mentioned, the best, or most popular are: Twenty Mile Creek, Sixteen Mile Creek, Twelve Mile Creek, Elk Creek, Walnut Creek and the mouth of Trout Run.

Western Streams

Walnut Creek

The first tributary west of the city, Walnut Creek usually is one of the most crowded, especially on weekends. The reason is the presence of a public boat launch. Walnut Creek at its mouth is surrounded by parking lots, mooring slips, maintenance sheds,

and a Fish Commission field office. Over its last 50 yards or so, it flows through a concrete and stone chute. The main purpose of the chute is to make it easier for boats to reach the lake, but it is also one of the most popular fishing locations. "The Wall" at Walnut Creek is the place where anglers can see salmon fishing the way it shouldn't be; i.e., shoulder to shoulder in a tangle of lines.

Walnut Creek is accessible and fishable immediately upstream of the wall. However, the scattering of pools that appear in this stretch draw smaller numbers than the wall only because of their tiny size. During low-water periods anglers can nearly jump many of them.

Because of its large launch facilities, a visiting angler might assume the road off Route 5 leading to the stream's mouth would be well-marked. Don't bet on it. The land around the lower stream holds some exclusive residences and the sign certainly does not intrude on the setting. It is the typical small wooden Fish Commission pointer. Traveling west on Route 5, the best way to keep from missing it is to look for the Presbyterian Manchester Lodge about five miles east of the city line. The sign and turn to the right is nearby.

In addition to the launch area, Walnut Creek also may be fished from Route 5. The stream is marked on Route 5 by an old iron sign, but motorists are better off looking for the bridge at the bottom of the dip in the road just past the access sign. The only parking is on the berm of Route 5, and that is limited. Anglers who choose to try this upstream portion of Walnut Creek should be careful not to cause any traffic problems or they could end up with a ticket.

Trout Run

Fishing is prohibited in Trout Run. However, the lake near the mouth of this tiny tributary stream is a very popular (translation crowded), and productive spot.

Trout Run can be found by turning right at the intersection of Route 5 and Route 98. The intersection is marked by a traffic light. Fish Commission regulations forbid fishing the lake shore within 50 yards east and west of the stream's mouth between 10 p.m. and 5 a.m., Labor Day to November 30.

Godfrey Run

Another miniscule tributary in which fishing is prohibited. Godfrey Run, nonetheless, draws some anglers, especially boaters, to the area around its mouth. It can be reached by taking Godfrey Road off Route 5. As at Trout Run, Fish Commission regulations forbid fishing within 50 yards east and west of the stream's mouth between 10 p.m. and 5 a.m. during the salmon season, Labor Day through November 30.

A few years back, the Western Pennsylvania Conservancy acquired lands around the mouth of Godfrey Run, and then resold them to the state for the Fish Commission to use the stream as nursery water for salmon and steelhead. So every angler who enjoys fishing for these species wants to make sure to obey all regulations along this stream. Or else risk not having fish in the future.

Elk Creek

Beginning almost in the dead center of Erie County, Elk Creek is the largest salmon and steelhead stream entirely within Pennsylvania. It also is among the most popular. Kerosene and propane lanterns can make the lower stretch near the mouth resemble new York's "Great White Way" during the height of a run. The glare from the lights on the banks are often bright enough to blind a wading angler, and often make it possible to land a fish at 4 a.m. without a flashlight.

Forgetting about the large number of fishermen who find their way to the stream, Elk Creek is probably the best tributary on which to use fly fishing gear. Its size gives fly fishermen space in which to fight a fish. This fighting room also allows the use of lighter leaders, which sometime spells the difference between success and failure.

Elk Creek's mouth may be found by following Route 5 west past the intersection of Pennsylvania Route 18. Approximately a mile beyond that intersection the road will start to bend down a hill and cross the stream. Access is available to a stretch of water maybe a mile above the mouth by parking near the bridge at the bottom of the hill. The stream will be clearly visible on the left. Be careful, though, as the only public parking is alongside the road, and a ticket is a possibility if a vehicle is interfering with the flow of traffic.

The entrance to the Fish Commission access at Elk Creek lies about a quarter of a mile west of the bridge near where the road starts to flatten out again. The road is on the right. It is well-marked along the entrance road, but there is no sign directly on Route 5.

A short distance before the turn-off for the access area, there will be a sign for North Creek Road on the left. This mostly dirt and gravel road leads back to Elk Park Road, where access to more upper water is available by making a left turn and parking near the bridge at the bottom of the hill.

Further upstream access may be found by continuing on Elk Park Road to its junction with Route 18 in Lake City. Turn right on Route 18 and follow it south into Girard. At the traffic light on Route 18 and Hathaway Street turn right and continue on to the stop sign. The entrance to Girard Borough Park will be almost across from the stop sign on Park Street at Lake Drive. The road leading to the park's picnic area also runs down to the stream.

Later in the fall, once the fish have reached the area, Elk Creek

may be fished off Pennsylvania Route 98, south of Interstate 90 Exit 4. Route 98 crosses over the stream.

Elk Creek contains some nursery water in which no fishing is permitted. These areas are wired off and posted. It also is closed to fishing south of Pennsylvania Route 20 between 10 p.m. and 5 a.m. from Labor Day to November 30.

Crooked Creek

A yellow traffic sign showing a truck heading downhill, an uncommon sight along the flat lake shore, should alert anglers to the approach of Crooked Creek. The stream itself will appear immediately before the sign for North Springfield and Pennsylvania Route 215. Access is off Route 5, and fishing prohibited between 10 p.m. and 5 a.m. on the south side of Route 5 between Labor Day and November 30.

Crooked Creek might be considered a medium-sized tributary stream. But that is relatively speaking. Since, except for Elk Creek in its lower reaches, none of Pennsylvania's salmon and steelhead streams are very large. Along Route 5 it flows through pastures and woods, and is generally pleasant. As usual, be careful about parking along Route 5.

Raccoon Creek

Locating Raccoon Creek is simply a matter of following the "County Park" signs. The entrance to Raccoon County Park, and the lower portion of the stream, is clearly marked with a sign on Route 5.

The last Lake Erie tributary on the west side of Erie entirely in Pennsylvania, Raccoon Creek is a small, bush-lined stream. Like Crooked Creek and Elk Creek, it is closed to fishing between the hours of 10 p.m. and 5 a.m. from Labor Day to November 30.

Until 1792, the northern triangle of Erie County was claimed,

Chinook salmon.

at various times, by four states—Connecticut, Virginia, New York and Massachusetts. The bottom of this triangle passed over Raccoon Creek and is remembered today by a historical marker along Route 5. The dispute over ownership was settled when Congress ceded the "Triangle," more than 200,000 acres, to Pennsylvania for $151,640.25, or 75 cents an acre. As cheap as that might sound, it actually was more than William Penn paid for the rest of the state. The ceding of the Triangle gave the state a lake shoreline of 46 miles and the Port of Erie, named after the Erie Indian Tribe which once lived in the region.

Eastern Streams

Four Mile Creek
Comparatively large, but still not of substantial size, Four Mile Creek sits on the very edge of the city of Erie. Access is off Route 5. The stream, which is closed between 10 p.m. and 5 a.m., Labor Day to November 30, can be identified by looking for Rockledge Road.

Six Mile Creek
Maybe five yards across on Route 5, this little stream is open to fishing north of the highway near the mouth. Look for the signs announcing the 10 p.m. to 5 a.m. no fishing period.

Seven Mile Creek
Another mile east on Route 5 is Seven Mile Creek. Like Six Mile, it might be five yards wide. Fishing is prohibited between 10 p.m. and 5 a.m. during the salmon season.

Eight Mile Creek
Slightly larger, and one more mile further east on Route 5, is Eight Mile Creek. It flows near the Lake Shore Terrace housing plan. Once again fishing is permitted along the stream except for the period 10 p.m. to 5 a.m., Labor Day through November 30.

Twelve Mile Creek
The first stream of any consequence, and the first one to lose its urban feel, on the eastern side of Erie is Twelve Mile Creek. It can be found on Route 5 at the intersection of Mooreheadville Road.

Access to the stream's upper water also is available along Mooreheadville Road. However, a water fall keeps salmon from going very far upstream. It, too, is closed to fishing from 10 p.m. to 5 a.m. during the salmon season.

Sixteen Mile Creek
The intersection of Route 5 and Pennsylvania Route 89 north of the town of North East marks Sixteen Mile Creek. The intersection has a flashing yellow light, so it is impossible to miss.

Sixteen Mile Creek is more country than city, with cornfields and especially vineyards abounding. Access is by walking off Route 5. Signs indicate that it is closed to fishing during the regular evening hours of 10 p.m. to 5 a.m., Labor Day to November 30.

Twenty Mile Creek
Most of Twenty Mile Creek flows through New York State. It is the largest salmon stream on the eastern side of Erie and easily spotted while driving on Route 5. The angler who does miss it will soon know he's gone too far when the sign welcoming him to New York appears.

A shale-bottom stream, like most of the tributaries, it is quite

picturesque even along the highway. Parking is along Route 5, and signs will greet the angler who is willing to "walk-in" and not fish between Labor Day and November 30 from 10 p.m. to 5 a.m.

Conneaut Creek
Erie and Crawford Counties

"It is a long time since they are gone" is the way George Donehoo translates the word "Conneaut" in his book *A History of the Indian Villages and Place Names in Pennsylvania.* And Conneaut Creek certainly does measure up to that description. All a person has to do to confirm the translation is follow the stream's crude L-shaped path from its headwaters between Pymatuning Reservoir and Conneaut Lake in Crawford County, about 25 miles as the crow flies from Lake Erie, through the southwest corner of Erie County on into Ohio where it enters the lake north of the town of Conneaut. Any Indian traveling it certainly would have gone a long time, even if he would have only covered about 25 miles in a straight line.

Conneaut Creek's width is a good match for its length. it remains a respectable size into Crawford County, and even then is larger than most of the other tributaries. Because much of its Pennsylvania water is so far away from the lake, however, the fish normally don't reach it until late in the season, especially if the fall has been a warm and dry one. Crawford County waters do not see any steelhead until February. And, since the stream is stocked with trout, no fishing is permitted in it from March 1 to the middle of April when the trout season opens. The number of fish that make the entire trip to Crawford County is very small.

Access to some of Conneaut Creek's lower water in Erie County may be had by taking Interstate Route 90 Exit 1 and following U.S. Route 6N east. The road crosses the stream on a large bridge in Conneaut Twp. just before the village of Cherry Hill.

State Route 3002 crosses Route 6N east at Cherry Hill. It also parallels the creek at varying distances both up and downstream. By turning right and then taking the first road to the right, about one mile off Route 6N, an angler can find access to the stream.

A portion of upstream water may be reached by taking a left turn off Route 6N at Cherry Hill and onto S.R. 3002. Approximately a mile down S.R. 3002 a crossroad marker will appear. The road to the left, marked by a bridge weight limit sign, leads down to the stream and a covered bridge.

Continuing on S.R. 3002 from the crossroads, the angler will eventually reach Pennsylvania Route 215. A left turn on Route 215 north will lead to a bridge and more access to Conneaut Creek. The character of the stream starts to change at this point, losing some of its size and turning from a rocky, shale bottom to more of a pasture stream.

Following Route 215 south fishermen will find the next access point on Route 6N east outside the town of Albion.

Access to the remainder of the stream in both Erie and Crawford Counties centers around Pennsylvania Route 18. Most township and state routes marked by yellow road signs running off Route 18 to the right will eventually lead to the stream. These include S.R 3004, S.R. 3011, S.R. 4012 in Shadeland, Beaver Street in Springboro, Pennsylvania Route 198 west in Conneautville, Crozier Road and S.R. 4004.

Conneaut Creek is stocked with rainbow and brown trout in Crawford County from about Dicksonburg to Springboro, and so also is a possible destination for the trout angler.

The Erie Extension Canal traced a path similar to that of Route 18 from Lake Erie through Crawford County. It was opened in 1844 and helped to link the city of Erie, Pennsylvania's third largest, to Pittsburgh via the Ohio River. Historical markers highlighting the canal appear both on Route 18 and Route 20.

Stream Index

*Denotes special regulation water.
**Denotes salmon and steelhead water.